The Central Intelligence Agency

Recent Titles in
Understanding Our Government

The Environmental Protection Agency: Cleaning Up America's Act

Robert W. Collin

THE CENTRAL INTELLIGENCE AGENCY

☆ ★ ☆

Security under Scrutiny

Edited by Athan Theoharis with Richard Immerman, Loch Johnson, Kathryn Olmsted, and John Prados

Understanding Our Government

Greenwood Press
Westport, Connecticut • London

Library of Congress Cataloging-in-Publication Data

The Central Intelligence Agency : security under scrutiny / edited by Athan
  Theoharis with Richard Immerman . . . [et al.].
      p. cm. — (Understanding our government, ISSN 1556–8512)
    Includes bibliographical references and index.
    ISBN 0–313–33282–7 (alk. paper)
    1. United States. Central Intelligence Agency.   I. Theoharis, Athan G.
  II. Immerman, Richard.   III. Series.
  JK468.I6C465   2006
    327.1273—dc22   2005020914

British Library Cataloguing in Publication Data is available.

Library of Congress Catalog Card Number: 2005020914
ISBN: 0–313–33282–7
ISSN: 1556–8512

First published in 2006

Greenwood Press, 88 Post Road West, Westport, CT 06881
An imprint of Greenwood Publishing Group, Inc.
www.greenwood.com

Printed in the United States of America

The paper used in this book complies with the
Permanent Paper Standard issued by the National
Information Standards Organization (Z39.48–1984).

10 9 8 7 6 5 4 3 2 1

Contents

Series Foreword

Since the founding of our country in 1776, the U.S. government has transformed significantly. Changing societies and events, both domestic and international, have greatly affected the actions and development of our country. The Industrial Revolution, World War II, the civil rights movement, and the more recent "war on terrorism" are just a few of the events that have changed our government and its functions. Depending on the needs of our country at any given time, agencies are developed or terminated, their size and/or budget increased or decreased, or even transferred to another department within the government, in order to meet policy makers' objectives. Whether an independent agency or part of the fifteen executive branch departments overseen by the president and the cabinet, each is given specific responsibilities and all are formed to fulfill an important role for the country and its people.

The Understanding Our Government series was developed to offer an in-depth view of the most powerful, controversial, and misunderstood agencies of the U.S. government and how they have changed American society and, in some cases, the world. Well-known agencies frequently in the media spotlight, such as the Central Intelligence Agency and the National Aeronautics and Space Administration, are included, as well as lesser-known, but important, agencies such as the Bureau of Indian Affairs and the Forest Service. Written by experts on the particular agencies, including former employees or advisory committee members, each volume provides a historical overview of an agency and includes narrative chapters describing such aspects as organization, programs, significant events, controversies, key people, and influence on society, as well as additional topics tailored to the particular agency. Subjects vary greatly among the different titles. Depending on readers' interests or needs, some will be able to find information including the Central Intelligence Agency's role in the Cuban missile crisis, as well as its history of covert operations, while others may be interested in the Environmental Protection Agency's response to environmental disasters such as the *Exxon Valdez* oil spill and the Three Mile Island nuclear accident. Still others may be curious to learn about the Federal Communication Commission's role in communications policy and regulation of the media, and the fine line between censorship and freedom of speech, or the Drug Enforcement Administration's enforcement of drug laws and methods of combating drug trafficking, and how the legalization of certain illegal drugs would affect the agency and the country in general.

Whether readers are students conducting research on a specific agency for a high school or college assignment, or just want to learn more about one or how the government works, our hope is that each will gain further knowledge about the U.S. government and its employees. We want readers to comprehend our nation's significant achievements, yet also understand its failures and how we can learn from them. Over the years, our country has performed great feats, from creating lifesaving drugs to space exploration, but it has also experienced tragedies including environmental catastrophes and terrorist attacks. Readers will learn of how such events shape legislation and public policy, and how they affect everyday life for the citizens of this country. While many agencies have been portrayed in certain ways in newspapers, on television, and in films, such representations have not always been realistic or impartial. As a result, this series attempts to offer fair, objective views of U.S. government agencies, and to allow readers to think about them and form their own opinions.

Steven Vetrano
Greenwood Press

Acronyms

A

ADDO: Assistant Deputy Director of Operations

AFL-CIO: American Federation of Labor–Congress of Industrial Organizations

AIOC: Anglo-Iranian Oil Company

B

BND: Bundes Nachrichten Diest (German intelligence service)

BNE: Board of National Estimates

BW: Biological Warfare

C

CAT: Civil Air Transport

CENIS: Center for International Studies

CFC: Chlorofluorocarbon

CICV: Combined Intelligence Center Vietnam

CIG: Central Intelligence Group

COI: Office of Coordinator of Intelligence

COMOR: Committee on Overhead Reconnaissance

CORDS: Civil Operations and Rural Development Support

COS: Chief of Station

CSIS: Center for Strategic and International Studies

CTC: Counterterrorist Center

D

DCI: Director of Central Intelligence (or CIA Director)

DDCI: Deputy Director of Central Intelligence

DDI: Deputy Director for Intelligence

DDNI: Deputy Director of National Intelligence

DDO: Deputy Director of Operations

DDP: Deputy Director for Plans

DDR: Directorate for Research

DHS: Department of Homeland Security

DI: Directorate of Intelligence

DIA: Defense Intelligence Agency

DNI: Director of National Intelligence

DO: Directorate of Operations

DoD: Department of Defense

DP: Directorate of Plans

DRV: Democratic Republic of Vietnam (North Vietnam)

DS&T: Directorate of Science and Technology

E

ECA: Economic Cooperation Administration

ELINT: electronic intelligence

EPA: Environmental Protection Agency

F

FBI: Federal Bureau of Investigation

FBIS: Foreign Broadcast Intelligence Service (renamed Foreign Broadcast Information Service)

FMLN: Faribundo Martí National Liberation Front

FNLA: National Front for the Liberation of Angola

G

GDP: Gross Domestic Product

GID: General Intelligence Department

GRU: Glavnoe Razvedyvatelnoe Upravlenie (Soviet military intelligence agency)

GVN: Government of Vietnam

H

HPSCI: House Permanent Select Committee on Intelligence

HUMINT: human intelligence

I

IAEA: International Atomic Energy Agency

ICBM: Intercontinental Ballistic Missile

ICIS: Interdepartmental Committee on Internal Security

IG: Inspector General

IIC: Interdepartmental Intelligence Conference

IMINT: imagery intelligence

INC: Iraqi National Congress

INF: Intermediate Range Nuclear Forces

INR: (State Department) Bureau of Intelligence and Research

IOB: Intelligence Oversight Board

IOR: Office of Research and Intelligence

IRBM: Intermediate-Range Ballistic Missile

ISI: Inter-Services Intelligence

ITT: International Telephone and Telegraph Corporation

J

JCS: Joint Chiefs of Staff

K

KDP: Kurdistan Democratic Party

KGB: Komitet Gosudorstvennoi Bezopasnosti (chief Soviet security agency)

KLA: Kosovo Liberation Army

M

MAAG: Military Advisory and Assistance Group

MACV: Military Advisory Committee Vietnam

MASINT: measurement and signature intelligence

MID: Military Intelligence Division (or G-2)

MIRV: Multiple Independently-Targeted Reentry Vehicle

MON: Memorandum Of Notification

MPLA: Popular Movement for the Liberation of Angola

MRBM: Medium-Range Ballistic Missile

N

NACA: National Advisory Committee for Aeronautics

NASA: National Aeronautics and Space Administration

NATO: North Atlantic Treaty Organization

NCTC: National Counterintelligence Center

NEC: National Economic Council

NESA: Near East and South Asia

NFAC: National Foreign Assessment Center

NFIB: National Foreign Intelligence Board

NFIP: National Foreign Intelligence Program

NGA: National Geospatial-Intelligence Agency

NGO: Non-Governmental Organization

NIA: National Intelligence Authority

NIC: National Intelligence Council

NIE: National Intelligence Estimate

NIO: National Intelligence Officers

NLF: National Liberation Front (National Front for the Liberation of South Vietnam)

NPIC: National Photographic Interpretation Center

NRO: National Reconnaissance Office

NSA: National Security Agency

NSC: National Security Council

NSCID: National Security Council Intelligence Directive

NSDD: National Security Decision Directive

NSDM: National Security Decision Memorandum

O

OCB: Operations Coordinating Board

OCI: Office of Current Intelligence

OGPU: Obedinennoe Gossudarstvennoe Politicheskoe Upravleniye (Soviet Intelligence Agency)

ONE: Office of National Estimates

ONI: Office of Naval Intelligence

OPC: Office of Policy Coordination

OPR: Office of Political Research

ORE: Office of Research and Evaluation (renamed Office of Reports and Estimates)

ORR: Office of Research and Reports

OSD: Office of the Secretary of Defense

OSINT: open source intelligence

OSO: Office of Special Operations

OSP: Office of Special Projects

OSS: Office of Strategic Services

P

PDB: President's Daily Brief

PFIAB: President's Foreign Intelligence Advisory Board

PID: Photo-Intelligence Division

PRC: People's Republic of China

PRU: Provisional Reconnaissance Unit

PSB: Psychological Strategy Board

PUK: Patriotic Union of Kurdistan

R

RIF: Reduction in Force

ROTC: Reserve Officer Training Corps

S

SALT: Strategic Arms Limitation Treaty

SAM: Surface-to-Air Missile

SAVA: Special Assistant for Vietnam Affairs

SAVAK: Sazamane Etelaat Va Amniate Kechvar (Iranian Security and Intelligence Service, 1956–1979)

SDI: Strategic Defense Initiative

SIGINT: signals intelligence

SIS: Secret Intelligence Service (British security agency)

SNIE: Special National Intelligence Estimate

SOVA: Office of Soviet Analysis

SRS: Senior Research Staff

SSCI: Senate Select Committee on Intelligence

SSU: Strategic Services Unit

SWNCC: State-War-Navy Coordinating Committee

T

TCP: Technological Capabilities Panel

TECHINT: Technical Intelligence

U

UAV: Unmanned Aerial Vehicle

UFCO: United Fruit Company

UNITA: National Union for the Total Independence of Angola

UNMOVIC: United Nations Monitoring, Verification and Inspection Commission

UNSCOM: United Nations Special Commission

USIB: United States Intelligence Board

USTR: United States Trade Representative

V

VC: Vietcong

W

WINPAC: Weapons Intelligence, Nonproliferation and Arms Control

WMD: weapons of mass destruction

Introduction

Athan Theoharis

In 1929, when justifying his decision to cease funding a Cipher Bureau (the codebreaking unit that the Departments of War and State had jointly funded since 1919), Secretary of State Henry Stimson observed "Gentlemen do not read each other's mail." The secretary of state's ethical qualms were reflective not of the naivete of an earlier innocent age but of the nature of the then U.S. international role and foreign policy priorities. U.S. policy makers during the 1920s (and earlier) did not believe that the United States should actively intervene in international conflicts—and, in consequence, forge military alliances with other nations or join international collective security organizations. Instead, they sought to advance U.S. security interests and avoid the need for military force, first by negotiating a treaty in 1921–1922 to limit the battleship forces of the major naval powers and thereby avert a destabilizing naval arms race, and then in 1928 by playing a leading role in negotiating another treaty to outlaw war as an instrument of national policy. Since 1783 when the United States formally gained independence, the primary goals of U.S. policy makers had been to protect the nation from a direct military attack and to promote foreign trade and investment. Consistent with this latter purpose, during the 1920s U.S. officials sought to professionalize the foreign service (through the enactment of the Rogers Act in 1924) and established a special division in the Department of Commerce, the Bureau of Domestic and Foreign Commerce, having the specific responsibility to compile statistical information about foreign trade and investment opportunities.

This all changed following the outbreak of World War II in Europe with the German invasion of Poland in September 1939. Dating from 1940 and even though the nation was formally neutral, U.S. military intelligence intercepted (and eventually succeeded in deciphering) the communications of Soviet, Japanese, German, and other Axis-aligned states—in the case of the Soviet

Union, consular and embassy telegraphic messages transmitted from New York and Washington to Moscow. Reading "each other's mail" came to be perceived as essential to advancing U.S. security interests.

Second, dramatically confirmed by the surprise Japanese attack on Pearl Harbor in December 1941, the United States could no longer avoid involvement in "foreign wars"—as counseled by President George Washington in his 1796 Farewell Address or by Congress when enacting neutrality legislation during the mid-1930s. President Franklin Roosevelt and his successors recognized the need to anticipate the hostile actions of powerful states or movements that had the intent and capability whether to upset the balance of power, to attack the United States, or to undermine support for U.S. policies and/or U.S. investments and commercial opportunities. Averting future "Pearl Harbors" and anticipating potentially destabilizing activities, moreover, required the creation of a more centralized and coordinated U.S. intelligence capability that could curb the bureaucratic rivalries of those departments (state, justice, war, navy—after 1948, defense) that already had international intelligence collection capabilities.

Third, dating from World War II and continuing during the Cold War and post–Cold War eras, presidents came to endorse the need for an intelligence agency that could also conduct covert actions, whether to destabilize hostile political movements or to promote the overthrow of hostile governments. To President Roosevelt and his successors, nations such as Nazi Germany and the Soviet Union were no longer considered as being merely powerful adversaries. These were "subversive" states which, in addition to their well-funded armies, could exploit the ideological sympathies of fascist and communist movements worldwide to achieve their expansionist objectives. Then, with the collapse of the Soviet Union and the unrelated emergence of the militant, anti-American Islamic fundamentalist movement, al Qaeda, in the 1990s a new concern emerged: the need to safeguard U.S. institutions abroad and within the United States from terrorist attacks.

The immediate byproduct of this shift in conception of the nation's foreign policy role and security interests was the enactment of legislation in 1947, the National Security Act, creating a Central Intelligence Agency (CIA). Then, in response to the apparent failure of the U.S. intelligence agencies to have anticipated the terrorist attack of September 11, 2001, Congress enacted legislation in 2004 creating a national intelligence director having oversight responsibilities over all U.S. intelligence agencies and reporting directly to the president—a major reorganization that affected the role and authority of the CIA.

The history of the CIA's creation, future expansion, and then the subsequent reassessment of its role and authority offers insights into the priorities, tactics, and objectives of U.S. intelligence policy after 1947. As importantly, this history extends our understanding of the U.S. international role and of the major policy decisions and commitments of U.S. policy makers during the post–World War II era; the dominant role that American presidents played after 1947 in conducting the nation's foreign and national security policy; the changes in executive-legislative relations triggered by the inherently secretive conduct of espionage, counterintelligence, counterterrorism, and covert actions; and the consequences posed by the creation and expansion of an inherently secret centralized intelligence system for a democratic society, reflected most pointedly in the difficulties members of Congress and American reporters encountered when seeking to fulfill their traditional role to inform the public about important governmental decisions and objectives.

This research guide will offer readers a fuller understanding of the CIA's historic role, activities, and personnel—integrating and correlating the findings of monographs that either: focus on specific events (the U-2 incident) or covert actions (Bay of Pigs), treat separately intelligence and counterintelligence activities, or survey the lives and careers of specific CIA officers and senior officials. Yet, because of the secrecy shrouding the Agency's history dating from its creation in 1947 and then the continuing classification restrictions which limit contemporary access to relevant records, our understanding of the CIA's history is inevitably incomplete.[1] Selected records have been declassified or released in response to Freedom of Information Act requests, congressional hearings (most notably, the hearings and reports of the so-called Church and Pike Committees in 1975–1976, the Joint House-Senate inquiry into the so-called Iran-Contra affair of 1987, the Joint House-Senate Intelligence Committee inquiry of 2002–2003 into the terrorist attack of September 11, 2001, the Senate Intelligence Committee inquiry of 2003–2004 into Iraq's pre-war programs of weapons of mass destruction), the independent inquiry into the September 11, 2001 terrorist attack conducted by the so-called Kean Commission in 2003–2004, and the independent inquiry into Iraq's, Iran's, North Korea's, Libya's, and al Qaeda's weapons of mass destruction programs and capabilities conducted by the so-called Silberman-Robb Commission in 2004–2005.

In light of these restrictions, this survey of the CIA's programs, personnel, and activities is qualifiedly comprehensive based on what is known or knowable about this secret agency. In addition, rather than compiling a series of discrete entries on specific events and personalities, the editor has solicited thematic chapters written by experts having specialized knowledge of aspects of the Agency's history, personnel, and activities. Each contributor will place key events and decisions relating to the CIA's history in a broader context, thereby offering a better understanding of the Agency's evolution, programs, and methods. These chapters trace the history of the Agency since its creation in 1947 through December 2004, describing its role in influencing and implementing key foreign policy objectives. Specific chapters will decribe the Agency's organization and liaison relations with the White House, other U.S. and foreign intelligence agencies, Congress, and the media; the personnel who have shaped the Agency's history ranging from the powerful CIA Director

Allen Dulles and the controversial head of the Agency's counterintelligence division James Angleton to renegade CIA officer Philip Agee; the Agency's intelligence and counterintelligence authority and programs (such as the U-2 and Corona); the Agency's known covert operations ranging from assassination planning to covert actions in Cuba, Iran, Guatemala, and Afghanistan; and the publicized controversies involving the Agency's programs that have raised questions, whether about its violations of academic freedom, its involvement in domestic surveillance, its attempts to suppress critical books and news stories, and its perceived failure to have anticipated the suicide bombing attacks on the World Trade Center and the Pentagon on September 11, 2001 or to confirm the Iraq government's ties with al Qaeda and weapons of mass destruction capabilities. The chapters will also briefly survey Congress's initial response to reforms proposed by the Kean Commission in 2004 and the Silberman-Robb Commission in 2005, whether to create a national intelligence director to ensure better coordination among all the U.S. intelligence agencies, to vest in the military responsibility over covert and other paramilitary operations, or to enhance intelligence collection and assessment relating to weapons of mass destruction. Furthermore, the authors of the chapters have explored how the Agency's actual and suspected activities have influenced the contradictory actions of the U.S. Congress—at times avoiding any attempt to oversee Agency operations and at other times examining critically perceived Agency failures and abuses of power.

Because many readers will only be interested in specific events and personalities, each chapter contains descriptive subheadings which are listed in a detailed Table of Contents, along with a separate chapter (Chapter 6) containing biographies in alphabetical order. In addition, a comprehensive, cross-referenced index will enable readers to locate all relevant information described in the thematic chapters about a specific event, program, or personality. Where appropriate, photographs, graphs, and tables will clarify aspects of the Agency's history. In addition, an annotated bibliography identifies relevant books and their specific subject matter, while a detailed chronology provides a ready reference of the important developments that have informed the Agency's history.

NOTE

1. This research problem is highlighted by a recent unsuccessful court suit to force the CIA to release annual budgets for the years 1947–1970. CIA officer Paul Gimigliano justified this refusal, claiming "The budget remains classified to prevent America's adversaries from piecing together the national security priorities set for the CIA."

A Brief History of the CIA

Richard Immerman

The Central Intelligence Agency (CIA) had become one of the most well-known institutions of the U.S. government by September 11, 2001, the date of the tragic attacks on the Pentagon and World Trade Center. Even more remarkable for an agency shrouded in secrecy, it had also become a cultural icon. Three popular network series focusing on the CIA debuted that year: *Alias* on ABC, *The Agency* on CBS, and *24* on Fox. All feature an attractive (and frequently sexy) cast of racially and ethnically diverse men *and* women who are committed, competent, and courageous. There is no moral ambiguity in these agents' battles against the forces of evil. The writers do not allow that any trick of covert trade can be classified as "dirty." Blockbuster movies such as *Spy Game* (also 2001) and *The Recruit* (2003) project these same dynamics, portraying the CIA as both a bastion of patriotism and a dream job. In the former megastars Robert Redford and Brad Pitt engage in virtually criminal behavior, but the viewer cannot help but applaud their professionalism and nobility. As an MIT-trained computer whiz in *The Recruit*, Colin Farrell forfeits the certainty of earning great wealth, endures the rigors of training at the "farm," and becomes a dazzling and dashing mole-hunter simply because, as Al Pacino explains, he "believes." Small wonder that the CIA hired Jennifer Garner, the seductive Sydney Bristow in *Alias*, to introduce the recruitment video it shows at college job fairs.

Amid intensifying public criticism of the intelligence failures associated with the terrorist attacks on 9/11, Osama bin Laden's escaping capture in Afghanistan, and the futile search for weapons of mass destruction (WMD) in Iraq following the defeat of Saddam Hussein in 2003, Hollywood's depiction of the CIA became more nuanced, and more critical. In the 2004 summer miniseries *The Grid*, which premiered in a two-hour special the week that the report of the National Commission on Terrorist Attacks upon the United

States became public, the War on Terrorism is marred by wars over turf within the intelligence community. The chief culprit is the Tom Skerritt–played CIA director, who is only slightly less dastardly than the Middle Eastern terrorists. Whether perceived or represented as virtuous or villainous, nevertheless, the CIA is as central to America's popular and political culture as it is to its national security. This phenomenon is both extraordinary and anomalous given the Agency's controversial origins, checkered record, and brief and highly classified history.

Only with memories of the devastation wrought by the Japanese attack at Pearl Harbor still vivid, and when confronted with what many Americans perceived as a life or death struggle against an evil greater than Nazi Germany, the godless Soviet empire, did the United States establish a central intelligence agency in 1947. Its subsequent history has left an indelible impression on American politics, American institutions, American culture, and America's image around the world. A few years short of three decades ago, in the wake of the Vietnam War, the Watergate affair, and the Church Committee hearings and reports, Hollywood, even as it thrilled audiences with the British James Bond, portrayed the CIA as a rogue agency in *Three Days of the Condor*. Some three decades before that, the very concept of a permanent intelligence agency seemed anathema to American ideals and values. Not that Americans did not recognize the contributions of espionage to their history. Although he did not succeed in providing George Washington with any useful intelligence, and although prior to hanging in 1776 he probably never said, "I regret that I have but one life to give for my country," Nathan Hale, the nation's first spy, remains among the pantheon of martyred heroes in American memory.

U.S. INTELLIGENCE FROM THE REVOLUTION THROUGH WORLD WAR II

Espionage was in fact crucial to America's growth and security. The Revolutionary War did produce the Culper Ring, America's initial organized spy network organized in New York City in 1778, and the Civil War gave rise to the Pinkertons. In 1889, as the United States began its ascent to global power, the Navy Department established the Office of Naval Intelligence (ONI), and shortly thereafter the War Department followed suit with the Division of Military Information (soon renamed the Military Intelligence Division [MID] and organized under the General Staff as G-2). The State Department, moreover, had long relied on its foreign-service officers for vital intelligence.

Successive U.S. administrations made no attempt to coordinate intelligence collection. During World War I, for example, the War Department created an effective signals intelligence (codebreaking or cryptanalytic) unit, known instructively as the Black Chamber. It continued in the war's aftermath under the leadership of Herbert Yardley and the joint direction and funding of the War and State Departments. Allegedly uttering the infamous sentence

"Gentlemen do not read each other's mail," Secretary of State Henry Stimson shut it down in 1929, just as the Versailles system began to unravel. For more than a century Americans had, of course, read others' mail. Yet to Stimson and the nation's elite, sanctioning such behavior as a permanent feature of the state would undermine U.S. distinctiveness—its exceptionalism.

America's antipathy toward spying ameliorated substantially with the shock of Pearl Harbor and the U.S. entry into World War II. And ironically, America's "gentlemen" led the way. Convinced that the reports on the situation in Europe he received in the late 1930s from his ambassador to Great Britain, Joseph Kennedy, were unreliable, President Franklin D. Roosevelt sent William "Wild Bill" Donovan to England to provide a second opinion. Roosevelt appreciated that Donovan, a prominent Republican attorney, Medal of Honor recipient, and intimate of Secretary of the Navy Frank Knox would insulate the administration from criticism from partisan isolationists. Not only did Donovan portray the British chances against the Germans, particularly with U.S. assistance, more positively than did Kennedy, but he also became a fan of the British Secret Intelligence Service (SIS or, more commonly, MI6) and developed a close relationship with William Stephenson, London's intelligence liaison to Washington. Donovan recommended that the United States set up a comparable institution. Roosevelt was sympathetic to the idea. In July 1941, while the United States was still at peace, by executive order the president established the Office of the Coordinator of Intelligence (COI), appointing Donovan as its chief. Some six months after Pearl Harbor in June 1942 Roosevelt abolished the COI and replaced it with the Office of Strategic Services (OSS), following Donovan's advice that it would be less bureaucratically divisive if the intelligence organization reported to the military. Donovan remained in charge; his soldiers tended to be overwhelmingly Ivy League "gentlemen."

Four future directors of the CIA (DCI) served in the OSS: Allen W. Dulles, Richard Helms, William Colby, and William Casey. Other OSS veterans included Ray Cline and Frank Wisner, who later became CIA deputy directors, and subsequent government officials and public intellectuals such as Arthur M. Schlesinger, Jr., David Bruce, Walt Rostow, Carl Kaysen, and Douglas Cater. More generally, its ranks included an inordinate number of the Ivy League's "Best and the Brightest," the majority of whom worked with the OSS's Research and Analysis Branch. Indeed, represented by such later CIA legends as Sherman Kent and Walter Pforzheimer, more than forty members of the Yale class of 1943 worked in World War II intelligence.

THE DISSOLUTION OF OSS AND THE ORIGINS OF THE CIA

The continuation of a centralized U.S. intelligence agency once the war was over was anything but inevitable. Despite the dramatic expansion of the OSS between 1941 and 1945 and its panoply of activities, ranging from espionage, sabotage, and "black propaganda" to code-breaking and intelligence analysis, from the start Donovan's efforts to ensure its permanency and make it the equal of the other military services generated heated opposition from myriad fronts. Even during the war itself the Army's G-2, the Navy's ONI, and the Department of State resisted what all construed as Donovan's infringements on their autonomy, and J. Edgar Hoover of the Federal Bureau of Investigation (FBI, which at the time had a branch for Latin American intelligence, the Special Intelligence Service), fiercely defended his turf. Those in and out of government with fewer vested interests, moreover, feared that Donovan sought to use an institutionalized intelligence organization to further his political ambitions. In addition, the question of whether a powerful, permanent spy agency could be reconciled with the democratic ideals for which the United States fought troubled a broad spectrum of Americans.

Donovan's only hope to defeat these powerful forces arrayed against his plans was the burgeoning Executive Office of the President, and more specifically, Franklin Roosevelt. He proposed to remove the OSS from the military and make it accountable directly to the president. Although Roosevelt also harbored reservations about Donovan, his own propensity to champion the unconventional, to innovate, and to centralize made him the most likely supporter of a permanent postwar intelligence agency. On April 12, 1945, however, Roosevelt died. His successor, Harry S Truman, had little interest in becoming Donovan's ally. A novice in matters of international relations let alone foreign intelligence, he was loath to do battle with those military and government experts on whom he would need desperately to rely on. The war was winding down, and Truman thought his best chance of successfully riding the presidential tiger was for the country to return to some semblance of normalcy as rapidly as possible. The establishment of a peacetime agency of superspies in the United States seemed unambiguously abnormal. As far as Truman was concerned, Donovan was walking too fine a line between a liberal democracy and a police state.

On September 20, 1945, Truman ordered that the OSS disband effective October 1. Nevertheless, recognizing that the fluidity of the global environment and the deterioration of relations with the Soviet Union demanded that his administration maintain its guard and keep abreast of developments overseas, he assigned responsibility for counterintelligence and gathering foreign intelligence to the Strategic Services Unit (SSU), which he placed under the War Department, and responsibility for assessing this intelligence to the State Department's Interim Research and Intelligence Service. To a large degree Truman was responding to Donovan's military and civilian critics. By consensus they wanted a peacetime national agency that would synthesize the intelligence procured by different sources and coordinate intelligence activities. What they did not want was for this authority to be overly centralized or for the empire-building "Wild Bill" to direct it. As the president wrote

Donovan, he intended for the United States to benefit from "a coordinated system of foreign intelligence within the permanent framework of the Government."

A consensus could not be reached as to what form this system would take, and the ensuing bureaucratic battle, in the words of one participant, was "tougher than I'd seen before; as tough as anything I saw afterwards." The Departments of War and the Navy, in conjunction with the service chiefs, initially proposed establishing a "National Intelligence Authority." Composed of a representative of the Joint Chiefs of Staff and the secretaries of War, Navy, and State, this authority, to be funded by the participating departments, would assume responsibility for overall intelligence planning and development. Its instrument for doing so would be a "Central Intelligence Agency," directed by either a military officer with appropriate experience or a "specially qualified civilian." Appointed by the president, this director would be advised by an "Intelligence Advisory Board." State, supported by the Bureau of the Budget and, ultimately, the Department of Justice, vigorously objected to the proposal. Already concerned that the influx of OSS personnel would overwhelm its foreign-service officers, Foggy Bottom balked at the premise that the military services "should have a voice reaching the President as unmistakable as that of the State Department." It held that the secretary of state should "control America's intelligence effort" by "determin[ing] the character of the intelligence furnished the President." The secretary of state, in fact, should chair the National Intelligence Authority.

In this bureaucratic battle royale State's authority on intelligence and most aggressive advocate, Alfred McCormack, special assistant to Secretary of State James Byrnes, proved no match for Secretary of the Navy James Forrestal. Forrestal was not only in the vanguard of government officials convinced that the Soviet Union posed a serious threat to the United States and its allies, but he was also in the vanguard of government officials convinced that the United States required a substantially improved national security machinery to assess that threat. Forrestal commissioned his friend Ferdinand Eberstadt, a prominent investment banker, to recommend measures to reorganize America's defense establishment and promote more coherent decisionmaking. Eberstadt concluded that the effectiveness of any national security structure, no matter how coordinated, required an intelligence agency that could provide "authoritative information on conditions and developments in the outside world." To draft the section of his report outlining the organization and character of that agency, Eberstadt turned to Rear Admiral Sidney W. Souers. A reserve naval officer who served under Forrestal during World War II, Souers, at the time the deputy chief of naval intelligence, reflected the perspective of the Departments of War and Navy. Souers's contribution to the Eberstadt report echoed this perspective. McCormack's advocacy of a central intelligence agency that institutionalized the supremacy of the Department of State fell by the wayside.

Driven largely by the Eberstadt report, Truman's initial effort at forging a compromise tilted significantly toward the military's preference. In January 1946 he created its proposed National Intelligence Authority (NIA). In fact, his memorandum announcing the NIA's establishment repeated verbatim much of the wording produced by the Joint Chiefs of Staff six months earlier. Rather than its representative joining with the secretaries of War, Navy, and State on it, however, a personal representative of the president would. The NIA would supervise a Central Intelligence Group (CIG), responsible for the coordination, collection, evaluation, and dissemination of intelligence. But each department's intelligence service would retain its personnel and "continue to collect, evaluate, correlate, and disseminate departmental intelligence." Neither the NIA nor the CIG could engage in domestic intelligence gathering or surveillance, and Truman's memo made no mention of covert operations. The choice of CIG director, to be called the Director of Central Intelligence (DCI) and serve as a nonvoting member of the NIA, was the prerogative of the president. President Truman chose Rear Admiral Sidney Souers.

Officially activated on February 8, 1946, and housed in sundry office buildings and prefabricated huts along the reflecting pool around the Lincoln memorial in Washington, the CIG manifested confusion from the start as to its precise charge. Its primary components were a Central Planning Staff, to coordinate intelligence activities, and a Central Reports Staff, responsible for producing "national policy intelligence." At issue was what defined national policy, or strategic intelligence, and through what channels it would flow. Truman wanted "current intelligence," daily summaries that would make it unnecessary for him to read lengthy reports or the volumes of intelligence data that the CIG received. For this purpose Souers directed the Central Reports Staff to produce succinct briefs that excluded all material that the president did not need to know immediately. Truman normally read these summaries each evening and used them for his discussions the next day with his personal military advisor and the presiding officer of the JCS, Admiral William D. Leahy.

Yet Truman's memorandum establishing the CIG directed it to "Accomplish the correlation and evaluation of intelligence relating to the national security, and the appropriate dissemination within the government of the resulting strategic and national policy intelligence." Not only did the Central Reports Staff lack the resources to produce both "current" and "strategic and national policy intelligence," but also at the NIA's first meeting Secretary of State Byrnes insisted that it was the responsibility of the State Department to furnish the president with "current intelligence." Souers formulated a compromise. The Central Reports Staff would produce national intelligence. The production of current intelligence, however, would be its "first priority." Even as the State Department remained dissatisfied, preparing current intelligence for the president's use came to dominate the "culture" of the Central Reports

Staff, which Souers's successor, Lt. Gen. Hoyt S. Vandenberg, renamed the Office of Reports and Estimates (ORE). "National estimative intelligence was reduced to also-ran status." Souers tried to square the circle by also instructing the Central Reports Staff to produce weekly summaries; this product satisfied no one.

Souers only agreed to accept the position of DCI on an interim basis, and his brief tenure was hardly successful. During the three months prior to his departure in July 1946, the NIA met but three times. With Forrestal's star still rising in the administration and Byrnes's poised to fall, the likelihood of Truman's selecting someone from outside the military to succeed Souers was exceedingly remote. Souers's recommendation of Lt. General Hoyt Vandenberg, and Vandenberg's willingness to accept the position despite his concerns that it could interrupt his career trajectory, all but assured his appointment. The chief of the Army's G-2, Vandenberg had the necessary experience—and the connections. He was the nephew of Michigan's Arthur Vandenberg, the ranking Republican on the Senate Foreign Relations Committee and pivotal to whatever bipartisan support Truman could hope to engender on Capitol Hill. The combination of General Vandenberg's ambitions and Senator Vandenberg's political skill and influence augured well for the CIG's future development.

Almost immediately after succeeding Souers, DCI Vandenberg had grand plans for the CIG. Because of his standing within the military, he was more willing than Souers to step on the service chiefs' toes. Indeed, Vandenberg was eager to challenge the status quo of the military establishment: His ultimate goal, moreover, was to become chief of staff of an independent Air Force. Hence whereas Souers premised his stewardship of the CIG on the primacy of the services' (and State's) intelligence assets, Vandenberg sympathized with Donovan's proposal of a strong, highly centralized intelligence agency that exceeded the sum of its parts. As the autonomy and the authority of the CIG increased, so would Vandenberg's. He had no intention of serving merely in a custodial role for the National Intelligence Authority. From his point of view, the DCI should exercise preponderant control of all foreign intelligence and counterintelligence operations.

Vandenberg's initial reform, not surprisingly, was administrative and focused especially on the budget. Because it was the executive agent of the NIA and not an independent agency, the CIG could not request appropriations directly from Congress. It derived its funds from the Departments of War, Navy, and State. But those departments did not have lines in their budgets for the CIG. This meant that the DCI had to depend on the generosity of each department's secretary. To rectify this inherent weakness, Vandenberg insisted that each department earmark appropriations for the CIG and empower him, as DCI, to disperse them. Predictably the secretaries objected, but influenced by the advice of his chief of staff, William Leahy, Truman sided with Vandenberg. The CIG, however, still lacked a sufficient independent budget.

Vandenberg nonetheless received sufficient funds through vouchers (so that the precise amount of department funds targeted for the CIG could remain secret) to purchase supplies and hire his own personnel.

Acquiring what was tantamount to an independent budget was but a small step in the CIG's growth and maturity. And each additional step that Vandenberg sought to take encountered resistance, for the CIG's gain meant a loss to a department. Chief among these were his efforts in the fall of 1946 to enhance the DCI's control over the production and assessment of strategic intelligence. Yet improving America's capacity to produce such intelligence assessments had been the raison d'etre for the CIG's establishment. Nonetheless, it played a decidedly subordinate role, to the War Department's Joint Intelligence Committee above all.

One of Vandenberg's gambits was to phase out the SSU, the OSS's foreign intelligence component that Truman had assigned to the Department of War. Vandenberg enveloped its responsibilities within an Office of Special Operations (OSO), which would operate under the CIG as he directed. The mission of the OSO was to conduct "all organized Federal espionage and counterespionage operations outside of the U.S. and its possessions for the collection of foreign intelligence information required for national security." FBI Director J. Edgar Hoover refused to relinquish the FBI's responsibility for Latin America until 1947, and even then he instructed his agents not to share their files with their replacements from the OSO. Vandenberg scored related victories when he won approval from the NIA to cede the CIG responsibility for intelligence pertaining to the field of atomic energy and award it the Foreign Broadcast Intelligence Service (FBIS, later renamed the Foreign Broadcast Information Service).

In Vandenberg's eyes, institutionalizing the CIG's authority for evaluating and disseminating intelligence was even more critical for its future legitimacy and clout than its mandate to procure it. This capacity would make it central, indeed indispensable, to the formulation of national policy. The State Department, never reconciled to sharing power equally with the Navy and War Departments on the NIA, vigorously opposed the proposal that it now take a backseat to the CIG. Vandenberg's opening salvo was to reconstitute the Central Reports Staff in July 1946 as the Office of Research and Evaluation (ORE). Unlike the CRS, ORE's personnel would not be borrowed from other departments but hired independently. When State complained that it was in charge of research and evaluation, Vandenberg renamed his bureau the Office of Reports and Estimates.

At issue, of course, was not the name. The basis of the conflict was what kind of reports and estimates the ORE would produce, and who would be the consumers. Essentially the debate reflected the earlier confusion between "current" and "national" intelligence and who would produce what for whom. The debate raged for months, finally reaching closure at a meeting in February 1947. There the NIA agreed to the definition of strategic intelligence that

Vandenberg proposed, a definition that assured that the "reports" and "estimates" produced by the ORE would be the linchpin of the national security policymaking process. The approved wording read,

> Strategic and national policy intelligence is that composite intelligence, *interdepartmental in character*, which is required by the President and other high officers and staffs to assist them in determining policies with respect to national planning and security in peace and war and for the advancement of broad national policy. It is in that political-economic-military area of concern to more than one agency, must be objective, and *must transcend the exclusive competence of any one department.*

THE CREATION OF THE CIA

For Vandenberg, the pieces were falling into place. The CIG's fundamental weakness remained, nevertheless. It was, as described by Lawrence Houston, "a stepchild of three separate departments." Houston's vantage point enabled him not only to speak with authority, but also to appreciate fully the implications of the predicament. Souers had appointed him general counsel for the CIG. This appointment required Houston to examine the paper trail that led to its establishment. The problem went beyond the constraints imposed by Truman's memorandum of January 1946 that so circumscribed the power of the CIG as to define its role as more of a coordinator for the NIA than an operating agency in its own right. It did not have any "authority to act on its own responsibility in other than an advisory and directing capacity." What Houston also learned was that the CIG lacked its own statutory basis, and without this basis, federal guidelines precluded it from continuing to function legally in any capacity for more than a year. With Souers's blessing, then, Houston began to draft the enabling legislation that would enable the CIG to survive.

To facilitate his task Houston drew heavily on Donovan's 1944 memorandum. This made sense; more than any other participant in the debates over the character of a U.S. intelligence agency during peacetime, Donovan had argued that it should be an autonomous component of the Executive Office of the President. Souers did not sympathize with Donovan's proposals, but he supported Houston's borrowing portions of it in order to place the CIG on a more solid legal footing. By the time Houston had prepared his initial recommendations, moreover, pivotal members of his "audience" had become more receptive to an independent and empowered CIG. On the one hand, Houston submitted his report three days after Souers had retired, on June 13, 1946. In other words, he submitted it to the more aggrandizing Hoyt Vandenberg. On the other hand, by June 1946 the U.S. government and its informed public were substantially more disposed toward a powerful spy agency and other aspects of a national security state. George Kennan's "Long Telegram" from Moscow and Winston Churchill's Iron Curtain speech had become the talk of Washington, the Soviets had behaved badly in Iran, the Council of Foreign Ministers meeting in Paris was degenerating into acrimony, and the hope of reaching an understanding between the Soviets and Americans to control atomic weapons was about to be dashed in the United Nations. Dramatic institutional initiatives were becoming integral to the Truman administration's nascent Cold War arsenal.

Progress was slow, nevertheless. Not only did Houston's enabling legislation for the CIG run up against the expected bureaucratic interests and the problem of providing it with a confidential budget, but it also became caught in the quagmire over the proposed unification of the armed services. The legislation to establish an autonomous, "enabled" central intelligence agency had become incorporated into a broader national security bill, a key feature of which was the establishment of an Air Force independent from and equal to the other military services. Vandenberg resigned so that he could receive his fourth star and become available to become its first chief of staff.

Truman submitted the proposed National Security Act to Congress on February 26, 1947. The single section authorizing a central intelligence agency was remarkably brief. It included virtually none of Houston's initial recommendations, and, for that reason, owed little directly to Donovan's vision. The Act called for the establishment of an Office of the Secretary of Defense; an independent Air Force; a coordinating committee comprising the service chiefs, the Joint Chiefs of Staff; and a National Security Council (NSC) composed of the president, the vice president, the secretary of state, and the secretary of defense as statutory members. The NSC would be situated in the Executive Office of the President, and subordinate to it was the CIG, which the legislation renamed the Central Intelligence Agency. The president would still appoint the director, but the appointee would now require confirmation by the Senate. If a military officer, the DCI could retain his commission and rank. Although the CIA would inherit all the responsibilities of the CIG, the National Security Act enumerated only in the most general terms what those responsibilities were to be. It did, however, abolish the NIA and include an elastic clause stipulating that the CIA's duties would include performing "such additional services of common concern as the National Security Council determines can be more efficiently accomplished centrally." Congress passed the National Security Act overwhelmingly, and Truman signed it into law on July 26, 1947. He appointed Admiral Roscoe H. Hillenkoetter, who had taken over from Vandenberg while Congress considered the legislation, as the first director of Central Intelligence (as opposed to director of "just" the CIA). Truman also appointed Sidney Souers executive secretary of the NSC.

In the fear-ridden Cold War environment of 1947, Congress and the president established the CIA as one component of the largest reorganization of America's national security machinery. The significance of this synergy cannot be exaggerated. Although a consensus had developed even before the end of the World War II on the need for a central authority to coordinate the intelligence services, officials in Washington conceived the CIA as an instrument to fight the cold war. What is more, the juxtaposition of the CIA's birth with that of the Office of the Secretary of Defense (OSD), the JCS, and the NSC all but assured that the confusion and discord that had afflicted its predecessor, the CIG, would abate but not cease.

THE EARLY YEARS OF THE CIA, 1947–1949

The conundrum encountered by the CIA because of the circumstances of its founding was manifest in identifying its priorities and defining the role of the director. In the latter case, conflicts inhered in the dichotomy between directing central intelligence (the community) and directing the CIA. The tension between producing national and current intelligence surfaced again. The fundamental reason for support for a central intelligence agency throughout the Washington and public communities was the need to coordinate assessments of the Soviet threat. Indeed, Moscow's intentions became the subject of the first intelligence estimate produced by the Office of Research and Evaluation when Vandenberg, to the chagrin of the State Department, established this CIG bureau in 1946. ORE 1, "Soviet Foreign and Military Policy," reflected the influence of George Kennan. As counselor to the embassy in Moscow, Kennan had earlier that year dispatched his "Long Telegram" to Washington, and he was one of America's few experts on the Soviet Union. Souers had appointed him his special consultant. ORE-1 closely paralleled Kennan's analyses and predictions. Although the estimate expected the Kremlin leadership to postpone "overt conflict for an indefinite period," it stressed that "the Soviet Union anticipates an inevitable conflict with the capitalist world," and its "ultimate objective may be world domination."

CIG's subsequent ORE estimates were similarly imprecise. Their utility for Truman and his key national security managers was no greater than the reports and evaluations produced by the other intelligence agencies. The same held true for ORE estimates on other areas and topics because its resources were no better, and sometimes worse. "[O]ur information relating to this subject is meager," began ORE 3/1, "Soviet Capabilities for the Development and Production of Certain Types of Weapons and Equipment," written in 1946. It forecast that "the capability of the U.S.S.R. to develop weapons based on atomic energy will be limited to the possible development of an atomic bomb to the stage of production at some time between 1950 and 1953." As late as 1948, after the CIA's creation and the intensification of the Cold War, only thirty-eight analysts worked in ORE's Soviet and East European branch. Of these, nine had lived there, twelve spoke any Russian, and one had a Ph.D. Six had no college degrees at all.

The institutional interests of the ORE and the career aspirations of its staff militated against producing national intelligence. This was especially so because these estimates reaped few bureaucratic awards, and risked provoking scorn if not wrath from the department secretaries. The assessments of Soviet intentions and capabilities of Forrestal and the military intelligence services especially were significantly more alarmist than those of the CIA's Soviet experts. Hence ORE was content to oblige President Truman's priority on current intelligence rather than risk a confrontation with Forrestal and his powerful allies over matters of strategic intelligence. Whereas national estimates normally began with a set of conclusions followed by detailed analysis, the daily and weekly summaries were by and large limited to descriptions of events and developments. These summaries were what the president most wanted; antiseptically noncontroversial, they were less likely to generate a backlash. As a result, intelligence produced by the CIA tended to contribute remarkably little to policy formulation, especially policy related to the Soviet Union.

The establishment of the CIA reinforced this dynamic. In what seemed like a logical organizational initiative, Hillenkoetter divided the ORE into regional branches. Personnel with particular expertise staffed the appropriate branch. The most effective way for an individual staff member to gain recognition and hence career advancement was to contribute to an ORE publication. The daily and weekly summaries provided many more opportunities than a long-term estimate. The CIA's own official history lamented that because of their ambitions, "individuals in ORE perpetuated and contributed to the current intelligence stranglehold."

To his credit Hillenkoetter sought to accord higher priority and status to the production of national intelligence. He was not one to rock the boat, however, and even if so inclined, the CIA's inherent weaknesses in 1947 and his own ambiguous role as its director severely undermined his influence. By statute the DCI wore three distinct hats: head of the agency itself, intelligence provider to the president and the NSC, and supervisor to all the elements that make up the U.S. intelligence community. The last of these responsibilities caused problems from the start, and severely constrained Hillenkoetter's ability to produce the kind of national intelligence he preferred. The best he could do was to integrate the descriptive daily and weekly summaries into slightly more analytical documents that he thought the CIA's customers would value: digests entitled "Review of the World Situation as it Relates to the Security of the United States."

When Souers had instructed Houston to prepare enabling legislation for the CIG, he had assumed that the DCI would reign supreme over the intelligence community's other components and their heads. Houston, building on Donovan's model, proceeded accordingly. The National Security Act, however, did not incorporate Houston's prose. Its general wording did anoint the DCI the nation's chief intelligence officer, but did not specify how and to what extent he would control other intelligence organs. In addition, although it abolished the NIA, the same cabinet officers who composed it now served on the NSC, to which the CIA was subordinate. And Forrestal, as the first secretary of defense, combined in his person the authority of the secretaries of war and navy. Neither he nor Secretary of State George Marshall, whose background drove him to link intelligence to the military, were inclined to cede supremacy to the DCI. Vandenberg probably would have fought to achieve dominance. Hillenkoetter did not. Doubtless he understood that Forrestal and Marshall could derail the CIA's development before it could establish itself, and thus he could not afford to alienate either. Whatever the reason, Hillenkoetter conceded that the position of DCI was subservient to the secretaries of state and defense. By doing so he forfeited the best opportunity for the director of central intelligence really to direct central intelligence.

The intensification of the Cold War in 1948, punctuated by the Soviet blockade of Berlin and the communist coup and the death of Jan Masaryk in Czechoslovakia (neither of which the CIA predicted), persuaded Truman that U.S. security required additional reorganization of the executive branch. In this regard the confusion in Washington over what to make of General Lucius Clay's early 1948 cable expressing his concern that a war with the U.S.S.R. might erupt with "dramatic suddenness" underscored the need to strengthen the CIA's analytical capabilities—and its authority over competing intelligence agencies. Truman had already created a commission under former President Herbert Hoover to recommend measures to improve the effectiveness and efficiency of the federal bureaucracy. In 1948 the Hoover commission established a task force on intelligence directed by Ferdinand Eberstadt, whose 1945 report had contributed to the creation of the CIG. The task force's report card on the CIA's first year was not good. It faulted the agency for failing to become a "major source of coordinated and evaluated intelligence." For this, however, the CIA alone was not to blame. The "relationships of this agency to some of the other intelligence agencies of government...have been and still are unsatisfactory," the Eberstadt task force concluded. "The Central Intelligence Agency deserves and must have a greater degree of acceptance and support from old-line intelligence services."

These judgments prompted Truman's national security managers to recommend a comprehensive review of the fledgling CIA. At Souers's urging the NSC appointed Allen W. Dulles, an OSS stalwart who had been one of the favorites in 1946 to be DCI, to chair the examining committee. Dulles's Republican credentials and ties to Truman's presidential opponent Thomas Dewey also influenced his selection. Serving with Dulles were William H. Jackson, another New York lawyer and veteran of World War II intelligence, and Mathias F. Correa, a former aide to Forrestal in the Department of the Navy.

THE CENTRAL INTELLIGENCE AGENCY ACT OF 1949
AND REORGANIZING THE CIA

The Dulles-Jackson-Correa committee submitted its report on January 1, 1949. Its diagnoses had by then become conventional wisdom. They included such standard fare as the CIA's responsibility to coordinate intelligence activities was "not being adequately exercised," and the ORE had "been concerned with a wide variety of activities and with the production of miscellaneous reports and summaries that by no stretch of the imagination could be considered national estimates." The report took aim at the CIA's leadership and it did not mince words. It is "necessarily a reflection of inadequacies of direction" that the agency has become "just one more intelligence agency producing intelligence in competition with older established agencies of the Government departments." It concluded with scores of specific recommendations, almost all of which were organizational. "While organizational charts can never replace individual initiative and ability, the Central Intelligence Agency, reorganized along the functional lines indicated in this report, should be able more effectively to carry out the duties assigned it by law and thus bring our over-all intelligence system closer to that point of efficiency that our national security demands."

The initial impact of the report was minimal. The NSC adopted most of its proposed reforms, but it did so incrementally and without acknowledging that the problems were fundamental. The influence of the report over the long term, however, was more substantial. For one thing, submitted in the anxiety-ridden climate of the Cold War that had carried Truman to reelection, the report motivated Congress to enact the enabling legislation that Vandenberg had sought since 1946 and Houston had begun to draft. The objective was to provide the agency with the explicit authority to fulfill its responsibilities and defend its turf, and to fund these purposes without congressional or public scrutiny. Signed into law in June, the Central Intelligence Agency Act of 1949 "was everything that the 'intelligence professionals' wanted it to be." The report also prescribed an administrative reform that generated little attention at the time but that dramatically affected the agency's future. The Dulles-Jackson-Correa committee proposed the creation of five overarching divisions to replace the multitude of offices that deterred coordination in the CIA. The first four of these divisions were predictable and anodyne: Administration, Coordination, Research and Reports, and Estimates. The fifth recommended division was a Division of Operations. Its responsibility would include espionage and counterintelligence, functions considered integral to the CIA from its inception. What distinguished this division, however, is that it could exercise "a considerable degree of autonomy" because its mandate embraced covert operations. The juxtaposition of the creation of the Division of Operations with the CIA Act of 1949 bestowed upon the Agency "the power to wage secret war."

THE ORIGINS OF CIA COVERT OPERATIONS

The requirement for greater coordination of America's intelligence services drove the decision to establish a peacetime successor to the OSS. Those who contributed to the discussions about the organization and authority of this central intelligence agency paid little attention to providing it with the capability to conduct covert political, paramilitary, or psychological activities. These are the activities associated with influencing government officials, labor leaders, intellectuals and artists, and others in foreign countries; supporting insurgent movements, counterrevolutionaries, and even terrorists and assassins; and engaging in black propaganda and other forms of psychological warfare. During World War II the OSS had engaged in this shadow warfare frequently. For a liberal democracy to sanction such unsavory behavior when not at war seemed intolerable for "gentlemen" who had only reluctantly endorsed reading others' mail. In their view sub rosa conduct reflected too radical a break with the nation's traditions. Besides, the OSS had engaged in covert operations under the aegis of the military, and were such operations to be undertaken again, the services had no intention of ceding the responsibility to another institution or agency. In theory the CIG had inherited the OSS's license for dirty tricks when Truman transferred to it the War Department's Strategic Services Unit. But the essential tasks of the SSU were intelligence collection and counterintelligence, and Vandenberg made no mention of covert operations when he replaced the SSU with the Office of Special Operations (OSO).

With the outbreak of civil war in Greece and China and a crisis in Iran, the Soviets bearing down on Eastern Europe, the economic and political instability of Western Europe, the failure of U.S. efforts to secure an agreement on control of atomic weapons, and Kennan's description of the Kremlin leadership as fanatics with whom there could be no *modus vivendi*, by the end of 1946 officials in the Truman administration concluded that the United States confronted a different kind of war that required a different kind of thinking. America could not afford to "play fair" because the communists would not. In his quest to expand Stalin probably would not initiate a military attack. "Because of the ravages of war, the Soviets have vital need for a long peace before embarking upon a major war," estimated the CIG, reflecting the thinking of most in Washington. The greatest threat was that the Kremlin, relying on propaganda, exploiting political unrest and economic instability, and providing assistance to "indigenous" parties and labor movements, would successfully subvert local governments and institutions. In defense the United States had to develop its own political and psychological warfare capabilities.

The military predictably took the lead in urging President Truman in 1946 to add covert operations to the administration's Cold War arsenal. Evidently Secretary of War Robert Patterson was the first high-level official to broach the subject formally. He quickly gained an ally in Secretary of the Navy

Forrestal, and by December 1946 a subcommittee of the State-War-Navy Coordinating Committee (SWNCC, predecessor to the NSC) had formulated guidelines for conducting psychological and political warfare. By mid-1947 under the supervision of SWNCC, a Special Studies and Evaluations Sub-committee came into existence for the purpose of planning such efforts. The issue was no longer whether the United States would undertake them, but who would, how, and when. In December 1947 the newly created NSC determined that the "similarity of operational methods involved in covert psychological and intelligence activities and the need to insure their secrecy and obviate costly duplications renders the Central Intelligence Agency the logical agency to conduct such operations."

The NSC directed the CIA to begin immediately to

> initiate and conduct, within the limits of available funds, covert psychological operations designed to counteract Soviet and Soviet-inspired activities which constitute a threat to world peace and security or are designed to discredit and defeat the United States in its endeavors to promote world peace and security.

Although the focus at the time was on a potential Communist victory in the 1948 Italian elections, the NSC did not identify any specific threats, nor did it advise the CIA about how and with what assets it should implement its new assignment. DCI Hillenkoetter quickly set up a Special Procedures Group within the OSO for the purpose of planning and implementing "all measures of information and persuasion short of physical in which the originating role of the United States Government will always be kept concealed."

Even as the NSC directed the CIA to become the agent for America's covert operations, a broader definition of shadow warfare became a fundamental feature of U.S. national security policy. The consequences of this development on the future of the CIA, U.S. foreign policy, and the structure of the U.S. government cannot be exaggerated. In this context, George Kennan played a pivotal role. Kennan's star had risen meteorically since as the counselor to America's embassy in Moscow he had written the "Long Telegram." In April 1947 Secretary of State George Marshall appointed him director of the department's new Policy Planning Staff. No sooner had the NSC mandated the CIA to undertake covert operations than Kennan argued that America's security demanded that the administration not limit covert actions to psychological warfare.

Kennan recommended that the NSC establish a "directorate of political warfare operations" with "complete authority over covert political warfare operations conducted by this Government" and authorized to "initiate new operations." These operations would promote the liberation of communist dominated areas by more aggressive means than previously envisioned. For example, in the case of Italy the United States would intervene directly in the electoral process in contrast to "merely" seeking to influence public opinion. Rather than directly implicate the NSC in actions that if detected could contaminate its other foreign policy initiatives and embarrass the administration, nevertheless, the council's members, Marshall above all, suggested that the CIA, with its clandestine budget and many OSS veterans, expand its covert mission by supplementing its psychological warfare programs with political ones. Left unresolved was whether the agency's capabilities were already stretched too thin and whether, if it had the authority to "initiate" new operations, State and Defense would be involved in decision making.

The NSC assigned State's Policy Planning Staff the task of drafting a document to place covert operations in U.S. national security strategy and to address the NSC's structural concerns. Kennan did most of the writing himself, and in June 1948 the NSC approved his handiwork as NSC 10/2. This policy directive stressed that conducting covert operations was essential to the achievement of U.S. national security objectives, and, going well beyond Kennan's initial recommendation, extended the parameters of covert operations to encompass political, economic, and paramilitary activities, including sabotage and demolition. NSC 10/2 made the CIA responsible for planning and executing these operations, but created a highly unorthodox structure to carry out this responsibility. The Special Procedures Group within the OSO would be replaced by an Office of Special Projects (OSP) autonomous from the OSO. The NSC and CIA soon agreed to rename the OSP the Office of Policy Coordination (OPC). Although this unit was funded through the CIA's secret appropriations, for reasons of "security and flexibility" it would operate independently of other "components" of the agency, and the DCI would have very little say in its activities. NSC 10/2 vested primary authority for the behavior of the OPC in its director, to be appointed by the secretary of state. Further, the OPC director would be guided by instructions jointly issued by State and Defense.

Shortly after Truman approved NSC 10/2, Lawrence Houston drafted a memorandum providing retroactive legal justification. In August 1948 the NSC endorsed State's nomination for OPC director the OSS veteran Frank Wisner, who at the time was serving as the assistant secretary of state for Occupied Areas. Wealthy, well connected, and highly respected, Wisner was an avid advocate of covert operations and entrusting them to "intelligence professionals." It soon became apparent that he could pursue his most imaginative projects with few constraints. For guidance Wisner met regularly with representatives from Defense and State. For the next two years that meant meeting with General Joseph McNarney and George Kennan. The commander of U.S. forces during the initial years of the Cold War, McNarney sympathized with any anti-Soviet initiative. And having played the pivotal role in creating the OPC and defining its mission, Kennan was enthusiastic about Wisner's plans.

The NSC approved Kennan's unconventional design for the OPC for two overarching reasons. First, the connection between the OPC and the NSC, and by extension, the president, was sufficiently convoluted as to shield the executive branch from explicit culpability, allowing it to "plausibly disclaim any responsibility" for operations it had approved. Second, the design reflected the administration's lack of confidence in DCI Hillenkoetter, who had opposed the arrangement. Ironically, shortly before Truman signed off on NSC 10/2, the CIA registered its first covert action success: Italy. Funneling an estimated \$10–30 million to several groups and parties, particularly the Christian Democrat party, contributed to the defeat of the Italian communists in the April 1948 election. But under Hillenkoetter's watch the CIA had failed to predict either the February 1948 communist coup in Czechoslovakia or, in April, the riots that broke out during the Inter-American Foreign Ministers Meeting in Bogotá, Colombia. Things became worse for the CIA, and U.S. foreign policy, in 1949 with the successful Soviet test of an atomic device and the communist victory in the Chinese civil war. 1949 was also the beginning of the disastrous joint operation between OPC and Britain's SIS to overthrow the communist government of Enver Hoxha in Albania by surreptitiously offloading or airdropping agents. The project finally ended four years later with the death or capture of virtually all of the operatives and many indigenous Albanians, probably because of advance notice provided by the British double-agent Kim Philby. Then in June 1950 came the surprise North Korean invasion of South Korea. Hillenkoetter was but one of many who shared responsibility for these intelligence failures. He was the DCI, however, and he had never exercised this authority with sufficient dynamism or, some claim, conviction. In addition, Hillenkoetter proved incapable of untying the bureaucratic knot that entangled the hybrid OPC and, for that matter, the CIA itself.

THE DIRECTORSHIP OF WALTER BEDELL SMITH

During the fall of 1950 President Truman took two huge steps to address the perceived degradation of U.S. security. Establishing a pattern for future presidents, in September he approved NSC-68, a new statement of national security that—all but disregarding CIA estimates of the Soviet Union, which were less alarmist than other intelligence assessments— essentially placed America on a war footing. Then in October, shortly before the most egregious U.S. intelligence failure to date, to predict Communist China's intervention in Korea, he replaced DCI Hillenkoetter with Walter Bedell Smith. Beetle, the name used by Smith's friends, was in many ways everything that Hillenkoetter was not. A four-star general who had served as Dwight D. Eisenhower's chief of staff during World War II and afterward as ambassador to the Soviet Union, Smith had the prestige and clout to compete with any military officer or cabinet secretary. And he had the appropriate personality. Strong-willed and frequently irascible, Smith could be fearsome as well as intimidating. An ardent Cold Warrior with vast administrative experience, he was perfectly suited to lead the CIA into a new era. Ray Cline, an OSS veteran who was present at the creation of the CIA and ultimately became its deputy director, exulted in Smith's appointment: "For the first time since Donovan, central intelligence was in the hands of a man with vision and drive, a man with the prestige persuasive to military commanders, ambassadors, and Congressmen, and, finally, a man with the full support of the President."

The day after the Senate unanimously confirmed Smith's appointment, he received a lengthy memorandum from general counsel Lawrence Houston spelling out the challenges the new DCI would face. They were substantial. Houston seemed to suggest that despite the 1949 CIA Act, NSC 10/2, and the CIA's revised organization and accreted mission, it was in truth no more effective than it had been under Vandenberg. Because other agencies still resisted providing the Agency with the intelligence it required, its estimates remained inadequate. The military was the worst offender, but the CIA had not been able to do anything about it. From Houston's perspective, the CIA had yet to establish its authority over the government's other intelligence services, nor had the DCI established his authority over the other members of the Intelligence Advisory Committee. This had to change. As for the hybrid character of the OPC, it was worse than inefficient—it was unworkable. Houston also opposed the establishment of the OPC as independent of the CIA's other components, especially clandestine intelligence collection.

Smith lost no time instituting reforms aimed at making right what Houston said was wrong. He was assisted by the experienced William Jackson. Then, when Jackson returned to private business in 1951, Smith replaced him as DDCI with Allen Dulles. While Dulles was a valuable asset, predisposed toward planning and executing covert actions, he demonstrated less concern for the reorganizational initiatives that Smith considered vital. Smith undertook them virtually unilaterally. To begin with he established a directorate of administration to manage the Agency's personnel, financial, and other support functions. Concurrently, to improve the CIA's capacity for producing national intelligence estimates, which still suffered from a misplaced priority on current intelligence as well as the lack of cooperation from other intelligence services, Smith divided ORE into three different offices: the Office of National Estimates (ONE), the Office of Research and Reports (ORR), and the Office of Current Intelligence (OCI). To head ONE, Smith named former OSS Chief of Research and Analysis and Harvard Professor William Langer. MIT's Max Millikan became the director of ORR and wrote the guidelines for this office's priority on providing economic analyses of present and future threats—in other words, economic analyses of the Soviet Union and its allies and clients. The OCI housed the individual country analysts and focused on political intelligence. By separating ONE from both ORR and OCI, moreover,

19

Smith distinguished institutionally between the production of national and current intelligence. As Langer's deputy and expected successor, Smith appointed Yale's Sherman Kent, who had also served in the OSS. Kent, who in 1949 published the acclaimed *Strategic Intelligence for American and World Policy*, succeeded Langer in 1952 and became a legend over the subsequent decades.

ONE, ORR, and OCI were in turn supervised by a Board of National Estimates (BNE), comprised of leading military and civilian intelligence experts. It would review all estimates produced to ensure that they both incorporated the necessary material from the appropriate departments and underscored differences in their judgments. Of its initial eight members, five held doctorates in history; one, a doctorate in economics; one was a prominent attorney; and the final member was a four-star general who had recently retired after commanding U.S. forces in Europe. Then in 1952 Smith established a Directorate of Intelligence (DI), appointing Loftus Becker, a lawyer who served as an advisor at the Nuremberg trials, deputy director for intelligence. In addition to ONE, ORR, and OCI, Becker's directorate included the Office of Collection and Dissemination and the Office of Scientific Intelligence. A year later Robert Amory, another OSS veteran and Harvard professor, succeeded Becker as DDI.

Smith firmly believed that intelligence collection and analysis was the CIA's chief mission. Ambivalent about the efficacy of covert operations, he thought the military should undertake them. Still, because the NSC had assigned the CIA responsibility for these operations, Smith could not countenance the Agency's inadequate capacity to fulfill that responsibility. Nor could he countenance accepting a subordinate role in covert action decision making. Perhaps even more than any of his other initiatives, Smith's reforms of the organizational chart for covert operations radically affected the agency's future direction. Ironically, Smith all but assured that within the CIA's structure intelligence collection and analysis would play second fiddle to operations.

Smith attacked the question of the CIA's contribution to and responsibility for covert operations from a variety of angles. As an initial step, the month he took over as DCI he proposed a "reinterpretation" of NSC 10/2. What the document *really* intended, he argued to representatives from State and Defense, is that the DCI receive their *advice*, not instructions, on the priorities for and planning of covert operations. By this time Kennan was in Moscow as America's ambassador and Forrestal had committed suicide. Confronted with the indomitable Smith, State and Defense acquiesced without objection. As a result, in practice Smith integrated the OPC into the CIA. A year later the NSC replaced NSC 10/2 with NSC 10/5. It confirmed the DCI's authority over covert operations even as it mandated their "intensification." Implementing Houston's recommendation, and the recommendation of the Dulles-Jackson-Correa report, Smith then folded the OSO, responsible for espionage, counterespionage, and foreign intelligence collection, into the OPC. The OPC would now be responsible for all clandestine operations. He also established new Offices of Foreign Intelligence, Political and Psychological Warfare, Paramilitary Operations, Technical Support, and Administration, placing all within a Directorate of Plans (DP). Allen Dulles was its first director (DDP).

Although Smith achieved his goal of transforming the CIA, he was not altogether pleased with his accomplishments or his legacy. He strengthened the agency's capacity for covert operations because that was his mandate as DCI. But he continued to fret that in doing so he would undermine its capacity as an intelligence collecting and assessing agency. In the anxiety-ridden climate that infected the final years of the Truman administration, his fears proved well founded. With its appropriations concealed in the Defense Department budget, congressional "oversight" confined to general briefings of ranking members of the House and Senate Armed Services Committee, and NSC 10/5's directive for an "intensification" of covert operations, OPC's budget increased three-fold during Smith's tenure as DCI (and in 1952 the Truman administration created a Contingency Reserve Fund to provide the CIA with more flexibility for its operations). In 1949 OPC's budget was $4.7 million; in 1952 the budget for clandestine projects and intelligence collection ballooned to $82 million, or an estimated 70–80 percent of the CIA's entire budget. In the same years between 1949 and 1952, the number of overseas stations grew from seven to forty-seven. OPC's personnel numbered only 302 in 1949; it skyrocketed from 584 to 1531 between fiscal years 1950 and 1951 alone.

Initially the OPC concentrated largely on Western Europe. It intervened in elections in France as well as Italy, and established networks with labor unions and among Soviet and East European emigrés in Germany and Vienna. OPC did, nevertheless and with little success, seek to promote resistance organizations in Eastern Europe, such as Poland's Freedom and Independence Movement (known by its Polish initials, WIN), and it funded "liberationist" broadcasts through Radio Free Europe and Radio Liberty. Propelled by the outbreak of the Korean War, such operations expanded exponentially—and geographically. Before June 1950 the CIA had purchased "subsidiaries" in the Far East such as the Civil Air Transport, an outgrowth of Claire Chennault's and Whiting Willauer's Flying Tigers in China that later became better known as Air America, and established bases in Formosa for raids on the mainland. After the North Korean attack, the CIA established a paramilitary capability that it would employ in Asia for the next two decades, most prominently in Vietnam, Laos, and elsewhere in Southeast Asia. In the Philippines, directed by the soon-to-be notorious Edward Lansdale (the model for the lead characters in both *The Quiet American* and *The Ugly American*), the CIA played a vital clandestine role in the defeat of the Huk (Hukbong Mapaspalaya ng Bayan or Hukbalahaps) rebellion and the elevation of Ramon

Magsaysay to the presidency. By 1952 OPC's reach had extended to Latin America, where the aborted 1952 Project FORTUNE (resurrected the next year as PBSUCCESS) intended to oust the perceived communist-influenced government of Jacobo Arbenz Guzmán.

THE DIRECTORSHIP OF ALLEN DULLES

Smith had no qualms about the objectives of these operations. He had serious qualms, however, about their implications for the CIA's future. When President-elect Dwight D. Eisenhower offered him the opportunity to move to the State Department as its undersecretary, Smith readily accepted. Eisenhower had two motives for the appointment. On the one hand, he was not well acquainted with his choice for secretary of state, John Foster Dulles. It was comforting for him to place his former chief of staff at Dulles's side. On the other hand, because of Eisenhower's experiences during World War II, he placed a premium on intelligence operations, whether defined in terms of gathering and assessing intelligence or pursuing covert projects. In either instance greater coordination between the CIA and the State Department should produce greater effectiveness. Smith's transfer to State would clear the path to promote the CIA's deputy director, Allen Dulles. Who better to coordinate with Foster Dulles than his brother?

Thus began the heyday of the CIA. Without question the Agency grew in stature among the constellation of government organs and in notoriety throughout the American public and world community, developing a legend of invincibility. The widespread identification of the CIA with DCI Dulles contributed in large measure to this evolution. Allen Dulles was much more than the younger brother of the secretary of state. He began his intelligence career while a foreign service officer during World War I. His alleged refusal to answer a telephone call from Vladimir Lenin actually enhanced his reputation. That reputation expanded with his OSS service during World War II. Dulles spent the bulk of the war running the office in Bern, Switzerland, the center of an array of operations directed against both the Germans and the Italians. In the most famous of these, Operation SUNRISE, Dulles caused a stir within the Grand Alliance by coming within a hairbreadth of arranging the secret surrender of the German forces in Italy. Dulles was a risk-taker who took naturally—and enthusiastically—to the world of cloaks and daggers.

He was also well connected, an indispensable attribute for the CIA's ascent. A Princeton graduate, when not working for the government Dulles was a lawyer with the prominent Wall Street firm of Sullivan and Cromwell. Outgoing and gregarious, he readily developed excellent personal and working relationships. Many of the CIA's top officers—individuals like Wisner, Richard Helms, Tracy Barnes, and Richard Bissell—shared Dulles's background and values, and welcomed his leadership. He endeared himself to the CIA's personnel even more when, unlike other high officials in the

Eisenhower administration, he openly rebuffed Senator Joseph McCarthy's charges that the Agency harbored communist agents and sympathizers. When McCarthy targeted William Bundy, an ONE analyst and son-in-law of Truman's secretary of state, Dean Acheson, Dulles intervened to thwart the senator's effort to subpoena Bundy to appear before his investigative sub-committee. He also moved comfortably through the halls of Congress and counted among his friends movers and shakers from the worlds of business, law, and, perhaps most importantly, journalism. And no DCI ever had such intimate ties to Foggy Bottom, the Pentagon, and the White House.

Dulles's leadership, stature, and bureaucratic acumen were pivotal to the CIA's transformation from the NSC's stepchild to its vital instrument. More pivotal, nevertheless, were the president's priorities and policies. Eisenhower had campaigned on a platform calling for the aggressive "liberation" of "captive peoples." In part his rhetoric can be attributed to partisan posturing. Still, having come to appreciate the potential of clandestine operations and deception when serving as supreme commander during World War II, Eisenhower firmly believed that shadow warfare provided a low-risk means to achieve Cold War gains, whether defined as reversing perceived communist successes, especially in the developing world, or forcing the Soviets onto the defensive. The growth in the size and power of the atomic and then nuclear arsenals of both Washington and London heightened the appeal of covert projects. In addition, as a military man Eisenhower desperately sought to improve U.S. intelligence capabilities for operational reasons, and as a long-range planner, he believed that grand strategy had to be informed by more reliable national estimates.

In his first term President Eisenhower approved two NSC directives, NSC 5412/1 and NSC 5412/2, that set up a "Special Group" of representatives from State and Defense for the purpose of reviewing plans for covert projects and providing better cover for the president to "plausibly deny" authorizing them. (The group was renamed the 303 Committee during the administration of Lyndon B. Johnson, after the room in which it met in the White House Annex; under Richard Nixon the Special Group became the 40 Committee, following the number of the president's new directive, National Security Decision Memorandum [NSDM] 40, issued on February 17, 1970.) Eisenhower also established the President's Board of Consultants on Foreign Intelligence Activities (PBCFIA), composed of retired military officials, distinguished educators, business leaders, and others of that ilk to provide him with expert advice. More pointedly, he created a committee under the chairmanship of Air Force ace James Doolittle to "make any recommendations calculated to improve the conduct of these operations." The Doolittle Committee reported that America's security demanded that it possess a "covert psychological, political, and paramilitary organization more effective, more unique, and if necessary, more ruthless than that employed by the enemy." This organization must "subvert, sabotage and destroy our enemies by more clever, more sophisticated and more effective methods than those used against us." It must reconsider "long-standing American concepts of 'fair play.'"

The Doolittle Committee concluded that institutionally and organizationally the CIA's structure and its relationships with other departments and arms of the government were quite satisfactory. The Special Group (or "5412" committee) met infrequently and never arrived at sufficiently precise criteria by which to evaluate CIA projects. That left the initiative with the agency itself, which is what Allen Dulles preferred. Intrinsically drawn to covert actions and recognizing that the more of them there were the more integral to security strategy the CIA would become, and the larger its budget, Dulles encouraged Wisner and his staff to develop the most imaginative plans. "[N]o matter how important [intelligence] collection is," Richard Helms quotes Dulles as explaining in 1953, "in the short and even the long run, it just doesn't *cost* very much." While comparatively inexpensive, covert operations did cost, and that was the name of Washington's bureaucratic game. "If there's no real money involved," Dulles continued, neither those in Congress nor in the administration itself would accord the CIA the respect it craved.

Although Dulles did need to confront the complication of camouflaging the increasingly large appropriations earmarked for the CIA's covert operations (the norm was to bury these appropriations in the budgets for State and Defense), he did not need to worry about congressional backing. A bipartisan consensus held that the CIA represented "a first line defense against Communism." As DCI, moreover, Dulles cultivated outstanding relations with the ranking committee members who counted most. It did not matter that for all but Congress's first session during President Eisenhower's two terms of office these members were Democrats. The most influential were Richard Russell (D-GA), who chaired the Senate Armed Services Committee, the House Armed Services Committee Chair, Carl Vinson (D-GA), and House Appropriations Committee Chair Clarence Cannon (D-MO). The committee members preferred to remain in the dark about the CIA's activities. They did not ask; Dulles did not tell. When the DCI appeared before the committees, recalled Senator Leverett Saltonstall (R-MA), a ranking member of both the Senate Armed Forces and Appropriations Committees, "members would ask few questions which dealt with internal Agency matters or with specific operations." The most sensitive discussions were reserved for one-to-one sessions between Dulles and individual committee chairmen.

On several occasions during the 1950s members of Congress did propose structural reforms intended to strengthen legislative oversight. For three primary reasons these attempts made little headway. Most fundamentally, Dulles and others in the executive branch sincerely believed that the greater the involvement of Congress in the CIA's affairs, the greater the risk of a breach of security. Second, the chairs and other senior members of the committee whom Dulles did brief supported the executive branch. What drove their perspective was a reluctance to cede the prerogatives that attended their seniority. The third reason reflected a more temporal concern of Eisenhower and his inner circle. They feared that establishing a formal committee with the responsibility for CIA oversight could provide another platform for Senator McCarthy. In the end Congress and the administration agreed to several almost meaningless compromises. The legislative leaders established CIA subcommittees in both the Armed Services and the Appropriations Committees. In each case, however, the members of these committees were the same who had previously been privy to Dulles's briefings—Richard Russell, Carl Vinson, and Clarence Cannon.

CIA COVERT OPERATIONS DURING THE 1950s

The CIA consequently operated under few formal controls during the 1950s. This is not to say that it could implement unauthorized covert operations. Under Wisner's direction, the DP developed plans for a broad array of contingencies in a broad array of areas. Dulles would often bounce the ideas off his brother when the two regularly lunched on Sundays at the home of sister Eleanor Lansing Dulles, who also worked for State. For approval he would meet informally with the president and his chief advisors; only after Foster Dulles's death in 1959 did the Special Group emerge as a significant cog in the covert operation wheel. To an extent unimaginable but a few years before, much of the 1950s history of U.S. foreign policy was the history of the CIA.

The CIA directed its first major covert operation during the Eisenhower administration, which established a precedent for its future, toward the government of Prime Minister Mohammed Mossadegh in Iran—Operation TPAJAX. Mossadegh had locked horns with the British-dominated Anglo-Iranian Oil Company (AIOC) when he nationalized the company months after becoming Iran's prime minister, following the assassination of his predecessor in 1951. The CIA's intelligence capabilities in Iran at the time were negligible. The country had long been within Britain's sphere of influence, and as a consequence the CIA had developed few assets of its own. Given the thinking in Washington at that time, therefore, the Agency saw no reason to challenge the judgment of the British Secret Intelligence Service (SIS) that Mossadegh's nationalization of the AIOC was more than an attack on British economic interests; it was evidence of the pervasive influence of the communist Tudeh party. Truman's security advisers agreed, but opposed a plan developed by the SIS to topple Mossadegh, a plan that London proposed to pursue in collaboration with the CIA, when an effort to remove Mossadegh by the Iranian shah, Mohammed Reza Pahlavi, failed. DCI Smith never embraced the scheme. Acheson and the State Department, moreover, fretted that an unsuccessful action against Mossadegh could produce a serious disruption of the global oil supply even as it provided grist for the communists' propaganda mill. There was also a risk that the Soviets would use the opportunity to regain the influence that it had lost in 1946.

The Eisenhower administration found the SIS's plan more appealing. In part this was because President Eisenhower and Secretary of State Dulles saw the ouster of Mossadegh as a low-risk means to set the tone for the new administration. No less a contributing factor was the transition from Smith to Allen Dulles as DCI. Much more than his predecessor, Dulles wanted the agency actively involved in the business of covert operations. Representing the CIA in Iran, CIA officer Kermit Roosevelt tweaked the SIS plan to ensure that the Agency was the leading partner and the British financial interests would not benefit at the expense of justified Iranian ones. That accomplished, first John Foster Dulles and then President Eisenhower approved. TPAJAX began in August 1953, and despite the shah's loss of nerve, through strategically placed bribes and staged demonstrations, by the end of the month Mossadegh was in prison. The CIA had come of age.

TPAJAX turned out to be but a prelude. The next year the CIA registered what the Eisenhower administration considered its greatest covert coup—ousting the regime of Jacobo Arbenz Guzmán in Guatemala. As was the case with Iran, Eisenhower inherited a situation in Guatemala in which communists appeared poised to gain predominant power. In fact, the threat seemed more imminent and more severe than in Iran. A 1944 revolution had overthrown the long-time *caudillo* Jorge Ubico Castañeda, leading to the election of Juan José Arévalo, a "spiritual socialist." When the Arévalo government began to implement its agenda of social and economic reform by instituting such programs as rent control and a labor code, the United Fruit Company (UFCO), Guatemala's largest landholder, sounded the alarm that communists had penetrated Arévalo's regime. Initially the State Department discounted these warnings. Yet U.S. intelligence increasingly corroborated the United Fruit Company's assessment. Then, in the last year of Truman's tenure, Guatemala's National Assembly enacted legislation proposed by Arévalo's successor Jacobo Arbenz Guzmán to nationalize massive swatches of United Fruit's holdings. UFCO's charge that communism had come to Guatemala now seemed compelling.

President Truman nevertheless aborted a plan, code named FORTUNE, to orchestrate a collective effort by Guatemala's Central American neighbors to oust Arbenz. Nicaragua's Anastasio Somoza had proposed the idea to Truman, who turned it over to DCI Smith. Prior to implementation, however, Truman called the operation off. Allen Dulles had no such reservations, and neither did his brother or President Eisenhower. There was no need to reexamine the case against the Arbenz regime. In the latter months of 1953, buoyed by the success of Operation AJAX in Iran, the CIA prepared a revised plan, Operation PBSUCCESS.

Proceeding on the premise that the army was the ultimate arbiter of Guatemala's political order, the objective of PBSUCCESS was to induce the military's chief officers to abandon Arbenz in favor of a counterrevolutionary regime. The CIA strategy in Iran had been to buttress bribery with psychological warfare. The CIA reversed the equation in Guatemala and added assassination as a variable to hold in reserve. By early 1954 it had financed the creation in Nicaragua of an "Army of Liberation" headed by Colonel Carlos Castillo Armas, a veteran of past antigovernment uprisings, and composed largely of mercenaries. It concurrently established a "Voice of Liberation," which broadcast inflated accounts of the size and quality of the Army of Liberation. On June 18, 1954, the Voice of Liberation broadcast that the invasion had begun. In reality, little happened on the military front of great significance. The invasion was not intended "in any sense [as] a conventional military operation," explained a CIA official. The goal of PBSUCCESS was to convince the army, or more specifically its leadership, that it could not avoid choosing between continuing to support Arbenz or defecting to the counter-revolutionary forces. Because the United States stood behind the latter, the army's very survival depended on its making the "right" choice. Should the army continue to collaborate with Arbenz, as an institution it would suffer "a terrible fate."

Less than a year after the success in Iran, the CIA's covert operation in Guatemala succeeded even more brilliantly. Certain complications required more direct and heavy-handed involvement than Eisenhower would have preferred. Britain and France threatened to support a Guatemalan-sponsored resolution to the Security Council calling for a United Nations investigation of Washington's role. But both relented after some arm-twisting from the administration. Moreover, when Arbenz resigned on July 27 before fleeing the country, he turned over power to General Enrique Diáz, the chief of his armed forces. Castillo Armas remained distant from Guatemala City. Consequently, it took the not-at-all-subtle engagement of U.S. Ambassador John Peurifoy to arrange for Castillo Armas to march triumphantly into the city to wrest control of the government from other aspirants. While DCI Allen Dulles savored the victory in silence, his brother Foster proclaimed to the world "the biggest success in the last five years against Communism."

Although the CIA's legend of invincibility derived largely from its successful operations in Iran and Guatemala, these were the exceptions more than the rule. Propaganda from sources such as Radio Free Europe encouraged uprisings in East Germany in 1953 and Hungary in 1956. In neither case, however, did the CIA take any significant action to support the insurrectionists. Subsequent CIA projects, most notoriously its effort to oust Sukarno in Indonesia, but also in Syria, the Congo, the Dominican Republic, Tibet, and Southeast Asia, were either abject failures or achieved little of consequence. Evidence suggests that the CIA saved Nasser's life before unsuccessfully trying to kill him.

Just as Operation PBSUCCESS neared execution, Allen Dulles recruited Richard Bissell to join the agency. Bissell, unlike most of the CIA's early leadership, lacked prior intelligence experience. His education at Groton, Yale, and the London School of Economics had led him to Ivy League professorships and then the Commerce Department during World War II, where he coordinated allied shipping. In the war's aftermath he played a vital role in the formative years of the Marshall Plan, after which he followed his former boss at the Economic Cooperation Administration (which administered the Marshall Plan), Paul Hoffman, to the Ford Foundation. But by 1954 Bissell had become restless, and his close relationships with such CIA stalwarts as Tracy Barnes and Frank Wisner, coupled with the Ford Foundation's intimate connection with the Agency, induced him to change careers. Dulles welcomed him to the CIA and immediately placed him high up in the chain of command of PBSUCCESS as his personal assistant.

Later in 1954 Dulles placed Bissell in charge of a different kind of covert operation, one that reflected President Eisenhower's commitment to improving intelligence on Soviet capabilities. In his capacity as DCI, Allen Dulles began each meeting of Eisenhower's NSC with an intelligence briefing. With regard to the Soviet Union, he conceded at an early briefing that U.S. intelligence manifested "shortcomings of a serious nature." Indeed, the surprise by which the administration was caught by the death of Joseph Stalin in March 1953, and its struggle to provide confident estimates of the successor regime, proved to be one of its greatest embarrassments. The series of "CAESAR" reports, produced by a small group of "Kremlinologists" established within the CIA's Office of Current Intelligence to focus exclusively on Soviet internal developments, showed little improvement. The problem, it became evident, was that the CIA lacked the human assets (HUMINT) capable of penetrating the Soviet Union's veil of secrecy. Extant Signals Intelligence (SIGNINT) and Electronic Intelligence (ELINT) could not compensate.

THE ORIGINS OF CIA TECHNICAL INTELLIGENCE—
THE U-2 AND CORONA

As early as 1946 the United States had considered photography through aerial surveillance as a potentially valuable instrument for monitoring scientific and technical (S&T) developments in the "denied areas" within the Soviet Union especially, but also the People's Republic of China and the Eastern Bloc. It fully appreciated, however, that the Kremlin would likely perceive such overflights as hostile in intent. In addition U.S. public opinion might have reservations about such provocative and devious acts. Hence, even the advocates of overflights stressed that it "is extraordinarily important that a means of long-range aerial reconnaissance be devised which cannot be detected."

By 1948 photographs taken with a 100-inch focal length camera from F-13 aircraft detected Soviet military installations that previous "oblique photography" had missed. Two years later, following the successful Soviet test of an atomic device and the outbreak of the Korean War, the urgency to enhance aerial surveillance intensified. The need to collect intelligence on possible Soviet intentions to launch an attack drove President Truman to authorize overflights of Soviet and Chinese "denied territory." RB-45C air-refuelable reconnaissance bombers and modified B-47B jet bombers flew out of Britain's Sculthorpe Royal Air Force Base and Yokota Air Base, west of Tokyo. When Eisenhower took office in 1953, he expanded such aerial surveillance by using additional bases in Alaska and Greenland. The Eisenhower administration claimed that these overflights did not violate international law because the assistance provided by the Soviets to the communist Chinese, including MiG pilots, "qualified" them as "unannounced belligerents" in the ongoing Korean War.

Notwithstanding the CIA's establishment in 1949 of a Scientific Intelligence Committee to coordinate America's S&T effort, the CIA initially played a subordinate role to the Air Force in the evolution of the aerial surveillance program. Near the end of his tenure as DCI, however, Smith received an invitation from the Air Force's Deputy Chief of Staff for Development to develop a more equal partnership. "I believe that CIA participation in this study [of intelligence and reconnaissance] on a continuing basis would be mutually beneficial," wrote Lt. General L. C. Craigie. "It would inform you of our trends and development plans as well as avail us of CIA experience and working knowledge. Furthermore, it would give us a more intimate working knowledge of CIA needs for national intelligence which might influence our own development programs, especially our vehicle programs." Craigie suggested that as a first step Smith establish a liaison office to the Air Force.

Smith was surprisingly unenthusiastic. Ideally, he replied, the Air Force should establish liaison offices with the entire spectrum of U.S. intelligence agencies, but that would produce a very cumbersome process. He preferred that the Intelligence Advisory Committee approve the creation of a standing group to advise the Air Force on intelligence needs. There matters stood through the first eighteen months of the Eisenhower administration. Using reconfigured jet bombers (such as the RB-57A-1, nicknamed the "Heart Throb"), the Air Force conducted overflights of Eastern Europe and Asia in order to acquire intelligence. The targets were somewhat hit-or-miss, however, and no attempts were made to overfly the Soviet Union proper.

DCI Allen Dulles remained reluctant to assume greater responsibility for aerial surveillance because he feared that the effort required to achieve effectiveness would inevitably cost the CIA the opportunity to improve its capabilities in other areas. As Wisner's deputy Richard Helms wrote, "I am persuaded that this Agency should stick to its knitting and not permit itself to be pushed into an area of activity which would inevitably overstrain its resources." As a compromise, the CIA adopted a policy that stipulated that the "primary" mission of its overflights would continue to be dropping, supplying, and retrieving agents, distributing leaflets, and the like. Only as a "secondary mission" would it collect ELINT, and even then "no methods will be used which will in any way militate against the success or security of the primary mission." The CIA officials further insisted that the Department of Defense should assume financial responsibility for development and data analysis and agree to share with the CIA the cost for purchasing, installing, and maintaining equipment.

During this same eighteen-month period the successful Soviet test of a thermonuclear device, the debates over the framing of the New Look strategy, the findings of the Surprise Attack [officially, Technological Capabilities] Panel set up by President Eisenhower, and the decision of the Eisenhower administration to rely extensively on a nuclear deterrent brought about a change in the CIA's attitude. In May 1954 DCI Dulles warned Air Force Chief of Staff Nathan Twining that Eisenhower's national security planners had "a critical need for intelligence information on Soviet capabilities for the delivery of mass destruction warheads, particularly against the continental United States." At issue was how to monitor Soviet progress in the areas of nuclear weapons, long-range bombers, and intercontinental missiles. Increased and improved aerial overflights seemed the only answer because "[c]landestine penetration efforts have not been sufficiently rewarding, and the electronic intercept approach is slow and the data is inherently difficult to analyze and interpret." Dulles urged Twining to "spare no effort to develop the specialized aircraft and operational capabilities necessary for such operations [air photographic and electronic reconnaissance]."

Eisenhower assigned the CIA with the task of developing the "specialized aircraft and operational capabilities." Dulles turned this assignment over to Bissell, who had on hand invaluable resources. Edwin H. Land, the Polaroid camera's inventor, had headed the Surprise Attack Panel's intelligence subcommittee. Also on the subcommittee was Edward Purcell, a Nobel Prize–winning physics professor from Harvard. Both recognized the vast potential for aerial surveillance because each appreciated that advancements in the quality of cameras, film, and lenses made possible very high-altitude photography. The key was to design an appropriate aircraft. Clarence "Kelly" Johnson of Lockheed had actually submitted such a design, the CL-282, but the Air Force had rejected it, preferring to stick with its commitment to a proposed twin-engine spy plane, the X-16, and experimenting with balloons that could overfly the Soviet Union and then splash down in the Pacific. But early trial runs had failed.

Exacerbating the Air Force's frustration, Land became a proponent of Kelly's CL-282 and lobbied to have the CIA take over the overflight program. With more than a little reluctance, by late fall 1954 Allen Dulles accepted the "offer." With greater reluctance, the Air Force surrendered its claim. After a meeting with DCI Dulles, Secretary of State Dulles, Secretary of Defense Charles Wilson, and Air Force Chief of Staff Twining on Wednesday,

November 24, President Eisenhower authorized the CIA to oversee and finance (through its secret contingency reserve fund) Lockheed's development of Kelly Johnson's initial design. Dulles put Bissell in charge of Project AQUATONE the day after Thanksgiving. While Lockheed went to work on constructing what came to be called the U[tility]-2 at its "Skunk Works" hanger in Burbank, California, Bissell set up a small office in downtown Washington, D.C. Provided virtually unencumbered rein by the free-wheeling style of management that became Bissell's trademark, by mid-1955, after only about a half-year of development, Lockheed informed him that the first plane, "Kelly's Angel," was ready to test. As insisted upon by Eisenhower, pilots could be recruited from the Strategic Air Command, but they would fly as private citizens under contract to the CIA.

The U-2's rapid development influenced Eisenhower's decision to redefine the objective of the 1955 Geneva summit by proposing his dramatic Open Skies initiative. Predictably Soviet Prime Minister Nikita Khrushchev dismissed it as a ruse to allow the United States to spy on the Soviets. Ironically, Khrushchev had allowed the United States to spy unilaterally. Tests of the U-2 began in July 1955 and were completed by early 1956. Rebuffing Air Force efforts to wrest control of the project from the CIA, Bissell arranged with Chancellor Konrad Adenauer to use the West German base at Wiesbaden. Under the direction of Arthur Lundahl, the Photo-Intelligence Division (PID), a secret agency capable of interpreting the expected volume of photographic intelligence, was established. In May and June came the first missions. They targeted the Mediterranean and the Middle East. (A U-2 mission surreptitiously photographed military preparations integral to the October 1956 Suez crisis.)

The initial overflight of the Soviet Union occurred, ironically, on July 4, 1956. Eisenhower, however, had imposed a regimented system of control. A proposal for a flight could originate in the military, the State Department, or the CIA. The initiator would send the proposal to Lt. General John K. Gerhart, the Air Force deputy chief of staff for plans and programs. Once he approved it, he would send it on to the Air Force chief of staff, and then it went to the chair of the Joint Chiefs of Staff, to the DCI, to the secretary of state, and then the White House. Normally Eisenhower's staff secretary, General Andrew Goodpaster, would hand-deliver the "proposal" to the president. Occasionally Bissell, usually accompanied by both Dulles brothers, would discuss a proposal with the president directly. Eisenhower reviewed every mission personally, and more than once revised the flight plan before signing off on it. Less than a handful in Congress ever learned officially that the United States overflew the Soviet Union.

Most of the U-2 flights probed radar defenses and obtained oblique photographs of military installations on the periphery of Soviet Union. About twenty of them directly overflew Soviet territory in an effort to uncover military preparations for a possible surprise Soviet attack. Although far from perfect, information from such flights provided Eisenhower with the confidence he needed when subsequently confronted with such allegations of U.S. strategic inferiority and vulnerability—manifested most publicly in claims of first a "bomber gap" and then a "missile gap"—that followed the successful Soviet test of an intercontinental missile in August 1957, the Sputnik satellites that circled the earth in October, and the release of the Gaither Report in December. Significantly, largely because of information acquired through the U-2, CIA estimates of Soviet bomber and ICBM capabilities were lower than military projections, particularly those of Air Force intelligence. For these reasons Eisenhower continued to approve the flights even though the Soviets from the start tracked the flights. Whereas U.S. radar could not detect the U-2 at an altitude of more than 70,000 feet, the Soviets' could. Although furious, the Kremlin refrained from any public protest. To do so would have meant publicly conceding that the Soviet military could not protect its own air space. And the CIA lost not a single U-2 flight until May 1, 1960.

Although the Soviet downing of Francis Gary Powers's flight on May 1, 1960, realized Eisenhower's recurrent nightmare and was the catalyst for

U-2 spy plane pilot Francis Gary Powers sits in the witness chair of the Senate Armed Services Committee in Washington, D.C. on March 6, 1962. He is holding a U-2 model plane. (AP/Wide World Photos)

Khrushchev's scuttling the Paris summit that spring while ending U-2 over-flights of the Soviet Union, the effect of this suspension on America's strategic intelligence was minimal. In part this was because Eisenhower never doubted that America retained a strategic retaliatory capacity sufficient to deter a Soviet strike. In larger part, by this date the CIA, which under Eisenhower progressively became the equal of the military services in estimating Soviet military power, had been trying for several years to produce a sleek supersonic jet successor to the U-2, code named OXCART. More significant still, CIA officials intended to rely primarily on satellite photography for aerial sur-veillance, and the indefatigable Richard Bissell was also in charge of devel-oping this project. As a spin-off from Air Force directed satellite-development programs, the CIA launched the CORONA project in 1958. Massive tech-nological obstacles and another, and more serious, turf battle with the Air Force plagued the early years of this satellite project. Compounding the problem was Bissell's need to balance his supervision of CORONA with his continuing responsibilities overseeing the U-2 and his new responsibilities as the CIA's Deputy Director for Plans, a post to which he had been appointed in January 1959. To his disappointment and the frustration of President Eisenhower, tests of the booster (first THOR and then ATLAS), the satel-lite with camera and film (AGENA), and the recovery system failed re-peatedly. Had the CORONA system come online by May 1, 1960, Eisenhower would not have felt compelled to approve one last U-2 flight to prepare for the forthcoming arms limitation talks with Soviet premier Khrushchev at Geneva.

The first successful CORONA launch and "catch" did not take place until August 18–19, 1960, the same day that the Soviets sentenced Francis Gary Powers to ten years in prison. (The Soviets subsequently agreed to exchange Powers two years later for captured Soviet spy Rudolf Abel.) Before returning its payload, Discoverer XIV had completed seven passes over the Soviet Union, thereby providing "more photographic coverage of the Soviet Union than all previous U-2 missions." For more than a decade afterward CORONA, overseen by the CIA's Committee on Overhead Reconnaissance (COMOR), produced a progressively greater volume of progressively higher quality pic-tures of the Soviet Union—and elsewhere. Not even the most sophisticated advances in technology, however, could keep precise track of the buildup of Soviet strategic forces. Nevertheless, the intelligence that CORONA and its successor satellite programs provided about Soviet missile capabilities, Chi-nese nuclear developments, damage incurred during the 1967 Middle East War, and much more was invaluable, frequently providing the foundation for National Intelligence Estimates (NIEs) and Special National Intelligence Estimates (SNIEs). These estimates, notwithstanding dissent of the military services, bolstered successive administrations' confidence in the efficacy of a deterrence strategy. CORONA remained officially a secret until President Bill Clinton ordered its declassification in 1995.

THE BAY OF PIGS INVASION

The CIA could classify few of its other activities during the era of CORONA as successes. Even after the establishment in 1956 of an autonomous Senior Research Staff (SRS) on International Communism, which reported directly to the Deputy Director for Intelligence, the progress it made in estimating Soviet intentions fell woefully short of that which it made with regard to Soviet capabilities. Analysts remained largely in the dark in the area of assessing political and economic developments within the Soviet Union and its bloc of satellites. A senior official within the Office of National Estimates lamented, "We had constructed for ourselves a picture of the U.S.S.R., and whatever happened had to be made to fit into that picture. Intelligence estimators can hardly commit a more abominable sin." Richard Bissell's career and reputation mirrored the CIA's fall from grace. On the first day of January 1959, Fidel Castro and the 26th of July Movement forced long-time dictator Fulgencio Batista into exile and declared the start of a new Cuba. That same month Allen Dulles appointed Bissell deputy director for plans. Bissell's first assignment for the CIA had been to assist Dulles in overthrowing the Arbenz regime in Guatemala. As DDP, his final assignment for the CIA would be to plan an operation to overthrow the Castro regime in Cuba.

Although the Eisenhower administration had quickly recognized the Castro government, each passing month brought seemingly more robust evidence of communist influence and sympathies. Castro instituted an agrarian reform that, as had Arbenz's a half-dozen years earlier, primarily targeted U.S. interests. It expropriated some $1 billion of U.S. property. Castro then took a page out of Stalinist books by holding public trials leading to the execution of Batista's henchmen. More generally, the bearded self-proclaimed revolutionary railed against the Yanqui imperialists from the north. Convinced that U.S. spies abounded, he demanded that the United States relinquish its naval base on Guantánamo Bay and reduce the size of its Embassy. Eisenhower responded by embargoing Cuban exports to the United States. Castro responded by concluding a treaty with the Soviet Union by which Cuba exchanged its sugar for arms, machinery, and advisors.

By fall 1959 Eisenhower approved a State Department proposal that the CIA formulate a plan to overthrow Castro. DDP Bissell was placed in charge. Not surprisingly, he used PBSUCCESS as the model. The world must conclude that Cubans, not Americans, had overthrown Castro and restored liberty. Bissell established a task force within the agency's Western Hemisphere division to devise the strategy. Its first step was to train exiles in preparation for an invasion of Cuba. Initially the camps were located in the United States and Panama Canal Zone, but by spring 1960 they were moved to Guatemala. Soon thereafter David Atlee Phillips reprised his role in Guatemala by establishing an anti-Castro "black" radio station on Swan

Island off the coast of Honduras. Phillips was able to use some of the equipment that remained on the island from the 1954 operation. In March, even as he stressed that "our hand should not show in anything that is done," Eisenhower gave the CIA the go-ahead to continue preparations for "A Program of Covert Action Against the Castro Regime." Radio Swan began to broadcast two months later.

The project was far from ready for implementation, however. Even as CIA planners began to cooperate with the Mafia in schemes to assassinate Castro, they came to appreciate that an amphibious invasion of Cuba presented considerably more problems than had the Army of Liberation's entry into Guatemala from neighboring Honduras in 1954. Conducting guerrilla warfare from beachheads would likewise be difficult. Hence Bissell modified the original plan. Now code-named TRINIDAD, the plan called for a significantly larger force of better-trained and equipped exiles to land at Trinidad on Cuba's southern coast. It would receive air support from unidentifiable planes based in Nicaragua. The premise was that the combination of the invasion, air strikes, and black propaganda would incite disenchanted Cubans to revolt and/or cause Castro's military to defect and his government to disintegrate. The worst scenario Bissell envisioned was of a stalemate between Castro and the invading force. In that circumstance Bissell predicted that the Organization of American States would intervene owing to U.S. control.

Bissell seems not to have fully briefed Eisenhower or the 5412 (Special) committee on the rationale for and the implications of the revised plan. In any event President Eisenhower never approved its execution. He did, however, encourage the CIA to continue to be "bold and imaginative" in its planning, and then bequeathed what plan resulted to successor, John F. Kennedy. The appeal to President Kennedy was all but irresistible. Not only was Operation TRINIDAD directed against an island he had called "a dagger pointed at America's heart" during the 1960 presidential campaign, not only was it imaginative and bold (resonating with Kennedy's fascination with James Bond and the image he sought to project), but also its salesperson was Richard Bissell. Kennedy had already decided that Bissell was the logical and worthy successor to Allen Dulles as DCI.

Still, President Kennedy's civilian and military advisors expressed doubts whether the invading force, even when buttressed by propaganda and supported by air strikes, was sufficient to achieve Castro's ouster. Undaunted, Kennedy instructed the CIA to step up its campaign of propaganda and sabotage on the one hand, and to concert more systematically with the Pentagon on the other. The military, however, remained wary, but refused to rule out the possibility of success. State Department advisors were more skeptical. Although having his own reservations, Kennedy intrinsically preferred the CIA's creativity to State's conservatism. Further, Bissell continued to argue that the plan would work and, moreover, that to abort now would anger and alienate the trained Cuban exile force. By March Kennedy had decided to go ahead, but he insisted that the invasion be scaled back to make it less likely that the United States would be implicated. As a result, the CIA reformulated TRINIDAD as Operation ZAPATA (the Pentagon's code name). Supported by less dramatic air strikes both on D-day and two days before, in the early morning hours the Cuban exiles (2506 Brigade) would seek to establish a quieter beachhead (actually three beachheads) at the more remote Bay of Pigs. These revisions convinced many of Bissell's chief lieutenants that the plan was doomed. Bissell retained his belief in it, however, and Kennedy retained his faith in Bissell. On April 14 the president greenlighted the operation.

ZAPATA turned into the CIA's greatest fiasco, costing the agency the leadership of both Bissell and Allen Dulles. Before authorizing ZAPATA, Kennedy had cut in half the number of B-26 air strikes scheduled for April 15 from sixteen to eight. That made the second raid, scheduled for D-day, that much more crucial to knocking out Castro's capacity to retaliate. On the advice of Secretary of State Dean Rusk, though, Kennedy cancelled the second raid. The subsequent conclusion of the Taylor Committee's post mortem assessment of this failed operation was that this cancellation—notwithstanding all the other problems of the overlooked lighthouse that illuminated the advancing landing craft, the protruding coral (mistakenly identified as seaweed by CIA photographic interpreters) that prevented many of the craft from reaching the beach, the swamp that separated the beach from the Escambray Mountains—as the chief cause of the debacle. Success depended on neutralizing Castro's T-33s, and the failure to do so exposed the invaders to certain capture. The Taylor Committee's assessment, however, missed the most fundamental cause. Bissell and his allies in the CIA fully appreciated the risks, and that the odds of success diminished as both Eisenhower and Kennedy modified the plan. Yet flushed with the pride and arrogance produced by the successes in Iran and Guatemala, and the U-2 and CORONA, Bissell and his allies perceived no reason why they could not beat those odds once again.

They paid the price. Allen Dulles was a leading member of the Taylor Committee. It was his final substantive act as DCI. During the summer 1961 Berlin Crisis Dulles did restore some of his credibility with Kennedy by briefing him on the vital intelligence the CIA (in collaboration with the British SIS) had gained through the defection of Colonel Oleg Penkovsky, the deputy head of the foreign section of the Soviet military's Office of Scientific Research. Penkovsky, whom the KGB soon arrested and executed, argued that the United States should respond resolutely to Soviet premier Khrushchev's bluster. He supported his argument with photographs of classified documents that assured the administration that the Soviets lacked the nuclear capability to go to war over Berlin. Kennedy perceived Khrushchev's retreat from his threat to terminate the joint occupation of Berlin and sign a peace treaty with the German Democratic Republic as a triumph for U.S. intelligence, allowing

This is a general view of the headquarters of the Central Intelligence Agency, at Langley, Virginia, in 1962. The building is located about eight miles from downtown Washington, D.C. (AP/Wide World Photos)

Dulles to retire on a high note in November 1961, shortly after he had dedicated CIA's new headquarters on 125 acres in Langley, Virginia.

In a role far different from Dulles's, Richard Bissell provided some of the most consequential testimony to the Taylor Committee. It was almost his final act as DDP. Bissell's promotion to DCI was now out of the question. Kennedy did ask him to remain with the CIA to continue to supervise CORONA and future technological espionage. Bissell, understandably, declined. Before he left the agency in February 1962, however, he reactivated the program to assassinate Castro. He then turned over the DP to his long-time rival in the agency, Richard Helms.

THE DIRECTORSHIP OF JOHN McCONE AND THE CUBAN MISSILE CRISIS

John McCone succeeded Allen Dulles as DCI. McCone had little previous experience in intelligence. But Kennedy wanted someone like McCone, a successful corporate executive who had served as undersecretary of the air force and chaired the Atomic Energy Commission under Eisenhower, to get the CIA back on track. A conservative Republican, he could help win Kennedy support from across the aisle even as he personified the ideal that the CIA was above politics. In addition, McCone was the opposite of Dulles as his priority for the agency was intelligence analysis. That suited Kennedy fine, both because the Bay of Pigs was above all a failure of intelligence, and because the president intended to run covert operations directly out of the White House to the extent that he could without jeopardizing a capacity for plausible deniability. Although CIA personnel contributed to Operation MONGOOSE, the continued effort to assassinate Castro and otherwise undermine his regime, Attorney General Robert Kennedy was the de facto director of this project. Moreover, the connection to the CIA of Edward Lansdale, MONGOOSE's field commander, was highly ambiguous. In addition, at the suggestion of the president's Foreign Intelligence Advisory Board, an enhanced version of Eisenhower's Board of Consultants, President Kennedy in October 1961 created the Defense Intelligence Agency (DIA). Its purpose was to institutionalize the transfer to the Pentagon of many paramilitary and other intelligence activities associated with the CIA. The agency's role as the vanguard of America's Cold War crusade appeared to be over.

Ironically, McCone proved to be pivotal to the CIA's resurrection. With Operation MONGOOSE in full swing and the Castro regime entrenching itself in the Soviet camp, by 1962 Washington's relations with Havana had deteriorated to the point that a crisis appeared inevitable. McCone's focus on Cuba centered on its capability to threaten the United States, not America's capability to overthrow or assassinate Castro. During three consecutive meetings with Kennedy's chief advisors in August 1962, two of which the president attended personally, McCone underscored that it was probable that Castro was concealing the installation of medium-range ballistic missiles (MRBMs) on the island nation.

McCone's warnings at first caused little alarm. Probably the lessons of the bomber and missile gap controversies made veteran intelligence analysts wary of once again overestimating an adversary's capabilities. And there existed no precedent for the Soviets to accept this kind of risk. Even McCone's chief deputy in the CIA, General Marshall "Pat" Carter, concluded that the Cubans were installing defensive surface-to-air missiles (SAMs), not offensive MRBMs. Sherman Kent and the Board of National Estimates concurred. Sporadic U-2 flights, however, failed to confirm McCone's suspicions, and the Kennedy administration had insufficient confidence in the plane to approve multiple missions. Finally, on October 9 McCone received approval to have U-2s directly overfly suspected SAM sites. The first of three missions flew on October 14. By late in the evening of Monday, October 15, "the latest readout from Cuban U-2 photography indicated initial deployment of Medium Range Ballistic Missiles" at San Cristobal. As Secretary of State Dean Rusk commented to the NSC the next day, "Mr. McCone had predicted such a possibility back in mid-August."

The next thirteen days were among the most dramatic in modern American history. Although McCone normally receives high marks for his insight and foresight, the CIA as an institution receives little credit for the outcome. Whether fan or critic of the administration's crisis management, scholars, journalists, and others who write about the Cuban Missile Crisis overwhelming stress the roles played by President Kennedy, Attorney General Kennedy, and the members of Excomm, the Executive Committee of the National Security Council that the president established to debate the options and decide upon a response. That a succession of U-2 missions that overflew Cuba throughout the crisis and NSA eavesdropping operations (SIGINT) provided the members of Excomm with a steady stream of intelligence on the number and likely operational state of the missile sites, on Soviet and Warsaw Pact military preparations, and on the progress made by Soviet ships headed toward the quarantine line have received scant if any attention.

Although slow to detect the Soviet emplacement of missiles in Cuba and plagued by the lack of clandestine agents within Cuba and the Soviet Union (HUMINT), the CIA performed well during October 1962. U-2 photography revealed six MRBM and three IRBM (Intermediate-Range Ballistic Missiles; McCone had limited his warnings to MRBMs) sites that collectively enveloped some three dozen launch pads. Based on this imagery the Agency correctly inferred that nuclear warheads as well as missiles had arrived. This imagery also provided U.S. Ambassador to the United Nations Adlai Stevenson with the necessary ammunition to demolish his Soviet counterpart Valerian Zorin's protestations of innocence during their public debate in the UN Security Council. What is more, the NSA's SIGINT allowed for careful monitoring of Soviet and Warsaw Pact military communications, and additional information provided by Penkovsky prior to his arrest on October 20 was extremely valuable for Kennedy and his advisors as Excomm debated U.S. options and Soviet ships approached the quarantine line. And McCone personally contributed positively, both through his participation at meetings and his memoranda, throughout the crisis.

In the end it was U.S. resolve, Soviet concessions, backchannel exchanges between KGB agent Aleksandr Feklisov and ABC correspondent John Scali, and President Kennedy's judgment that were responsible for the peaceful resolution of the Cuban Missile Crisis. The early detection of the sites by the CIA, nevertheless, provided the administration with a critical window to frame its response, and the subsequent intelligence it provided militated against a precipitate employment of U.S. force. In this context the two Special National Intelligence Estimates that the CIA had produced by October 20 assessing the likely Soviet responses to and consequences of a variety of U.S. actions promoted more rigorous discussion and debate. Further, Kennedy, because of the confidence he had gained in the CIA's capacity for aerial reconnaissance, was unconcerned when Castro forbade on-site inspection of the dismantling of the missile bases. In stark contrast to the Bay of Pigs' Operation ZAPATA, the CIA's performance during the Cuban Missile Crisis, the president concluded, was "very well done."

Covert schemes to rid Cuba of Castro continued up to and beyond the day of President Kennedy's assassination, generating enduring rumors of Cuba's culpability in it. In this context, on October 16, in the interval between two of the most significant of the Cuban Missile Crisis meetings, Attorney General Kennedy met with Lansdale, Helms, and others to express the "general dissatisfaction of the President" with U.S. efforts to execute "acts of sabotage" against the Cuban regime and to announce that accordingly he (the attorney general) "was going to give Operation MONGOOSE more personal attention." Toward this end, beginning the next day he intended to meet with MONGOOSE's "operational representatives" at 9:30 A.M. *every morning*. And he did, although not for long. As the missile crisis unfolded and the need for further intelligence gathering and military preparation became more urgent, officials in both the CIA and the military came to perceive MONGOOSE as an intolerable loose cannon. Moreover, officials in the White House and Foggy Bottom, including Robert Kennedy himself, concluded that acts of sabotage committed by agents not held on a tight leash by Washington were incompatible with the diplomacy necessary to finalize the removal of the missiles and put into place an inspection regime. While sporadic efforts to undermine Castro persisted, the administration in early 1963 closed down MONGOOSE as a set program. In light of the priority Kennedy's successor Lyndon Johnson placed on his domestic programs and the apparent relaxation of the Cold War that followed October 1962, it stood to reason that the CIA, relieved of the harebrained activities associated with MONGOOSE, would retain the respect and standing that it had recovered during the Cuban Missile Crisis.

THE CIA AND THE VIETNAM CRISIS

The CIA performed better than other arms of the U.S. government during the controversial conflict in Vietnam. Yet domestically and abroad, during the 1960s and 1970s the agency came to be identified as synonymous with U.S. foreign policy, and it suffered commensurately. That it did so is more than a little ironic. Vietnam had been one of the primary sites where the fledgling U.S. covert operatives gained their spurs, and many in the CIA were familiar with Indochina long before it became common to be so. During World War II, OSS units forged close relationships with Vietminh nationalists and the organization's leader, Ho Chi Minh, in their fight against the Japanese occupiers and their surrogate French administrators in Indochina. Following the Japanese surrender most OSS veterans of this theater supported Vietnamese independence from France. By that time, however, the Truman administration had adopted a Cold War perspective that gave top priority to the Western alliance and defined geopolitics as a zero-sum game.

In Indochina this perspective translated into a policy of supporting the French effort to regain control of their colony in the face of indigenous opposition. CIA operatives dutifully executed the president's policy. In 1950 the CIA had, through a holding company, the American Airdale Corporation, assumed proprietary control over the Civil Air Transport (CAT), founded in 1946 by General Claire Chennault and Whiting Willauer of Flying Tigers fame to aid Chiang Kai-Shek's Kuomintang in the Chinese Civil War. Following the communist victory in 1949, CAT pilots airlifted thousands of Chinese Nationalists to the island of Taiwan (Formosa). Subsequently, the CIA made CAT an agency asset in order to carry out operations in the Far East, just in time for its engagement in the Korean War. But it was in Indochina that CAT distinguished itself as a covert arm of the U.S. government by its pilots' daring airdrops of supplies to the besieged French at Dien Bien Phu in 1954.

Shortly thereafter the CIA dispatched Colonel Edward Lansdale to Saigon. An OSS veteran who shortly before Dien Bien Phu had played a pivotal role assisting the governments of Elpido Quirino and Ramon Magsaysay to defeat the communist-influenced Huk insurgency in the Philippines, Lansdale led a team of a dozen CIA agents assigned to the U.S. Military Advisory and Assistance Group (MAAG). His tasks were manifold. With the Geneva Accords of July 1954 having established Vietnam as an independent state but divided at the seventeenth parallel pending unification elections in 1956, Lansdale's initial assignment was to mount a propaganda campaign aimed to dissuade Vietnamese in the south from voting for the communists, organize the migration of noncommunist Vietnamese from the communist north to the south, and carry out acts of sabotage in the north. Concurrently, Lansdale manipulated an election in the south to ensure Prime Minister Ngo Dinh Diem's overwhelming triumph over the former Emperor Bao Dai, and orchestrated Diem's defeat of the rival sects and consolidation of his regime. With the support of Lansdale, Diem resisted efforts to hold the unifying elections scheduled for 1956. By 1957, the U.S. government was proclaiming Diem a miracle worker, and Lansdale had become the model for Graham Greene's classic *The Quiet American*.

Diem worked no miracles in Vietnam, and by Kennedy's inauguration civil wars consumed all the former French colonies (Laos, Vietnam) that comprised the former French Indochina. The CIA remained active throughout America's involvement in these conflicts, although during the early years its presence and influence remained small. In 1960, for example, its station in Saigon was but a fraction of the size of that in Cuba. By 1967, however, the Saigon station had become the CIA's largest, and the Agency had contributed significantly to some of the great watersheds in America's deepening commitment to the war (which the United States directly entered in 1965). These included the coup and assassination of Diem in 1963; OPLAN 34-A, the psychological warfare operations and sustained program of covert airborne and maritime sabotage operations directed at bridges, small islands, storage dumps, and other targets in the north that precipitated the Gulf of Tonkin incident in 1964; and the prosecution of a secret war in allegedly neutral Laos. More notoriously, from 1967 the CIA collaborated with Military Advisory Command Vietnam (MACV) to manage the Phoenix Program. Conceived by CIA operative and then NSC staffer Robert Komer but directed primarily by future DCI William Colby, who had been station chief in Saigon from 1959 until he took charge of the CIA's Far Eastern Division in 1962, the program established Provisional Reconnaissance Units (PRUs) that relied on local intelligence assets to target Vietnamese communists and other members of the National Liberation Front (NLF) in the south so that they could be "neutralized" by South Vietnamese security forces or elite U.S. commandos. But because the intelligence acted upon was often either inaccurate, out of date, or intentionally corrupt, the number of innocents who were neutralized (imprisoned or assassinated) overwhelmed those who in fact mattered to the enemy's infrastructure. The CIA also ran Project Heavy Green, a top-secret radar facility at Lima Site 85 in Laos that provided instruction for U.S. bombers flying ROLLING THUNDER bombing missions over North Vietnam. The U.S. government never acknowledged the existence of this site in neutral Laos, even after enemy forces overran it in the aftermath of the Tet offensive in 1968.

Notwithstanding the above list of CIA projects in Vietnam, the agency's primary contribution to the U.S. war effort was intelligence collection and analysis. On this dimension its performance was superior. As with almost all sectors of the U.S. government, the CIA was largely ignorant about Vietnam and the Vietnamese. This lack of expertise was most manifest in the area of providing the military with both tactical and strategic intelligence. Because of the surveillance capabilities of the National Security Agency and photographic reconnaissance units, and the combined assets of the CIA, the DIA, the Army's G-2, and MACV's intelligence structure, U.S. military commanders in the field received relatively accurate information about enemy movements and strength. But in an unconventional war, political will, psychological initiatives, and parallel intangibles are often decisive. In these areas the CIA was at a decided disadvantage. It lacked expertise and depended on indigenous assets, too many of whom were either unreliable or more concerned with jockeying for position against political or even family rivals. Hence even after the establishment in 1967 of the Combined Intelligence Center Vietnam (CICV), a unit that included both South Vietnamese and American analysts, U.S. tactical and strategic intelligence paled in comparison to Hanoi's.

Yet the most salient chapters of the history of the CIA's performance in Vietnam concern its production of national intelligence, the National Intelligence Estimates and Special National Intelligence Estimates. In Vietnam the relationship between the producers and consumers of intelligence was far from ideal. From early on in America's involvement, the judgments of CIA analysts were consistently pessimistic. The consensus was that the French were unlikely to prevail, and as late as the 1954 Geneva Conference CIA analysts estimated that the chances were better than even that the People's Republic of China would respond in kind to U.S. military intervention. As America's commitment to South Vietnam increased subsequent to the Geneva Accords of 1954 and the Eisenhower administration's decision to prop up the Diem regime, the CIA considered Chinese intervention less likely, but it remained less sanguine than policymakers about the war's prospects. Pervading its estimates were doubts about the strength and, equally important, the cohesion of the Republic of Vietnam. Throughout this time, nevertheless, the CIA's role was largely passive; it collected intelligence from the field and provided Washington with finished products: NIEs and SNIEs.

This dynamic began to change following the Bay of Pigs fiasco of 1961 and Allen Dulles's replacement as DCI by John McCone. Not that McCone was initially more optimistic than other CIA analysts, including Office of National Estimates' chief Sherman Kent. McCone did differ from Kent and others, however, in pinpointing the source of the problem. In contrast to the ONE's assessment, which stressed South Vietnam's internal weaknesses, McCone attributed the gains made by Hanoi and the NLF (between which he did not differentiate) to the support provided by China. He agreed with the ONE, nevertheless, that in terms of the objective of creating a viable, stable bulwark against communist expansion in Southeast Asia, South Vietnam was making little progress, and America's military assistance contributed minimally toward this end. As late as June 1962, McCone informed Secretary of Defense Robert McNamara point blank that the United States could not prevail in this "war," adding that "we were merely chipping away at the toe of the glacier from the North."

McCone's perspective changed dramatically at the end of 1962, however, and with it did the character of the CIA's contribution to Vietnam policymaking. Shortly prior to the Cuban Missile Crisis, the ONE began to draft a new NIE (53–63), entitled "Prospects in Vietnam." The draft, which was congruent with previously pessimistic assessments, reached McCone through his membership on the United States Intelligence Board (USIB, established by Eisenhower in 1958 and later renamed the National Foreign Intelligence Board, NFIB) some six months later. McCone erupted in fury, demanding to know why the ONE dissented so intensely from the military, State, and almost every senior official "who knew Vietnam best." He insisted that Kent and his staff consult Joint Chiefs of Staff (JCS) chair Earle Wheeler, MACV commander Paul Harkins, Ambassador in Saigon Frederick "Fritz" Nolting, Assistant Secretary of State for Far Eastern Affairs Roger Hillsman, and other senior officials, all of whom maintained that the enemy had suffered severely over the past few years. McCone instructed Kent to revise the NIE to take into account their input. The ONE at first resisted this pressure, but ultimately succumbed. In April 1963 it produced a new NIE that began, "We believe that the Communist progress has been blunted and that the situation is improving." This estimate indicated, McCone told President Kennedy, "we could win."

Plausible explanations for McCone's behavior include the not-uncommon phenomenon that intelligence officers tend to tell superiors what they want to hear for the purpose of career advancement. Yet McCone appeared not to harbor political ambitions, had prior to the discovery of the Soviet missiles in Cuba manifested little reluctance to speak his mind independently, and during those thirteen days of the October Cuban Missile Crisis experienced Kennedy's thirst for multiple sources of information. The most salient lesson he probably learned from the Missile Crisis was not to trust the ONE. Its analysts had not predicted that the Soviets would seek to sneak missiles onto Cuban soil. McCone may well have hesitated to endorse its position now, especially because the estimates of the DIA varied considerably. Conversely, McCone did trust former President Eisenhower and Victor Krulak, then a Marine Major General serving as the JCS's special assistant for counterinsurgency activities, both of whom maintained that the United States and South Vietnam were making progress.

McCone's intervention and the resultant new NIE fueled the enthusiasm of the interventionists and compromised the CIA as an objective producer of intelligence. One consequence was that the Agency's estimates' influence on policy became more marginal, a condition exacerbated by increased tensions with MACV and State on the one hand, and among its own analysts on the other. That held true even for McCone. Along with Saigon station chief John Richardson, for example, McCone in 1963 opposed any effort to remove the Diem government because he could not identify a successor. Yet George Carver, the ONE's expert on Vietnam, was inclined to support a coup, having determined that any alternative to Diem would be a positive development, and in the field CIA operative Lucien Conein collaborated with the conspirators. With the State Department also split, the only role the United States played in the overthrow and assassination of Diem and his brother in November 1963 was to abandon him to his fate. But the CIA ended up farther on the periphery.

On the periphery it stayed during the momentous debates of 1964–1965 over military escalation. By this time McCone had conceded his mistake in corrupting the 1963 NIE and resurrected his pessimistic prognosis. In doing so he rejoined hands with almost all of the CIA's experts on Vietnam, although unlike them he remained convinced of the validity of the domino theory. McCone supported ONE estimates in 1964 that characterized the South Vietnamese leadership as mired in "increasing defeatism" and "paralysis" and portrayed the position of South Vietnam as steadily deteriorating. Where he parted company was his assessment of what to do about it. Pentagon planners, recognizing that progress was in fact not being made, began to assess the impact of a program of intensified air attacks on the north. In the estimates of CIA specialists, any positive effects of such program, which would ultimately lead to the formulation and approval of Operation ROLLING THUNDER in February 1965, would at best be temporary. McCone disagreed. In his view air attacks could at least curtail the deterioration of the situation in the north, but only if implementation was sudden and virtually unlimited. McCone advised against worrying about possible Chinese retaliation and advocated targeting industrial centers and POLs (Petroleum, Oil, and Lubricant supply centers) wherever they were located. To confine the objective to interdiction and promoting negotiations, McNamara's formula, promised disaster.

McCone was no more effective than anyone at the ONE in winning acceptance of his prescriptions. President Lyndon Johnson increasingly froze him out of his deliberations, and the implementation of ROLLING THUNDER in March 1965 was gradual and limited. A month later the ONE's Harold Ford wrote that Johnson's chief advisors were "becoming progressively divorced from reality in Vietnam...and are proceeding with far more courage than wisdom." In his view, increased U.S. military engagement in Vietnam, on the ground as well as in the air, was unlikely to prove decisive because the "VC [Vietcong] insurrection remains essentially an indigenous phenomenon, the product of GVN [Government of Vietnam] fecklessness, VC power, and peasant hopelessness." McCone resigned on April 28; his successor, Vice Admiral William F. Raborn, Jr., served as DCI only long enough for his advice to be ignored and the United States to increase exponentially the introduction of conventional U.S. forces into Vietnam. Raborn gained the confidence of neither the White House nor Langley, and in 1966 Johnson, with neither the time nor inclination to conduct an extensive search for a replacement, appointed Richard Helms, Raborn's deputy, as his successor.

"Vietnam was my nightmare for a good ten years," Helms recalled. Doubtless it was, although the politically savvy DCI kept his distance from Johnson when it came to Vietnam policy. He delegated much of the responsibility to George Carver, his special assistant for Vietnam affairs. Carver had years of service as an "eloquent" ONE analyst in addition to his experience as a junior case officer in Saigon. He had contributed significantly to many of the CIA's NIEs and SNIEs. Even though Carver was on record as sharing the pessimistic assessment that pervaded the Agency, he had the reputation for expertise and insight that Helms sought.

After 1968 Carver's reputation would never be the same. As a result Vietnam caused greater damage to the Agency's standing in Washington. The catalyst was the controversy over the enemy's strength, the Order of Battle (O/B) estimates, that attended the finger-pointing subsequent to the January 1968 Tet Offensive. The antecedents for this internal debate can be found in 1966. By the end of that year Sam Adams, one of the CIA's most "diligent" researchers who would soon be transferred to Carver's office, began to sound alarms that the military's estimates of the enemy's strength were dangerously low. Using SIGINT in contrast to MACV's interrogations and captured documents, Adams assessed the enemy's strength as numbering 600,000, double that of MACV. While few in the CIA accepted Adams's number, most, including Carver, considered it closer to the mark than MACV's "guesstimate." By 1967 McNamara had also come to doubt the military's estimates and to rely on the CIA's intelligence.

MACV insisted that its estimates were right. Helms demanded that the rivals reach an agreement, and in fall 1967 he dispatched a CIA team led by Carver and including Adams to Saigon to hammer one out. Encountering a "MACV brickwall," on September 14 Carver, who until then had supported the CIA's position, unconditionally surrendered. It is certain that he took to heart the argument of MACV commander General William Westmoreland, Ambassador Ellsworth Bunker, and others in the Saigon embassy that accepting Adams's estimate would signal the failure of the strategy of attrition. The compromise agreement reached between the CIA (at least Carver), MACV, the DIA, and State (INR) set enemy strength at 249,000. Shortly thereafter, moreover, MACV publicly announced an estimate of 208,000, and the next SNIE used that number.

CIA officers in Vietnam never accepted the O/B estimate, and the Tet Offensive of January 1968 provided robust evidence that they were right. They were also right in sending a succession of intelligence reports in November and December 1967 warning of an impending enemy offensive. This field reporting, according to General Bruce Palmer, constituted "an uncannily accurate forecast." It made little impression on the Johnson administration or MACV, however. Carver was now committed to providing an optimistic prognosis, and he commanded the greatest attention in Washington. Small wonder, then, that President Johnson and other key advisors were so surprised not only by the Tet Offensive itself but also afterward, when during the debate over Westmoreland's request for two hundred thousand additional troops, the briefing presented by intelligence experts, especially the CIA's William Dupuy and State's Philip Habib, was so discouraging. Ironically, it may well have been Carver himself who most decisively influenced President Johnson's decision to turn Westmoreland down, order a bombing pause and seek a negotiated settlement, and abandon the quest for reelection. Carver had been the one intelligence expert who attributed success to the strategy of attrition. By March 1968 he could no longer do so.

THE NIXON PRESIDENCY AND THE CIA

The CIA never received credit for being more right than wrong during those pivotal years of the Vietnam War. To the contrary, the agency was identified with and blamed for the Tet debacle. Its failure to predict the 1968 Soviet invasion of Czechoslovakia poured salt on its wound. For a time Richard Nixon retained Helms as his DCI, and to improve estimates of the Soviet Union and China, the foci of détente and triangular diplomacy, he supported the abolition of the ONE and SRS and their replacement by a new Office of

Political Research (OPR). Eventually (in 1973) a system of National Intelligence Officers (NIO) replaced the Board of Estimates. Still, President Nixon kept his personal meetings with Helms to a minimum, and as an independent source of intelligence the CIA "counted for little." He preferred to rely on sources over which he had more control, especially the staff of National Security advisor Henry Kissinger, to whom on all matters of intelligence Helms took a back seat. To Nixon, the effectiveness of the CIA had declined steadily since the resignation of Allen Dulles. Besides, "Ivy League" liberals who historically opposed him infected it. Nixon's relations with the CIA, to use Helms's word, were "cranky."

What value Nixon did place in the CIA was as an instrument for covert operations, toward which he was predisposed owing to both his experience as Eisenhower's vice president and his secretive personality. Hence, although the CIA played virtually no role in Nixon's Vietnam endgame, it played a significant role in the president's foreign policies. The chief target was Chile. For decades perceived by Washington as an ally and major bulwark against communism and by American multinationals as a hospitable place to do business, Chile attracted more attention from the CIA than one might have expected in light of its stable and pro-American history throughout the twentieth century. During Chile's 1964 presidential election, the Agency covertly provided Eduardo Frei, the opponent of the Marxist candidate Salvadore Allende Gossens, with several million dollars of support. Frei won. But in September 1970, on his third attempt, Allende, heading a united front ticket known as Unidad Popular (Popular Unity), achieved a plurality. Nixon saw him as a Chilean Castro.

The CIA had again in the 1970 Chilean election spent money to defeat Allende. In this effort it received cooperation and additional funds from private American businesses, particularly International Telephone and Telegraph (ITT), whose chairman was former DCI John McCone. McCone feared Allende's potential both for spreading communism and nationalizing U.S. properties. Anaconda and Kennecott corporations, which owned copper mines in Chile, also contributed. Still, the total sum available did not approach the millions that had been available in 1964, and although CIA station chief Henry Hecksher and U.S. Ambassador Edward Korry supervised the anti-Allende campaign, coordination was imperfect. Moreover, according to Henry Kissinger, Nixon's national security advisor, the CIA underestimated the threat Allende posed and behaved too complacently.

President Nixon, however, refused to concede defeat. Because Allende won by a plurality, Chile's Congress would decide the election's ultimate outcome at the end of October. The president authorized Helms to spend up to $10 million and accept all necessary risks to reverse the September results under a two-track assault. Track I concentrated on manipulating the political process. Track II involved orchestrating a coup. The CIA focused on Track II. A special task force was set up at Langley that, rather than rely on the CIA's station in Chile, supervised a dedicated team of agents who operated under deep cover.

Despite the CIA's success in encouraging indigenous military officers to assassinate Rene Schneider, the commander of the Chilean armed forces who refused to subvert the constitutional process, a coup never occurred in 1970. On October 24, two days after Schneider's assassination, Allende assumed the presidency. The CIA's covert operations against him nonetheless intensified. Even as the United States halted economic assistance to the Allende administration, prevented its receipt of loans from the World Bank and other multilateral institutions, and instituted an embargo, the CIA channeled funds to the Chilean military, which increasingly came to perceive Allende as a liability. Meanwhile, Chile's population, especially the middle class, increasingly perceived him as responsible for its North American–induced travails. Within this polarized environment in fall 1972 Chile's truckers accelerated the economic distress by initiating a series of national strikes that for months at a time disrupted internal transportation. Evidence is not available to support the allegation that the CIA funding allowed the truckers to sustain the strikes for a year. Regardless, Chile's economy further deteriorated and its political tensions further escalated. Protected by Schneider's successor, General Carlos Prats, who shared the slain commander of the Armed Forces' respect for the constitution, Allende survived. In fact, his Popular Unity party gained seats in the March 1973 elections for Congress. But following a demonstration outside his home by the wives of his officer corps, Prats resigned. His successor, General Augusto José Ramón Pinochet Ugarte, viewed Chile's constitution, the interests of the country and the military, and Allende very differently. Whereas he had helped to crush an attempted coup in June, Pinochet led a successful one in September. Allende died in the assault on the Le Moneda presidential palace. In 1973 Richard Helms, by then having been removed as DCI and appointed ambassador to Iran, testified that the CIA had never sought the overthrow of Allende. For this testimony Helms was convicted of perjury four years later.

Pinochet took over the reins of government as head of a junta that immediately and with dire consequences repressed all dissent, real and imagined. Declaring a state of siege, he turned the military loose. It killed or "disappeared" thousands of Chileans and at least two Americans, Charles Horman and Frank Teruggi. Recent evidence supports long-time allegations, portrayed in the popular movie *Missing*, of U.S. complicity in Horman's and Teruggi's murders. Subsequently, with the cooperation of the CIA and right-wing allies in Latin America, Pinochet ran Operation Candor, assassinating opponents who had fled Chile. One victim, Allende's former foreign minister Orlando Letelier, along with his American assistant Ronni Moffitt, died when his car exploded in Washington, D.C. Pinochet reigned until 1990, two years following his defeat in a plebiscite on continuing his rule.

WATERGATE AND THE CHURCH AND PIKE
COMMITTEE INVESTIGATIONS

The CIA's operations in Chile accelerated its downward spiral but not because of the bloodbath that followed the coup against Allende that brought Pinochet to power. The CIA had played a more direct role in the overthrow of Arbenz in Guatemala, for example, the catalyst for greater slaughter. The difference is that whereas PBSUCCESS remained largely insulated from public scrutiny, Chile became the focus of a Congressional investigation. And whereas the American people and much of the international community never lost confidence in and trust for Eisenhower, Nixon's penchant for secrecy and duplicity, and his disregard for the Constitution, led to his disgrace and in 1974 his resigning the presidency. The CIA's fall accompanied that of Nixon. Already widely in disfavor because of its identification with a foreign policy responsible for the American tragedy in Vietnam, for much of the American public the CIA became inseparable from the web of dirty tricks that in aggregate is called "Watergate."

The CIA was first ensnared in the Watergate affair because of its indirect culpability in the break-in of the Democratic National Committee headquarters and in other illegal Nixon campaign and attendant activities. Among those caught in the break-in were such CIA veterans as E. Howard Hunt and James W. McCord, Jr., and Cuban exiles with whom the CIA had contracted for the Bay of Pigs invasion. Although Hunt's relationship with the Agency had by the 1970s become tenuous, the agency did provide him with limited assistance. For one, the CIA had acceded to Nixon's request that it develop psychological profiles of the president's "enemies." Toward this end Hunt and others involved in the 1972 Watergate break-in had broken into the office of Daniel Ellsberg's psychiatrist earlier in 1971 in order to obtain files on the former defense official who had leaked the Pentagon Papers to the *New York Times*.

More fundamentally, with the Vietnam War undermining the Cold War consensus on which the efficacy of plausible deniability depended as much as did institutions such as the 40 Committee, Watergate presented an opportunity to air the CIA's dirty laundry to an extent previously unimaginable. On December 22, 1974, in the wake of the sensational hearings on Watergate and impeachment resolutions and Nixon's subsequent resignation and pardon, Seymour Hersh published a front-page article in the *New York Times* on the CIA's role in domestic surveillance. Hersh identified Operation CHAOS, run by the agency's counterintelligence guru James Jesus Angleton, in an effort to unmask foreign influences on the student protest movement.

President Gerald Ford, who less than a year before succeeded the disgraced Spiro Agnew as Nixon's vice president and had inhabited the Oval Office with Nixon's resignation, asked DCI Colby whether, so soon after the Watergate revelations, the government could weather another storm. During

President Nixon addressing the investigation of the Watergate break-in at a brief news conference on April 17, 1973. (Courtesy of Photofest)

his brief tenure as DCI bookended by Helms's departure in February 1973 and Colby's appointment in September, James Schlesinger had instructed the Agency to compile a highly sensitive report on its more questionable practices, including its involvement in political assassinations, a report which grew to more than 600 pages. To the chagrin of most CIA veterans, Colby responded to Ford's inquiry by providing him with a copy of these "family jewels." Ford in response established a blue-ribbon commission under Vice President Nelson Rockefeller to look into the matter, confident that Rockefeller would exercise judicious discretion. Rockefeller behaved as expected, but CBS correspondent Daniel Schorr learned of the report's reference to assassinations and went public with the story. Allegations concerning the CIA's involvement in the coup against and possibly the assassination of Allende in Chile also surfaced. Congress seized the initiative from the White House. In response, in December 1974 Congress enacted the Hughes-Ryan Amendment (Public Law 93-559) to require the president to make a "finding" that a covert operation was vital to the national interest and describe its scope to Congress. Then in January 1975 the Senate mandated the establishment of a Select Committee to Study Governmental Operations with Respect to Intelligence Activities, chaired by Democratic Senator Frank Church. The next month the House followed suit. Initially chaired by Lucien Nedzi, the House Select Committee on Intelligence was reconstituted five months later with Nedzi replaced by New York Democrat Otis Pike.

President Ford's objective in appointing the Rockefeller Commission was to restore confidence in the presidency and "heal" the wounds of Watergate. Events conspired against him. On April 30, 1975, the government of South Vietnam surrendered, forcing the United States to withdraw under humiliating conditions. In May Cambodians seized the U.S. merchant ship *Mayaguez* in international waters. Rather than accept another blow to America's credibility, Ford, relying on the CIA's intelligence, ordered a three-pronged military mission to rescue the crew. Over forty Americans died in the operation, which rescued not a single captive as the Cambodians had already released the entire crew. Meanwhile, a civil war erupted in Angola following its independence from Portugal in January 1975. Ford approved a CIA covert mission, IAFEATURE, to combat the Cuba-assisted pro-Marxist forces, the MPLA (Popular Movement for the Liberation of Angola). IAFEATURE accomplished little other than to exacerbate tension between the White House and Congress. In 1976 Congress approved the Clark Amendment (to a foreign aid bill) prohibiting U.S. assistance to any faction in Angola and reaffirming Congress's authority to oversee intelligence operations.

Against this backdrop congressional hearings into the abuses of power of the U.S. intelligence agencies (CIA, FBI, NSA) began earning 1975 the title, "Year of Intelligence." Even as the Church Committee started to call witnesses and its staff began pouring through volumes of classified archives, in June the White House released portions of the Rockefeller Commission's report. In addition to confirming and elaborating upon the CIA's domestic spying exposed in Hersh's article, it included descriptions of such practices as the Agency's use of unsuspecting Americans to test the effects of various drugs. In one case a military officer who had unknowingly ingested LSD committed suicide. President Ford, moreover, kept classified the material in the Rockefeller Report dealing with assassinations. Inheriting this issue, Chairperson Frank Church condemned U.S. involvement in assassinations as morally reprehensible and anticipated that the committee's investigation of them and other abuses would prove to be a boon to his presidential aspirations. Also, as a leading congressional opponent of the Vietnam War, he seized on the opportunity to bring to light the CIA's covert operations as a means to indict the conduct of U.S. foreign policy.

Although the hearings uncovered robust evidence of the CIA's complicity in assassination plots, the effectiveness of the 40 Committee and its predecessors in constructing a shield of plausible deniability prevented the Church Committee from determining that any president had explicitly authorized an assassination. To the consternation of his Republican colleagues, moreover, Church was reluctant to tarnish the reputations of Democratic as well as Republican presidents; the attempts on Castro's life had occurred under the watch of Presidents Kennedy and Johnson. That the CIA operated as an out-of-control "rogue elephant" seemed to church the only viable conclusion. Over in the House, the Pike Committee suffered from more intense partisan sniping. Pike, however, resisted White House and CIA efforts to suppress the release of sensitive intelligence material, including that acquired by the still-unacknowledged National Security Agency. He likewise challenged the rogue elephant metaphor by placing responsibility for CIA deeds and misdeeds squarely in the Oval Office. After the Pike Committee in January voted to reject the more than one hundred deletions insisted on by the CIA, the full House voted not to release the report to the public.

THE POST-1975 DEBATE OVER THE CIA

The publication of the Church Committee's multi-volume reports in December 1975 and April 1976 proved to be anticlimactic. Their most sensational revelations had already become public, and they failed to provide a systematic evaluation of America's intelligence assets and effectiveness. The portrayal of the CIA as a rogue elephant stuck, but the Ford administration had already enacted several minor reforms to ensure greater oversight. Further, the assassination of Richard Welch, the CIA station chief in Athens, on December 23, 1975, reminded congressional and public critics of the dangers confronted by Agency personnel even as it hardened attitudes against exposés.

Ford had the benefit of the politically experienced and connected George H. W. Bush as Colby's successor as DCI. The president soon confronted another problem, namely allegations from hard-line conservatives and neoconservatives, some of whom were members of the President's Foreign Intelligence Advisory Board (PFIAB), that the CIA's NIEs underestimated Soviet nuclear capabilities, amount of military spending, and most importantly aggressive intentions, and failed to detect violations of the SALT I agreement (Strategic Arms Limitation Treaty), thereby making negotiations for SALT II a reckless venture. As DCI Bush acquiesced to allowing the NSC to establish a "Team B," composed of rabid anti-Soviets like its head, Harvard's professor of Russian history Richard Pipes, to prepare an estimate that would compete with that of the CIA's "Team A." Team B's report sharply criticized the Agency analysts' assessment of Soviet capabilities, intentions, and doctrine. Much of the criticism leaked to the press, while the notoriety generated by the exercise undermined the Agency's credibility and authority to produce national intelligence estimates. Still, the Team B report's influence on the subsequent NIE (11-3/8-76) was minimal; the CIA's assessments prevailed.

With great difficulty in 1976, Gerald Ford fought off Reagan's challenge to his candidacy for the Republican presidential nomination. But he did not win the presidential election in 1976. Neither did Frank Church who failed even to secure the Democratic nomination. The party chose and Americans instead elected as president Jimmy Carter, a Washington outsider who pledged to right the country's moral compass and conduct a foreign policy consistent with America's ideals as well as interests. By definition and tradition, covert operations, let alone assassinations, were incompatible with those ideals. While Carter aligned with the Agency's experts in their battle with Team B ideologues, he signaled during the campaign and interregnum that he was no friend of the Agency. Neither was his vice president, Walter Mondale, who had been a vocal critic of the Agency during his service on the Church Committee.

The day that Carter took office, photographs from the newest generation of U.S. spy satellites, the KH-11 (code-named Kennan), reached Washington. Unlike previous images, these digitalized transmissions required no film to retrieve and develop. In "real time" computers received and converted the coded data into pictures, which could be readily manipulated and enhanced. This success excited the new president, a technology enthusiast who recognized how valuable the KH-11 could be in pushing forward the SALT II negotiations. Yet his skepticism about the CIA remained undiminished. Indeed, Carter took the unprecedented step of dismissing Bush, who lobbied to remain DCI, because of his association with the previous administration. After his preferred successor, Theodore Sorensen, withdrew his name from consideration amidst criticism that he was too dovish and a potential security risk to boot, President Carter turned to his former Annapolis classmate, Admiral Stansfield Turner. Although more extensive that Carter's, Turner's experience with intelligence was limited—he described himself as an "outsider to the intelligence profession." Carter was confident, nevertheless, that he could revolutionize the CIA's culture. Congruent with this goal, and much to the chagrin of Carter's hawkish national security advisor, Zbigniew Brzezinski, Turner requested a budget that allocated the lowest funding for covert operations since President Truman's first term. He revealingly entitled his 1985 memoir, *Secrecy and Democracy: The CIA in Transition.*

CIA veterans, many still smarting from what they perceived as Colby's betrayal, their harsh treatment by the Church and Pike Commissions, and the establishment in 1976 of the Senate Select Committee on Intelligence and House Permanent Subcommittee on Intelligence to institutionalize congressional oversight, viewed Richard Helms's receipt of a fine and two-year suspended sentence in November 1977 for deceiving Congress about the Agency's operations in Chile as adding insult to injury. From their perspective Carter and Turner piled on the insults. Sharing the president's distaste for the CIA's behavior, Turner pared the budget for clandestine projects and cashiered long-time operatives as relics of an irrational Cold War mindset. To "put the CIA's much criticized past behind us," he shut down operations in Moscow and supported Carter's abolition of the PFIAB on the premise that it had been too eager to sanction covert actions. Turner also reorganized the CIA's analytical architecture. In particular he established the National Intelligence Council (NIC) to prepare National Intelligence Estimates, and selected as its head Robert R. Bowie. Bowie was the highly respected director of Harvard University's Center for International Affairs, who had served under Eisenhower as the assistant secretary of state for policy planning. His selection was tantamount to conceding the poor quality of previous NIEs. Morale in the agency plummeted, and the veterans who remained with it became increasingly risk-averse.

Even as the Carter administration achieved some hard-fought and significant achievements during its first three years in office, culminating in 1978 with approval of two Panama Canal Treaties and, in 1979, the signing of the Egyptian-Israeli Peace Treaty (Camp David Accords) and then the SALT II Treaty with the Soviets, the president's foreign policies appeared erratic and incoherent. In part the problem evolved from Carter's inexperience and his inability to articulate a vision that embraced both containment and the promotion of human rights. No less responsible were the conflicting views between Secretary of State Cyrus Vance, a proponent of détente who preferred diplomacy to force, and National Security Advisor Zbigniew Brzezinski, an ardent and hard-line Cold Warrior. In this battle for Carter's heart and mind, Brzezinski gradually gained the upper hand. As national security advisor, he insisted that he, not the director of the CIA, deliver the president's "intelligence briefing," which he pointedly renamed the "national security briefing." Indeed, Brzezinski all but boasts in his memoir about how successfully he limited Turner's direct contact with Carter. He writes that "throughout the four years [Turner had] practically no one-on-one meetings with the President, and all CIA reporting was funneled to the President through me."

THE IRANIAN HOSTAGE CRISIS

The administration's internal pathologies and the upheavals within the CIA were not, however, the causes of the grief that befell it in the latter half of Carter's presidency. But they contributed. The specific catalyst was growing unrest in Iran. By 1978 a quarter of a century had passed since the CIA-orchestrated coup (TPAJAX) had restored Shah Mohammed Reza Pahlavi to the Peacock Throne. During that time the shah had turned Iran into an oasis of stability in the Middle East, the linchpin of American efforts to contain communism and preserve ready access to the region's vital resources, oil above all. Successive U.S. administrations had also perceived Iran as a developmental model for its neighbors and for the Third World in general. For his part the shah, appreciating his value to U.S. strategy, saw no reason to heed advice to relax the repressive regime he had methodically constructed over the decades. For their part American policy makers and analysts accepted his iron-fisted authority as an immutable dimension of Iran's political environment. Its contacts limited to the shah's inner circle, armed forces, and internal police (the dreaded SAVAK, Sazamane Etelaat va Amniate Kechvar), the administration, as had its predecessors, relied almost exclusively on SIGINT and IMINT for intelligence assessments. Washington could not fathom that any substantial segment of Iran's population took seriously the calls of eighty-one-year-old Ayatollah Ruhollah Khomeini from Paris, where he had been in exile for sixteen years, for a revolution aimed at establishing a theocratic state. After a year in office Carter was still toasting the shah as "an island of stability in a turbulent corner of the world," and the CIA assessed the country as "not in a revolutionary or even a prerevolutionary situation."

The CIA's assessment proved to be fatally flawed; its underestimation of Khomeini almost criminally negligent. A very large percentage of Iranians were fundamentalist Shi'ite Muslims whose disaffection with the shah's secular ways had reached a climax by 1978. Middle-class youth produced by Iran's U.S.-financed modernization were equally resentful of his disregard for civil liberties and refusal to provide them a voice in his government. United only in their opposition to the current regime, these factions allied to overthrow it. Outbursts of violence forced the shah to declare martial law and, when that fueled more unrest, to appoint in December a civilian government headed by the moderate Shahpour Bakhtiar. It was too little too late. On January 19, 1979, the shah fled the country. On February 1 Ayatollah Khomeini returned; less than two weeks later he replaced Bakhtiar with Mehdi Bazargan. On February 19, Khomeini triumphantly proclaimed the establishment of the Islamic Republic of Iran.

Carter rejected Brzezinski's recommendation that the United States dispatch military forces to restore the shah and yet was unwilling to negotiate with the new Islamic state. As a result the administration lost influence over Iran, which including losing two sites vital to the NSA's ability to monitor Soviet missile testing even as mounting opposition in the Senate to ratifying the SALT II treaty intensified the urgency of such monitoring. As the administration struggled to decide what to do next, the shah struggled to identify a country that would accept him. On Vance's advice Carter determined that the United States would not. But in October 1979 he learned that the shah was receiving chemotherapy for malignant lymphoma while in Mexico, and not responding to the treatment. Now accepting the advice of Brzezinski, backed up by Henry Kissinger and Chase Manhattan Bank's David Rockefeller, the president reversed himself. He invited the shah to come to the United States for medical treatment. Khomeini immediately denounced the invitation as evidence that the shah was conspiring with the "Great Satan" to make a comeback. On the morning of November 4, 1979, Carter awakened to news that thousands of Iranian "students" had seized the U.S. Embassy in Tehran and taken fifty-two American hostages, whom they paraded blindfolded for the world to see.

For Carter, his administration, and much of the American nation, throughout the 444 subsequent days required for the release of the hostages, the world was an unrelentingly hostile place. The CIA could take credit for the most notable exception. On January 28, 1980, its covert operation rescued six of America's foreign-service personnel in Iran who had managed to reach the safety of the Canadian Embassy. President Carter, however, could make no progress toward reclaiming the U.S. embassy and freeing the hostages imprisoned within it. By then Khomeini had ousted the Bazargan government, installing in its place a Revolutionary Council composed of militant clerics. Americans marked the days of captivity by adorning their property with yellow ribbons and watching Ted Koppel on *Nightline* each evening.

The Hostage Crisis consumed time that neither the White House, State Department, nor CIA could afford to give. To the surprise of all three, on Christmas Eve of 1979 the Soviet Union invaded Afghanistan to secure its communist client against insurgent Islamic *mujahedeen*. Three days later KGB forces assassinated Afghan President Hafizullah Amin, allowing Babrak Karmal to declare himself president and prime minister of the Democratic Republic of Afghanistan and general secretary of the People's Democratic Party of Afghanistan. The Carter administration had underestimated the power of Islamic fundamentalists in Iran and appeared helpless to do anything about it. Now the president admitted publicly that his assessment of the Soviet leadership was no more accurate. On January 3, 1980, he suspended his SALT II treaty ratification effort, and in April he announced that the United States would boycott that summer's Olympics, which Moscow would host.

Behind the Oval Office's closed doors, less than a month into the crisis Carter had authorized Brzezinski to orchestrate the development of contingency plans for a rescue mission to free the hostages. Brzezinski composed a steering committee, with himself as chair. It included DCI Turner, Secretary of Defense Harold Brown, and David C. Brown, chairman of the Joint Chiefs of Staff. The rescue mission, a military operation, would have to be covert. The plan that evolved, Operation EAGLE CLAW, was remarkably simple. Helicopters would sneak into Iran to a predetermined staging site in the remote Persian Desert (Desert One), where they would be met by a special unit of the Green Berets (Delta Force) and refueled by awaiting six C-130s. The helicopters would carry the Delta Force to a hideout near Tehran. From there the commandos would penetrate the embassy compound under cloak of darkness and rescue the hostages. Helicopters would then transport them from the compound to planes waiting at a nearby airport, which would fly them out of the country.

Carter, encouraged by Secretary of State Vance, resisted approving the mission in the hope that a combination of economic sanctions and skillful negotiations would produce a settlement. As winter turned to spring, however, that hope evaporated. In early April the president, having learned that a reconnaissance flight had eluded detection, selected a staging site. Less than a week later he severed diplomatic relations with Iran. Shortly thereafter, he approved the mission. It began on April 24 and rapidly turned into a disaster. An unexpected dust storm crippled three of the eight helicopters. With a minimum of six helicopters required to execute the evacuation, Carter aborted the mission. But during the withdrawal from Desert One, a helicopter that did reach the staging area crashed into a C-130, killing eight Americans and an Iranian interpreter. The operation was no less a calamity than the Bay of Pigs.

PRESIDENT REAGAN "UNLEASHES" THE CIA

The CIA had played a relatively minor role in the Iranian tragedy. The intelligence it provided was far from perfect, but under the circumstances, it performed satisfactorily. It could not predict the dust storm. Nevertheless, its history tied inextricably to covert operations and its reputation still reeling from its inability to provide warning about the embassy takeover in the first place, the CIA's image suffered another blow. But the greatest casualty of Operation EAGLE CLAW was President Carter. The failed mission took its place at the top of a seemingly endless list of examples of the president's alleged incompetence. During the 1980 campaign Republican challenger Ronald Reagan pledged to restore America's strength, its honor, and its pride. In November he won the presidency by more than eight million votes. As a lame duck Carter succeeded on January 18, 1981, to secure a settlement that would release the hostages. They arrived in Washington on January 20, following Reagan's inauguration.

Reagan had been willing to excuse CIA abuses when he was a member of the Rockefeller Commission that Gerald Ford established in 1975 to investigate the CIA's "family jewels." As president, he was unwilling to excuse what he considered its deplorable performance not only in Iran but, more importantly, also with regard to an array of intelligence matters concerning the Soviet Union. In his view, the CIA had grossly underestimated the Soviets' military power and its military spending. Worse, it grossly underestimated the Soviet success in paralyzing the United States by practicing nuclear blackmail while it expanded its global influence through proxies in the Third World. During the interregnum between his election and inauguration Reagan assembled a transition team to recommend measures to enhance the CIA's capabilities across the board. In the president-elect's judgment, improving the CIA required a DCI who appreciated that the United States was in danger and was willing to take risks to secure the national interest. It needed William Casey.

Although their personalities contrasted sharply and they were never close, Casey and Reagan saw eye to eye on the severity of the Soviet threat and the role the CIA must play in combating it. They already knew that the Soviet Union could not be trusted, and that it relentlessly sought to extend its evil empire to Central America, Africa, the Middle East—everywhere. The United States needed to be more aggressive in its response; that required "unleashing" the CIA. Effective covert operations would roll back the gains made by the Soviets since the end of the Vietnam War and produce victory in the Cold War. Casey, who had served in the OSS during World War II prior to embarking on a successful career as a New York City lawyer, investor, and entrepreneur, was the president's immediate choice for the job. He was a risk-taker with a reputation as a rule-breaker, too. Signaling the prominent position that his former campaign manager would hold in his administration, Reagan made Casey the first DCI to have a seat at the cabinet table, and provided him with an office in the Old Executive Office Building next to the White House to go along with his headquarters at Langley.

Casey lost no time rebuilding the CIA by recruiting a new generation of personnel. No longer was the agency a welcome home for Ivy League–educated Cold War liberals committed to public service. Disillusioned by the Vietnam War and the investigative hearings on the CIA of the 1970s, they retreated to Wall Street and Madison Avenue. Many case officers in Casey's CIA had fought in the Vietnam War, not protested against it. *Their* president was Ronald Reagan, not John Kennedy. Throughout the CIA, "The tennis players were being replaced by the bowlers."

By the end of the administration's first year, Casey and his bowlers were taking dead aim at what they, the president, and Secretary of State Alexander Haig agreed was the phalanx of the Soviet attack, Central America. Supported by a White Paper issued by the State Department a month after Reagan's inauguration, they were convinced that the Sandinista Liberation Front, which had wrested control of the government of Nicaragua from the dictator Anastasio Somoza in July 1979, was funneling Cuban arms to the rebellious Faribundo Martí National Liberation Front (FMLN) in El Salvador. Their ambition was to gain dominion over all of Central America, from where they would move up north through Mexico to the United States proper. On December 1, 1981, Reagan approved a covert project to arm and train anti-Sandinistas based in Honduras, soon to be called the Contras (counterrevolutionaries). Although administration officials deceptively told Congress that the aim was to interdict weapons traffic to the FMLN in El Salvador, their real purpose was to liberate Nicaragua from the yoke of communism. The price tag reached $19 billion, and Casey oversaw the planning. Three days later, on December 4, Reagan issued Executive Order 12333, providing the CIA with exclusive authority to conduct covert operations "unless the President determines that another agency is more likely to achieve a particular objective." The implication of this qualification was that the president might want to call on the Delta Force or another unit of the military. It turned out that the Executive Order provided a loophole that the staff of the National Security Council would soon exploit.

A year later the covert operation had become a front-page story. The administration could no longer plausibly deny its involvement with the Contras, but it denied that it sought the overthrow of the Sandinista regime. Reagan's replacement of Secretary of State Haig by the less bellicose George Schultz did not diminish public and Congressional suspicions that the administration's anticommunist crusade continued unabated. President Reagan's and DCI Casey's commitment to the Contras appeared messianic in nature, consistent with the president's identification of them as the moral equivalent of the Founding Fathers and his definition of the Vietnam War as a noble cause. Congress put them both on notice that it would not trust their words alone. On December 8, 1982, the House passed the Boland Amendment to the Defense Appropriations Act for Fiscal Year 1983 (House Amendment 461 to HR 2968), prohibiting the CIA (or the military) from training, equipping, or even advising the Contras for the purpose of bringing down the Nicaraguan government. Initially attached to the classified 1983 Intelligence Authorization Bill in April by the House Select Committee on Intelligence, chaired by Edward Boland, the amendment did allow the CIA to carry on operations intended to interdict the export of Nicaraguan arms.

The administration would not be deterred. The attempted assassination of the Polish-born Pope John Paul II in 1981, for which Casey held the KGB responsible; Moscow's crackdown on the Solidarity Movement in Poland and declaration of martial law by General Wojciech Jaruzelski later that year; and the Soviets' downing in September 1983 of a South Korean Airliner, KAL 007, buttressed the perception that the Evil Empire had to be vigorously challenged. In early 1984 the CIA, disregarding the ban of the Boland Amendment, began to mine Nicaraguan harbors. Casey attributed the mining to the Contras, but the press again uncovered the true story. Acting on a petition of the Nicaraguan government, the International Court of Justice ruled that the United States had violated international law. The Senate Select Committee responded by demanding an apology from Casey and his agreement to inform it in advance of *any* covert actions. In contrast, the House of Representatives enacted an amendment to the Fiscal 1985 Continuing Appropriations Act, Boland II, prohibiting any organ of the U.S. government from providing any type of support to the contras. This more draconian prohibition laid the foundation for the Iran-Contra scandal that was to consume the administration during its final years.

THE IRAN-CONTRA AFFAIR

Iran-Contra paralleled Watergate in its unconstitutionality and abuse of executive power. The motive was simple: President Reagan and DCI Casey refused to deprive the Contras of U.S. support, notwithstanding their manifest ineptness and the Boland Amendments and the president was equally interested in addressing the problem posed by the Iranian government. President Reagan's familiarity with the particulars of the Iranian and Contra initiatives remains unknown; Casey was more deeply involved although he skirted Congress's prohibitions and obfuscated his participation by "delegating" responsibility for its management to the National Security Council. For this reason National Security Advisor Robert C. McFarlane and his deputy and then successor, Admiral John M. Poindexter, supervised the twin operations. From the basement of the White House, Marine Lieutenant Colonel Oliver North, a low-level NSC staffer, directed both initiatives. North's woeful ignorance of the global environment explains a great deal about how the Contras came to be linked with Iran in the scheme. And his woeful ignorance of covert operations explains a great deal about the ineptness of the plans and their execution. North's qualifications were his daring, deceptiveness, and true belief in the cause.

The premise was simple. The Contras required arms, but Congress had prohibited the administration from supplying them. Iran, at war with Iraq, also required arms, but since the hostage crisis of 1979 the administration was effectively prohibited from supplying them as well (given its militant stance on not negotiating with terrorists). Reagan felt no sympathy for the Iranians. But he felt a great deal of sympathy for five Americans, including the CIA station chief in Beirut, William Buckley, who had been kidnapped by the pro-Iranian terrorist organization Hezbollah and was said to be held in Lebanon. McFarlane convinced President Reagan that by using Iranian arms dealer Manucher Ghorbanifar as an intermediary to sell Israeli arms to Iran, and specifically TOW and HAWK missiles, he could strengthen a potentially powerful faction of moderate Iranians. These moderates would thereby be in a position to challenge fundamentalist rule in Iran and to intercede with Hezbollah to secure the release of the American hostages. North, meanwhile, concocted the idea of diverting the profits from the arms sales to Iran to fund the Contras.

With virtually no means to gather intelligence internal to Iran, the CIA knew nothing about the supposedly moderate faction or its putative influence on Hezbollah. In contrast intelligence on Ghorbanifar was that he was unreliable. With Casey remaining far in the background, McFarlane, Poindexter, and North set the plan in motion. Ghorbanifar orchestrated the sale of the Israeli missiles to Iran. He then arranged a series of clandestine meetings between McFarlane and North and several mid-level Iranian officials in May 1986. Iran's hostility to the United States remained just as intense, however, and there is no evidence that anyone from Iran sought the release of the U.S. hostages. Hezbollah did release some of them, but it kidnapped an equal number to compensate. CIA station chief Buckley died after more than a year of captivity and torture, apparently in Iran.

North managed to siphon to the Contras money from the sale of the arms to Iran. But that diversion ended no more happily. In October 1986 the Sandinistas captured the sole survivor of a cargo plane that had been shot down carrying arms and supplies to the Contras, publicly exposing the breach of the Boland Amendments. The next month a Lebanese newspaper published a story about the meeting of McFarlane and North in Teheran. Even as North began systematically to shred or doctor documents pertaining to the operations, the White House began to stonewall and issue incredible statements. A barrage of public and congressional criticism forced Poindexter's resignation, North's firing, and Reagan's appointment in November of a three-member commission consisting of former Senator John Tower (who served as chair); Edmund Muskie, who had succeeded Vance as Carter's secretary of state; and former national security advisor under Gerald Ford, Brent Scowcroft, to determine what had happened and under whose authority. Its investigation lasted ten weeks. Congress also launched an investigation into the Iran-Contra affair. The next month Attorney General Edwin Meese appointed Lawrence E. Walsh as special prosecutor to investigate the many violations of federal law. The mountains of testimony and other evidence produced by the Tower Commission, the congressional investigation, and Walsh's inquiry led to criminal convictions that included McFarlane, Poindexter, and North (the latter two were subsequently vacated because of their immunity agreements relating to their public congressional testimony). The testimony implicated Casey but never established his culpability. In May 1987, just as the Walsh investigation was starting up, Casey died. According to Bob Woodward, on his deathbed the DCI (who had resigned shortly before) answered an explicit question by nodding that he knew all.

What President Reagan knew and when he knew it remains unknown. Perhaps no covert operation better illustrates the effectiveness of the institutional cocoon that allows a president plausibly to deny complicity. But Reagan escaped the Iran-Contra scandal relatively unscathed because of other factors as well. The CIA had not shed the moniker rogue elephant, and neither Congress nor the public wanted to charge Reagan with anything more than being an amiable dunce with a poor memory who was incapable of controlling his subordinates. Probably more saliently, the administration's breakdown over Central America and the Middle East coincided with its breakthroughs over the Soviet Union. The progress Reagan made in improving relations with the Soviet Union during the last years of his presidency, and in laying the foundation for the end of the Cold War, distracted attention from the Iran-Contra revelations. It also took practically everyone by surprise, and no one more so than those who worked for the CIA.

THE END OF THE COLD WAR AND THE COLLAPSE OF COMMUNISM

The CIA's capability to collect intelligence on and produce estimates about the Soviet Union had been called into greater question after the challenge of the Team B exercise during the Ford administration. Turner's obliteration of the Moscow station had forced President Carter to rely overwhelmingly on technology for his estimates, which after the Soviet invasion of Afghanistan he conceded were mistaken. President Reagan and DCI Casey had their minds made up before entering office. One of Casey's early innovations was to bring under his direct control the National Intelligence Council and select as its chair Henry S. Rowen, whose views paralleled his own. Casey also established an Office of Soviet Analysis (SOVA), which, along with the also-newly-established Office of Global Issues, produced assessments to the DCI's liking.

The May 1981 SNIE 11/2-81, *Soviet Support for International Terrorism and Revolutionary Violence*, portrayed the Kremlin as "deeply engaged" in supporting global violence. This analysis probably reflected more than influenced Reagan's policies through much of his first term in office.

Mikhail Gorbachev took over as the Soviet president and communist party general secretary at the start of Reagan's second term. By then the U.S. president's stridency had already begun to mellow. In addition to the dictates of the 1984 campaign, Reagan seems to have been shaken when, in the aftermath of his announcing the Strategic Defense Initiative and NATO's exercise in nuclear release procedures, code named Able Archer, he realized that the Kremlin feared the United States was preparing for a first strike as much as he feared that it was.

But Gorbachev's "New Thinking" challenged Reagan's most fundamental beliefs about the Soviets, and he shocked almost everyone by revising them. In this regard the CIA proved to be of little value. On the one hand Casey, who did not share his predecessors' interest in intelligence analysis under any circumstances, succumbed to pressure from the Casper Weinberger-led Pentagon to give the Department of Defense a greater voice in preparing "net assessments"—the comparison of U.S. to U.S.S.R. capabilities. DoD rigidly adhered to a magnified estimate of the Soviet threat. On the other hand, those CIA analysts who argued that Gorbachev's New Thinking was really new—for example Melvin Goodman, the chief of SOVA—tended to be drowned out by less sanguine perspectives, such as those of Robert Gates. As Casey's Deputy Director for Intelligence, Gates, who had joined the CIA as an intelligence analyst in 1966 and served as the NSC expert on and National Intelligence Officer for the Soviet Union under President Carter, wielded greater influence. He perceived *glasnost* and perestroika as tactics Gorbachev was using to enhance achieving what remained the Soviet's strategic objective: the defeat of the West. Buttressing Gates's suspicions was the mid-1980s spy-versus-spy tangle that enveloped the defection and redefection of KGB Colonel Vitali Yurchenko, his identification of ex-CIA officer Edward Lee Howard as a Soviet mole, the FBI arrest of Gennadi Zakharov in New York City for recruiting spies, and the Soviet Union's retaliatory arrest of Moscow journalist Nicholas Daniloff for allegedly spying for the United States.

Reagan did not dismiss the CIA's caution and conservatism, or its alarmism. Yet his instincts drove his attitude toward Gorbachev more than his mantra, "Trust but verify." As time went on CIA assessments of the Soviet Union—although still reflecting the skepticism of Gates and NSA director Lt. General William Odom and an institutional disinclination to err on the side of optimism—did become increasingly more positive about Gorbachev's sincerity. What made a greater impact on the president, however, was his personal assessment of the Soviet leader. Each time Reagan met with Gorbachev, in Geneva in 1985, Reykjavik, Iceland, in 1986, Washington, D.C., in 1987, he became more convinced that cooperation was possible to bring about first an end to the nuclear arms race and then an end to the Cold War. The negotiations that produced the two SALT treaties were complicated and arduous because they were dependent heavily on intelligence capabilities. Reagan's agreement on the Intermediate Range Nuclear Forces Treaty depended on his relationship with Gorbachev. In contrast, his successor George H. W. Bush, the only president whose resume included the directorship of the CIA, embraced the Agency more enthusiastically. President Bush also paid closer attention to Gates, who, even before being elevated to DCI in 1991, was as DDI a more intimate adviser to the president than his boss, William Webster. As a result, Bush, who prized stability and perceived the unpredictable changes occurring in the Eastern Bloc as threatening, was less than eager to build on Reagan's foundation. But he no more than Gorbachev could control the forces that *glasnost*, perestroika, and new thinking had unleashed. Neither Bush nor the CIA had any idea that in 1989 the Berlin Wall would come tumbling down, and in 1991 the Soviet Union would implode.

AFGHANISTAN, IRAQ, THE BALKANS—AND THE CIA'S POST–COLD WAR ROLE

The improvement in U.S.-Soviet relations and conclusion of the INF Treaty, which went into force in June 1988, limited the damage Iran-Contra had caused President Reagan. Americans rejoiced in his commitment to ending peacefully the Cold War. Yet even though Gorbachev accompanied his accord on the INF treaty with a pledge to withdraw Soviet troops from Afghanistan, most Americans were largely ignorant of the critical significance of that Cold War theater. The CIA's intensive involvement in Afghanistan first began during the Carter administration but grew exponentially more intense under the direction of Reagan and William Casey. The CIA's support of the resistance to the Soviet-sponsored regime helped turn Afghanistan into the Kremlin's Vietnam.

The CIA's role in the events that unfolded in Afghanistan before the belated Soviet withdrawal in the late 1980s attracted little domestic or international attention. After the Soviet withdrawal, its role attracted virtually no attention at all. Indeed, the end of the Cold War triggered calls from some influential circles for the end of the CIA altogether. New York Senator Daniel Moynihan led this charge. Moynihan argued that the Agency's failure to predict the Soviet Union's collapse demonstrated its inadequacy as a collector and analyst of intelligence. He further argued that the secrecy that inhered in its mission and self-definition violated the ideals and values responsible for America prevailing over the Soviets. Citing the master spy novelist John le Carré as his authority, Moynihan thundered, "The Soviet Empire did not fall apart because the spooks had bugged the men's room in the Kremlin or put broken glass in Mrs. Brezhnev's bath, but because running a huge closed repressive society in the 1980s had become—economically, socially and militarily, and technologically—impossible." As early as 1991 Moynihan proposed folding its functions into the State Department. Then in 1995, following the arrest and sentencing to life in prison for treason of the CIA's former Soviet counterintelligence head Aldrich Ames, he sponsored the Abolition of the Central Intelligence Agency Act. His bill, however, gained few supporters.

Approaching its fortieth anniversary, the CIA was by then an entrenched institution. Its budget was no longer a high priority during the 1990s, but its abolition would be politically and bureaucratically more difficult than its establishment. Further, the phenomenon of globalization had elevated the risk of stealing U.S. economic and technological assets, which the CIA could help to deter. Furthermore, the end of the Cold War produced not so much global peace as global instability. The perception that the CIA was vital to U.S. security revived even as the Agency's intelligence collecting capabilities declined precipitously.

In fact, the CIA's image during the decade of the 1990s improved markedly, as attested to by the complimentary television series and films. The success in early 1991 of Operation DESERT STORM—the U.S.-led destruction of Saddam Hussein's army and forced evacuation of the Iraqis from Kuwait after less than two months of combat—were attributed in no small part to good intelligence. The CIA's responsibility was minor compared to that of the military, but it received credit for it nonetheless. And it received little blame for the massacre of thousands of Kurds in the Gulf War's aftermath, although it was culpable. Following Saddam Hussein's defeat, the United States and its allies established an ersatz Kurdistan, a safe area for Iraqi Kurds in the "no fly zone" north of the 36th parallel. There, authorized first under the administration of George H. W. Bush and then under that of Bill Clinton, the CIA embarked on a covert project to topple Saddam's regime. It funneled millions of dollars to two anti-Saddam organizations, Ahmed Chalabi's Iraqi National Congress (INC) and the Iraqi National Accord, or Wafik, led by Iyad (Ayad) Allawi, a former member of Saddam's Baath Party. The organizations and their leaders were bitter rivals, and the CIA shifted its support from one to the other, resulting only in acrimonious finger-pointing. CIA operatives also recruited Kurds eager to establish their independence from Iraq, but they, too, were divided between the Patriotic Union of Kurdistan (PUK) and the Kurdistan Democratic Party (KDP). Encouraged by the CIA, the two factions united temporarily to take up arms against Iraq in 1991 and 1995. Crushed militarily in the first instance, they aborted the insurrection in the second and turned for protection to either Iran or, showing their desperation, Saddam himself.

The CIA's involvement in the Balkan Wars during the George H. W. Bush and Clinton administrations was not dissimilar. On the one hand, along with other elements of the U.S. intelligence community, through aerial surveillance and other means the Agency collected valuable evidence of Serbia's campaign of "ethnic cleansing." On the other hand, its operation to destabilize the regime of Slobodan Milosevic contributed to the escalation and expansion of the fighting. The CIA helped to fund, train, and supply first the Army of Bosnia, then the Kosovo Liberation Army, and finally extremist offshoots of the KLA who launched campaigns in Southern Serbia and Macedonia. Few knew about these covert operations, however. Of the myriad actors in the Balkan tragedy, Milosevic was widely regarded as the most evil. Much of the world's opinion supported intervention to assist his victims, and the CIA's operations preceded those of NATO. In June 1999 the Agency emerged from the Kosovo War not only on the winning side, but also on the right side.

It became progressively more evident after 1999 that the CIA had been on the wrong side in Afghanistan. Or at least, it had failed to locate or identify a right side. The CIA's intervention in Afghanistan had dated from the Soviet intervention on Christmas Eve of 1979. Until then, the Agency's Afghan operations had been limited to targeting the Soviets for the purposing of stealing military secrets and recruiting assets. The Agency had focused so little on the Afghans themselves that it failed to predict the communist coup of 1978. Following the Soviet invasion, however, the Carter administration determined that it must deter Moscow from projecting greater power toward the Persian Gulf. Support of the *mujahedeen* could tie down Soviet troops in Afghanistan. In light of events in Iran, moreover, such assistance could deflect Muslim animosity away from Washington and toward Moscow. Carter nonetheless feared too much U.S. involvement. But following the advice of Brzezinksi, he did sign a "finding" that authorized the CIA to provide the rebels with nonlethal aid supplies and to undertake propaganda and psychological warfare projects.

The CIA's Afghan operations intensified dramatically with Reagan's election to the presidency and the arrival of William Casey to Langley. The Kremlin's naked aggression in Afghanistan and the Islamist dynamic of the Afghan resistance struck a responsive chord with Casey's militant Catholicism. "More than any other American," aptly writes Steven Coll in his authoritative study, "Casey saw the Afghan jihad not merely as statecraft, but as an important front in a worldwide struggle between communist atheism and God's community of believers." Disregarding the advice of such subordinates as the Agency's deputy director, Bobby Ray Inman, whom he considered "too timid," and manipulating the Pentagon's budget to siphon funds into the CIA's covert trove, Casey dedicated hundreds of millions of dollars to the Afghan theater. He also reached an arrangement with Saudi Arabia's royal family by which the Saudis, through their secret intelligence unit, the General Intelligence Department (GID), matched U.S. funding dollar for dollar. Casey collaborated even more closely with the Inter-Services Intelligence (ISI), the covert arm of Pakistan General Mohammed Zia-ul-Haq's military regime. The *mujahedeen* received training and ever more sophisticated and potent weaponry. Most notably, in 1986 the CIA provided the Afghans with Stinger antiaircraft missiles. Battery powered and guided by a remarkably effective yet portable heat-seeking system, the Stingers crippled the Soviet forces by downing scores of helicopters and transport aircraft. Casey's objective went beyond making the Soviets pay for invading Afghanistan. His goal for this "largest covert operation" in U.S. history was nothing less than to drive them out of the country and establish an indigenous government untainted by communism or communists.

Many factors contributed to the Soviet decision to withdraw from Afghanistan in 1988, but the CIA's role was among the leading ones. Casey, however, did not live long enough to witness what he doubtless would have regarded as his greatest success. He also did not live long enough to witness the consequences. In part because his priority had been to inflict a defeat on the Soviets, Casey had given little thought to what a Kremlin defeat would leave behind. CIA analysts were confident that without the support of Soviet troops, Afghanistan's communist regime, now headed by Mohammed Najibullah, would collapse. Other than that, they recognized that the aftermath would be highly unstable and unpredictable. The *mujahedeen* had long been divided under rival leaders, most prominently Ahmad Shah Massoud and Gulbuddin Hekmatyar, each of whom had an army loyal only to him. Pakistan supported the latter; the United States equivocated. In addition, as the Islamist resistance to Soviet rule grew in the 1980s, so did the number of Muslims from other states, fundamentalist Muslims, migrating to Afghanistan and Pakistan to join the Islamist cause. Among these was Osama bin Laden, who arrived in Afghanistan from Saudi Arabia in the mid-1980s. The CIA knew that bin Laden came from a very wealthy Saudi family, and that he had some kind of informal relationship with Saudi intelligence. It knew little else about him.

Even though the last Soviet troops evacuated Afghanistan in early 1989, Najibullah, with continued Soviet political and economic support, defied the CIA's predictions and clung to power. Nevertheless, with President George H. W. Bush fixated on the rapid deterioration of the Soviet state, the German question, and Iraqi aggression, CIA operations and interest in Afghanistan fell off significantly. The Agency unthinkingly followed the lead of Pakistan and backed Hekmatyar. Complicating matters, Bush's State Department favored Massoud, and relations with Pakistan deteriorated precipitously following the discovery of Islamabad's nuclear program. Further, by the end of the Bush presidency both the CIA and State Department had concluded that Afghanistan had become a breeding ground for potentially very dangerous Islamist jihadists. By that time as well the end had arrived for the Soviet Union, and with it the end of support for Najibullah. In February 1992 Massoud's forces took Kabul and placed Najibullah under house arrest.

In an effort to avoid civil war among the *mujahedeen*, Burhanuddin Rabbani became president of a coalition government. This compromise satisfied neither Massoud nor Hekmatyar, and within two years came the civil war.

Within those same two years, moreover, Pakistan threw its support to a united group of Islamist students, or *Taliban*, from the Pashtun region that traversed the border between Pakistan and Afghanistan. Although they had spent most of their lives studying at madrassas, the Taliban rapidly proved their military mettle and gathered a popular following. While Massoud and Hekmatyar fought each other, in 1996 the Taliban captured the vital city of Kandahar and then steamrolled into Kabul. They hung Najibullah, deposed Rabbani, and established their own fundamentalist government headed by Mullah Muhammad Omar.

A NEW THREAT—ISLAMIC TERRORISM

President Clinton had followed Bush's passive, watch-and-see posture toward Afghanistan. Foreign policy was not near the top of his agenda when he took office, and what policies he pursued in Central Asia concentrated on those republics that emerged from the former Soviet Union. Further, since the 1980s, when terrorism increasingly made headlines with reports of the bombing of the Marine barracks in Beirut (1983), the hijacking of the *Achille Lauro* in Italy (1985), the attack on a West Berlin discotheque (1986), and the explosion of Pan Am Flight 103 over Lockerbie, Scotland (1988), Washington debated whether terrorism was a law enforcement or national security problem. The antiterrorist policies that Clinton developed, moreover, with impetus provided by the bombings of New York's World Trade Center in 1993 and the Murrah Federal Building in Oklahoma City in 1995, concentrated primarily on domestic terrorism.

In 1986 CIA officials had established a Counterterrorist Center within the Directorate of Operations, but Clinton, whose relationship with DCI James Woolsey was distant at best, entrusted primary responsibility for counterterrorism to the FBI. The CIA's responsibility was getting rid of Saddam Hussein in Iraq. In fact, so focused was the agency on Iraq that al Qaeda's role in the 1993 attack on U.S. military forces in Mogadishu, Somalia, escaped its notice. As the Taliban marched toward Kabul, however, the CIA's priorities began to shift, and its subordinate position to the FBI began to reverse. Clinton replaced Woolsey with John Deutch in the aftermath of the Aldrich Ames scandal. Deutch, a professor of chemistry and provost at the Massachusetts Institute of Technology who had served in Clinton's Pentagon, was no fan of covert operations. But he was a great advocate of using the most advanced technologies to collect intelligence, and he had the respect of the president. Deutch pulled the CIA out of Clinton's doghouse even as the president's relationship with FBI director Louis Freeh grew frosty. By then international terrorism, especially that associated with Islamic fundamentalism, emerged as a grave security concern. In June 1995, Clinton signed Presidential Directive-39, "U.S. Policy on Counterterrorism." Highlighting the danger of terrorists acquiring weapons of mass destruction (WMD), it instructed the CIA to undertake "an aggressive program of foreign intelligence collection, analysis, counterintelligence, and covert action." Concurrently, though, Deutch's well-intentioned directive prohibiting the Agency's recruitment of personnel with records of criminal behavior or human rights abuses devastated the ranks of the CIA's indigenous counterterrorist assets. A year later nineteen U.S. servicemen died when terrorists bombed U.S. military barracks at Khobar Towers in Saudi Arabia.

Deutch never warmed to his job at the CIA. At the end of Clinton's first term he returned to MIT. Clinton first nominated National Security Advisor Anthony Lake as his successor, but Lake withdrew his name from consideration when Senate Republicans pilloried his record on both foreign policy and political fund-raising. Clinton then turned to George Tenet. In contrast to Deutch, Tenet was an ardent booster of the CIA, a skilled bureaucrat, and a political centrist without party ties. Prior to becoming the agency's deputy director under Deutch, Tenet had served on the staffs of the Senate Select Committee on Intelligence and the National Security Council. Expert at working the corridors of Congress as well as the machinery of the White House, Tenet recognized that for purposes of both safeguarding American security and restoring the CIA's reputation, budget, and élan, the agency had to reorient its emphases. Building on Presidential Directive-39, he immediately positioned the CIA as the linchpin of a much more aggressive and concerted effort to confront terrorism, the proliferation of WMD, and other unconventional threats to U.S. security far removed from dynamics associated with the Cold War. Tenet managed the CIA, he defended it, and he advocated for it.

Within a short time the CIA's morale improved and funding increased. Tenet placed particular emphasis on boosting recruitment of agents and rebuilding the DO's clandestine service. His success in combating the spread of terrorism and WMD, however, was not commensurate. By 1998 Osama bin Laden and his network of terrorists had replaced Saddam Hussein as America's number one enemy. Early that year the CIA formulated an elaborate scheme to kidnap bin Laden from Tarnak Farms, his Afghan compound in Kandahar, and bring him to the United States. Tenet decided that this plan was too risky, however, and called it off. But the hunt for bin Laden continued. To coordinate with Tenet and the CIA, Clinton appointed Richard Clarke as the White House counterterrorism "czar" and assigned him a seat at the Cabinet table. On August 7, nevertheless, terrorists bombed the U.S. East African embassies in Nairobi, Kenya, and in Dar es Salaam, Tanzania. Tenet quickly identified Osama bin Laden as the mastermind. For the CIA, bin Laden's profile as a terrorist rose along with its concern over the Taliban turning Afghanistan into terrorism's homeland (by providing bin Laden sanctuary). In hope of a quick fix Clinton ordered a missile strike on Zawhar Kili in Eastern Afghanistan, where the CIA thought bin Laden was attending a meeting. He was not. CIA officials were further concerned over public accusations, popularized in the film *Wag the Dog*, that Clinton had authorized the strike to divert attention from the Monica Lewinsky scandal, that politics might constrain its options and operations.

The administration's counterterrorism efforts intensified during Clinton's final years in office. To enhance coordination with Clarke in the White House and more effectively hunt down bin Laden, in 1999 Tenet appointed J. Cofer Black to head up the CIA's Counterterrorist Center. Black had been following bin Laden's trail since serving as the CIA station chief in Khartoum, Sudan, in 1993, and had kept close tabs on the progress of the "bin Laden station" (known as the Alec Station), the special unit led by Michael F. Scheuer that the CIA (to which FBI personnel contributed) established in 1996 exclusively to track the wealthy Saudi. Clinton, moreover, signed a Memorandum of Notification (MON) authorizing the use of lethal force if necessary, but bin Laden continued to elude capture. CIA operatives were also unable to make any progress penetrating al Qaeda. Neither the Counterterrorist Center nor the bin Laden station "acquired intelligence from anyone that could be acted upon."

Along with other CIA officials, Black viewed the Taliban as no less dangerous than bin Laden and al Qaeda. Pursuing both targets placed terrific stresses on the CIA's resources, and the military, mindful of the failed mission to rescue the Iran hostages during the Carter administration, resisted committing its Special Forces. Furthermore, not only had the CIA's partnership with Pakistan's ISI ruptured years earlier, but Pakistan continued to support the Taliban as an ally in its conflict with India over Kashmir and as a prophylactic to its own Pashtun population. Some CIA officials opposed assisting Massoud and other rebel forces associated with the Northern Alliance fighting the Taliban for fear of a "blowback effect" (detrimental unintended consequences) paralleling its initial assistance to the mujahedeen, yet Tenet and Black carried the day. The Agency's counterterrorist operations aggressively expanded in the last months of the Clinton administration, but to little avail. On October 12, 2000, terrorists blew up the U.S.S. *Cole*, docked in the harbor of Aden, Yemen. Seventeen Americans died. The CIA eventually determined that bin Laden was responsible. By then, Clinton was a lame-duck president.

President George W. Bush retained George Tenet as his CIA director. The bond established between the DCI and president was immediate and strong. Tenet was about the only Clinton legacy whom Bush retained. Advised during the campaign and transition by a band of hard-line conservatives and neoconservatives, President Bush and his team of national security managers, notably Vice President Dick Cheney, Defense Secretary Donald Rumsfeld and his Chief Deputy, Paul Wolfowitz, and National Security Advisor Condoleezza Rice, took office convinced that Clinton's foreign policies were fatally flawed. Among the most serious and deleterious of these flaws was a misplaced obsession with bin Laden, al Qaeda, and the Taliban. In their view Saddam Hussein's Iraq, owing to its present and potential capabilities, and sponsorship of other terrorists' capabilities, represented a far more severe threat than did the "little terrorist in Afghanistan." The new administration intended defense against nuclear missiles, not terrorism, to be the cornerstone of its national security strategy. On September 11, 2001, Rice was scheduled to give a major speech justifying that priority.

THE SEPTEMBER 11, 2001, TERRORIST ATTACK

She never gave it. Throughout the initial eight months of the George W. Bush presidency, DCI Tenet had sought to impress on the national security "principals" that al Qaeda was the gravest contemporary threat confronting the United States and the non-Muslim world. Indeed, Tenet counseled that al Qaeda was plotting an attack that would kill many Americans. Having declared in 1998 that the U.S. intelligence community was "at war" against terrorism, Tenet began to brief administration officials on the severity of al Qaeda's threat during the transition. He briefed Bush personally about bin Laden some forty times, even as the CIA instructed its overseas station chiefs to warn their host governments that al Qaeda planned "High Profile Attacks."

Tenet did not meet with the president during August 2001, when Bush was vacationing at his ranch in Crawford, Texas. One of his subordinates, however, delivered to the president the President's Daily Brief (PDB) for August 6, 2001. Entitled "Bin Laden Determined to Strike in U.S.," the PDB stipulated that al Qaeda's leader "has wanted to conduct terrorist attacks in the U.S." since 1997, that he planned his operations years in advance, that sleeper cells of al Qaeda members residing in America provided support for them, and that uncorroborated sources claimed that these plans included hijacking U.S. aircraft. Apparently administration officials considered this PDB no different from others they had previously received. Tenet, moreover, did not update an NIE produced in 1995 on the threat of a foreign terrorist attack on the United States to incorporate the intelligence analyses that emphasized the growing menace of bin Laden and al Qaeda. National Security Advisor Rice first convened a meeting of the principals on September 4 to discuss a strategy paper drafted in June explicitly designed to combat terrorism. The next week she completed the text of her speech on missile defense.

Shortly before 9:00 A.M. Eastern Time on September 11, 2001, a hijacked airliner slammed into the north tower of the World Trade Center. Before the morning was over, a second airliner struck the other Twin Tower, a third crashed into the Pentagon, and a fourth, probably on route to the Capitol Building in Washington, D.C., was brought down in rural Pennsylvania by courageous passengers on board. Claiming almost as many victims (2,973 deaths) as the Japanese attack on Pearl Harbor that was the catalyst for the establishment of the CIA, the 9/11 disaster became an equally transformative event for the Agency, for the intelligence community, and for the influence of intelligence on America's society and culture as well as its national security.

Even as the CIA identified al Qaeda as responsible for the calamity, it conceded the obvious—its effort to monitor bin Laden and his network had not detected preparations for the attack. Nevertheless, with notable exceptions, particularly the ranking Republican on the Senate Select Committee on Intelligence, Richard Shelby, Americans muted their criticism of the catastrophic intelligence failure. Within a month, moreover, Congress had appropriated supplementary funds for the CIA, and its operatives had reentered Afghanistan. Indeed, the military operation to overthrow the Taliban government, Operation ENDURING FREEDOM, was the plan of the CIA, not the Pentagon. Preceding and then to an unprecedented extent collaborating closely with Special Operations Forces from the U.S. and British militaries, the Agency's paramilitary operatives (the Northern Afghanistan Liaison Team, code-named Jawbreaker) quickly reestablished contacts with the Northern Alliance's anti-Taliban warlords, providing them with intelligence, money, and supplies. They coordinated with other operatives previously stationed in Uzbekistan to direct Predator drones (unmanned aircraft) on surveillance missions over Afghanistan. Once the United States launched Operation ENDURING FREEDOM on October 7, CIA agents in the field (ultimately about 110 in total), although unable to capture and/or kill bin Laden or Mullah Mohammad Omar, provided vital real-time, "actionable" intelligence, identifying and then helping to guide American bombs to designated targets, and interrogating prisoners. By November 25 the allied Taliban and al Qaeda forces had lost the battles for Mazar-e-Sharif and Kabul in the north and with CIA assistance were being pummeled in the Tora Bora cave complex near Afghanistan's eastern border.

THE SECOND IRAQ WAR

In early December the Taliban's southern stronghold of Kandahar fell and its leader, Mullah Omar, fled into hiding. Major combat operations ended in March 2002 following Operation ANACONDA's defeat of the remnants of al Qaeda and the Taliban. By then, bin Laden, Mullah Omar, and other survivors had escaped, probably over the border to Pakistan. The Bush administration had by then redirected its proclaimed War on Terrorism to target Saddam Hussein's regime in Iraq. Having presumed, without reliable intelligence from the CIA or any other agency, that Saddam Hussein had assisted bin Laden in executing the 9/11 attacks, the Bush administration began to develop war plans against Iraq in early November 2002.

Former DCI James Woolsey was a leading champion of the theory that tied Saddam Hussein to bin Laden, a view shared by Secretary of Defense Rumsfeld. But the CIA's intelligence did not support it. Agency analysts did conclude that Saddam Hussein possessed WMD (chemical and biological) and sought actively to develop nuclear weapons, which the president subsequently cited to claim that Saddam was prepared to supply them to bin Laden and

71

other terrorists. This syllogism implicated the CIA in the president's subsequent public justification for a preemptive attack on Iraq. DCI Tenet played along zealously. Even if Tenet initially did not share the view that Iraq was in league with al Qaeda, he did not challenge the assessment of Bush, Cheney, Rumsfeld, Wolfowitz, and Secretary of State Powell that Saddam was seeking to supplement a cache of WMD he had concealed since expelling UN inspectors in 1998 with a nuclear capability and therefore posed an imminent threat to U.S. security. The administration was committed to "regime change" in Iraq. Through its support of Saddam's opponents and conduct of covert operations, the CIA had been pursuing this objective through most of the Clinton years. The advice of Tenet's experts in the DI was that such measures were doomed to failure. The CIA had a vital role to play in overthrowing Saddam, but that role was to support a military invasion. The White House reached that same conclusion, and it counted on Tenet to bolster its position. The DCI fully appreciated that his personal relationship with President Bush and the institutional interests of the CIA required his providing the president with the service he sought.

Although the CIA expended great energy and resources in an unsuccessful effort to penetrate Iraq through U-2s, Predator drones, and other means for gathering intelligence the military needed, it expended greater energy and resources seeking to assess the danger posed by Saddam. This assessment was more important for gaining the support of allies and the American people for an attack on Iraq than it was for formulating policy. Driven by an unshakeable belief in Saddam's guilt that pervaded the top ranks of the administration, policy already was essentially set. In his January 2002 State of the Union speech, Bush cited Iraq's effort "to develop anthrax, and nerve gas, and nuclear weapons for over a decade." The challenge for the CIA and other components of the intelligence community was to confirm that this effort continued and, moreover, that Saddam Hussein had available for his use and that of al Qaeda the products of this effort: WMD.

Drawing inferences from discrepancies between information collected previously by UN inspectors and current accounts, the CIA strongly suspected that Saddam had hidden in Iraq at least a small stockpile of WMD. But with virtually no assets of its own within Iraq, and lacking a critical mass of analysts fluent in Arabic, it could not be sure. Consequently, to the frustration of key hawks like Secretary of Defense Rumsfeld and his deputy Wolfowitz, Agency officials continued to hedge. Both Wolfowitz and Rumsfeld interpreted the CIA's hedging as symptomatic of its decades-long pathology of underestimating threats. As a remedy, Wolfowitz set up a small Office of Special Plans, directed by Abram Shulsky, to produce intelligence assessments on Iraq independent of—and to many observers in competition with—those of the CIA. Rumsfeld had earlier established the even smaller Policy Counterterrorism Evaluation Center for the same purpose. He also established the position of undersecretary of defense for intelligence to accent the Pentagon's voice over national intelligence, appointing to the position Stephen Cambone, Rumsfeld's "most trusted troubleshooter" and "favored bureaucratic commando."

Finally in the fall of 2002 Tenet reluctantly agreed to produce rapidly a new NIE. The goal was to express conclusions with a minimum of equivocation. The authors, who included representatives from the U.S. intelligence agencies that comprised the NIC, completed their assignment in less than a month, on October 1. To an extent that their evidence could not justify, they indeed wrote without equivocation. Their first key judgment, pointedly entitled "Iraq's Continuing Program for Weapons of Mass Destruction," read, "We judge that Iraq has continued its weapons of mass destruction (WMD) programs in defiance of UN resolutions and restrictions. Baghdad has chemical and biological weapons as well as missiles with ranges in excess of UN restrictions; if left unchecked, it probably will have a nuclear weapon during this decade." The NIE also cited specific facts, which proved to be mere speculation or misinformation. Still, interspersed throughout the ninety-two-page document were admissions that significant gaps remained in the intelligence relied on. The authors further conceded that they had "low confidence in our ability to assess when Saddam would use WMD," had "no specific intelligence information" that Saddam Hussein had in any way contributed to al Qaeda's attack on the United States, and estimated that the Iraqi leader might provide WMD to Islamist terrorists only "if sufficiently desperate" and saw such assistance as "his last chance to exact vengeance by taking a large number of victims with him." To these qualifications the State Department's Bureau of Intelligence and Research (INR) added that it lacked evidence to make a "compelling case that Iraq is currently pursuing what INR would consider to be an integrated and comprehensive approach to acquire nuclear weapons."

Two years later the *New York Times* referred to this NIE as "one of the most flawed documents in the history of American intelligence." The CIA's internal "Tradecraft Review" completed at this same time (concurred later by the Silberman-Robb Commission) identified numerous defects in the NIE, particularly the failure of the analysts to substantiate all of their conclusions, but nonetheless described the NIE as "reasonable" in light of the information then available. The sanitized White Paper based on the NIE that the CIA issued on October 4, 2002, however, included none of the caveats and dissents, even that of the INR. The Bush administration, in its consistent pattern of transforming ambiguous evidence and contradictory interpretations into statements of certainty, did not make public these qualifications until pressured to release excerpts from the NIE in September 2003. It further distorted the threat assessment by folding biological, chemical, and nuclear weapons into the single category of "WMD."

As the administration ramped up its campaign to generate support for a military attack on Iraq, the CIA became more of an accomplice. Some agency officials reported being pressured by the administration. If "Bush wants to go to war," quotes one case officer in the DO about the instructions he received from his superior, "it's your job to give him a reason to do so." In any event, during the lead-up to the war the CIA's leadership fell in line behind the president. At a meeting in the Oval Office in December 2002 DCI Tenet expressed no concern over the quality of the intelligence collected or the reservations held by analysts within and outside the CIA and characterized the "case" for invading Iraq as a "slam dunk." Referring implicitly to the NIE in his January 2003 State of the Union speech, the president averred unequivocally that Saddam possessed chemical and biological weapons and the capability to deliver them. He also cited unidentified "intelligence sources, secret communications, and statements by people now in custody [that] reveal that Saddam Hussein aids and protects terrorists, including members of al Qaeda. Secretly, and without fingerprints, he could provide one of his hidden weapons to terrorists, or help them develop their own." The president then zeroed in on what Americans for decades identified as the most severe WMD capability: nuclear weapons. Saddam Hussein recently sought to acquire "significant quantities of uranium from Africa," Bush told the nation. He explained why: "Our intelligence sources tell us that he has attempted to purchase high-strength aluminum tubes suitable for nuclear weapons production."

CIA analysts in fact harbored serious reservations about reports that Saddam Hussein had attempted to obtain raw "yellow cake" uranium, specifically from Niger. For this reason they had advised the White House to delete the allegation when it appeared in a draft of a speech that President Bush had delivered the previous October in Cincinnati. At that time the president obliged, albeit he publicly claimed that for the purpose of reconstituting his nuclear program Saddam had held "numerous meetings" with his "nuclear mujahadeen," his "nuclear holy warriors." But the president's close advisors, notably Rumsfeld and Wolfowitz, counseled that the CIA was once again emphasizing too much the lacunae in its intelligence and refusing to draw patently obvious inferences from the available intelligence. They were supported by Vice President Cheney, who prepared the public by explaining, "Intelligence is an uncertain business, even in the best of circumstances." Reminded that the CIA had failed to estimate how close Saddam had come to developing nuclear weapons prior to the first Gulf War, Bush allowed the charge to remain in the State of the Union. With Tenet's approval, however, he cited British intelligence as his source. When it turned out that the British relied on forged documents, the administration claimed neither it nor the CIA warranted blame.

Nevertheless, when on February 5, 2003, before evidence of the forgery surfaced, Secretary of State Colin Powell indicted Iraq for possessing WMD in a major address to the United Nations' Security Council, he omitted any reference to the yellow cake uranium. His department's INR had always held the report to be "highly dubious." In fact, virtually alone among all the U.S. intelligence agencies, the INR doubted that Saddam intended to reconstitute his nuclear program. Powell nonetheless did claim that the aluminum tube purchases were intended for use in hidden Iraqi uranium centrifuges. The press later disclosed that a junior CIA analyst assigned to WINPAC (Weapons Intelligence, Nonproliferation and Arms Control) had virtually by himself advanced that theory, and almost a year before it had been discredited by nuclear experts, particularly those in the Energy Department. Powell still relied on the CIA's allegation about the aluminum tubes to indict Saddam before the United Nations. Unlike the president, he acknowledged unspecified sources who considered conventional rocket launchers the tubes' likely destination. But he quickly added that all experts agreed that they "can" be used for nuclear centrifuges, and then explained, as an "old army trooper," why logically that could only be their purpose.

Powell's speech to a rapt audience in the UN Security Council more systematically than Bush's State of the Union address drew on the available intelligence to close the administration's case against Saddam Hussein. With Tenet seated at his shoulder, the secretary of state expressed his confidence in information acquired through intercepted telephone conversations and satellite photos of weapons and weapons sites. Gratefully acknowledging "people who have risked their lives to let the world know what Saddam Hussein is really up to," he pronounced that "every statement I make today is backed up by sources, solid sources." Highlighting these sources with unprecedented frequency, Powell charged Saddam Hussein with taking extraordinary measures to conceal his possession of a range of banned weapons and continuing efforts to develop others. One illustration, which he labeled as one "of the most worrisome things that emerges from the thick intelligence file," received exceptionally widespread attention because it was so "dramatic." Citing four different sources, including a defector "currently hiding in another country with the certain knowledge that Saddam Hussein will kill him if he finds him," Powell indicted Iraq for maintaining mobile production facilities capable of producing "a quantity of biological poison equal to the entire amount that Iraq claimed to have produced in the years prior to the Gulf War." Playing tape recordings and displaying graphs and imagery, the secretary of state was explicit and his case seemingly conclusive. At one time he projected a diagram of the facilities mounted on both a truck and a railroad car, and stipulated that Iraq had at least seven of these mobile "factories," some with multiple trucks.

Because the intelligence that Powell interspersed throughout his powerful address seemed so robust, his allegations were invulnerable to criticism. Not even the international inspectors who opposed Washington's rush to judgment, especially Hans Blix, chief of the UN Monitoring, Verification and Inspection Commission (UNMOVIC), and the director of the International Atomic Energy Agency (IAEA), Dr. Mohamed El Baradei, could rebut Powell's evidence. The U.S. press expressed virtually no reservations. Bolstered by both national and international belief in the credibility of both the intelligence and Powell, on March 19, 2003, the United States launched

Operation IRAQI FREEDOM, a preemptive attack on Iraq. Although the CIA's role in the military operations was relatively minor, it was crucial to the timing and nature of the war's origins. For the agency had provided Bush with the intelligence that Saddam Hussein and his two sons were in an underground bunker at the Dora Farms compound south of Baghdad that evening. Following a lengthy meeting with his key advisers, President Bush ordered U.S. missiles to obliterate the compound. It immediately became apparent that either the CIA had incorrect intelligence on the location of Saddam and his family, or had misinterpreted the word "bunker" for "compound." Saddam survived. Dozens of other air strikes, also based on CIA intelligence, were subsequently launched that targeted senior Iraq leaders. These strikes caused the deaths only of civilians.

In less than two months Baghdad fell and Saddam and his lieutenants fled into hiding. Ironically, the swiftness and what seemed the totality of the U.S. military success eventually proved to be a source of the administration's (and further, the CIA's) problems. The stockpiles of WMD, factories and laboratories that produced them, and data documenting illicit programs and activities that had eluded detection by UN inspectors but was putatively uncovered by U.S. intelligence sources were never found. In April American and Kurdish troops did locate two trailers near Mosul, Iraq. By May 28 the CIA had in cooperation with the Defense Intelligence Agency made public a White Paper describing the trailers as "the strongest evidence to date that Iraq was hiding a biological warfare program." Referring to the "striking similarities" between the trailers and the diagrams Powell had projected during his speech to the UN, the White Paper asserted that "BW [biological warfare] agent production is the only consistent, logical purpose for these vehicles." The CIA was "confident that this trailer is a mobile BW production plant because of the source's description, equipment, and design."

Its confidence was misplaced. Led by the State Department's INR, within days of the White Paper's posting on the CIA's web site, America's own intelligence analysts disputed the assertion that the trailers were in fact mobile biological warfare producers. The configuration was incongruous for this purpose, and the trailers were devoid of any biological agents. More likely they were used to manufacture hydrogen for weather balloons, to produce rocket fuel, or to refuel extant Iraqi missiles. President Bush began to backtrack. He first claimed publicly that even if the trailers were not used to produce WMD, their discovery demonstrated that Saddam Hussein was *capable* of producing WMD. Further weakening the president's authority was the failure to locate evidence of any nuclear program, all but confirming the contention of UN officials that the sanctions imposed after 1991 had been remarkably successful.

The administration's credibility, and that of the CIA and the entire U.S. intelligence community, became increasingly suspect, compounded further by the growing frequency and intensity of indigenous attacks on American troops in now-occupied Iraq. Along with other members of the NIC, the CIA had in

January 2003, two months prior to IRAQI FREEDOM, contributed to a report, "Principal Challenges in Post-Saddam Iraq," that predicted a U.S. invasion would generate violent factions within Iraq. This report, however, had less stature than an NIE, and it was not disclosed to the public until September 2004. Further, the warning about a potential insurgency was buried in the last paragraph of a thirty-eight-page document. In contrast, some CIA officials repeatedly expressed optimistic predictions that initially the Iraqis would greet U.S. troops warmly as liberators; not until July 2004 did the NIC prepare another NIE that pessimistically forecast scenarios ranging from instability to civil war. For the growing legion of CIA critics, the mounting toll of casualties spawned by post-invasion Iraq's spiral of violence not only brought to mind Vietnam, but also the Bay of Pigs.

With his presidency under fire, in mid-June 2003 President Bush appointed David Kay, who had led three arms inspections for the UN in the 1990s and had repeatedly expressed his conviction that Saddam Hussein was guilty as America had charged, as a special advisor to DCI Tenet. Kay would lead a team of experts, the Iraq Survey Group, that Bush predicted would discover the WMD that had been cited as justification for IRAQI FREEDOM. Six months later Kay rendered his judgment. In January 2004 he announced that his investigation led to the inescapable conclusion that long before the U.S. invaded Iraq Saddam Hussein "got rid" of his unconventional weapons: chemical, biological, and nuclear. The CIA had relied on both out-of-date and unreliable intelligence. Kay opined that the mistakes were honest. Over the next half-year he became less forgiving: "Iraq was an overwhelming systemic failure of the Central Intelligence Agency," he said. Kay's conclusions were subsequently reaffirmed by the Silberman-Robb Commission and the Senate Select Committee on Intelligence.

The reputation of the CIA concurrently came under attack for other reasons. It was tarred with the DIA's feather when that agency's Ana B. Montes was arrested for spying for Cuba. Shortly thereafter, Los Angeles businesswoman Katrina Leung, whose current handler for the FBI, James J. Smith, had won the CIA's National Intelligence Medal of Achievement in 2000, was arrested for funneling classified information to the People's Republic of China. But Tenet and the CIA received the most severe criticism from individuals and institutions who doubted Kay's initial judgment that its mistakes were honest—doubts reinforced by revelations that the agency seemed to have downplayed credible evidence that North Korea had come closer to developing a nuclear capability than had Iraq, and had done so with the assistance of Pakistan. These juxtapositions suggested to critics that Tenet especially had allowed the administration to politicize the intelligence process by "cooking the books" for the purpose of justifying regime change in Iraq. The appointment of Iyad Allawi as Iraq's first post-Saddam prime minister added more fuel to critics' fire. Allawi had been a favorite of the CIA since his founding of the Iraqi National Congress in 1991.

Lending credence to these suppositions was the controversy that erupted over the president's "16 word" reference in his 2003 State of the Union to Saddam Hussein's effort to purchase uranium from Niger. In commentary published in the *New York Times* on July 6, 2003, former ambassador Joseph Wilson recounted how after a CIA-mandated investigative trip to Niger he had reported to the administration that intelligence concerning the alleged attempted purchase was based on forged documents. Consequently, Wilson wrote in the *Times*, in light of the president's State of the Union address and decision to invade Iraq, "I have little choice but to conclude that some of the intelligence related to Iraq's nuclear weapons program was twisted to exaggerate the Iraqi threat." Within a week DCI Tenet issued a statement explaining that the CIA had mistakenly cleared the inclusion of the reference to uranium in the speech; he, not President Bush, was responsible for the gaffe. Three days later, however, syndicated columnist Robert Novak publicly disclosed that he had learned from two Bush administration officials that Wilson's wife, Valerie Plame, was a CIA operative who specialized in WMD and that she had arranged his trip to Niger. The public disclosure of the name of a CIA officer under cover, because it violated the Intelligence Identities Protection Act of 1982, led to a criminal investigation to identify the Bush administration officials who had leaked Plame's name to Novak, providing additional support for Wilson's conclusion that the administration—and Tenet—were vigorously seeking to avert critical scrutiny of the purported evidence. The ensuing criminal investigation, led by U.S. Attorney Patrick Fitzgerald, resulted in a five-count indictment of I. Lewis Libby, Jr., on October 28, 2005, for perjury, false statements, and obstruction of justice.

Against this background, in June 2003 the Senate Select Committee on Intelligence began to investigate, according to its vice chairman, John D. Rockefeller IV, "the accuracy of our pre-war intelligence and the use of that intelligence by the Executive—specifically, a reference in the President's State of the Union message that has now been acknowledged to be erroneous." A year later it issued its report—a devastating critique of the CIA. Covering more than 400 pages, the report rendered 117 different judgments that, in sum, pronounced virtually every product to which the CIA contributed—the October NIE, the speeches by President Bush, Secretary of State Powell, and others, additional assessments and analyses—fatally and unconscionably flawed. In part the committee attributed the problems to the CIA's sources, especially its lack of HUMINT. But in larger part the fault lay with the CIA's performance—what it did with the intelligence it did have. In the unanimous, bipartisan opinion of the Senate Select Committee, not only had CIA analysts insufficiently distinguished between credible intelligence and conjecture, not only had they repeatedly used unsubstantiated judgments as the foundation on which to layer additional unsubstantiated conclusions which none of the analysts dared to challenge (manifesting "groupthink"), not only had they ignored contradictory evidence, but they also withheld discordant or even disconfirming intelligence from other analysts and policymakers.

The inclusion in the State of the Union address of the possible sale of Niger yellow cake uranium to Iraq was assessed by the committee as one of the CIA's less egregious offenses. Far more serious transgressions included the Agency's withholding testimony from the families of Iraqi scientists about the cessation of Saddam's programs to produce WMD during the years following the withdrawal of the UN inspectors; the summary dismissal, without any evidentiary basis, of the judgment of both UN experts and American experts that certain aluminum tubes discovered in Iraq were used for conventional rockets permitted by the UN Security Council and not, as CIA analysts claimed, to be used as centrifuges to enrich the uranium essential for nuclear weapons; reliance on multiple occasions on a single source for information, one defector code-named CURVEBALL, despite having received explicit warnings, particularly from the DIA, about the source's reliability. Ironically, the leader of the exile organization the Iraqi National Congress, Ahmad Chalabi, had introduced CURVEBALL to the CIA, and the CIA had spearheaded the opposition in Washington to the Pentagon's advocacy of Chalabi to head the post-Saddam Iraqi government. CURVEBALL received so much attention from the committee because he was a primary source for Secretary of State Powell's claim during his UN address that Saddam Hussein was using trailers as mobile WMD factories.

Entitling its editorial about the Senate Report "The Intelligence Mess," the staff of the *Washington Post* described the performance of the CIA in evaluating Iraq's WMD capabilities as "shockingly incompetent." Not long thereafter Charles Duelfer, David Kay's successor as head of the Iraq Survey Group, provided more substance for the *Post*'s description. Dated September 30, 2004, the more than 900-page *Comprehensive Report of the Special Advisor to the DCI on Iraq's WMD* concluded that Saddam Hussein had not made any attempt to restart his nuclear program after its destruction in 1991, and that the last Iraqi factory that produced illicit weapons had been shut down in 1996. With regard to Iraq's WMD, Duefel told a Senate panel, "We were almost all wrong."

REORGANIZING THE INTELLIGENCE COMMUNITY

The Senate Report explicitly pointed its finger at the CIA and the intelligence community, not President George W. Bush and the policymaking community. Further, the chief culprit—the fall guy—was DCI George Tenet. On cue, Tenet resigned a month before the report's official release to the public. The crescendo of doubt and suspicion lent weight to more far-reaching questions about the CIA. Although Democratic voices were the loudest, within days after the 9/11 attack legislators from both sides of the aisle had called on President Bush to establish an independent commission to investigate the seeming failure of the U.S. intelligence community to have anticipated this terrorist attack. Then in December Senators John McCain (R-AR) and Joseph Lieberman (D-CT) officially introduced legislation to establish a bipartisan commission and provide it with subpoena power. The White House initially resisted, although the House and Senate Select Intelligence committees decided in February 2002 to launch a joint investigation. Confronted by a groundswell of support for an independent, bipartisan commission, support that received vital impetus from the families of the victims of the attack and grew in intensity as the hearings conducted by the joint inquiry of the House-Senate Intelligence committees revealed embarrassing mistakes of both the CIA and FBI, Bush relented. In November 2002 he signed legislation creating the National Commission on Terrorist Attacks upon the United States (the so-called Kean or 9/11 Commission).

The 9/11 Commission completed its organization in December 2002. Simultaneously the Joint House-Senate Inquiry issued its report. The report set the tone for what the 9/11 Commission would ultimately conclude. The Joint House-Senate committee report faulted all the components of U.S. intelligence, each of which had exacerbated its lack of resources dedicated to tracking al Qaeda and its insensitivity to the importance of the intelligence that it did gather by making little effort to coordinate with other components. The prime example of this "stovepipe problem" was the Keystone-Cops-type blunders of both the CIA and the FBI that allowed two of the hijackers, Khalid al-Mihdhar and Nawaq al-Hazmi, to enter the United States and to operate with impunity within it notwithstanding having been identified in 2000 by the CIA as al Qaeda sympathizers. The report quoted an FBI agent's testimony that had the CIA shared its intelligence on al-Mihdhar and al-Hazmi with the FBI that this could have made a "huge difference" in the uncovering the 9/11 plot in time to prevent its execution.

For some eighteen months the 9/11 Commission methodically and at times sensationally built on the Joint House-Senate Report's foundation, overcoming obstacles presented by the White House "at nearly every turn." It pried loose documents the administration sought to withhold, and it heard testimony not only from Tenet, Rumsfeld, Clarke, and others whom it could subpoena, but also from those it could not: Rice, Cheney, and Bush (the president, however, insisted that he and the vice president testify together and not under oath). It even forced an extension of its deadline. Using evidence judiciously and assessing its credibility, the commission's energetic staff produced a dozen distinct reports. Along with excerpts from the testimony of more than a dozen witnesses, it made these reports available to the public in June 2004, only weeks after Tenet's resignation and weeks before the release of the Senate Select Committee's report on pre-Iraq War intelligence. At the end of July 2004, on the eve of first the Democratic and then the Republican national conventions, the CIA suffered its most systematic, comprehensive, and scorching critique when the 9/11 Commission released its final report.

What distinguished the report was not so much its narrative of the events, or for that matter, its identification of the mistakes made by the CIA and its cognate agencies but the report's central conclusion, that while a "shock" the 9/11 attacks "should not have come as a surprise" because for months if not years the intelligence alert was "blinking red" and, paraphrasing the testimony of a CIA supervisor, that "No one looked at the big picture; no analytic work foresaw the lightning that could connect the thundercloud to the ground." The report's criticisms of the intelligence community for its lack of imagination, manifest in its failure to envision the nature of the attacks, was by then widely shared, in part because of the earlier release of the staff reports, and in part because of almost three years of extensive, and more analytical, press coverage. What readers may have anticipated the least in light of this advance publicity is that even as it chronicled the litany of CIA errors and miscalculations, the 9/11 Commission treated almost as an aside the one critical judgment that the agency got right: its finding that no evidence surfaced to support the allegation that bin Laden and Saddam Hussein developed "collaborative operational relationship" or that "Iraq cooperated with al Qaeda in developing or carrying out any attacks against the United States." As reported repeatedly by the press during the months leading up to the start of Operation IRAQI FREEDOM, the CIA had openly clashed with the White House and the Pentagon over efforts to implicate Iraq officials in 9/11.

The lack of evidence connecting Saddam Hussein to the terrorist attack severely undercut one of the Bush administration's most salient rationales for invading Iraq. The 9/11 Commission, however, was no more willing than the Senate Select Committee to hold the administration accountable for this decision and instead reinforced the judgment that blame fell all but exclusively on the intelligence community, the CIA above all. The shortcomings of the CIA manifest before and after 9/11, the report read, confirmed criticism expressed throughout the 1990s that with the end of the Cold War the agency was plagued by a "dispersal of effort on too many priorities," a "declining attention to the craft of strategic analysis," and "security rules that prevented adequate sharing of information." In terms of covert action and paramilitary operations, moreover, the capacity of the CIA was "not large." Hence although "no agency had more responsibility—or did more—to attack al Qaeda, working day and night, than the CIA," its capability, in the words of one officer, was limited to "holding the ring until the cavalry gets here." For this reason the most distinctive feature of this report was its proposal that the CIA and the entire U.S. intelligence community undergo fundamental reform, by far the most extensive since the Agency's creation in 1947.

The publication of the 9/11 Commission's conclusions and recommendations represents a watershed in the CIA's history. Having overcome intense opposition when established in the crucible of the Cold War, and having evolved over the next half-century to iconic stature, the agency's influence on policy, prominence within the constellation of agencies comprising the intelligence community, and hold on the popular imagination is bound to diminish. Indeed, one of the commission's chief proposals for remedying the "stovepipe problem" was to unify the agencies responsible for strategic intelligence and operational planning through the creation of a National Counterterrorism Center headquartered in the Executive Office of the President. This center would institutionalize the sharing of intelligence information, but at the expense of the CIA. More dramatically, the commission proposed the establishment of a Director of National Intelligence (DNI) also within the Executive Office of the President. The DNI would oversee all fifteen components of the intelligence community and command the entire intelligence budget, replacing the DCI as the president's principal advisor on intelligence. The DCI's priorities, the report continued, must be to improve the agency's intelligence-gathering and analytic capabilities, including placing more emphasis on HUMINT and language proficiency in Arabic, Persian, Pashto, Urdu, and other critical languages, and rebuilding a capacity for undertaking covert operations. The commission further recommended that the authority for these operations should be ceded to the Pentagon—a recommendation subsequently rejected by President Bush. In addition, the 9/11 Commission recommended significantly strengthening congressional oversight, either by establishing a joint committee or dedicated committees in each house that would exercise control over both appropriations and authorization for all intelligence matters.

Challenging a myriad of institutional interests, the commission's recommendations immediately attracted heated controversy. They were far-reaching, in some cases radical. But they were not original. Proposals to strengthen congressional oversight of the CIA had been advanced periodically since the 1950s; they gained impetus and some success following the Church Committee hearings and the Iran-Contra scandal. Once again Congress did not endorse this proposed change. The development of the military's Special Operations Forces can be traced to the CIA's fiasco at the Bay of Pigs. And President Carter's instrument for securing the Iran hostages was Delta Force, not the CIA. Congress, moreover, had created a Special Operations Command in 1987, while wresting control of paramilitary and covert operations had been at the top of Rumsfeld's agenda from the time of his appointment as secretary of defense in 2001.

In this same vein, recognizing that the stovepipe problem impaired the intelligence community's capability to thwart the 9/11 attacks, a joint CIA-FBI "Terrorist Threat Integration Center" began to operate at Langley in early 2003. By this time restrictions on recruiting spies had already been eased for the purpose of enhancing HUMINT. DCI Tenet's goal following 9/11 was to increase the size of the Directorate of Operations by 25 percent, and within the DO, to increase the number of U.S. spies by up to 70 percent. Moreover, months before the investigations of 9/11, numerous experts had endorsed proposals to create a national intelligence director. Indeed, in the mid-1990s former two-time national security advisor Brent Scowcroft had recommended establishing this kind of "intelligence Czar," a decade before his White House-appointed "Scowcroft Commission" made the same recommendation.

More radical proposals to abolish the CIA altogether and devolve its responsibilities to new agencies, however, never gained traction. Owing to the authority and bipartisanship of the 9/11 Commission, in contrast, and given the widespread perception in and out of Washington that the U.S. intelligence system needed fixing, enactment of intelligence reform legislation was never in doubt. The sole question was how soon and how extensively such legislation would be enacted, given the diverse strategies for revising Congressional oversight advanced by leaders from each chamber of Congress and each party. Officials of the various U.S. intelligence agencies—whether from the CIA, the Department of Homeland Security, or the Pentagon—moreover, vigorously opposed establishing an DNI, with Pentagon officials claiming that such a change would gravely imperil U.S. defense capabilities by interrupting the chain of command and establishing an additional bureaucratic layer. White House support for an DNI was also lukewarm. As a result, not until December 7, 2004, did House Republicans agree to compromise legislation. The 600-page bill authorized the establishment of a National Counterterrorism Center and of an DNI. The bill, however, limited the DNI's authority over the budget, personnel, and covert operations, ensuring that whomever occupied the position would not "abrogate the statutory responsibilities" of the Defense Department. The bill passed the Senate the next day, and on December 17 President Bush signed it into law.

Although the reforms might lessen competitive analyses, they are likely to benefit U.S. intelligence capabilities and will take time to implement and to clarify the revised responsibilities and authorities of the fifteen U.S. intelligence agencies. Changes in the organization chart are not likely to resolve the fundamental problem that has plagued the CIA since its origins, a problem exacerbated but not caused by turf wars, stovepipe dynamics, budgetary capriciousness, and congressional laxity. The root of this problem stems from the CIA's position as a planet within the policymaking universe. Yet, even as the CIA's stature and status within the intelligence community declines, its analytical and covert capabilities can be improved. Its success will be dependent on who resides in the White House and his or her most trusted and influential advisors. The CIA only produces the intelligence that presidents and their subordinates consume for the purpose of reaching informed decisions about policy and strategy. The historical record provides robust evidence that they have not done very well.

The intelligence failures that occurred under President George W. Bush's watch may prove to be the most egregious of any president since the CIA's origin. His appointment of the partisan Porter Goss as DCI may well exacerbate the agency's politicization. Goss, moreover, selected for his chief aides veteran GOP Hill staffers. Within weeks of Bush's reelection, he purged the agency of many career professionals, including former Acting DCI John E. McLaughlin and a slew of top officials in the Directorate of Operations, Goss's "main target." So public became the Republican DCI's allegation that the agency was insufficiently loyal to the president that McLaughlin broke protocol and wrote an op-ed piece proclaiming "The CIA is No 'Rogue Agency.'"

Nevertheless, President George W. Bush, perhaps the most blatant in his efforts to politicize the CIA, is but the most recent in a succession of occupants of the Oval Office who accepted that intelligence that confirmed their preexisting beliefs and strategic doctrines and discarded or distorted those which were discordant with them. Under any circumstances individuals are loath to revise that in which they deeply believe. Presidents are normally elected because they hold strong beliefs, or, as politicians, because they have convinced the electorate that the beliefs they hold are sound. The surprise is not that their policies and strategies reflect these beliefs; the surprise is that they ever change them. In the rare cases when intelligence was the decisive factor, its influence demanded the kind of unambiguous and dramatic evidence that the U-2 produced when overflying Cuba in 1962. With the CIA unable to provide intelligence this unambiguous and dramatic during the period 2001–2003, Bush, Cheney, Rumsfeld, and their associates interpreted intelligence that the CIA did provide as they were predisposed to interpret it. This had been the case for all the Cold War presidents with regard to the Soviets. Their perceptions of the Soviet threat may have varied, but the intelligence they received had little effect on their perceptions. President Carter was the most dramatic exception to this norm, and he paid for publicly conceding that he changed his views.

Both the Senate Select Committee investigating the Iraq War and the 9/11 Commission followed a familiar pattern of blaming the intelligence producers for the mistakes of the intelligence consumers. This syndrome is apt to generate greater timidity within the CIA, decreasing the Agency's effectiveness. While it will never be perfect, the intelligence capacity of the CIA or a successor agency can be improved. Its direction, management, and funding can contribute to this improvement. Still, the value of the resultant intelligence for the national security will remain contingent on its use by those who make the decisions.

The Liaison Arrangements of the Central Intelligence Agency

Loch Johnson

THE ORGANIZATIONAL FRAMEWORK OF AMERICAN INTELLIGENCE

The American intelligence establishment, referred to widely in government circles as the "intelligence community," grew into a colossus during the Cold War years. Its fifteen major agencies, some 200,000 employees, vast array of collection platforms (such as surveillance satellites and unmanned aerial vehicles or UAVs), and an annual budget of approximately $40 billion make it the largest producer of information in the history of the world. The primary job of the intelligence community is to provide timely, accurate, and relevant information and insight (analysis) for decision makers, from the president and other members of the National Command Authority (which includes cabinet members and the Joint Chiefs of Staff) to members of Congress on the two intelligence oversight committees. In addition, the intelligence agencies are expected to maintain tight security over sources and methods, as well as the content of the information they gather (a duty known as counterintelligence); and the Central Intelligence Agency (CIA, known by insiders as "The Agency" or "The Company") is also expected to carry out operations designed to influence affairs in other countries through secret propaganda, political, economic, and paramilitary or warlike activities (covert action). The various programs and operations dedicated to intelligence collection and analysis, counterintelligence, and covert action are known collectively as the National Foreign Intelligence Program (NFIP). The main components of the intelligence community (something of a misnomer, given the distinctive cultures and competition for resources among this diverse collection of government agencies) are led, since passage of the Intelligence Reform and Terrorism Prevention Act in December 2004, by a Director of National Intelligence or DNI.

The National Security Council

Each of the intelligence agencies is ultimately responsible to the president, the preeminent official on the National Security Council (NSC)—the most important foreign policy and security panel in the American government, created at the same time as the CIA by the National Security Act of 1947. In addition to the president, the NSC is composed of the vice president, the secretary of state, and the secretary of defense. At the behest of the president, a national security adviser is responsible for coordinating NSC meetings and paperwork, guiding the council's staff, and assisting in the public advocacy of the administration's foreign policy objectives. The top official in the intelligence community, the DNI (as of December 2004), is a regular attender of NSC meetings, and several other officials—among them the chairman of the Joint Chiefs of Staff, the secretary of the treasury, the director of the Office of Management and Budget, the attorney general, and the director of the Federal Bureau of Investigation (FBI)—are invited from time to time, depending on the council's agenda.

The NSC has several subcommittees related to intelligence, including a Net Assessment Group for analyzing the military capabilities of foreign adversaries; a Verification Panel to monitor the allegiance of other nations to international agreements entered into by the United States; a covert action panel, which has had various names over the years (such as the 40 Committee under President Richard M. Nixon); and a Senior Interagency Group for Intelligence (SIG/I), responsible for deciding on global collection requirements and intelligence resource allocations among the fifteen secret agencies. Emanating from the NSC are National Security Council Intelligence Directives or NSCIDs (pronounced "n-skids"), which serve as the foundation for America's clandestine collection and counterintelligence operations around the world; and "presidential findings," which provide written authority for covert actions ("The president finds that this covert action is important to the national security of the United States").

The Director of National Intelligence

The crafting of operational specifics is left for the most part to the Director of National Intelligence, in coordination with the "program managers" that head up each of the intelligence agencies, such as the director of the Central Intelligence Agency (CIA) and the director of the National Security Agency (NSA). The DNI is in charge of the National Foreign Intelligence Program (NFIP), which includes the operations of the CIA—the only agency in the community that stands independent from a policy department; the eight military intelligence agencies placed within the framework of the Department of Defense; and the remaining intelligence agencies embedded in the five civilian departments of the intelligence community, including the Departments

FIGURE 2.1. The Intelligence Community (IC) 2005*

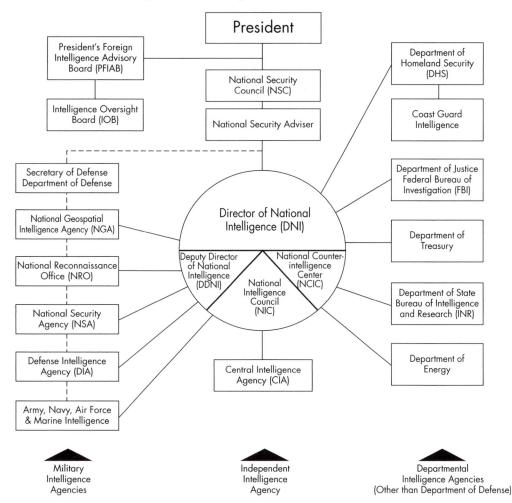

President

President's Foreign Intelligence Advisory Board (PFIAB)

Intelligence Oversight Board (IOB)

National Security Council (NSC)

National Security Adviser

Department of Homeland Security (DHS)

Coast Guard Intelligence

Secretary of Defense Department of Defense

National Geospatial Intelligence Agency (NGA)

National Reconnaissance Office (NRO)

National Security Agency (NSA)

Defense Intelligence Agency (DIA)

Army, Navy, Air Force & Marine Intelligence

Director of National Intelligence (DNI)

Deputy Director of National Intelligence (DDNI)

National Intelligence Council (NIC)

National Counterintelligence Center (NCIC)

Central Intelligence Agency (CIA)

Department of Justice Federal Bureau of Investigation (FBI)

Department of Treasury

Department of State Bureau of Intelligence and Research (INR)

Department of Energy

Military Intelligence Agencies

Independent Intelligence Agency

Departmental Intelligence Agencies (Other than Department of Defense)

*From 1947 to 2004, a Director of Central Intelligence (DCI) led the IC, rather than a DNI. The Department of Homeland Security and the Coast Guard did not become part of the IC until 2003.

of Energy, Homeland Security, Justice, State, and Treasury. These agencies carry out a number of intelligence activities or "ints," each referred to by intelligence professionals with specific acronyms. Chief among them are OSINT or open-source intelligence (information derived from the public domain, which provides the important background setting for understanding clandestinely acquired information); HUMINT or human intelligence (classic espionage); SIGINT or signals intelligence (mainly the interception of telephone and other electronic communications); IMINT or imagery intelligence (photography, as with spy cameras on reconnaissance aircraft and surveillance satellites); and MASINT or measurement and signature intelligence (the capture of energy emissions from weapons systems and industrial sites). Together, these last three technical sources of intelligence are sometimes referred to as TECHINT.

Accountability

In a democracy, executive power is held accountable by external review ("oversight") panels. With respect to intelligence, these panels include the

FIGURE 2.2. Intelligence Oversight Committees, Before and After 1976*

Oversight Committees 1947–1976	*Oversight Committees 1977–2005*
House of Representatives:	House of Representatives:
Appropriations	Appropriations
Armed Services	Armed Services
Judiciary	Judiciary
Foreign Affairs	Permanent Selection Committee on Intelligence (HPSCI)
Senate:	Senate:
Appropriations	Appropriations
Armed Services	Armed Services
Judiciary	Judiciary
Foreign Relations	Select Committee on Intelligence (SSCI)

*Excluding the many committees that claim jurisdiction over the Department of Homeland Security.

President's Foreign Intelligence Advisory Board (PFIAB), the Intelligence Oversight Board (IOB), and a new Privacy and Civil Liberties Oversight Board established as part of the Intelligence Reform and Terrorism Prevention Act of 2004. They are all under the auspices of the Executive Office of the President. The PFIAB focuses on TECHINT and questions related to the quality of intelligence coming to decision makers, while the IOB examines allegations of misconduct inside the intelligence community. The Privacy Board will examine specific charges related to questions of civil liberties. Each of the intelligence agencies also has an inspector general (IG) charged with maintaining internal accountability. The CIA's IG is an office confirmed by the Senate and its incumbent is expected to report to Congress twice a year, as well as whenever serious cases of impropriety or illegality arise within the Agency.

On Capitol Hill, the key oversight entities are the Senate Select Committee on Intelligence (SSCI) and the House Permanent Select Committee on Intelligence (HPSCI), along with the House and Senate Appropriations subcommittees on intelligence. The House and Senate Judiciary Committees have supervisory responsibilities over the Federal Bureau of Investigation (FBI), and the House and Senate Armed Services Committees handle oversight for tactical intelligence. All in all, this tangle of supervisory lines in Congress cries out for reform and consolidation.

It is sobering to note that none of these review panels succeeded in pushing the intelligence agencies toward better sharing of information prior to the terrorist attacks of 9/11.

THE ORGANIZATION OF THE CENTRAL INTELLIGENCE AGENCY

Surrounded by an electric barbwire fence and patrolled by stern-faced guards in dark blue fatigues with black pistols at their hips and German shepherds at their heels, the CIA is housed in a 219-acre leafy, campuslike compound on the west bank of the Potomac River, twelve miles from

FIGURE 2.3. CIA Domestic and Foreign Liaison

Liaison connections between the CIA and other government organizations, at home and abroad:

downtown Washington, D.C. The Agency enjoys a special stature in the intelligence community by virtue of its early establishment in 1947, predating most of the other agencies, and President Truman's emphasis that he expected the CIA to lead and coordinate the entire community.

The CIA is divided into four main components: the Office of the Director and, beneath that office, three functional directorates: the Directorate of Intelligence (DI), the Directorate of Science and Technology (DS&T), and the Directorate of Operations (DO). The Agency reportedly accounts for less than 15 percent of the total annual expenditures of the community. The military intelligence agencies consume the lion's share of the spending, especially for the costly construction, launching, and management of surveillance satellites.

Internally, whoever is the director of the CIA has often confronted considerable management challenges—especially before passage of the Intelligence Reform and Terrorism Prevention Act of 2004, when the director of the CIA was also the director of Central Intelligence (DCI) in charge of all fifteen agencies in the intelligence community. Admiral Stansfield Turner, DCI during the Carter administration, observed that running the CIA was like "operating a power plant from a control room with a wall containing many impressive levers that, on the other side of the wall, had been disconnected."

Cultures in Conflict

The Directorate of Intelligence (DI)

Part of the problem has to do with the different cultures inside the CIA. The Directorate of Intelligence, for example, is where the CIA's research work is conducted: the scrubbing, sorting, and interpretation of data—the essence of the intelligence mission. The analysts in the DI are the Agency's scholars, usually Ph.D.'s and area specialists, replete (in the stereotype) with elbow-patched tweed jackets, button-down collars, and regimental ties. However exaggerated this stereotype, it remains true that the DI is a place of study and reflection, with an academic air about it. The job of the analyst is to sift through secret information (acquired overseas by collectors in the DO), blend it with OSINT, and prepare either short, up-to-date reports on world conditions ("current intelligence") or longer in-depth "estimates" ("research intelligence"). The milieu of the analyst is the library, increasingly the virtual one inside a personal computer.

The Directorate of Operations (DO)

In contrast, the DO is field oriented. It is the largest (two-thirds of the Agency's staff) and most controversial component of the CIA, subdivided into geographic and other specialized staffs. Overseas within each country, the DO has a chief of station (COS) under diplomatic cover in the U.S. Embassy.

Supervised by the COS are American "case officers"—hired less for their postgraduate educational achievements than for their gregarious nature—who attempt to recruit indigenous spies ("agents" or "assets") to steal secrets—for cash or some other incentive—from their own country to give to the United States via the CIA. The case officer often believes that his or her on-the-ground knowledge of a country is superior to whatever the analyst may derive from library research. In an attempt to overcome this breach between the two cultures, the CIA has experimented with a "co-location" or "partnership" scheme to place analysts and case officers cheek-by-jowl in the same suite of offices, so their combined sources of knowledge can lead to valuable synergisms in the search for all-source fusion. So far the experiment has produced limited results.

Also within the DO are covert action specialists who plan and manage operations to influence—and sometimes overthrow—foreign governments. These intelligence officers, often husky males sporting blue-tinted aviation glasses and rolled shirt sleeves, relish the risks of unmarked air flights behind enemy lines and the command of speedboats in hostile waters—the James Bonds of the CIA, rather removed from the desk-bound cerebral activities of the analysts. Paramilitary officers within the DO's Covert Action Staff have earned the monikers "knuckle-draggers" and "snake eaters," evoking the image of Rambos crawling on their bellies through foreign jungles. As a DCI once observed, "The analysts are a bunch of academics, while the DO types would be entirely comfortable in the Marine Corps."

Complicating matters further, within the DO are officers in charge of counterintelligence, a painstaking search for evidence that the CIA may have been penetrated by a mole recruited by a hostile intelligence service. Like Talmudic scholars, counterintelligence specialists must pore over faded intelligence archives in search of mole tracks. Further, they probe for opportunities to recruit moles of their own overseas, since the best way of discovering what operations the enemy is running against the Untied States is to penetrate its foreign intelligence service with a spy of one's own.

The Directorate of Science and Technology (DS&T)

This directorate, the newest and smallest of the CIA's major divisions, is devoted to the application of technology to espionage—notable through spying with satellites and high-altitude airplanes. It is yet another separate world within the Agency, a lab-based support service where reside the CIA equivalent of Major Boothroyd (aka "Q") of the Bond movies. In the early days, DS&T helped the air force build airplane and satellite "spy platforms," including most famously the U-2. It also experiments with drugs and other chemicals, like the deadly poisonous pill encased in a hollow silver dollar that U-2 pilot Francis Gary Powers was supposed to swallow if his plane was shot down over the U.S.S.R. during the Cold War (but chose not to); constructs such handy objects as fake rocks and trees with hollowed-out spaces for hiding messages ("dead drops"), or listening and sensing devices (e.g., for registering the presence of radioactive materials—nuclear weapons—on passing trucks); and handles many of the Agency's computer-processing tasks. Most notoriously, the Directorate's scientists have constructed killing instruments for assassination plots, including a highly efficient poison dart gun ("non-discernible microbioinoculator"). More prosaically, they fashion tools for picking locks and disguises that rival the best produced in Hollywood.

The Difficulties of Managing the CIA

DCI Stansfield Turner described the difficulties in dealing with the CIA's disparate cultures:

> The differing outlooks give rise to a lot of pushing and pulling on what position the Agency as a whole should take on specific questions. In any other organization such disputes would be brought to the person at the top, who would have to adjudicate them. Not so at the CIA. There, the branch heads go a very long way to compromise with each other rather than let an issue reach the DCI for resolution. The last thing [the directorates] want is for the DCI to become a strong central authority. In adjudicating between them he might favor one or the other, and the others would lose some of their traditional freedom.

Turner attributes the independence of the CIA's directorates to a combination of three influences: their initial separateness at the beginning of the Agency's history; the philosophy of a need-to-know "compartmentation" of activities that, for security reasons, fractures the sharing of information along directorate (and even office) lines; and their differing responsibilities: analysis, collection, covert action, counterintelligence, and technical support.

In what manner does the CIA's professional intelligence bureaucracy want the Agency's director to perform his or her duties? In Turner's opinion, by leaving the Agency alone and concentrating on external matters: on the CIA's relationship to the White House, the Congress, the public, and foreign governments. Here is the domain of liaison, the primary focus of this chapter—at home, a blend of public relations and Washington infighting to protect Agency budgets and programs; abroad, an attempt to persuade others to help the United States acquire the information it seeks as a shield against harm to the national interest.

While no DNI and no agency director (whether of the CIA, FBI, or NSA) is going to concentrate exclusively on external relations—no matter how much this approach might appeal to the internal directorates of the individual agencies—the director nonetheless must spend considerable time and effort on trying to ensure that the CIA has strong ties with its various constituencies beyond Langley. No man is an island, noted the poet John Donne. Nor is any government agency, even the most secretive. The CIA illustrates the point. It has an extensive network of ties with other government entities within the United States, with private groups, and with foreign intelligence services. Together, these relationships comprise a liaison system, through which Agency personnel communicate and receive information from a wide range of external sources.

CIA LIAISON WITHIN THE EXECUTIVE BRANCH

The White House

The CIA, like its sister agencies, exists primarily to serve the information needs of high-level policy makers, the most important of whom is the president of the United States. Early every morning (with rare exceptions, as when the president is traveling in remote regions of the world—and often even then), the president is presented with the CIA's most exclusive intelligence report, the President's Daily Brief (PDB). Behind the preparation of this glossy four-color document is a team of researchers and information synthesizers who pull together the most significant findings available from open and clandestine sources regarding world events over the past twenty-four hours. The objective, as with all intelligence reports, is to provide the president and other top officials (some half-dozen notables in the George W. Bush administration receive the PDB) with facts and insights about global affairs to help illuminate their decision options.

As part of the PDB effort, the CIA provides a liaison briefing team on call to the DNI and the CIA director. According to a president's preferences, the DNI (and formerly the DCI) may bring along to the White House one or more PDB briefers to answer questions the president or other officials may have. Some presidents, notably both Presidents Bush, have enthusiastically requested oral briefings to flesh out the PDB; others, such as President Nixon, have been satisfied to read the written document alone. As with all good liaison relationships, the PDB liaison is a two-way street. On the one hand, the briefers offer further insight; on the other hand, the policy maker can probe for more information, perhaps charging the liaison officers to return to the CIA with the message that the president wants a follow-up analysis on subjects X, Y, or Z.

The PDB liaison team is but one of the CIA's bridges to the White House. The most important foreign policy and national security entity in the U.S. government is the NSC. Beneath the senior policy officials ("principals") on the council, the NSC boasts a staff of experts numbering more than fifty. A few are hired directly by the national security adviser, usually from academe or the nation's think tanks, but the NSC's budget is small and most of the staff are on loan ("detailed") from various agencies or services in the government. Invariably, a few are from the CIA and serve as liaisons between the NSC and the Agency—conduits of incoming intelligence expertise at the highest reaches of government, as well as channels for NSC solicitation of fresh information requests. Since the DNI (as formerly the DCI) is also a regular attender at NSC meetings, he or she plays the role, too, of a high-level liaison officer connecting the intelligence community (the producers of intelligence) to the principals on the council (important consumers of intelligence).

One of the dilemmas facing the DNI and the intelligence community will be to determine which policy officials need to know what kinds of information and when. Through liaison relationships, the intelligence director seeks to inform policy officials about dangers and opportunities facing the United States that have been uncovered by CIA assets in the field, and about new intelligence reports that have been prepared by analysts throughout the community. Often the wrong or unneeded information is gathered by the intelligence community because of inadequate liaison relationships between the consumers and producers of intelligence. One part of the government is all too often unaware of what another, related part is doing about a specific security concern, even at high echelons. For example, a recent senior NSC staffer had never met the top NIO dealing with global health issues, even though both individuals had been in their respective positions for almost a year.

The Policy Departments and Agencies

As with the NSC, so do cabinet departments and other agencies in the executive branch with foreign policy responsibilities have CIA and other intelligence liaison personnel in their buildings. There is no single way for the intelligence community to build bridges to the policy departments. Rather, top intelligence administrators (the DNI and the program managers) must regularly consult with policy makers to determine their preferences for a liaison relationship with intelligence analysts.

Some departments and agencies prefer to have analysts or oral briefers (perhaps both) directly in their building, just down the hallway from where important policy decisions are made and available for consultation at a moment's notice. This "forward observer" model of liaison has been successful in some locations. The Commerce Department, for example, has several intelligence officers on loan from the intelligence community to service top policy officials in the department. Other policy makers may prefer an early morning briefing on the way to work or the first thing at the office, or perhaps exchanges throughout the day using secure fax or e-mail facilities. Still others may want a briefing on demand or an opportunity to gather with a group of analysts from time to time. One innovative official in the George H. W. Bush administration established an ad hoc study group that became known as the "East Asian Informals"—various collectors, analysts, and policy officials discussing that region of the world.

The newest effort to develop liaison bridges between the community and a policy department arose with the creation of a Department of Homeland

Security (DHS) in 2002. This department is responsible for guarding the shores, harbors, skyways, water supply, industrial infrastructure, communications facilities, and many other aspects of American society—an overwhelming responsibility. The department's success will depend in large part on having good intelligence about threats; if information sharing is to work, strong ties must be developed between the new department and the intelligence community. Intelligence sharing has seriously faltered over the years, even between just the CIA and the FBI. For example, in the early 1960s, FBI Director J. Edgar Hoover formally severed liaison between the two agencies in a fit of pique over the Agency's criticism of the bona fides of a Soviet defector resettled by the FBI in the United States. (At a lower level, though, the liaison that had been built on personal trust between CIA and FBI officers continued unabated, despite the FBI director's intemperate decree.) So seeking extensive ties between DHS and fifteen intelligence agencies will require considerable energy and diplomacy.

The subject of international economic intelligence provides a window into a highly successful liaison relationship that arose between the White House and the intelligence community. A leading economic analysis at the CIA provides this perspective on the relationship:

> Those of us on the economic side are not in competition with the *Wall Street Journal*. We try to provide information on broad economic trends. Our consumers include, for example the National Economic Council, the U.S.T.R. [United States Trade Representative], and the Commerce Department. The NEC is a new institution [established in 1993 inside the jurisdiction of the White House, as an economic analogue to the NSC] and had to be convinced that we can be useful. The kind of support we now give is probably divided fifty-fifty between day-to-day, direct "tactical" intelligence and the longer-term finished intelligence that we have always done.

The neophyte National Economic Council soon responded to the liaison feelers put out by the CIA during the Clinton administration. As a senior Agency official told a reporter, "Just about every day, [NEC deputy director] Bo Cutter is asking the CIA for information on economic issues. The National Economic Council is treating the CIA like an extension of its own staff." While this relationship between intelligence producers and consumers in the economic domain has prospered, liaison is not always so successful.

The Intelligence Community

Several liaison organizations have been created to help the DNI overcome the imposing centrifugal forces of fragmentation in the community, as the intelligence agencies jockey for influence and funding, and (with the exception of the independent status of the CIA) had often deferred more to the cabinet secretary above them than to the titular head of the intelligence community, the DCI. There are interagency coordinating panels for each of the "ints," as well as a National Intelligence Council—a prestigious committee of senior analysts (National Intelligence Officers or NIOs) drawn from across the community. The Intelligence Reform and Terrorism Prevention Act of 2004 also established an overarching National Center for Counterterrorism and a National Nonproliferation Center.

Dikes to Contain Centrifugal Forces

The DNI also heads a community-wide management staff, established to help bring the fifteen components of the community closer together through interagency discussions of common intelligence challenges. Moreover, the DNI is chair of a new National Joint Intelligence Committee, whose members include all the program managers from the community. This committee will meet periodically to review how well the agencies are functioning and co-operating.

Recent DCIs had also experimented with interagency "fusion centers" and special task forces that concentrate on specific intelligence problems, which the new DNI will inherit. These entities consist of intelligence officers from a cross-section of the community, brought together (usually at CIA Head-quarters, in part because parking is less problematic than at some of the other agencies in the center of Washington, D.C.) to provide a sustained all-source focus on especially contentious threats facing the United States. They are meant to offer planning, research, analysis, technical support, and operations all in one place—"one-stop shoppping," officials in the centers boast. They seek to encourage the sharing of information across agencies, in contrast to the more traditional emphasis on separate agency hierarchies (the stovepipes), competition, and the hoarding of data and insights.

Among the fusion centers are the Counterterrorist Center, the Counter-intelligence Center, the National HUMINT Requirements Tasking Center, the Crime and Narcotics Center, and the Environmental Center. In addition, ad hoc task forces have been set up from time to time, usually to assist the DCI in the gathering and interpretation of information related to battlefield situations. For instance, during the wars in the Balkans in the 1990s, the DCI had highly regarded Bosnia and (later) Kosovo Task Forces—interagency in composition, like the fusion centers, but even more focused and with a shorter life span.

The DNI will also enjoy the benefits of a team of legal counselors, legis-lative liaison officers, and arms control experts. They can help to overcome the divisions throughout the community, as they promulgate on behalf of the director guidelines giving direction for all of the intelligence agencies with respect to legal questions, reporting to Congress, and the monitoring of in-ternational arms-control forums.

Gorillas in the Stovepipes

Despite the various organizational measures adopted to assist the DCI in becoming a true leader of the community and not just a figurehead, the results failed to meet President Truman's expectations of a centralized intelligence establishment. The reality is that each of the agencies remained quite distinct and separate from the others, as if they were organized into individual "stovepipes" that often defied the DCI's best efforts at coordination. Each agency had a program manager or director with significant authority over internal personnel and budgets—strong "gorillas in the stovepipes," a phrase that DCIs used in the past to lament their plight, and probably will be used by future DNIs. In a different metaphor, the community can be described as a "tribal federation" more than a cohesive team of agencies pulling together in the same harness. As one study has concluded, the community "has developed into an interlocking, overlapping maze of organizations, each with its own goals." Another observer looks upon the pre-2004 intelligence community as "a Hobbesian state of nature."

While some degree of diversity is healthy in any set of agencies, critics view the newly created Office of DNI as too weak, still lacking meaningful budget and appointment powers over each of the agencies (except the CIA)—even though the purpose of the Intelligence Reform and Terrorism Prevention Act of 2004 was to give the DNI full budget and appointment powers over the entire intelligence community. Consider the military intelligence agencies. They remain within the ambit of the secretary of defense, sometimes described as the "800-pound gorilla" in the political maneuvering that takes place in Washington. Torn between allegiance to the secretary of defense on the one hand, and the DNI on the other hand, the military agencies are usually more worried about crossing the mighty gorilla than the new and comparatively weak Office of the DNI.

The CIA resides at the center of this extensive intelligence apparatus. Its creation in 1947 was intended to pull all the parts together into a harmonious working relationship, so that the president and other top officials could receive a full picture of world events and conditions. This is known as "all-source fusion" or "jointness," in the jargon of intelligence professionals—in plain English, the sharing of information. Improved coordination of the intelligence agencies was the whole rationale behind President Truman's proposed creation of a *Central* Intelligence Agency in 1947. Prior to the attack on Pearl Harbor on December 7, 1941, the existing U.S. intelligence agencies had failed to gather together fragments of information in the different military units of the Pentagon bureaucracy about an impending attack. The available clues were never pulled together and reported to theater military commanders. With this failure in mind, along with the rising threat of global communism, President Truman was receptive after the war to proposals for major intelligence reform that would bring about better coordination of information, under the leadership of a DCI and a CIA.

As tragically demonstrated by the September 11, 2001, terrorist attacks against the United States, the end result of a fragmented intelligence community is (as with Pearl Harbor) ongoing failure to coordinate information, move it to the White House in a timely fashion, and avoid disaster. At least two of the nineteen "9/11" terrorists had been spotted in suspicious activities prior to the attack and were known to be within the United States, yet neither the CIA nor the FBI adequately shared this information with each other or with policy officials.

Liaison Challenges within the Executive Branch

The proper approach to liaison in any given case must be decided by the consumers of intelligence in the executive branch and Congress. Some consumers might decide they want no liaison with the intelligence community. "Many policymaking entities jealously guard their analytic functions," states an expert on international economic policy, "and [they] see intelligence analysis as an unwanted and not very useful intrusion into their territory." Moreover, sometimes government agencies have information that is as good as, if not better than, the intelligence community's. First-rate economists at the Departments of Treasury, Commerce, and State may know more about particular questions of international finance than any CIA analyst.

Value Added

Yet, through a liaison relationship, the intelligence community often can provide a perspective that other agencies and departments may have overlooked, especially "nuggets" of secret information derived from, say, a telephone tap or an asset deep within the trade ministry of a foreign economic rival. As a top CIA analyst has commented:

> Our strength—and our principal mission—lies in winkling out the key bits of non-public information and then blending this non-public information with, typically, a much larger volume of openly available material to build a picture of foreign government plans and intentions that is comprehensive (the phrase we often use is "all-source") and, equally important, tailored to the specific immediate needs of U.S. policymakers.

Furthermore, U.S. government departments involved in foreign affairs are understaffed (especially the Department of State) and too busy with their day-to-day duties to prepare detailed intelligence reports—or any other reports—for other policy officials. Even the basic chore of collecting open information on international events and conditions has been eroded by substantial cutbacks in State Department personnel posted in American embassies around the globe. In response to these staff cuts, officials have relied increasingly on their liaison with the intelligence community to take up the slack of a wide range of foreign policy issues. According to an experienced government official, "Intelligence analysts—essentially DI analysts—do 90 percent of the analysis of the USG [U.S. government] on foreign affairs."

George Tenet, DCI under Presidents Bill Clinton and George W. Bush, maintained as well that the policy departments already have a heavy load without taking on the added task of gathering and disseminating information. "If the CIA did not pull [information] together, sort it out, and present it [through its network of liaisons], who would?" he asks. "Some argue that individual agencies, such as State and Defense, should do it; but, in my view, this would place an unfair burden on them. Our democratic system obliges these agencies to formulate policies on behalf of the president and to defend them in public and before the Congress. That is a heavy responsibility."

Such obstacles notwithstanding, the CIA has historically taken a leadership role in government liaison within the national security establishment. The Agency has been able to take on this role because it has the staff and facilities to carry out the necessary liaison tasks, and a worldwide espionage network to add often valuable insights to more readily available information. The CIA enjoys an elaborate around-the-clock publishing capability, allowing its analysts to prepare eye-catching, four-color reports on glossy paper, all attractively bound. Over the years the CIA has become skillful, too, at writing reports that can be easily absorbed by busy and distracted policy officials, with an emphasis on plain English and minimal jargon.

In addition, the Agency has developed a quick distribution system for passing its reports through the hands of intelligence liaison officers and into the in-boxes of the government's highest echelons. Even though the intelligence agencies are not necessarily smarter about international developments than the rest of the national security establishment, they have an edge in the processing and dissemination of information. "The capacity to handle both open and clandestine sources of information for now remains uniquely within the intelligence community," notes an expert, "rendering it the sole choice for all-source intelligence." For the most part, the policy departments wisely understand another advantage of letting the CIA and its sister agencies fill their information gaps: liaison support from the intelligence community is available to them at zero marginal cost.

The Importance of Marketing

In some instances, policy officials may simply fail to realize that intelligence liaison can deliver to them valuable information. Interviews with staff personnel at the Environmental Protection Agency (EPA) and the NSC reveal, for example, that decision makers can be quite unaware of global environmental research findings generated by the intelligence agencies. A senior EPA official was pleased to receive high quality intelligence reports from the community on the suspected Russian dumping of radioactive materials into the Arctic; of industrial plants illegally producing chlorofluorocarbons (CFCs) in different parts of the world; and of evidence of pollution in sundry global watersheds. Yet he was surprised to learn that the intelligence agencies also give policy officials (on request) daily liaison briefings regarding whatever international topics interest them, including information on fast-breaking environmental developments around the world. This official did not know that some policy makers have intelligence "forward observers" in their own buildings, that is, liaison officials from the intelligence community who convey classified information and requests for further analysis back and forth between the policy officials and the intelligence analysts.

Moreover, the EPA official was surprised to learn that policy officials may regularly request from the intelligence community written materials on specific topics of concern to them—so-called niche intelligence. He expressed an interest in having all these services support his global environmental responsibilities at EPA. Similarly, a senior NSC staffer in charge of environmental affairs had little contact with either the National Intelligence Officer for global environmental issues on the National Intelligence Council or any of the individual intelligence agencies. She was unaware of the environmental reports available form the intelligence community.

Blame for this failure of liaison between the producers and the consumers of intelligence lies on both sides. Policy officials could be more assertive in seeking assistance from the intelligence community; but, clearly, the intelligence agencies could advertise their products better. As one high-level official complained, "The intelligence community must become more user friendly."

Intelligence managers and analysts are aware of the need to improve liaison relationships throughout the government. "We used to throw things over the transom," remembers a senior analyst. "Now we market." One CIA technique is to have liaison officers present policy officials with a brief typescript memorandum on a subject, as a door opener. "The more provocative we are," notes former DCI Robert M. Gates, "the more likely we are to be read." The policy official may then want access to longer, more formal documents, yielding a growing liaison relationship between the producer and the consumer of intelligence. A leading manager of intelligence in the CIA, Douglas MacEachin, Jr., has emphasized the importance in liaison efforts of packaging, timing, and the building of rapport. "Good packaging is vital," he observes. "You must focus the policymaker's attention. They are busy. They like pictures and graphs." Intelligence videotapes were popular with the Reagan White House, especially in portraying international personalities such as [Soviet Premier] Brezhnev or the Libyan leader Col. Muammar Qaddafi.

Liaison timing is crucial. "You have to get [your data and analysis] in early," MacEachin further notes. "This is risky, because you can be wrong, especially on current intelligence—just as the best golden-glove shortstop is going to make more errors than the right fielder. But if you don't get in early, the *Washington Post* or the wire services will scoop you. This means hitting the consumer [in other words, contacting him or her through an intelligence liaison officer] before his second cup of coffee, prior to the 8:15 staff meeting." Nor is it simply a matter of being there first in the morning; the analyst also has to hit the right day. "You have to be there when the options are being formed," MacEachin stresses.

Intelligence agency officials have learned that many policy officials will not seek out a liaison relationship of their own accord. Typically, an intelligence liaison officer will manage to place a report into the hands of a junior aide. If the "executive summary" on the cover of the report grabs the aide's attention, he or she will read the underlying document, highlighting key points. The principal will then look at the highlights and, if interested, perhaps request an oral briefing from the liaison officer or directly with the senior analyst who wrote the report (a meeting arranged by the liaison officer). Once in the policy maker's office, the skillful liaison officer and analyst will then use the opportunity to draw attention toward other pages in the report, along with a new graph or two.

Rapport, Yes—Politicization, No

To improve the chances of gaining access to the principal in the first place, CIA officials encourage the growth of closer personal ties between liaison officers and analysts, on the one hand, and policy officials, on the other hand. This is easier said than done, given the harried existence of those in high office. Personal chemistry may be the most important aspect of the liaison relationship; but, even when consumers and producers hit it off, a senior intelligence manager has emphasized that "getting on the policymaker's calendar is hard."

From the standpoint of chemistry, the CIA never had a better relationship with the most important policy maker—the president—than under DCI William J. Casey, who served President Ronald Reagan. The president and Casey had been long-time personal friends; Casey had even served as his national campaign manger in Reagan's first successful bid for the White House in 1980. The DCI often saw the president, frequently in private. In contrast, some former DCIs—including William E. Colby under President Gerald R. Ford and Richard Helms under President Nixon—were rarely invited to the White House.

"It's very nice to have someone who has the ear of the president," observes Charles Briggs, a CIA executive director, though he pointed out an important liability as well: "This has sometimes led to a perception of the politicizing of intelligence." As the Iran-Contra scandal of 1986–1987 reveals, it can also hold danger that a president and a DCI—or, now, a DNI—who are that close will enter into questionable operations based on personal trust, without adhering to established decision procedures involving others in the CIA, the

NSC, and Congress. The more recent charges that the close personal ties between President George W. Bush and DCI Tenet may have led to exaggerated intelligence ("intelligence to please") about the danger of weapons of mass destruction (WMDs) in Iraq, in support of the second Persian Gulf War, is another example—if true—of the risks than can accompany too tight a relationship between policy officials and the intelligence community.

The cardinal rule of intelligence must be objectivity. If the CIA fails to remain detached from policy, if it fails to concentrate exclusively on bringing the facts to the table, it becomes just another policy advocate arguing in the Roosevelt Room of the White House. Smart presidents and effective democracies need someone at hand in the high echelons of government dedicated solely to the unembroidered facts of world developments, as best they can be ascertained in a world that will never be fully transparent.

CIA LIAISON WITH THE LEGISLATIVE BRANCH

The CIA's legislative liaison efforts, though belated (the FBI learned the importance of good relations on Capitol Hill much earlier), sprang into action after the intelligence scandal of 1975, when the Agency's illegal domestic spying and questionable foreign assassination plots came to light. As a result the CIA Office of Congressional Affairs expanded from two staffers in 1974 to more than a dozen in 2004; and the CIA Office of General Counsel, which also keeps an eye on the handiwork of lawmakers, soared from two in 1974 to over sixty in 2004. In 1993, for example, 1,512 meetings took place between lawmakers and the CIA's legislative liaison staff, as well as 154 one-on-one or small-group meetings between lawmakers and the DCI. In addition, the Office of Congressional Affairs prepared the DCI to appear as a witness in twenty-six congressional hearings, along with preparing other lower-ranked CIA officials as witnesses in another 128 hearings. Further, the Office recorded 317 other contacts with lawmakers, and 887 meetings and contacts with legislative staff—a 29 percent increase over 1992. In 1993, the CIA provided 4,976 classified documents to legislators, along with 4,668 unclassified documents and 233 responses to constituency inquiries.

The degree of liaison openness between the CIA and Congress, however, should not be overstated. That lawmakers are still kept in the dark on key aspects of intelligence activities has been startlingly underscored in recent years, even if (relatively speaking) Congress is kept much more informed than during the "age of darkness" prior to the 1975 intelligence scandal that led to tighter supervision over America's secret agencies. In the pre-1975 era, lawmakers often seemed to want no liaison with the CIA at all. A former DCI, James R. Schlesinger, recalls seeking out a top legislative overseer in the Senate in 1973 to brief him on the latest Agency operations. The response of Senator John Stennis (D-MS) was: "No, no, my boy, don't tell me. Just go ahead and do it—but I don't want to know!"

Even in the post-1975 era, lawmakers have frequently been approached as if they were greenhouse mushrooms: kept in the dark and fed manure. In 1994, for instance, lawmakers learned only through a chance audit that the National Reconnaissance Office (NRO, one of the military intelligence agencies) had incurred cost overruns amounting to some $159 million for its new head-quarters building in the Virginia countryside. Subsequent reports in 1995–1996 revealed further that the NRO had amassed a $4 billion slush fund of appropriations, without keeping Congress informed of its magnitude. DCI R. James Woolsey produced a raft of paperwork purporting to show that law-makers had been briefed on the NRO budget nine different times; but a CIA/Department of Defense inquiry subsequently indicated that the NRO had presented its budget numbers to the lawmakers in piecemeal fashion that (to quote the report) "left unclear the total project cost." However inadvertent the inadequacy of the briefings may have been, the fact remained that liaison between the NRO and the intelligence oversight committees had broken down; the NRO had failed to keep Congress fully informed of its activities, as the spirit and the letter of the oversight laws since 1975 intend.

A Failure to Communicate

More unsettling still, in 1995 Congress discovered that the CIA had failed to report that one of its Guatemalan assets (Colonel Julio Roberto Alpirez) may have been involved in the murder of an American citizen—the kind of questionable Agency connection abroad that the intelligence community was now expected (by law) to report without hesitation to their overseers on Capitol Hill. According to the established liaison rules, the CIA should have reviewed with the congressional oversight panels the propriety of an ongoing relationship with the colonel. "Guatemala's most important lesson," concluded the *New York Times*, "is that the C.I.A. cannot be trusted to police itself"—or honor its liaison commitments, the newspaper might have added.

In 1999, an intelligence manager in the Energy Department (whose intelligence unit monitors the worldwide flow of fissionable and fusionable materials that might be converted into nuclear weapons) displayed a profound misunderstanding of the importance of liaison relationships with lawmakers. He publicly criticized SSCI and HPSCI for requiring him to testify "before fourteen different committees for two months" about counterintelligence problems revealed by an alleged spying incident at the Los Alamos National Laboratory, under the control of the Energy Department. Yet the security shortcomings at the lab were serious and lawmakers had a right to know what was going to be done to protect America's weapons secrets; it is an important part of an intelligence manager's job to provide the liaison necessary to keep representatives of the American people informed about such matters affecting the national security. After all, Congress—a debating club of elected individuals—provides a vital form of popular control, the very anchor of democracy. As a wiser former CIA officer acknowledges: "Dealing with the public is as much a function of intelligence these days as the recruiting of agents or the forecasting of future events."

At least the Energy Department official eschewed the worst sin of intelligence liaison: lying to lawmakers. Or the next worst thing: failing to inform Congress—the treat-them-like-mushrooms approach. In an attempt to explain why he deceived lawmakers during the Iran-Contra affair, the CIA's chief of the Central American Task Force argued that in his sworn testimony he had been "technically correct, [if] specifically evasive"—semantic gobbledygook for attempting to conceal, and reflective of a basic disdain that some intelligence officers have for keeping Congress informed of intelligence activities through close liaison. Other officials in the Energy Department have come close to the low Iran-Contra standard of liaison. In 1998, the department failed to file an annual report on the status of security at the nation's labs, as required by Congress; and two of its senior officials, including its acting head of intelligence, withheld information on the Los Alamos scandal from the House Armed Services Subcommittee on Military Procurement, even under oath and in executive (closed) session.

For some people, the lessons of the Iran-Contra affair failed to stick. "To my mind, to disclose as little as necessary to Congress, if they can get away with it, is not a bad thing," a former intelligence officer has candidly observed. "I have trouble myself blaming any of those guys [involved in the Iran-Contra affair]." A recent NRO director has commented that the old ethic at his organization, which he vows to change, was at best a grudging acceptance of liaison with Capitol Hill. "Legislators were considered pimples on the face of progress," he recalls. "The attitude was: 'we're not going to tell you and you can't make us.'" Yet, as a former SSCI staff member has stressed, intelligence accountability—vital in a democracy—will work only if there is "honesty and completeness in what the members of the intelligence community tell their congressional overseers."

During lawmakers' inquiries in 1999 into the reliability of Los Alamos security procedures, even DCI Tenet—formerly the SSCI staff director and well versed in the theory of accountability—refused to provide information about the spy case to his former committee (evidently so ordered by the Department of Justice). The SSCI chairman, Senator Richard Shelby (R-AL), correctly asserted his panel's right to "have access to all information in unredacted form that pertains to our oversight responsibility." Without an unfettered flow of information through liaison channels from the intelligence community to the oversight committees, Congress could not provide the institutional balance envisioned by the nation's founders as a safeguard against the abuse of power.

The evolution of reliable liaison between the intelligence community and lawmakers was dealt another blow when it came to light in 2000 that the CIA had never reported to the congressional oversight committees or the Justice Department evidence that implicated former DCI John Deutch in the improper handling of classified materials. While director, Deutch had taken large numbers of documents home to work on, a violation of security regulations.

There was "no excuse" for failing to report this incident to Congress, conceded Deutch's successor, George Tenet, who concluded: "It should have been done promptly, certainly by the spring of 1997 [after Deutch had resigned as DCI]."

The Key to Successful Legislative Liaison: Executive Branch Cooperation

As these examples make clear, the cooperation of the White House, the Justice Department, and the intelligence agencies is vital if proper liaison is to exist with lawmakers. Members of Congress only know about intelligence activities to the extent that the president and the DCI allow them to know. As a former HPSCI staff director has emphasized: a "spirit of comity" between the branches is essential. Yet this sine qua non is often missing. During its investigation in 1975, the Church Committee ran into one roadblock after another erected by the Ford administration to slow the panel's progress. At one point, a Defense Department truck dumped enough documents at the committee's doorstep in the Dirksen Office Building to keep it busy for weeks, without a single significant paper in the whole lot.

More recently, in 2002 a Joint Committee (composed of SSCI and HPSCI members) complained about stonewalling by the second Bush administration. During that probe into the CIA's failure to anticipate the 9/11 attacks, DCI Tenet tried to put the committee on the defensive during public hearings with aggressive responses to questions from lawmakers. Allotted ten minutes to speak, he went on in a "somewhat defiant tone" (according to a newspaper report) for fifty minutes, despite a request from cochair Senator Bob Graham (D-FL) that he abbreviate his remarks. Tenet also refused to declassify information that the Joint Committee asked to make public, and, just before a scheduled hearing, withdrew intelligence witnesses the Joint Committee had called to testify. "Witnesses are requested, refused, requested again, granted, and then—at the last minute—refused again," groused a committee member on the Senate floor.

When word leaked that the staff had cautioned members about the elusiveness of a scheduled CIA witness, Tenet blasted the committee for prejudging the veracity of CIA officers. The staff, though, could hardly be blamed for reminding members that, in past inquiries, CIA witnesses had not always been forthcoming; indeed, some had misled Congress—even under oath—during the Iran-Contra investigation. Moreover, officers from the CIA had "flat lied" to SSCI in 1995–1996, according to a senior staffer on the committee, when it attempted to investigate the Agency's ties with a controversial military officer in Guatemala, Col. Alpirez.

Having become increasingly dissatisfied with Tenet's belligerent posture before the Joint Committee, Senator Graham "toughened his stance toward the intelligence agencies when the administration began to stonewall," recalls an aide on the panel. When the DCI refused to provide SSCI with CIA documents on Iraq—closing down the liaison lines altogether on this important topic—and then failed to appear at a closed hearing, Graham accused the CIA of "obstructionism" and said that its behavior was "unacceptable." A former Hill staffer, who follows intelligence closely, concluded that the CIA had "stuck its fingers in the eye of the oversight committee, which—under Graham—was waking up very late to the fact that it is being rolled." Though Senators Graham and Shelby seemed agitated over the collapse of meaningful liaison, most of their colleagues adopted a more benign view of the intelligence community's behavior and preferred to concentrate on the terrorist threat.

Open lines of communication between overseers and the DCI, who is the president's primary liaison to Congress on intelligence matters, is of utmost importance for effective accountability. Yet Tenet invariably ignored the rank-and-file membership, preferring to discuss issues one-on-one with the Intelligence Committee chairs and ranking minority members. In the past this liaison approach had at times been used by DCIs to honor "oversight" more in the breach than in the observance, whispering into the ear of the chair, then counting on him to support the intelligence community if an operation crash landed and the rank-and-file members wanted to know why they were never informed before take-off.

At least the rank-and-file have access to liaison officers from the separate agencies. Often these individuals are personable and knowledgeable, and they can build bridges of trust between the community and its overseers. Lately, however, the turnover rate of liaison officers at the CIA and most other intelligence agencies has been excessively high (the exceptions are the NSA, the U.S. Army, and the Defense Intelligence Agency), undermining rapport between the Hill and the intelligence community.

The Barrier of Excessive Secrecy

Any discussion of CIA legislative liaison invariably leads to the issue of secrecy. As former HPSCI chair Lee Hamilton (D-IN) has stated, "the great task is to strike a balance between the need to ensure accountability and the intelligence community's need to gather and protect information. It's the balance between oversight and secrecy." In democracies, the presumption is that openness leads to better decision making and a more informed electorate. Yet the second Bush administration has shifted the balance far toward the secrecy side. Throughout 2002, the Justice Department routinely snubbed queries from the Senate Judiciary Committee; and the chairman of the Senate Armed Services Committee, the usually reliable administration supporter John Warner (R-VA), grumbled about being left "out of the loop" on important defense and national security issues. "I will not tolerate a continuation of what's been going on the last two years," he warned. A *New York Times* reporter further observed "exhibiting a penchant for secrecy that has been striking." Indeed, the number of classification actions increased in 2001 by 44 percent over the previous year, to a record 33,020,887 instances.

One canard about protecting secrets can be dismissed quickly: a jibe from former Senator Barry Goldwater (R-AZ) that Congress has more leaks than the men's room at Anheuser-Busch. Every study and every DCI has been laudatory of the HPSCI and SSCI record on keeping secrets. The only significant exception occurred in 1995, when HPSCI member Robert Torricelli (D-NJ) disclosed information related to CIA activities in Guatemala that should not have been released by an individual representative. This record is remarkable for over twenty-five years of oversight on Capitol Hill. In fact almost all leaks come from the executive branch. Moreover, virtually every study on secrecy has concluded that far too much information is unnecessarily classified, another realm of intelligence policy that lawmakers have failed to address adequately.

Another question relating to secrecy is to what extent can intelligence overseers inform the public of their activities? While executive classification of documents has shot up during the second Bush administration, public hearings on intelligence on Capitol Hill have declined. The emphasis on secrecy in the government is greater than ever before. "Too many people in the world today know how we go about our business," argues Timothy R. Sample, the HPSCI staff director, which suggests that even congressional overseers wish to further limit public access to information about how the taxpayers' money is being spent on intelligence activities.

Member Motivation

As critical for effective liaison is the willingness of individual lawmakers to engage in the meaningful examination of intelligence programs. For the period from 1975–1990, a study on the quality of intelligence oversight in public hearings found that although members will show up (along with the network television crews) for televised sessions dealing with scandals, attendance at hearings of a more routine nature was spotty—approximately one-third of the total SSCI and HPSCI membership, on average, during these years. Citing Woodrow Wilson's adage that "Congress in committee-rooms is Congress at work," the study concluded that "a good many legislators failed to show up for work." The study further found that even among those who did show up at hearings the quality of the questioning of CIA witnesses varied greatly. Usually congressional hearings have been more of an opportunity for lawmakers to advocate the case for intelligence operations than questioning their effectiveness or morality.

Even DCIs have been critical of congressional laxity in maintaining serious liaison with the intelligence community. "Congress is informed to the degree that Congress wants to be informed," testified former DCI William E. Colby, noting that several overseers had expressed little interest in being briefed. Another DCI, Adm. Stansfield Turner, recollected: "I believe the committees of Congress could have been more rigorous with me [during the Carter Administration] . . . it would be more helpful if you are probing and rigorous." Several lawmakers, though, have a different view from Colby and Turner, preferring the role of advocate over adversary. For them, the president and the

DCI know best in this sensitive domain; better to follow than to second-guess and perhaps harm America's efforts against terrorism and other threats. Efficiency trumps accountability, and the doors to candid liasion between intelligence officers and lawmakers slam shut.

Reporting Requirements

At the heart of the liaison issue are the questions of what should the intelligence agencies tell the Congress, and when. Lawmakers now have, in theory at least, access to all information that the secret agencies provide to the executive branch, with the exception of the President's Daily Brief. In reality, members of Congress frequently have to throw a fit before the agencies are responsive, although it must be conceded that the degree of access accorded SSCI and HPSCI far outshines what overseers had received prior to 1975.

As a means of guaranteeing a more systematic flow of information to overseers about intelligence operations, Congress established formal reporting requirements—some in statutory form, others written or oral agreements between SSCI and HPSCI leaders and the DCI. The trailblazer in this regard was the Hughes-Ryan Act of 1974, the first effort by lawmakers since the creation of the CIA in 1947 to place tighter controls on its activities. The Hughes-Ryan Act required the president to authorize formally all major covert operations (through the "findings" process discussed earlier in this chapter), and then to report the approved covert action "in a timely manner" to eight congressional committees (narrowed to SSCI and HPSCI by the Intelligence Oversight Act of 1980). Subsequent legislation of 1991 clarified the reporting time limit to mean prior to the implementation of the covert action, and certainly within two days (except in extraordinary circumstances where the president decides that more time is needed).

Lawmakers and others cleave into two camps on the subject of formal reporting requirements. Some believe that they are indispensable points of leverage for forcing the intelligence community to keep open its liaison lines. Others balk at what they see as excessive involvement by lawmakers in the fine workings of intelligence leading to an unwarranted surcharge on the time of intelligence officials who could otherwise deal with terrorism and other threats—in a word, "micromanagement," the favorite slight used by critics of any form of oversight they oppose—often all forms.

For proponents of robust liaison, though, reporting requirements are essential for keeping the oversight committees informed. Intelligence managers might otherwise brief lawmakers merely when they are so inclined, or when forced to by a publicized scandal. Better to have important operations automatically brought to the attention of overseers, who might not otherwise know about them. Obviously, reporting requirements should not be excessive in number and should focus on important activities. An HPSCI request for eighty-seven reports due on May 1, 2002, from the intelligence community seems too many; but, at the same time, the community's 92 percent delinquency rate in providing those reports reflects poorly on its efforts to communicate well with congressional overseers.

The purpose of liaison is not to stifle the vital work of the intelligence agencies, but rather to keep Congress informed so that it can help preserve civil liberties, maintain budget discipline, and bring to bear—as former SSCI member William S. Cohen (R-ME) has put it—"the combined wisdom of both branches." Reporting requirements help ensure regular liaison and sharing of information with Congress to allow this pooling of wisdom. If one is dead set against Congress's role in intelligence matters, one is apt to endorse the characterization of lawmakers and their reporting requirements advanced by Admiral John M. Poindexter, national security adviser during the Reagan years, and an Iran-Contra conspirator: they are nothing but an "outside interference."

Co-optation

The danger always exists that lawmakers will "go native." Like ambassadors abroad accused of taking on the coloration of the country where they are living rather than the country they represent, HPSCI and SSCI members and staff can come to identify more with the intelligence agencies than with their roles as detached and objective supervisors. "They are awful nice to [overseers]," recalls former HPSCI chair Hamilton, "invite them to the CIA, give them a nice dinner, court them, seduce them." Liaison can take beguiling forms. Lawmakers and staff who come out of the intelligence community might be especially prone to favoring their old agencies. Like HPSCI chair Porter Goss (R-FL), a majority of staff members on the two Intelligence Committees had earlier careers in one or another of the secret agencies. A remarkable number of SSCI and HPSCI staffers also take up, or resume, positions in the intelligence community after a tour on the Hill, DCI Tenet most conspicuously.

By and large, though, co-optation seems less of a problem than the pervasive sense among members (especially in the Republican Party) that Congress should defer to the executive branch on matters of national security. Occasionally, some staffers do exhibit an inability to criticize their former agencies; but, just as often, the committees have benefited from having staffers who can tell whether their former colleagues in the intelligence community are playing it straight with Congress or spinning. Still, it would be prudent for the committees to recruit a higher percentage of non-intelligence professionals to provide ballast, even though this would involve some training costs.

When SSCI and HPSCI were created, co-optation was much on the mind of congressional leaders. They included a special provision in the committees' founding language to require a rotation of members from the panels after eight-year periods of service. This rule, so the thinking went, would help eliminate the development of cozy ties between lawmakers and intelligence officers that could undermine a meaningful liaison relationship. The growing consensus, however, is that rotation has harmed oversight, because as soon as members become sufficiently experienced and expert in arcane intelligence matters, they must depart the committee.

Further, since one can never count on serving as chair for long (if at all) in a rotation system, the incentives for joining the Intelligence Committees and working hard to learn the subject are diminished. Those who do rise to chair the committees generally occupy that position for only a couple of years, although House Republican leaders waived the limit to permit Goss a fourth term of leadership on HPSCI. Others insist, though, that it is valuable to have a large percentage of representatives flowing through the Intelligence Committees, not only to guard against co-optation but also to disseminate throughout the chambers expertise about this important and poorly understood aspect of American government. "It's better to have people with fresh eyes [on the committees]," reasons former Senator Fowler (D-GA) in favor of rotation. On balance, though, having continuity and experience on the Committees—liaison bonds that are not severed every few years—seem to trump the benefits of rotation. The eight-year ceiling should be razed, or at least raised.

CIA LIAISON WITH FOREIGN INTELLIGENCE SERVICES

"The main effect [intelligence liaison between nations] is to make national systems more productive than they would otherwise be," notes British intelligence scholar Michael Herman, "with more data and the technical advantages of dialogue with others. Governments get better views of the world at cut prices." Liaison relationships can vary from quite close (America's ties with Great Britain, New Zealand, Canada, and Australia) to rather weak (as with American and Russian cooperation on environmental intelligence). Germany is an example of a country that falls toward the close end of the spectrum, though short of the long-standing bonds between American and British intelligence. The U.S.-U.K. liaison relationship is a special case that draws on an extensive, intertwined history between two enduring democracies that share a common language and culture. The U.S.-German case nonetheless is closer to the norm.

The Raison d'Etre for Intelligence Cooperation

This planet is vast and nations, even wealthy ones, that try to achieve global transparency are bound by finite resources. The development of a human and technical spy network is expensive, especially if the nation is a world power (or so aspires). Even when a nation's focus is against a single adversary, resource investments can be high when the target is geographically large and well-protected, as was the U.S.S.R.

A number of nations, the United States and Great Britain among them, fund their intelligence activities at a rate roughly equivalent to 10 percent of their total defense expenditures. Spy satellites employed by some nations in this modern era of sophisticated long-distance surveillance are particularly expensive. These elaborate machines can be as large as a touring bus and cost a fortune just to propel into space, not to mention the expense of their design, construction, and management.

Costs are not the only limitation on a nation's ability to fashion an extensive intelligence network. A set of skills is also required and it can take a long time to refine. Human intelligence requires experience in the recruitment of foreign agents, which in turn rests upon a deep knowledge of the language and culture of other countries. Some nations—Great Britain and France are two—have a long and successful record of espionage, with traditions and lore going back to the Middle Ages. In contrast, U.S. intelligence remains in its infancy, with a modern organization dating only to the creation of the CIA in 1947. Technical intelligence requires sophisticated skills as well, including scientists with advanced research knowledge, elaborate management teams to build and deploy the spy machines, and highly trained operators. No nation, not even those having a lengthy history of intelligence activity, will possess all the requisite resources—money, experience, scientific skills, a dispersed array of mechanical eyes and ears—for perfect or even near-perfect global coverage. As a consequence, every nation will benefit from working with allies to share the burden of intelligence costs and thereby compensate for gaps in its own spy network. Indeed U.S. intelligence professionals often use the intelligence "burden sharing" phrase to describe cooperation with foreign intelligence services. Such ties are more formally referred to as "foreign intelligence liaison."

The Scope of Foreign Intelligence Liaison

America's intelligence activities include the cultivation of "an immense network of multiple liaison relationships," notes an intelligence expert. They include the sharing of information and insights on global affairs, as well as cooperation in training and support, access to facilities, and even collaborative operations. The most common and important form of cooperation is information sharing. For example, throughout the Cold War, the United States and West Germany had much to offer one another. For the Americans, the comparative advantage lay on the side of technical intelligence. From its constellation of space satellites that engaged in both photography (IMINT) and electronic listening (SIGINT), the United States knew the location of Soviet armies, tanks, warships, and missiles, along with information on their state of readiness—the most important military data one could hope for as a member of the Western alliance.

West Germany had no spy satellites of its own, but it did bring some comparative advantages to the table, preeminently human intelligence. The West German foreign intelligence service, the Bundes Nachrichten Dienst (BND), boasted a stable of agents in East Germany and elsewhere throughout the Soviet sphere of influence—of varying degrees of reliability and importance. They served as a (sometimes) helpful complement to the efforts of the

CIA, which prowled the same terrain in search of spy recruits but with fewer advantages of language proficiency and a cultural understanding of Europe.

West Germans had another advantage—geography. The Federal Republic of Germany provided an ideal base for U.S. intelligence operations directed against the Soviet bête noire. West Germany's eastern border stood as the longest contiguous boundary between the NATO alliance and the Warsaw Pact–a splendid launching pad for America's U-2 and other aerial reconnaissance flights over Eastern Europe and the U.S.S.R., as well as for the eastward infiltration of spy teams and propaganda materials. Moreover, the German cities of Berlin and Bonn were both important centers of diplomatic activity and were therefore infested with spies who pursued diplomats in hopes of acquiring useful information. What better place for the CIA (with the help of the BND) to recruit disaffected and avaricious officials from the Soviet Union and its allies posted in West Germany?

Even outside their comparative advantage, the West Germans and the Americans had other incentives that encouraged intelligence cooperation. West Germany possessed some aerial reconnaissance capabilities and was willing to share the "catch" hauled in from these observational platforms. The BND gathered additional information through the use of wiretaps and other ground-based modus operandi of a technical nature. The West Germans could assist in breaking foreign diplomatic and spy codes—a science heavily dependent on advanced mathematical and computer skills in which Germans have traditionally excelled.

As a source of espionage information—on Soviet weapons systems located in East Germany, for instance—and as a base for operations, West Germany thus contributed crucial resources to the Western intelligence effort. At the strategic level, the Federal Republic could not offer much that the CIA did not already know from America's more powerful surveillance platforms in space; but on such matters as the details of Soviet conventional weaponry throughout Eastern Europe, BND agents were able to add value to the Agency's intelligence estimates.

Bonn had every reason to cooperate with the West, even after the forced "partnership" that followed Germany's defeat in the Second World War. For one thing, the CIA had a few well-placed agents in the Soviet Bloc whose information was of continuing interest to Bonn. Moreover, the United States had vital satellite data to share, most importantly strategic "warning intelligence" if a tank blitzkrieg or missile attack from the east were to take place. Washington officials were also in a pivotal position to assist West German leaders in the pursuit of their broader political and economic objectives. The political quid from Washington for the intelligence pro quo from Bonn would, above all, further legitimize the rise of West German political and economic power in the European community. Intelligence cooperation, then, was another means for Bonn to ingratiate itself with the United States (and other Western powers with whom it carried out comparable liaison relationships), in return for its growing integration into the Western alliance. Intelligence goodwill would beget political goodwill, or so Bonn hoped.

The wooing was reciprocal. The United States stood to benefit from winning West Germany's allegiance in the tug-of-war with Moscow over world alignments. Intelligence enticements became a part of the wine and flowers in this courtship. In this sense, intelligence became an essential instrument for the expansion of U.S. power and influence abroad—what some might view as American imperialism. Or this use of liaison could be seen more benignly as simply a smart way to compensate for one's own intelligence weaknesses and to save money (economy through synergism), while at the same time forging bonds of political friendship within the pro-democracy Atlantic alliance.

Counterintelligence Liaison

The sharing of information and a base of operations were only two of many opportunities for U.S.-West German intelligence cooperation. Important as well was counterintelligence, the task of thwarting hostile operations carried out against the West by the secret services of the communist nations. At the end of World War II, Western intelligence agencies aggressively sought to acquire the espionage records of the Third Reich—a mother lode of information about possible agent recruitments in Eastern Europe and the Soviet Union. Even former Nazi intelligence officers with despicable records of war crimes were quietly eased out of post-war Germany and absorbed into the ranks of the CIA and other Allied intelligence agencies, as a means for tapping into expertise and contacts that would prove useful from a counterintelligence perspective in the new cold war against communism.

Covert Action Liaison

Covert action was yet another intelligence discipline in which the CIA and the BND found an opportunity to cooperate. By definition, covert action is the secret attempt to influence the affairs of other countries through the use of propaganda, political, economic, and, at the extreme, paramilitary activities. The classic illustration of CIA-BND solidarity in this domain during the Cold War involved the use of covert propaganda espousing pro-West and anticommunist views. The two intelligence agencies cooperated in fashioning propaganda themes and, of greatest value, in devising methods to infiltrate this propaganda into the Soviet camp (including such means as smugglers, balloons lofted over the Iron Curtain, and most effectively, radio transmission).

Radio Free Europe and Radio Liberty (Radio Liberation in the 1950s) were two important channels of propaganda. Beginning in 1949 and throughout the Cold War, the CIA operated both radio transmitters out of Munich with assistance from the BND. During the first few years of transmission, the American and West German governments frequently clashed over issues of policy and communications; these tensions gradually relaxed, however, as relations between Bonn and Washington settled into more of a routine. When the CIA connection to the radio stations was exposed in 1971, Congress began funding the broadcasts openly and created a small agency called the Board for International Broadcasting to supervise the propaganda transmissions.

A final, and unspoken, reason for intelligence liaison is the opportunity to spy on one's own partner. While rubbing elbows with BND officials, CIA liaison officers were also able to glean some idea about West Germany's foreign policy and intelligence objectives. Here is another source of information on the direction of German and European affairs that CIA officers could fold into their reports for Washington policymakers. The same held true for BND liaison officers, who in their visits with the CIA (and other U.S. intelligence agencies) could keep their eyes and ears open for extracurricular information.

The Risks of Foreign Liaison

However useful in some respects, intelligence liaison inevitably engenders an attitude of ambivalence in both parties, whether West Germany and the United States or even between the close wartime allies, Great Britain and the United States. Lord Palmerston pithily alluded to why some distance would always exist between friendly nations. "We have no eternal allies, and we have no perpetual enemies," he remarked. "Our interests are eternal and perpetual, and those interests it is our duty to follow."

To use the West German example again, its foreign policy objectives and those of the United States were often similar during the Cold War; but they were never precisely congruent, any more than was the case for the British and the Americans. After the Cold War, they diverged widely on the need for American military intervention in Iraq in the second Persian Gulf War of 2003. While "liaising," both sides are never completely on the same page. Both have a double agenda: some cooperation, combined with a constant eye out for a chance to learn more about the partner's global intentions and capabilities. As a savvy *New York Times* reporter observed, "When spies from two countries shake hands, they are often trying to pick one another's pockets." At the extreme, this could mean even attempting to recruit an intelligence officer from the ranks of the ally's secret service—perhaps someone on the liaison team itself. This is a highly risky venture, though, and is rarely undertaken because of the potential for rupturing ongoing intelligence cooperation and even higher government-to-government relations.

Ambivalence characterizes liaison partnerships for yet another reason: concern that the allied intelligence service may have been penetrated by a common adversary. During the 1960s, the CIA's chief of counterintelligence, James Angleton, wined and dined the visiting British liaison officer, the suave and witty Harold "Kim" Philby, for months in Georgetown's finest restaurants, sharing with him closely held CIA views on how best to battle the KGB and the GRU—only to discover at the time of Philby's defection to Moscow in 1963 that his clubby British counterintelligence companion had been in the service of the KGB since his student days at Cambridge University.

James Angleton, former chief of counterintelligence at the Central Intelligence Agency, answers questions before the Senate Intelligence Committee in Washington, D.C., on September 25, 1975. (AP/Wide World Photos)

The Israeli recruitment of a U.S. Navy civilian intelligence analyst, Jonathan Jay Pollard (arrested by the FBI in 1985 and sentenced to life in prison two years later), taught the lesson anew in the 1980s. Pollard claimed he was simply passing on information that had been unfairly denied by Washington to a trusted American ally. Beyond their disgust at Pollard's treachery, intelligence officials in the United States feared that Israel's intelligence service (Mossad) may have been penetrated by the KGB and, as a result, Pollard's acquisitions for Israel—thousands of top-secret U.S. intelligence documents, for which he was secretly paid—could have benefited the Soviet Union as well. They also feared that ordinary Israeli officials and Mossad officers might simply trade away America's secrets in their own negotiations with Moscow and the KGB.

Mindful of the ever-possible presence of a mole inside the partner's intelligence service, a liaison team will never reveal its most sensitive secrets (the "family jewels") to another country, even a close ally. If the CIA were to have shared intelligence fully during the Cold War, a penetration of the BND run by Moscow would have been tantamount to a CIA penetration. Moreover, America's intelligence agencies have suffered Soviet penetrations of their own, reminding the BND in turn of the risks to its agents involved in full espionage cooperation with the United States. Every liaison relationship is laced with suspicion.

The hush-hush details of tradecraft—the methods of espionage—also induce liaison ambivalence. While understanding and enjoying the fruits of a sharing relationship, both sides take care to protect both their own intelligence sources (the names and locations of agents) and methods (the specifics of their most advanced espionage techniques). This is particularly true in the case of America's desire to maintain an edge in the realm of satellite and other technical surveillance. The United States will rarely disclose the very best (that is, highest resolution) satellite imagery, even to close allies, for fear of revealing to other intelligence services—penetrated as they may be by an enemy agent—just how capable its spy cameras are. Made known to the enemy, this technical information could result in more effective methods for evading the camera's eye. Even liaison disclosures of tradecraft on miniature surveillance devices could possibly aid the enemy, or put the liaison partner on alert for methods that America's intelligence agencies might employ against him one day, should the friendship disintegrate.

During his confirmation hearings to become DCI in 2004, Representative Porter J. Goss (R-FL) argued that the United States has relied too much on foreign intelligence liaison with respect to the Middle East and South Asia, acquiring most of its information from these regions through liaison relationships. Goss, who was confirmed by the Senate, favored the CIA and its sister agencies standing on their own feet, using foreign liaison as a supplement to—not a crutch to replace—America's own circle of spies abroad.

LIAISON WITH INTERNATIONAL ORGANIZATIONS

Since the end of the Cold War, international organizations—especially the United Nations (UN) and the North Atlantic Treaty Organization (NATO)—have played an important part in America's foreign policy. During the first Persian Gulf War in 1991, the United States relied heavily on the UN as a framework for building a coalition of forces to repel the Iraq army from Kuwait. In the pursuit of this military objective, the U.S. intelligence community shared information and assessments with coalition members as the war unfolded. Even before the end of the Cold War, the United States had been sharing classified intelligence with NATO members for many years.

As a larger organization with less well-formulated security procedures (and with some members hostile toward America), the UN has received less information over the years than has NATO from the U.S. intelligence community—although, according to the Aspin-Brown Commission in 1996, the United States still provides the majority of information used by the UN in support of its worldwide activities (contrary to a CIA officer's claim to a reporter that "we don't get involved with international organizations"). When UN and NATO missions overlap, as they did in Bosnia in the early 1990s, the intelligence community provides one level of classified information to NATO participants and a more filtered version to UN participants.

Most of the U.S. intelligence shared with the United Nations is quite low-grade in classification—a special category of "UN Use Only," not to be

distributed to the media or anyone else outside the framework of the organization. This means that the information can go to 185 nations, including a
number of America's adversaries. As a result, the information is unlikely to
stay secret. With this in mind, the intelligence community provides to the
UN what one of its representatives has called "vanilla" information: somewhat bland, highly sanitized documents which, after various interagency
"pre-dissemination reviews," are usually less than timely in their arrival to
consumers at the United Nations. Nevertheless, the information is still considered useful by UN officials, for often it is the only reliable source of analysis
on some global issues.

If asked, the United States will sometimes provide information on specific
topics of interest to the United Nations, at a somewhat higher level of classification than normal—although still carefully sanitized to remove signs of
sources and methods before being passed along. A recent example was an
analysis of military, political, and economic developments in a war-torn developing nation. As a rule, the United States does not provide classified
documents to the UN, with the occasional exception of tactical battlefield
information in times of crisis for the UN's "Blue Helmet" troops.

Another venue of "information sharing" (the term the UN prefers over the
more intrusive sounding word "intelligence"), and one that avoids giving
sensitive documents to the United Nations, is the timely oral briefing. When
the intelligence community determines that the Blue Helmets are in jeopardy,
a member of the U.S. Mission to the United Nations will (with clearance from
the Department of State) present valuable battlefield information orally to the
appropriate UN officials, possibly saving lives but without leaving any intelligence documents behind.

The question of intelligence sharing with international organizations is
complex and nuanced, depending on the kind of organization (its size and
whether its members are U.S. allies, for example) and America's experience
with the organization. Whoever the recipient, the sharing of information
by the United States is carried out through the most exacting procedures.
The intelligence is usually given in a highly diluted fashion while more sensitive information is disseminated only to a small group of consumers. There
have been mishaps. In Somalia, for example, UN officials poorly handled U.S.
intelligence documents and left some behind during the withdrawal in 1994.
Subsequent inquiries into this case revealed, however, that the documents
were less sensitive than had been initially feared. More importantly, this
experience resulted in the tightening of security procedures by UN administrators to better safeguard intelligence documents in the field.

In all instances of U.S. information sharing with the United Nations, the
purpose is to advance America's national security interests, not to achieve
some ill-defined goal of enhancing good feelings among UN officials toward
Washington. Information that uncovers transgressions by Saddam Hussein,
protects peacekeepers in Bosnia, provides a realistic understanding of events

in Rwanda, or proves acts of atrocity by Serbian or Albanian soldiers—all are illustrations of information shared with the United Nations that benefits the United States as well. As a general proposition, America's best interests are served when the United Nations is in possession of accurate information about world affairs.

In many cases, UN officials are already well informed. As a result of their diplomatic contacts, world travel, and perusal of the standard sources of public information, most UN officials perceive no pressing need for secret information (short of tactical military intelligence when Blue Helmets are under fire). These officials would like, nonetheless, to receive from reliable member states more studies produced by their individual intelligence agencies on the issue of human rights, as well as on such broad topics as world population growth and global food supply.

The extent of U.S. liaison involvement with international organizations raises a significant question of the degree to which Washington's secret agencies undermine their credibility by making them appear lackeys of American foreign policy. This risk came to the public's attention in 1999, when news reports revealed that the CIA and the NSA had assisted the UN Special Commission (known as UNSCOM) in eavesdropping operations against some of Iraq's most sensitive communications. In this case, the United States had gone far beyond its normally low-level intelligence activities with respect to the United Nations.

The UN commissioned UNSCOM, a team of arms inspectors, to monitor Iraqi compliance with a 1991 cease-fire agreement requiring it to dismantle its program for strategic weapons. The team was nothing less than what one reporter called "an international intelligence service for the new world order . . . the first of its kind," adding: "More than 7,000 weapons inspectors from around the world served UNSCOM over seven years, spying on Iraq, surveying its military and industrial plants, trying to do what smart bombs could not: destroy nuclear, biological, chemical and missile programs hidden by Saddam Hussein." Germany provided helicopters to UNSCOM, for instance, with special radar to penetrate Iraqi sand dunes in search of buried weapons; Britain contributed sensitive scanners to intercept Iraqi military communications; and the United States loaned U-2 spy planes and even Navy divers to probe Iraqi lakes and rivers for submerged weapons. In the description of another reporter, "The spirit of post–Cold War cooperation promised a miracle: UNSCOM, operating on behalf of the U.N. Security Council, would utilize the secret intelligence agencies of its members states, Communist and non-Communist alike, to investigate the Iraqi arsenal."

Information acquired by the NSA, which can unscramble encrypted telephone conversations between Saddam and his aides, could assist the UN's search for weapons of mass destruction inside Iraq. At the same time, the U.S. intelligence community could exploit the UNSCOM relationship to advance its own agenda: namely, overthrowing Saddam Hussein. Under UNSCOM cover, the

NSA apparently had even wired a UN microwave transmission system (without the knowledge of UN officials), which allowed the eavesdropping agency to monitor a wide range of secret Iraqi military communications.

"The UN cannot be party to an operation to overthrow one of its member states," complained a confidant to UN Secretary-General Kofi Annan, when the U.S. intelligence ties to UNSCOM became a matter of public knowledge. "In the most fundamental way, that is what's wrong with the UNSCOM operation." Had the UNSCOM weapons inspectors restricted their activities solely to a nonproliferation agenda, which had widespread support in the world, they could have preserved the high esteem in which most member states held them. Instead, news leaks and speculation from one of the inspectors (a former U.S. Marine intelligence officer by the name of Scott Ritter) raised suspicions that UNSCOM had gone beyond just trying to find Saddam's weapons. According to these reports, the CIA had used UNSCOM in 1996 as an umbrella for its own intelligence collection operations, as well as for covert actions designed to topple Saddam Hussein. The Clinton administration conceded that the CIA had been assisting UNSCOM "through intelligence, logistical support, expertise, and personnel," but denied using the team as a medium for coup plotting against the Iraqi leader.

Wherever the truth may lie, UNSCOM had been fatally tarred by these charges. The independence of the United Nations was severely compromised, in perception if not in reality. In order to advance its plans to destroy Saddam Hussein, the UN liaison operations of the U.S. intelligence community (presumably acting under White House orders) had instead destroyed the most important international effort in the modern era to halt the proliferation of dangerous strategic weapons.

To avoid the problem of national bias that comes with reliance on individual national intelligence services for its information, the UN will need to create its own intelligence capabilities—a professional corps of intelligence officers with a commitment to making the UN work (with all the necessary safeguards against the misuse of shared information). The UN is already taking some steps in this direction. It has set up a Situation Center, which is building up a computer infrastructure for the collection, storage, and retrieval of open-source information on world affairs. Its modest resources, though, make this endeavor limited in scope.

The United Nations has also recently acquired authority to start up a satellite surveillance system that would allow its International Drug Control Program to monitor the cultivation of illegal drug crops in the major source countries. In this manner, the UN can establish an internationally accepted benchmark for measuring the faithfulness of promises by countries to reduce their production of drugs. "For the first time the international community will have a very reliable instrument to measure the extent of illegal crops," according to the executive director of the program. The European Space Agency is contributing the necessary satellites and technical expertise to support the operation.

These experiments in international intelligence remain alive, despite the UNSCOM setback. Still, it has been difficult to overcome the old mentality of viewing the UN as either a target or a cover for intelligence operations, rather than a customer for information and insight gathered by the secret agencies of member nations for the benefit of the whole world. This change in attitude is "ill thought out and haphazard," in the words of a former British Ambassador to the United Nations.

The relationship between international organizations and intelligence raises a paradox: how can these organizations be effective if they are so poorly informed about the outlaw nations they are expected to tame? The UN is meant to engage in conflict resolution, peacekeeping, peace enforcement, economic sanctions, controlling the spread of large-scale weapons, combating organized crime, fighting drugs, and bringing to justice war criminals and human rights violators. All of these tasks require intelligence, yet the UN has little at its disposal. International organizations cannot afford to develop their own full-service intelligence agencies. Besides, member nations are unlikely to tolerate the risk that the UN might end up peering into their own backyards. Member states could provide more intelligence assistance themselves, but they fear leaks of sensitive sources and methods. Further, the UN must worry about the national biases of intelligence emanating from member states.

Despite these dilemmas, one can envision nations and NGOs providing to the UN and other international organizations additional, second-hand satellites and other surveillance equipment for watching global environmental conditions, refugee flows, arms-control monitoring, and suspicious military mobilizations. Satellites can even track mosquito populations around the globe, by focusing on vegetation patterns and breeding grounds that attract the disease-bearing insects. The UN could establish an Assessment Board composed of retired senior intelligence analysts from member states: men and women with extensive analytic experience, known for their fierce independence and wisdom, who could evaluate the quality and objectivity of member-state intelligence reports solicited by the Secretary-General of the UN.

International organizations require reliable information on global conditions. As a specialist on the United Nations notes, "The UN must be given the means, including information-gathering and analysis, to make manifest its goal, as stated in the opening words of the UN Charter, of 'saving succeeding generations from the scourge of war.'" So far members of the UN have fallen far short of satisfactory intelligence cooperation, although some individual nations (such as Great Britain) have been responsive to requests from UN officials for intelligence assistance. Increased intelligence burden sharing within the framework of the United Nations would allow an opportunity for global dissemination of information to all member nations, carefully reviewed by an esteemed Assessment Board to filter out national biases. This would be a valuable contribution toward the search for solutions to the challenges that confront all the world's people—a crowning achievement for intelligence liaison.

———————————— ☆ **3** ☆ ————————————

A World of Secrets: Intelligence and Counterintelligence

John Prados

Intelligence work is about secrets. Divination of the adversary's secrets, the gaining of access to information that enables the possessor to know those secrets, the securing of one's own secrets and prevention of the adversary's doing the same thing, these are the very stuff of the endeavor. The "disciplines" of intelligence—a bit of jargon of relatively recent coinage—and the more familiar concept of tradecraft that apply in each area all aim at the fundamental objective of gaining or defending secrets. Here the focus will be on three of the disciplines: intelligence collection, analysis, and counterintelligence. The first is quintessentially the province of the spy, whether the human agent or the machine. The second is what you do with the information you collect. The third is the defensive function of avoiding someone else knowing what you know, or discovering how to prevent you from knowing it.

Current American practice owes much to the U.S. experience in World War II. Not only did the surprise attack inflicted on this country at Pearl Harbor in December 1941 serve as a powerful impetus to the creation of a peacetime intelligence agency but the substance of the work was greatly affected by what happened during the war. In fighting the war the United States established its first central intelligence organization, the Office of Strategic Services (OSS), an entity that broadly modeled itself on equivalent British agencies and benefited much from British tutelage. For example, the American counterintelligence unit within OSS, the specialized intelligence defense entity called X-2, worked directly with British security services in learning its trade. Similarly, American intelligence analysts were informed by the British practice of having their interagency Joint Intelligence Committee draw up "appreciations" for the government. The practice of compiling strategic assessments became commonplace during the war, as did a certain way of framing questions for analytical purposes. Beyond all this what can be termed the pillars of intelligence collection came of age: communications intelligence attained a level of sophistication beyond simple codebreaking; scientific and technical intelligence, previously unknown or rudimentary, grew into significant contributors to intelligence knowledge; overhead photography became standardized and widely utilized; prisoner interrogation (a variant of what is now known as "human intelligence") began to be approached in a systematic way; and the translation and review of documents (captured documents during the war, those purloined by espionage since then) plus speeches or broadcasts were regularly funneled into the reporting.

Technological development was also spurred by the war. Such developments have had important implications for intelligence work. Created for codebreaking and with certain military applications in mind, the computer now impacts every aspect of intelligence work as well as affecting society at large. Several generations of improvements in equipment have facilitated the efforts of intelligence agents to gain access to secrets and the communication of that information to case officers. Technological developments have also enhanced the capability of the counterintelligence experts. The same is true of instrumentalities for collecting certain information: better cameras permitted more detailed photographic coverage and more sensitive radios better monitoring of the electronic spectrum. And these improvements only accelerated after the war, to the point where satellites now supplement or even replace aircraft or ground stations for the collection of many types of overhead imagery, signal, electronic emission, or other measurement information.

The melding of all these materials with general knowledge or that from open sources became well understood during World War II and has been the model ever since. The net result has provided intelligence analysts with an unmatched (and previously unattainable) fund of material from which to draw their conclusions. These sources and methods developed in World War II became the mainstay of the Cold War CIA and have evolved further since.

The first and last of our subject functions, that is collection and counterintelligence, have forever been the staples of intelligence organizations the world over. Among the most distinctive properties of U.S. intelligence since World War II is its very intense focus on the *analysis* of information. Where most foreign equivalent agencies collect information but leave their bosses or overseers to draw what conclusions they may, from its very inception in 1947 the Central Intelligence Agency (CIA) created special offices for the interpretation of that information. From 1950 on the CIA has had a directorate—a component consisting of multiple offices—engaged in this work. Other agencies, most prominently the Defense Intelligence Agency, and armed services intelligence components, followed suit and created their own analytical offices. Some agencies, notably the Bureau of Intelligence and Research at the Department of State, exist *solely* as analytical units. In the U.S. system the interpretation of data has also been carried to a very high level with the elaboration of "National Intelligence Estimates" (NIEs), reports that not only interpret information but that incorporate the views of all the relevant agencies of the U.S. intelligence community.

One phenomenon largely absent during World War II, probably because of the unity of common purpose among participants, has been the effort of some, occasionally both players of the intelligence game or recipients of the intelligence product, to shape the contents of the reporting. This kind of intervention in the pure analytical process is often called "politicization" and it has exercised undue influence at various moments in the postwar history of U.S. intelligence.

Surveyed over the decades the modern U.S. intelligence community took and improved upon the World War II experience to become the most effective practitioners of the trade in the world, and probably in history. Some would argue that America's ability to spend as much money on intelligence as it did has been the main driver in this evolution. In truth without the synergism of understanding the pillars of intelligence collection plus the conscientious effort analysts apply to evaluating information from all sources, U.S. intelligence performance would be nowhere nearly as good as it has been.

Today, in the light of intelligence failures in preventing the September 11, 2001, attacks on the United States and the question of whether Iraq possessed weapons of mass destruction the following year, there is a tendency to see the CIA and other agencies as ineffective, poorly managed agencies incapable of coming to correct conclusions. In actuality the recent failures are merely the latest expressions of the tension that has constantly existed in the secrets race—grabbing and guessing at the inner truth as against defending it in the larger world of espionage and analysis versus counterintelligence, as affected by the political interests inherent in the system. Looking at the Cold War history of U.S. intelligence reveals many previous cycles in this race, with remarkable successes to match the failures. Making such a survey will also show much about the properties of the secrets race itself.

EARLY COLD WAR

By far the most important secret at the outset of the Cold War involved the design and details of how to build an atomic bomb. Especially since U.S. declassification of the VENONA decryption program in 1995 (about which more in a moment), whole forests have been felled to print texts that focused on Soviet acquisition of these secrets through espionage. Most of these accounts lose sight of basic realities of weapons innovation, development, and production. Every weapon is created through an essential process of intellectual conception, design, prototype testing and engineering development, and then production. Original concepts for the atomic bomb were inherent in the literature of physics, and the basic secret—that an atomic bomb could be created—the United States demonstrated publicly in an unmistakable way when it used these weapons against the Japanese cities Hiroshima and Nagasaki in August 1945.

Beyond that everything lay in the details. What we know today about Russian development of atomic weapons shows that the Soviet program began at a time when Soviet officials could not have had significant knowledge of the American program known as the "Manhattan Project." Soviet physicists had proposed creating a weapon using atomic separation in May 1942 and a laboratory was established in February 1943. In the United States the Manhattan Engineering District and the consequent Los Alamos laboratory were created in the summer of 1942. It would be more accurate to argue that the wartime strain on resources (and Russia's smaller resource base) hindered Soviet atomic development through much of the war, and that Russians could make U.S. nuclear weapons an intelligence target precisely because they were already interested in similar instrumentalities.

The Russians might have learned about what had to be the atomic bomb; nonetheless, no Soviet agent held a position with access to relevant technical information before May 1942, and there is no record of that agent at that time being actively in contact with Russian handlers. The first reference to "Enormoz," the dedicated project to obtain atomic secrets for Russia, occurs in a November 1942 cable and confirms that Soviet spies had yet to set up an effective network in this area. None of this is to say that agents like Alan Nunn May, Bruno Pontecorvo, Klaus Fuchs, David Greenglass, and Theodore Hall did not pass along U.S. bomb secrets to the Russians, but it does show that the best the atomic spies achieved would be to smooth the way for the Soviet atomic program, not to initiate it. The first Soviet atomic bomb, called RDS-1, would be detonated near Semipalatinsk on August 26, 1949, and is recorded as largely copied from one of the U.S. wartime designs.

The purpose of counterintelligence is to defend secrets, and strict security naturally applied to everything to do with the atomic bomb. But the spy-catchers never caught the agents at Los Alamos. Instead Nunn May, the first of the atomic spies to be uncovered, was first exposed by the defection of a Soviet intelligence officer in Canada in 1945. Fuchs confessed to British security after the exposure of his activities had been discovered through VENONA, the codename for a U.S. program that attempted to decrypt Soviet intelligence messages collected by the security services from the cable companies that transmitted them. Pontecorvo, who had worked with Fuchs, quickly fled to Russia, while the others, along with celebrated Soviet agents Harry Gold, David Greenglass, and Julius and Ethel Rosenberg, were swept up later as their espionage was also revealed from VENONA traffic. What exactly the Russians derived from their Enormoz effort, and who else may have been a Soviet spy—allegations include the physicist J. Robert Oppenheimer, scientific chief of the Manhattan Project—remains in dispute.

The atomic spy saga illustrates a key feature of the secrets war, one to do with the counterintelligence mission. Like the Russian spies in this early period, agents are most often caught as a result of defections of intelligence officers from the country for which they are spying (or revelations from such officers who remain in place to spy for the other side, so-called moles or double agents), or from problems with their communications with their handlers. This pattern has been replicated throughout the Cold War and beyond.

Meanwhile the question of the Russian development of the atomic bomb formed a key intelligence issue of the time for analysts as well. Projections made shortly after World War II by both the civilian predecessors to the CIA and the Joint Intelligence Group, a unit serving the Joint Chiefs of Staff that modeled itself on the British Joint Intelligence Committee, foresaw the Russians needing five years to craft an atomic bomb. In 1945 that estimate was nearly accurate for the Russian bomb *including whatever contributions resulted from Soviet espionage*. But as time passed after 1945 and there remained no hard data on Russian atomic development, the five-year interval was simply advanced into the future. As a result, when the Russians achieved their nuclear weapon in 1949 U.S. analysts would be caught out in an intelligence failure. The mistaken projection provides an early example of the huge importance of assumptions in making estimative projections, another recurrent issue in the intelligence business. At the same time the near-accuracy of the original U.S. estimate of the date at which the Soviets might achieve a nuclear weapon demonstrates the sterility of the VENONA debate over the impact of Russian espionage—without spies the U.S. estimate would have remained accurate, even given the postponements, for a longer period of time, and the Soviets would have needed more time to craft their weapon.

Now a comment on the relative importance of kinds of secrets: in spite of any value they drew from their atomic spying a fair argument can be made that in the immediate postwar years the Russians derived more value from scientific and technical intelligence. This is because they were able to draw on German and U.S. technology in the Soviet Union. By "reverse engineering," or systematically taking apart an item and copying it, which is made possible by technical intelligence, the Russians were able to produce their first long-range heavy bomber (a copy of the U.S. B-29, several of which had had to make forced landings in Russia) as well as a fleet of high performance submarines (copied from the German Types XXI and XXIII). These weapons systems gave Soviet officials a means of delivering an atomic bomb once they had it, as well as a way to challenge command of the seas, both of which were of huge military importance during that era.

After 1949 the key intelligence questions for CIA and Defense Department analysts shifted. When would the Russians have enough atomic bombs to mount a truly devastating attack on the United States (in other words, the size of the Soviet stockpile), when would they achieve the thermonuclear bomb, and when would they have an intercontinental bomber? American spies looked for information on Russian production and imports of weapons-grade uranium and associated strategic minerals, while analysts theorized on the quantity of nuclear materials consumed by the Soviet bomb design. By mid-1950 the CIA's National Intelligence Estimates projected a Soviet stockpile of 10–20 atomic bombs at that moment, rising to 70–135 by 1953 and 200 by the end of 1954. Other CIA reports held that once Russia attained a stockpile of 200 weapons with suitable intercontinental delivery systems, a crippling attack on the United States would become possible. We now know that the Soviets had assembled five atomic bombs by mid-1950 and that they began serial production of weapons late that year. The first stockpile estimate had been close to the mark. Even today, however, time-series data are not yet available to evaluate intelligence estimates of the Soviet weapons stockpile extending into the later 1950s.

Where we do have data is on delivery systems, specifically Soviet intercontinental bombers. The early Russian copy of the B-29 lacked the unrefueled range to reach targets in much of the United States. In 1953 and 1954 respectively the Soviets introduced a turboprop and then a jet bomber with intercontinental ranges. U.S. officials first learned of these aircraft from observation by military attachés in Moscow during ceremonial flyovers, that is to say, human intelligence. Other human intelligence efforts were mounted to obtain a sample of the metal used in the airframes of the planes. The intellectual ingenuity of the U.S. intelligence effort is illustrated by the fact that the CIA and other agencies then organized a panel that combined intelligence analysts with aviation engineers and experts to estimate the performance characteristics of the Russian heavy bombers and help attain production estimates. The difference in the numbers of bombers seen during successive flyovers was taken as an indication of production rates. Intelligence analysts also estimated the square footage of space in Soviet aircraft production plants (as would later be done for missiles), apportioning the total to various types of planes including the bombers.

The eventual NIE projections for the Soviet bomber inventory generated through the use of these methods were wild overestimates. Russian sources record that the jet bomber in its original version proved disappointing and failed to attain the range actually necessary to attack the United States. Just ten were built and an improved model only became available in 1958. As for the turboprop aircraft, the first two assembly-line models were completed in August 1955. Like the jet it suffered from underpowered engines. Russian designers tinkered with various versions for decades, but fewer than 150 ever entered service. Flying in the face of this history, the U.S. national estimate approved in May 1955 put *current* Soviet heavy bomber strength at 20 of each type, projecting 600 total by 1958 and peak strength of 700 by 1959. At these strengths Russian aircraft production would be greater than that of the United States, leading to a belief in a "Bomber Gap" that favored the Soviets. Instead the gap was between actual Soviet strength and that estimated in the NIEs.

Underestimates in projecting Soviet bomber strength were virtually un-avoidable given the paucity of hard intelligence on Soviet aircraft production capacity. Well aware of the information deficit, a 1954 scientific study carried out for the Eisenhower administration, the Technological Capabilities Panel (TCP), argued that the highest priority should be given to measures designed to enhance intelligence collection. Usually associated with the CIA's push to create the U-2 spyplane, developed in 1954–1955, the TCP report actually stimulated a broad range of intelligence technology programs that revolu-tionized the spy business.

INTELLIGENCE COMES OF AGE

The mid-1950s brought a new level of synergism to the pillars of intelli-gence collection. The Soviet Union and its bloc remained the main targets and yet they were "closed societies," controlling the movement of their populations (and almost everything else), making it extremely difficult for the CIA to recruit spies other than those who volunteered for that most dangerous job. But the push to acquire new sources of hard data brought the era of what the later CIA director Richard M. Helms would call the "machine spy." Gathering intelligence by technological means had a number of important advantages: activities of the machine collectors could be targeted, their output was reliable, it was massive, and performance could be monitored and re-directed with great ease. Though the technology systems were expensive, at the time the relief at access to hard information obscured that factor.

Technological Spying: The U-2 and Other Interception Projects

Between 1955 and 1961 a number of high technology intelligence collec-tion systems came on line. Possibly the best known is the tunnel that operated in Berlin (between 1954 and 1956) to tap a direct telephone cable in the Soviet zone that yielded masses of taped conversations between Moscow and senior Soviet officials (and intelligence officers) in East Germany. But the Berlin tunnel, which soon disappeared anyway, would be dwarfed by the other collectors. In 1955 the United States erected massive communications in-terception stations in Turkey to supplement those already in Germany. Sta-tions in Japan and the Philippines were upgraded. Similar arrangements were made with Norway with interception activity beginning that summer. Sta-tions to monitor the test signals (telemetry) sent by Russian rockets on their flight tests opened in Iran in the late 1950s, and to watch the tests by means of over-the-horizon radar from Pakistan in 1961. Submarine interception ac-tivities had begun off the Soviet coast in 1949 to a new high level. Aircraft were equipped to record the emissions of Soviet radars. The CIA formed a Photographic Interpretation Division in 1953 to extract national intelligence data from overhead imagery, and that unit received an armload of new business once the U-2 began flying. Agency scientists and aviation engineers designed a spyplane a generation past the U-2—the SR-71—which began flying in the early 1960s. Finally the CIA developed the necessary cameras and other systems to obtain useful overhead imagery from space, and designed reconnaissance satellites (code named CORONA) to carry that equipment, which became operational in 1960. The armload of photography became a boatload. In fact it would be in 1961 that the old imagery analysis unit at CIA had to be expanded into a new National Photographic Interpretation Center (NPIC). It was also at this time that computer data processing began to be applied to the task of comparing images with known data about and previous images of the same targets. In summary, a new tension developed between technological (expensive but easy) and human (serendipitous and difficult) collection.

The U-2 began the trend right away by debunking the Bomber Gap. Spyplanes photographed all of the Soviet strategic aircraft bases, and when the photo interpreters counted up the heavy bombers on the tarmac they added up to only a handful. The 1958 NIE put Soviet bomber strength at less than fifty and correctly surmised that the Russians might be building more of their turboprop aircraft than the jet ones, which seemed a technological throwback.

A new gap already stood on the horizon, however. The "Missile Gap" replicated the experience with bomber aircraft except this time the CIA and other analysts wrestled over the prospective numbers of Soviet intercontinental ballistic missiles (ICBMs). Again controversy focused on production rates and the number to be expected in the Soviet arsenal in future years.

An Air Force U-2 Dragon Lady flies a training mission. (Courtesy of U.S. Air Force, photo by Master Sgt. Rose Reynolds).

Once more U.S. analysts lacked hard data. The U-2 could not cover enough of Russia and its flights were personally controlled by President Eisenhower, while reconnaissance satellites were not yet available. The CIA employed an outside panel of experts to help hypothesize data for projections. Scraps of information were generalized to huge proportions. This time Americans were frightened by the Soviet launches of an ICBM carrying the first space satellite, Sputnik, into orbit on October 4 and November 3, 1957. The hint that America might be behind in the drive to develop science and technology, seized upon by Soviet premier Nikita Khrushchev to make a series of public claims about Soviet missile prowess, could not be refuted by the CIA's available information. By chance the U-2 had photographed the first Russian ICBM on the launch pad shortly before its test. The Agency knew that the Soviet claim to have flown such a rocket to be accurate.

Projections of the number of Soviet ICBMs to be expected three or five years hence soon grew into the thousands. The claims of military intelligence were even higher, sometimes at double the numbers. In 1954 a National Intelligence Estimate on Soviet guided missiles had predicted that the Russians might have an ICBM ready for series production by 1960 at the earliest. Just a month before the first Russian flight test, essentially the same prediction was written into a 1957 NIE. But a year later the national estimates predicted 500 Soviet ICBMs for 1960 and 1,000 for 1961. The 1959 NIE cut back this projection to 50 by 1960, but still anticipated 450–560 by mid-1963. Air Force estimates were even higher. The high resolution imagery from the U-2 could not settle the issue because it could not cover all of Russia, while the extensive machine spies aimed at Russian missile testing also could not help since they did not monitor production. In the summer of 1960, when the CORONA reconnaissance satellites became available, they failed to find the extensive base systems necessary to field the predicted Russian ICBM force. In this case human intelligence settled the problem. A Russian military intelligence officer, Colonel Oleg Penkovsky, had volunteered to spy for the CIA, and among his reports was the information that, even a year afterwards, the Russians had only *four* functional ICBMs.

As in the case of predictions about the Russian atomic bomb, the earliest American estimates of ICBM development had been accurate, but the projections became more and more erroneous as the anticipated events came closer. In the case of the alleged Missile Gap, Russian military power became a political issue in the days after Sputnik, triggering tremendous pressure on intelligence analysts to draw their conclusions a certain way. Data did improve, and by 1960 the estimates were already somewhat less alarmist, but in that year Democratic presidential candidate John F. Kennedy campaigned partly on the issue that the Eisenhower administration had ignored the Missile Gap. Kennedy was elected, and shortly after he took office in 1961 the CIA received the reports that confirmed that the Missile Gap ran in favor of the United States, not Russia.

The Cuban Missile Crisis

Almost immediately thereafter occurred the Cuban Missile Crisis of October 1962. Agent reports led to suspicions among senior CIA officials, including DCI John McCone, who argued that the arrival of Soviet surface-to-air missiles in Cuba had the purpose of shielding more serious activity. Liaison reports from foreign intelligence services, including those of the French and certain Latin American nations, were also important. Then U-2 flights secured imagery that showed missile bases under construction. The Penkovsky information gave photo interpreters the necessary knowledge to establish that the prospective missile bases were for Soviet intermediate- and medium-range ballistic missiles. The new data controverted a series of the Agency's Special National Intelligence Estimates (SNIEs) of March, August, and September 1962 that had concluded that the Russians would not send long-range missiles to Cuba. CIA analysts had assumed that the Soviet Union would not permit nuclear weapons to be stationed outside Russia. Decades later historical research established—and the CIA had apparently missed this at the time—that the Russians had had a brigade of nuclear-armed tactical missiles in East Germany in 1959.

The subsequent missile crisis became the showcase for current intelligence reporting—such publications as the *Central Intelligence Weekly* and *National Intelligence Daily*, along with the President's Daily Bulletin (then called the President's Intelligence Checklist) had been important throughout the history of Cold War intelligence, though they have not been touched upon here previously. The daily reporting converted the latest indications obtained from signals intelligence, field observations, military intelligence, and overhead imagery into a stream of data that constantly updated U.S. officials, enabling President John Kennedy and his Executive Committee of the National Security Council, for example, to make informed decisions on the crisis and, later, to watch the Soviet withdrawal of their offensive weapons from Cuba.

Events in Cuba also furnish a glimpse into how imagination can be brought to bear on the analyst's task. An excellent example was the new practice of "cratology," which identified items based upon their shipping containers. This practice sprang from 1961 exchanges between NPIC and the Office of Naval Intelligence over the creation of a collection guide that naval observers, especially at the Bosporus, could use to report on deck cargoes aboard Soviet vessels exiting the Black Sea. The Soviet jet bombers and fighters sent to Cuba would be recognized specifically as a result of cratology. Similar innovations in analytical technique have taken place throughout Cold War intelligence history, though some have been more successful than others. Statistical techniques applied to the Sino-Soviet border disputes of the late 1960s have consistently shown a much greater probability of full-scale war than events demonstrated (no war eventuated). In a most recent case, "alternative" analysis of an alleged alliance between Iraqi leader Saddam Hussein and terrorist chieftain Osama bin Laden showed such an alliance where none existed.

The CORONA Project and Communications Interception

Technical innovations matched the analytical ones. The CORONA spy satellites (which were first authorized in 1958 and became operational in 1960) became increasingly capable, with longer focal-length cameras and more film capsules to sustain a longer useful service life. The United States innovated separate lines of satellites for area coverage and detailed photography; infrared cameras for night photography, shadow elimination, and other applications; radar satellites for observation through cloud cover and to cover the sea; and early work would be performed on creating a "stealth" satellite, one that was not observable from the ground and which could therefore catch the adversary unaware of the spying. The 1960s also brought the advent of the communications intelligence satellite, replacing ground stations with "big ears" in space. In addition, naval vessels were equipped for communications interception, and for missile test tracking and telemetry interception. The Gulf of Tonkin incident of the Vietnam War (1964), the Middle East Six-day War incident involving the *Liberty* (1967), and the *Pueblo* incident off the North Korean coast (1968) all involved U.S. naval vessels engaged in intelligence collection.

The Polyakov Defection and HUMINT

By contrast, espionage through recruiting human spies (HUMINT) became more and more difficult. The agent Penkovsky, for example, whom the Soviets arrested at the height of the Cuban Missile Crisis, was executed in May 1963. Meanwhile, in 1961 another Soviet intelligence officer, Dimitri Polyakov, who rose to become a lieutenant general in the Russian military spy service, volunteered to spy for the United States. Over more than two decades case officers from both the FBI and CIA ran Polyakov, who proved crucial in identifying Soviet spies who were being sent to the West. Without doubt Polyakov became the most valuable U.S.-recruited agent of this period, but his case also demonstrates something else about human intelligence, at least in the arena of Cold War state-against-state espionage: spies most frequently affect the work of other spies rather than reveal great state secrets. The spies fuelled a sub rosa counterintelligence war between Russia and the United States. Indeed, the Soviets struck hard through the 1960s with a series of defectors whose information implicated all sorts of senior CIA and British secret service officers as possible Russian spies, and rocked these services back on their heels in futile efforts to find the real moles. One result was that the clandestine collection by the CIA was virtually paralyzed. By 1967 an Agency management survey (the Cunningham Report) comparing technical collection and espionage concluded that human intelligence absolutely had to be improved.

Not coincidentally, *every* policy or management review of U.S. intelligence since that time has concurred in the recommendation to improve human intelligence collection. Technological change remains more certain than spy recruitment and therefore more dependable. The machine spies have been in the ascendancy since the 1960s. At that time, however, the targets of U.S. collecting were the types most amenable to technical collection: missiles and rockets, nuclear submarines, tank divisions. The trend in recent years has been away from those targets and toward secret networks such as drug traffickers or terrorist groups. Human intelligence here is clearly more important than the machine spies.

To return to the period of the 1960s, the importance of acquiring intelligence on Soviet strategic missiles was equaled only by that of reporting on Soviet missile defenses. Both these debates proceeded simultaneously. The 1957 NIE had observed that no Soviet ballistic missile defense could be deployed before mid-1962. The national estimate for 1960 assessed missile defense as "overshadowing all other potential claimants for resources," but concluded that in spite of intensive effort over many years the Soviets had failed to develop a satisfactory defensive system. In late 1961 Russian leaders and military commanders claimed to have solved the problem of destroying ICBMs in flight. The CIA had some evidence that Russia had begun limited deployment of defensive forces, and photos from around Leningrad strengthened that impression. There were also the beginnings of development around Moscow, and an estimate that appeared in the midst of the Cuban crisis foresaw a dangerous Soviet defense potential by 1967. In the 1963 NIE the analysts concluded that the Leningrad system would achieve some operational capability that year, but that there was no concrete basis for a technical judgment, while the general state of Soviet technology remained such that it was unlikely that the Leningrad system could be effective. That same year satellites brought back imagery of construction around Tallinn (now in Estonia), and a new defensive missile appeared within months. Based on the notion of a nationwide deployment, estimates were written predicting a Russian missile defense with thousands of interceptors.

The Directorate of Science and Technology

The CIA moved to strengthen its analytical capability in science and technology fields in 1962–1963 with the establishment of a Directorate of Science and Technology (DS&T), and the scientists took the lead on analyzing the intelligence on Soviet missile defense. They quickly abandoned the notion that the Tallinn system had a missile defense purpose. In 1965 the NIE consensus predicted a small Russian missile defense capability around Moscow and saw the Tallinn system as intended for high-altitude air defense. The

Defense Intelligence Agency and Air Force intelligence disagreed, as they would continue to do through the 1960s and into the 1970s, when they argued that the missiles associated with the Tallinn system were designed in such a fashion as to permit an instant breach of arms control agreements by upgrading for use against ICBMs. The national estimates continued to maintain that Tallinn had no ballistic missile defense capability and the Soviets' Moscow system only a limited one. The NIEs proved correct.

Assessments of Soviet offensive nuclear forces continued to be the other side of the equation in the Soviet estimates. In the mid-1970s strategic analyst Albert Wohlstetter made a considerable splash with a series of studies in which he concluded that the NIEs of the 1960s had systematically underestimated the pace and scope of Soviet ICBM deployment due to pressures for conformity and the power of consensus. In general, however, the NIEs did a good job in their assessments on that which was directly observable—Soviet ICBM launchers that were under construction were reflected in projections for a few years into the future but after that the numbers the Russians actually built diverged more and more from those that U.S. intelligence predicted. Wohlstetter's charges were correct on one level: long-range prediction did fall short of Soviet achievements. But claims that the CIA systematically underestimated as a form of compensation for the exaggerations of the Missile Gap era were highly oversimplified and misleading. An element of fear of falling into another Missile Gap trap did exist, but no systematic underestimation occurred. During this same period CIA projections on Soviet ballistic missile defense *were* accurate (or overestimated), long-range bomber strengths were overestimated, and in a most vital area—the date at which the Soviets would field a multiple independently-targetable reentry vehicle (MIRV)–equipped ICBM—the NIEs were exactly accurate, *ten years* before the fact.

Aside from issues of intelligence evidence, this debate again turns on assumptions. A couple of hundred ICBMs in the discrepancies of the 1960s underestimates are accounted for by the assumption that the Soviets would retire their oldest, clunkiest rockets as they brought new ones online. The same thing happened in the early 1970s when Russia deployed fourth-generation ICBMs but retained the light missiles of the mid-1960s that the CIA assumed would be scrapped. Similarly the entire discrepancy in Soviet bomber numbers is accounted for by an assumption in the NIEs that wastage would reduce Soviet numbers whereas the Russians produced just enough aircraft to make good these losses.

In retrospect the most important intelligence dispute of this era that concerned nuclear forces had to do with qualitative improvements, specifically the issue of the Soviet MIRV. Treated as a purely technical proposition, in 1965 CIA scientific experts foresaw a Russian MIRV capability in a decade. As the Johnson administration gave way to Richard Nixon's in 1969, a new emphasis on deploying U.S. ballistic missile defenses led to Pentagon pressures on the CIA to project a near-term MIRV threat. A certain Soviet ICBM modification then in testing, the Pentagon argued, had this capability. The CIA resisted this analysis, despite pressures from both the Pentagon and the White House. DCI Richard M. Helms dropped a paragraph from the 1969 NIE that held that the Soviets were not seeking a first-strike nuclear capability based upon the SS-9 missile. This buckling to outside pressure, widely resented among CIA analysts, was far more representative of politicization than the ICBM projections that Wohlstetter had criticized. In observations of a 1970 test, the SS-9 Mod 4 ICBM exhibited some characteristics suggesting that the Soviets might have selected a certain path toward perfecting MIRV systems, as would then be noted in the national estimate. The Russians actually fielded a MIRVed system with their fourth-generation SS-18 missile in December 1974.

VIETNAM

With the Soviet-American rivalry in full swing, U.S. intelligence was simultaneously challenged by a regional conflict. That was the Vietnam War. The Vietnam experience also provides a window into intelligence effectiveness in wartime and is important for that reason. The United States had become embroiled in Vietnam dating from the late 1940s, when the conflict there pitted the Indochinese of Vietnam, Laos, and Cambodia against the French. The CIA had followed the war in some detail since at least 1950, and special estimates and NIEs on Vietnam began at that time. But the degree of U.S. effort built to a much higher level than the brief intelligence on Russian military developments. Beginning from 1952 and building throughout the decade and into the 1960s, the CIA became involved in action programs in South Vietnam and Laos especially, and to some degree in Cambodia as well. Though such projects are not our subject here, other aspects of U.S. intelligence activity in Southeast Asia had a definite impact upon the business of collecting information and following war developments and should therefore be kept in mind as we survey this history.

The Southeast Asian conflict especially highlights the importance of human intelligence. This war had an unusual twist, however. The South Vietnamese and Laotian governments were de facto U.S. allies. Their officials developed a wide range of connections to the CIA and other U.S. agencies as the result of operational programs, yet at the same time the governments were targets for U.S. spying. Thus there were phenomena such as the CIA bugging the offices of the Saigon leadership, and recruiting South Vietnamese officials as agents, at the same time many of those same officials were active in programs aimed at the adversary.

Meanwhile, that adversary combined a guerrilla insurgency, led by the National Front for the Liberation of South Vietnam (NLF), and the more conventional forces of the Democratic Republic of Vietnam (the DRV, or North Vietnam). Clandestine recruitment of agents on the other side proved extremely difficult. Even at the height of U.S. intelligence success, during the accelerated pacification campaigns of 1968–1971, the best U.S. sources (with one exception) tended to be low-level operatives of the guerrilla infrastructure. The exception, a senior DRV diplomat who worked in Hanoi and later served in the Vietnamese embassy in China, remains a shadowy figure of whom not a great deal is known, including just how useful he became to U.S. intelligence. In his memoirs Richard Helms acknowledges the virtual total absence of defectors from North Vietnam and the limited value of interrogating prisoners. He adds, "In the ten years of our most intense efforts we tried every operational approach in the book, and committed our most experienced field operatives to the effort to get inside the government in Hanoi. What had worked successfully against the U.S.S.R. and its Eastern European cohort failed in North Vietnam."

Technical means were plentiful but never made up the difference. Army radio intelligence detachments arrived in Vietnam as early as 1961. Tactical photographic reconnaissance began in 1962 and quickly became massive, continuing throughout the war. Naval vessels conducted intelligence interception from early 1964, and one of these missions resulted in the Gulf of Tonkin incident that August. There were periodic U-2 flights, and the CIA version of the SR-71 (Oxcart) was briefly active over North Vietnam in 1967. After 1971, when digital photography with radio readout became available on reconnaissance satellites, satellite photography also became more routine. Technical collection was massive throughout the conflict.

On the other side of the hill the adversary's intelligence collection against the United States relied upon the very human intelligence that CIA officials found impossible to conduct. Moreover, CIA and Saigon counterintelligence, despite occasional successes, were never able to eliminate the North Vietnamese or NLF networks. With Vietnamese families often divided on both sides of the war there were natural routes for potential recruiting. Even at official levels the desire to pass messages to the other side, send out secret diplomatic feelers, or just check the pulse on the other side increased the opportunities for spying. Being Vietnamese, the enemy also found it far easier to operate in the Vietnamese milieu than Americans. These problems were never solved, and with the fall of South Vietnam in 1975, the number and high posts of many of those who revealed themselves as agents suggests the huge dimensions of this problem.

In short, during the Vietnam conflict U.S. intelligence benefited from very good collection on our allies, on political, diplomatic, and military aspects of the war, coupled with very poor data on the enemy being fought. Conversely the North Vietnamese enjoyed excellent intelligence on South Vietnam, and very good collection against U.S. tactical targets if not strategic plans.

Despite difficulties in collection and problems in counterintelligence, American analysts compiled a record of substantial accuracy during the Vietnam War. The CIA furnished the White House excellent intelligence on

South Vietnamese political trends, good material on the National Liberation Front and North Vietnamese leaders—in terms of their backgrounds and policy incentives if not their actual decisions—and effective intelligence on the progress of the war. The CIA and the State Department's Bureau of Intelligence and Research (INR) saw mostly eye-to-eye in their assessments, which reported little progress in the U.S. effort. The military intelligence agencies tended to a more pessimistic view than the civilian agencies in their predictions of the threat, and more optimistic in their conclusions about U.S. military effectiveness. Possibly the key intelligence disputes of the war concerned the impact of U.S. bombing on North Vietnam, the likelihood of Chinese or Soviet intervention in the war, the size of the North Vietnamese and National Liberation Front armed forces, and certain associated questions of infiltration of Hanoi's troops and supplies into South Vietnam.

On the air war the civilian agencies remained cautious throughout. U.S. bombing of the DRV began in February 1965. Regularized in an air campaign called ROLLING THUNDER, and soon elevated to a program of thousands of attack sorties per month, the bombing campaign sought to impede North Vietnamese infiltration, raise the cost of that activity, and induce the DRV to negotiate with the United States. The military constantly reported progress, great strides in the effectiveness of bombing, including in certain special initiatives, such as a campaign against Hanoi's petroleum storage facilities in 1966, another against the DRV's electric power generation capacity in the spring of 1967, or one against Haiphong that summer. In time, Secretary of Defense Robert S. McNamara became so leery of military claims of progress that he asked the CIA to join with his Defense Intelligence Agency (DIA) in furnishing periodic analyses of the impact of the bombing, as a mechanism for forcing more realistic reporting by military intelligence. In the summer of 1967 McNamara publicly testified before Congress, based on the CIA reporting and in open disagreement with the Joint Chiefs of Staff, that the bombing of North Vietnam was ineffective.

The potential for Soviet and Chinese intervention in the Vietnam War, another key intelligence question, was also the subject of numerous Special National Intelligence Estimates (SNIEs) throughout the period, but especially during 1964–1966. The estimators showed a healthy wariness of the dangers, an assessment which informed President Johnson, who avoided policy choices that could have forced Moscow and Beijing to intervene. The CIA for a time underestimated the number of Chinese support troops serving in North Vietnam, and later failed to notice when Beijing began withdrawing its forces, but the Agency caught up on both counts. Inability to flag these events at the moment they occurred underscores the difficulties inherent in technical intelligence collection mechanisms tracking unconventional warfare activities. On the Soviet side, U.S. intelligence suspected but was never able to demonstrate that the Russians were actually flying North Vietnamese aircraft and operating DRV surface-to-air missiles, which they did do on a top-secret basis at various times during the war.

The size of DRV and NLF forces, the "order of battle" in conventional military terminology, remained a crucial issue throughout. During the period 1967–1969 it became caught up in the political question of the level of U.S. progress in the war. The U.S. command in Vietnam, supported by DIA in Washington and certain service intelligence branches, argued that the enemy had reached a "cross-over point" at which their rate of recruitment and in-filtration no longer matched their losses. Thus the enemy was shrinking and the war was being won (a variant of this dispute later took place regarding the size of the guerrilla infrastructure). CIA analysts believed the enemy to be stronger than the military admitted; their use of captured documents led to deriving a strength analysis higher than that of military intelligence. Con-ferences in Saigon and Washington in 1967 favored the military, though a few concessions were made to the CIA point of view. As a consequence, when the massive Tet Offensive occurred in January 1968 the U.S. military failed to anticipate the adversary's ability to act throughout the country, and over-estimated the degree of its success, since the enemy order of battle was sig-nificantly larger than it admitted.

Another question related to that of the North Vietnamese order of battle was that of DRV infiltration into the South. North Vietnamese troops had to come down the Ho Chi Minh Trail through Laos, but there were differ-ences in the analysts' estimates of the proportion of supplies that were moved overland through Laos versus those by sea through Cambodia. Beginning in late 1967 the United States attained improved communications intelligence interception against the Ho Chi Minh Trail and further refined its estimates of personnel infiltration. On the supply question, military intelligence performed better than the CIA, which held onto projections of seaborne infiltration through Cambodia that underestimated the adversary's supply flow by a large margin. In 1969–1970 clandestine collection, and then records revealed to the United States by the Cambodian government, confirmed that the military estimates had been within 5 percent of the actual amount.

Wartime conditions also raised the specific question of the ability of American intelligence to warn of various events, most prominently the assorted North Vietnamese offensives that took place. The Tet Offensive launched on January 30, 1968 came as one surprise. U.S. intelligence had expected a battle, but only a specific combat action on one front with a few diversionary attacks, but not the countrywide offensive that took place. An earlier North Viet-namese offensive of 1965, with its associated intervention of Hanoi's regular troops, had also come as a surprise, as did Hanoi's final war-winning offensive of 1975, when U.S. officials expected a continuation of a grinding-down opera-tion. On the other hand, the U.S. analysts successfully anticipated Hanoi's Easter Offensive of 1972, as well as the scale of its response to the Laotian invasion of 1971 (American and Saigon leaders in 1971 proceeded in the face of the intelligence to carry out this attack).

Meanwhile, propelled in part by revelations that the U.S. government had secretly spied upon American citizens who opposed the Vietnam War, in 1975 both the U.S. Senate and the House of Representatives launched investigations of the CIA and other agencies. While that is a subject for another page, a conclusion of one of the investigations, conducted by the Church Committee, is worth recording in this treatment of intelligence collection: the CIA did not put enough emphasis on human intelligence.

RETRENCHMENT AND REAGAN

The American war in Vietnam ended in 1975, and the major U.S. combat role in 1972. Afterwards the CIA and the U.S. intelligence community were reduced in size. These impacted mostly on the Directorate of Operations, but there was some retrenchment among the analysts as well. The system for drafting National Intelligence Estimates changed in 1973, replacing a corporate board–style process with a collection of National Intelligence Officers (NIOs) who held specific portfolios, commissioned the draft papers, and supervised the writing. In 1979 the set of NIOs became a National Intelligence Council, a system that still exists today. The final product had to meet the standards of the CIA director and the National Foreign Intelligence Board. This arrangement remains essentially the same today, except that the Director of National Intelligence is the official having final approval of the NIEs as a result of legislation enacted in 2004.

The first NIEs using this new procedure were crafted in 1975. More open than the previous system, this process is easier to influence. The old Board of National Estimates had had a certain corporate identity and integrity; the new National Intelligence Council, in contrast, is composed of individual National Intelligence Officers with concerns about getting along with others, reputations to uphold, and consciousness of expectations upon them. Immediately, the responsible NIO commissioned the 1975 Soviet estimate from a former agency analyst with known conservative views on Russia.

The Team B Exercise

The 1976 edition of the NIE would be powerfully influenced by an experiment in "alternative analysis" called the Team B exercise. This time an entire panel of conservative officials were assembled with a writ to write their own version of the NIE, a "competitive analysis." The group instead carried out a wide-ranging critique of CIA analysis on the Soviet Union, condemning the NIEs and the Agency's analysis on issue after issue, and advancing three specific technical areas where the panel felt the NIEs had been especially deficient. The Soviets wanted nuclear war and wanted to win it, according to Team B; the Soviets also had much higher ICBM accuracy than the CIA accepted, much better capability to combat U.S. missile submarines, and much more capable manned bombers than the CIA gave them credit for. By this view the Soviets were close to attaining a war survival capability and could disarm the United States in a nuclear first strike against American ICBMs. Team B's analysis, recorded in its report of December 2, 1976, was rejected by President-elect Carter but resurfaced during Ronald Reagan's campaign challenging President Carter in 1980 under what became known as the "window of vulnerability" issue. Reagan won the election partly on the strength of this allegation. By the mid-1980s observations of Russian ICBM tests and refining of earlier data demonstrated that the Soviets had never achieved the levels of accuracy and performance that would have made the window of vulnerability real.

The People's Republic of China

Another focus of intelligence involved the People's Republic of China (PRC). Between 1948 and 1976 U.S. intelligence produced no fewer than 240 estimates that dealt in some way with the PRC. Among key subjects during the earliest years were questions about Sino-Soviet relations—whether Moscow controlled Beijing, the relationship of both to the Third World and other communist countries, and the solidity of the Sino-Soviet alliance. CIA analysts also assessed questions of war and peace, Beijing's intentions vis-à-vis Taiwan, and whether the PRC would invade the offshore islands of Quemoy and Matsu or Taiwan itself. Analysts held that the PRC would not risk an open confrontation with the United States. In the 1960s U.S. intelligence described a variety of circumstances that could bring Chinese intervention in Vietnam, and they observed Beijing's involvement as it unfolded. The success of Mao Zedong's attempts at economic reform posed a key question, as did Chinese nuclear weapons development, especially once Beijing detonated its first nuclear blast in 1964. For CIA analysts, communist party politics were always important, given the major purges in China at the end of both the 1950s and 1960s, and the Great Cultural Revolution in between.

Intelligence collection against China always had its own peculiar difficulties. In contrast to the Soviet Union, the United States lacked diplomatic relations with the PRC until the mid-1970s, making it impossible to collect information directly, and even more difficult to run spies against the Chinese. A massive flow of information went to Taiwan through communications between friends and families divided by the Taiwan Strait and the ideological separation of communist from nationalist Chinese. But CIA analysts' ability to capitalize on that flow depended upon their relations with the Nationalist leadership on Taiwan, and the data would always be tainted with questions of what did Taiwan wish Washington to think about Beijing. Warm relations in the 1950s deteriorated into strains as the United States opened to China in 1972, and in 1975 established first a liaison office and then an embassy in Beijing. Through the entire period the only direct platform for U.S. operations into the PRC remained Hong Kong. There the CIA was hampered by British concerns regarding their own bilateral relations with the Chinese. At various times the British prohibited or posed obstacles to CIA human intelligence missions out of Hong Kong. The U.S. consulate there nevertheless provided a vital listening post on China, and devoured all manner of Chinese regional, local, and national publications, which became grist to the mills of American intelligence analysts. During the time of the Cultural Revolution the regional and local press became an especially valuable source as various Chinese factions justified themselves by publishing dirt about their enemies.

Other difficulties were compounded by the usual interplay of spy versus spy, not just with the Chinese but with the Russians. Defectors of the late 1950s and early 1960s brought Washington the message that apparently growing strain between Moscow and Beijing was phony, a smoke screen intended to make the United States believe in divisions within the world communist movement that did not exist. Some American analysts—and other CIA officers—were taken in. In a 1960 NIE, for example, CIA analysts were unable to call whether "cohesive forces in the Sino-Soviet relationships will remain stronger than divisive forces" through the five-year period of their estimate. By 1965, when clear distinctions emerged between Chinese and Russian approaches to the Vietnam War, it had become clear the Sino-Soviet split was real. In a 1966 estimate, U.S. intelligence advanced the proposition that "Sino-Soviet relations will continue to deteriorate" while Mao remained in power. By 1969 the Russians and Chinese were fighting along their common border and the CIA speculated on whether Moscow toyed with the notion of preemptive attacks on Chinese nuclear capabilities. Experiments with statistical methods of analysis by the Defense Intelligence Agency and others suggested war between China and Russia had become a virtual certainty. This, too, never transpired.

Intelligence reporting on PRC nuclear weapons exhibited features identical to those revealed by the Soviet estimates. Once again the assumptions of the analysts proved to be critical. The Chinese chose to emphasize their medium-range forces for the regional (Taiwan) context. Even decades later Chinese nuclear forces have major capability in the region but only a nominal strike potential against the United States or Russia west of the Urals (of course, China is today friendlier with Russia, as well, and a prime customer for Russian-built advanced weapons systems). At various times the NIEs assumed that the PRC would do as they did, would emphasize intercontinental capability, or projected both alternatives. As with their Soviet estimates, CIA analysts made assumptions about Chinese officials retiring weapons when they did not, or reaching initial operating capability with other weapons long before that actually became the case.

U.S. intelligence has only gradually caught up with the true state of affairs in China. As Sino-American relations advanced to feature even a degree of common purpose in the late 1970s and 1980s, to the extent of jointly-manned ground collection stations, Washington benefited from the resultant access to better information. Fortunately developments in China unfolded at a slow enough pace that the CIA's learning curve has not mattered.

Soviet Defense Capabilities

Another area confirming the importance of assumptions involves the question of estimates on Soviet spending for national defense, a debate that raged through the 1970s and into the Reagan years. Poor public understanding of this subject facilitated conservative attacks that CIA analysts had systematically underestimated Soviet defense spending, with the implication that the Russians were using even greater resources for national security than those factored into U.S. defense budgets. In effect this constituted a variant on the "window of vulnerability" thesis. The truth, however, was different and much more complex, and the arguments applied to China too, at that time, when these "closed societies" ran directed economies without free markets, published no reliable economic data, and had currencies not convertible on international money markets, making dollar-for-dollar comparisons impossible.

This is an area where intelligence collection has obvious difficulty. Real numbers in Soviet economic data existed only at the highest levels of the Russian government and of the Soviet communist party. It is rumored that U.S. intelligence had purloined a copy of the inner data in about 1972. If so, that is the only known true data that exists for establishing real Soviet prices and true defense costs. *Everything* else is speculation—informed analysis to be sure—but speculation nonetheless.

The CIA's Office for Research and Reports pioneered a novel method for calculating Soviet defense spending: first through calculations of Soviet currency (rubles), then using a building block model to determine the cost in dollars to produce the same military goods and services. The Defense Intelligence Agency began attacking the CIA's Soviet spending projections in 1970, and the emergence of a fourth generation of Soviet ICBM missiles in 1972 put yet greater pressure on the spending estimates. In 1976 CIA analysts doubled their assessment of the proportion of Soviet gross domestic product (GDP) being invested in defense. In the meantime, CIA reporting simultaneously showed the Soviet economy in grave difficulty, and by the 1980s projected that economy to be smaller than previously thought. Political circles converted this into an argument that the Russians were spending even more on military forces, because the burden on their economy could be seen to be higher. A 1983 paper revised the GDP estimate for defense investment downwards and found that a "plateau" had existed since at least 1976. When CIA analysts attempted to elucidate the consequences of that assessment in another paper the following year, however, DCI William J. Casey did not permit its publication.

Overlapping the administrations of Jimmy Carter and Ronald Reagan were issues of Soviet meddling abroad, particularly relating to the Soviet invasion of Afghanistan in December 1979, and the almost-intervention in Poland. In the Afghan case the CIA followed Soviet activities with its all-source intelligence, conditioned by observations of the military mission the Russians already had in the country to help combat an insurgency against its communist-led government. The CIA repeatedly reported the rising scale of Soviet involvement and Soviet frustration at the ineffectiveness of their client government in Afghanistan. Several months ahead of the invasion CIA director Admiral Stansfield Turner warned that the Russians "may be at the threshold of a decision to commit their own forces to prevent the collapse of the regime." The timing and scope of the actual Russian invasion—mounting a coup and sending major ground forces—accompanied by a coup against the communist faction then in power, however, took the CIA by surprise. But the trend of Russian activity had been anticipated.

U.S. intelligence had even better sources about Poland, the agent Colonel Ryzard Kuklinski on the Polish general staff, who furnished detailed data on Soviet contingency plans as revealed to the Polish military, and to the military's own preemptive imposition of martial law. Analysts did not go so far as justified by the reports they had received from Kuklinski. The CIA also appreciated that Soviet force mobilization remained insufficient to sustain an invasion—these moves were more properly seen as maneuvers to impress Warsaw. The CIA briefed the incoming Reagan administration that the Poles themselves might impose measures, rather than the Soviets invading, only days after the new president assumed office. For almost a year, until the Polish military actually moved, in December 1981, the intelligence reporting remained solid, even after Kuklinski defected to the United States several weeks ahead of the imposition of martial law. On balance intelligence performed well.

Probably the most controversial intelligence issue of the 1980s concerned the Soviet development program that paralleled President Ronald Reagan's Strategic Defense Initiative (SDI). The CIA continued to maintain through the 1970s that there was little evidence of major improvement in existing Soviet ballistic missile defenses. Air Force intelligence and some at DIA began arguing that the Russians would break out of the defense logjam by novel means—using a "particle beam" or laser antiballistic missile system. The CIA insisted that Russian technology was not advanced enough to support these applications. With the Reagan administration, Soviet SDI progress became a key development to be countered by an equivalent U.S. system.

DCI Casey commissioned scientific papers, a special estimate, and a publicly released issue paper on Soviet SDI to advance the case for a Soviet anti-missile defense system. Numerous CIA analysts disagreed. Pentagon officials argued that Russian ground-based laser defenses could be active by 1990 and a space-based system by the mid-1990s. The 1983 NIE posited instead that the Soviets might exhibit a prototype space-based system in the mid-1990s with an operational capability after the year 2000. Years passed with little evidence of Soviet advances in this field. In December 1988 the last Soviet estimate of the Reagan era maintained that a ground-based laser prototype could be tested around 2000 and operational perhaps ten years after initial testing. The "feasibility demonstrator" for a space-based system was estimated not to be available before 2000, and not to be deployable "until much later, perhaps around 2010." By August 1991, however, the National Intelligence Council had retreated. By then the U.S. analysts conceded "large uncertainties and differences of views among agencies" and claimed no more than that "The Soviets continue to be interested in developing space-based laser weapons." At this writing, in 2005, the Russians have yet to exhibit the weaponry predicted by alarmists in the 1970s.

NIEs dealing with Soviet offensive force modernization exhibited similar alarming tendencies. The creation of a series of diplomatic agreements for nuclear force reduction reduced the visibility of this issue, so the facts about the Soviet estimates have been obscured. Nevertheless, from 1973 through at least 1988 the Soviet NIEs consistently overestimated future Soviet nuclear warheads on launchers, and more often than not predicted specific modernization measures (new ICBMs, new warhead configurations) to emerge sooner than they did so. A postmortem analysis conducted by the Directorate of Intelligence under Douglas MacEachin demonstrates that the basic reason for the discrepancy is that analysts calculated the maximum feasible force increases for each of the Soviet systems in their projections, then simply stapled together all the results. This was the opposite of the 1960s, when assumptions had been made that Russia would drop and retire various weapons systems, and thus overall projections had fallen short of the mark. In fact, faced with a rapidly worsening economy, Russia lacked resources to carry on the robust force modernization program envisioned in these national estimates.

Skewed perceptions were articulated on so many issues during the 1980s that the Soviet estimates become only one piece of a larger story. Intelligence reports posited that the Russians were behind most global terrorism, then specifically behind an assassination attempt against Pope John Paul II carried out by a Turkish fanatic. On Lebanon, where the United States intervened after the Israeli invasion of 1982, the State Department's Bureau of Intelligence and Research (INR) warned in advance that Washington would be unable to avoid taking sides in the civil war. No NIE was requested. One would finally be assembled late in 1983, in which the CIA, INR, and the military were unusually united in their assessment that shifting politics and cross-cutting interests among all the players made this enterprise an extremely dangerous one. DCI William Casey closely questioned the NIE before finally approving it in October, just days before a truck bomb destroyed the U.S. Marine barracks in Beirut with the loss of 243 Marines.

Central America, the Nicaraguan Contras, and Afghanistan

In Central America, where the Reagan administration fought a counterinsurgency war in El Salvador and launched a CIA-directed covert campaign against neighboring Nicaragua, intelligence alleging that Salvadoran guerrillas were getting all their arms from Nicaragua was used to support initiating the CIA operation, then reports claiming that the CIA-backed rebels had better prospects than, in fact, they had. In 1984, when funding for the administration's covert campaign had become controversial, the administration suddenly leaked allegations that the Soviets were sending advanced jet aircraft to Nicaragua, while withholding CIA and DIA intelligence reports that concluded that Moscow would do no such thing. In 1984 and 1985 NIEs were compiled on Nicaragua that credited the rebels with greater capability than they had acquired, while other passages concluded that the Nicaraguan government faced numerous social and political obstacles in establishing itself firmly in power.

On Afghanistan, where the United States engaged in another secret war, CIA analysts estimated that the Soviets were escalating their involvement, and missed the Russian government's decision to get out of the war. On Iran, in a case where the Reagan White House wanted to reverse its announced policy of refusing to negotiate with terrorists, the CIA was induced to produce an estimate that found evidence of moderation in Iran's theocratic regime that might indicate an opening for relations. That became the basis for the notorious Iran-Contra affair.

So much questionable intelligence passed Langley's doors during the Reagan years that some explanation is needed. Bill Casey, an activist director with policy interests, rode close herd on the CIA analysts who produced the national estimates, as in the Lebanon case cited above, and that is part of the explanation. Casey demanded aggressive and timely reporting, and hated it when NIEs lacked concrete evidence for their assertions, as recorded by Robert Gates, who through this period served successively as NIO for the Soviet Union, deputy director for intelligence, and deputy director of central intelligence, the number two man behind Casey. Such arguments also served as clubs to push particular conclusions in the papers, and when Gates himself went up for confirmation as director for central intelligence in 1991 a number of former CIA analysts testified before the Senate Select Committee on Intelligence that it had been Gates himself pushing for slanted analysis. A major public debate then ensued, its outcome inconclusive; declassified documents seemed to bear out a number of the analysts' charges, while Robert Gates mounted a spirited defense of his approach during the Casey years at the CIA. Gates eventually won confirmation as CIA director and served in that post from 1991 to 1993.

The middle years of the Reagan era were punctuated by a new focus on espionage. It sometimes seems that efforts at counterintelligence proceed cyclically. Having been virtually paralyzed by its molehunts of the 1960s, beginning in about 1973, when William E. Colby headed the DO and later the CIA as a whole, the Agency made a concerted effort to take the wraps off efforts to recruit human intelligence sources, especially Russians. The former chief of CIA counterintelligence, James Jesus Angleton, was forced into retirement late in 1974. The United States did enjoy some notable results, including the defections of Soviet diplomats Arkady Shevchenko and Anatoli Filatov. By the early 1980s a bevy of Soviets were working for the CIA, among them Adolf Tolkachev, a wellspring of material on Soviet military technology, and Dmitri Polyakov, by this time a general and probably the longest-running U.S. human intelligence source of the Cold War.

1985—"The Year of the Spy"

Pundits have dubbed 1985 the "Year of the Spy" because of the number of key cases that arose. There were at least five major penetrations of U.S. secrets uncovered that year: the Walker spy ring (John A. Walker, his brother, and an accomplice) had compromised U.S. machine codes along with Navy material; Ronald A. Pelton of the NSA gave away more code secrets, including U.S. tapping of Soviet undersea phone cables; Jonathan Pollard, a naval intelligence analyst who furnished an array of Middle East material to Israel; Larry Wu-tai Chin, who spied for the People's Republic of China; and CIA officer Edward L. Howard, who defected to Russia with knowledge of CIA activities in the U.S.S.R. Suddenly it seemed that counterintelligence had failed, and renewed emphasis was put upon it. But *under* the surface matters were even worse. It was that very year that another CIA officer, Aldrich L. Ames, decided to spy for the Russians while remaining in place. Ames betrayed all the spies that the CIA had recruited in Russia, with Tolkachev, Polyakov and their colleagues swept up over the next months and years. The

Former CIA agent Aldrich Ames leaves federal court in Alexandria, Virginia, in 1994. (AP/Wide World Photos)

145

Ames channel remained open for a decade, supplemented after about 1991 by FBI officer Robert L. Hanssen, who accomplished the same great level of destruction.

For all its intensity, the spy war mostly concerned the compromising of other spies. At least a dozen agents were providing inside knowledge of other spy services for each spy reporting on the inner thoughts of a Soviet or Chinese leader. Human intelligence nonetheless remained important, and became even more so as the world moved away from the Cold War. Right through the 1980s the machine spies held center stage with their photos of rockets in silos, factories in production, grain ripening in the field. This intelligence was supplemented by NSA interception of voice communications. NSA interceptions retained value as the world moved to cell phones and forms of wireless communication that required the electromagnetic spectrum. Photo satellites, however, became much less valuable as the weapons of choice of America's enemies shifted from nuclear warheads on ICBMs to car bombs on streets. Satellites had once merited the label of "national technical means of verification," but knowledge of the plans of terrorists and drug smugglers at times could only be accessible through recruited spies. There are still armies on the move and countries developing missiles and nuclear weapons, of course, and satellites track that activity. Nevertheless, in recent years the relative value of agents has increased much more rapidly than that of the machine spies.

BRAVE NEW WORLD

While the nature of intelligence collection gradually changed, the Cold War played out its final years. Probably the key questions challenging CIA analysts during the waning Cold War years of the mid-to-late 1980s involved the viability of Mikhail Gorbachev's communist leadership in Russia, and the question of whether the Soviet Union might do down fighting. On both issues U.S. intelligence had its say. In the years immediately following the end of the Cold War it became fashionable to say that the CIA had "missed" the fall of the Soviet Union. This is accurate only in the narrow sense that Agency analysts had failed to predict the specific abortive coup d'etat that sparked the final end, or the actual disintegration of the country. The forces that challenged Gorbachev had long been identified by not only the CIA but other U.S. agencies, and their impact had for years been under frequent review. CIA analysts had long been aware of the centrifugal pressure of the "nationalities question" in the Soviet Union, the weaknesses of the Soviet economy, specific problem areas in resources such as petroleum and agriculture, the brittleness of the production sector, and the rising frustrations of communist conservatives. Indeed, by the time the end came it had been a guessing game in Washington for months to put a time on when Gorbachev would fall or face a serious challenge.

The general suspicion of many elites concerning Gorbachev's motives, including at the White House, and specifically about Gorbachev's moves toward unilateral military pullbacks and force reductions, hindered a proper appreciation of the underlying meaning of CIA reporting, and also (in terms of "politicization") made it more difficult for analysts to put judgments on paper that questioned whether the future would still include a Soviet Union. In a sense this problem replicated the difficulty that CIA analysts had confronted in the 1950s when attempting to appreciate the existence of a Sino-Soviet split. The prospect posed was simply so huge that it was difficult to get one's mind around it, for analysts as much as policy makers, and the result was to inhibit U.S. intelligence from drawing the consequences of its own predictions.

Change in the Soviet Union was not going to appear on satellite photographs. Nor were the CIA's recruited spies within the ranks of Soviet officialdom—their ranks radically reduced by the efforts of Ames and Hanssen—going to get the inside story to Washington. On the other hand, due to Gorbachev's policies of perestroika, U.S. analysts suddenly had unprecedented access to Soviet officials at many levels, and a more open flow of information to the West about Russia than had ever been the case during the Cold War.

In any case, the NIEs reported as early as 1988 to the effect that Gorbachev's economic reforms were not working. On the military side estimators recognized the Soviet need to retrench but foresaw Soviet efforts to preserve numerical advantages. Estimates on Eastern Europe foresaw the possibility of anti-Soviet reformist movements in several countries, but the NIE saw no reason to doubt Soviet willingness to intervene, nor any potential for reduction in the Soviet alliance's military threat to the West within the timeframe of the estimate. In fact, Eastern Europe did leave the Soviet alliance in 1989 and the threat level was radically transformed. The following year estimates openly acknowledged differences between analysts who viewed Soviet moves as tactical, and others who felt Gorbachev was engaged in a fundamental rethinking of the Soviet enterprise. The NIO supervising nuclear force estimates, for one, appears to have belonged to the former school. On the other hand, as early as September 1989 the CIA's Office of Soviet Analysis released a study finding the Gorbachev reforms flawed and based on wishful thinking, with the implication that Gorbachev might have to resort to repression, abandoning his reforms, or losing power. This dynamic is precisely what occurred, but CIA analysts could not or would not view the end of the Soviet Union as one form of "losing power." By December 1990, however, the analysts had come around, and the consensus of the NIE was squarely that "the old communist order is in its death throes" and it identified Boris Yeltsin, who in fact subsequently led the successor government, as a key figure in future political developments. In April 1991 an intelligence memorandum on "The Soviet Cauldron" observed that "explosive events have become increasingly possible," and saw the Soviet military and security services as "making preparations for a broad use of force in the political process." A June

1991 NIE projected a hardline military coup—the specific failure mode in the final collapse—as one of four possible futures, and it assessed that that maneuver "could unravel quickly if the center were unable to quash democratic resistance." In August 1991 hardline communists with the military and the security service mounted a coup against Gorbachev, which failed with a heroic stand by democrats led by Boris Yeltsin. Within months the Soviet Union was no more and the Cold War had ended.

THE NEW WORLD OF SNAKES

While the drama of the fall of the Soviet Union dominated the public's mind during the 1990s, both in the United States and elsewhere, and speculations as to whether any intelligence failure lay in the CIA's reporting on Russian events percolated on the surface, in the shadow world of the agencies the rules for spies were changing quickly. As Moscow's Eastern European bloc disintegrated and newly resurgent nations asserted their independence from Russia by moving toward the West, these territories ceased to be "denied areas." American intelligence collection became more open and aggressive. Indeed, the Soviets offered changes even at home—a delegation of senior Soviet intelligence officials met with CIA officers in Helsinki at the end of 1989 and actually suggested that the opposing services reach a mutual agreement on spying tactics. Though nothing came of that initiative it is a fact that CIA and Russian intelligence people—up to the level of director—began to meet periodically in what became something akin to diplomatic conferences.

The Russians, preoccupied by developments in their own country or perhaps satiated with the spying done for them by Aldrich Ames and Robert Hanssen, virtually got out of the espionage business, at least as measured by spies uncovered by U.S. counterintelligence. Where there had been a dozen spies caught in 1984 and eleven in 1985, and the levels remained high with ten and nine respectively in 1988 and 1989, only one person was prosecuted for espionage in 1990, three in 1991, and two in 1992. In addition, many of the spies caught turned out to be agents for other countries—from Ecuador to Nigeria to Saudi Arabia—rather than Russia. U.S. counterintelligence nonetheless remained fearful of a Russian mole, and the CIA set up a special task force in addition to its regular counterintelligence unit to focus specifically on the Russian spy hunt. At the time Aldrich Ames actually held a desk job at the CIA's Counterintelligence Center and had already become one of the suspects, but would not be caught until 1995. Hanssen remained at large, not to be ferreted out until 2001, interestingly, partly as a result of files from the former Soviet spy agency purchased from human sources by the CIA.

The Counterterrorist Center

A word about "centers": the CIA Counterintelligence Center worked directly for the DCI. It was one of a number of new so-called fusion centers, and represented a notable agency innovation of the 1980s and 1990s. These fusion centers were supposed to break down barriers between intelligence analysts and clandestine service operators by grouping them in the same office and giving them access to "all source" material, as well as permitting analysts to contribute to the planning for espionage and other operational efforts. Starting with terrorism, such centers were developed on a number of subjects, including narcotics and transnational crime, counterintelligence, and proliferation. "Fusion" at the centers, however, proved to be less than completely successful: the Directorate of Operations (DO) really did *not* want to share everything with the Directorate of Intelligence (DI); the analysts on substantive subjects looked askance at those who "went over" to the centers as perhaps not completely loyal; the centers, told that they would plan and carry out operations, found themselves carrying out progressively fewer. The experience of Michael Scheuer, who headed the Counterterrorist Center in the late 1990s, offers one glimpse into this area: Scheuer later told investigators of the 9/11 attacks that he had proposed more than three dozen operations against terrorist chieftain Osama bin Laden without obtaining approval to execute any of them.

The Clinton Presidency and the New Terrorist Threat

Intelligence organization underwent its own transformation during the 1990s, especially during the Clinton presidency, by which time the changes in Eastern Europe had become clear trends, and successor states to the former Soviet Union had emerged throughout central Asia. The old Soviet Divisions in both the DI and DO disappeared, first absorbed into rebooted European divisions, more recently into "Eurasian" divisions that would attempt to cover everything from the Atlantic coast of Europe to the Bering Strait in the Far East. These changes also partly reflected the post–Cold War "peace dividend," that had reduced the size of the CIA and other U.S. agencies. The Directorate of Operations, for example, consolidated some of its field activities, eliminating whole stations in Africa, and cut back the number of its personnel somewhere between 17 and 25 percent.

Some have criticized these cuts as, in effect, crippling U.S. intelligence, but such criticisms were overdone. *After* the cuts the DO remained larger than it had been, for example, at the time of the Vietnam War. And post–Cold War cuts were dwarfed by intelligence cuts after World War II, which were on the order of 85 percent. Moreover, the post–Cold War DO, whatever its size, had less on its plate, with covert operations seriously reduced and much activity absorbed into the fusion centers.

Changes in intelligence analysis arguably wrought greater overall impact on the effectiveness of the U.S. intelligence community. The Clinton years brought a marked emphasis on current intelligence reporting to the detriment of long-range forecasting as in the National Intelligence Estimates.

Peacekeeping operations in Somalia and Bosnia in addition triggered charges of poor intelligence cooperation, making "support to military operations" a new term of jargon in the community of the 1990s, both at the Pentagon and the CIA. Great gains were made in this area, but by the same token such support quintessentially represented an emphasis on current intelligence. Within analytical staffs the drive to be relevant and responsive to consumers at the White House and elsewhere contributed to this trend as well. The creation of a dedicated intelligence "architecture," a classified network like the internet but containing secret data and analyses called Intellink, further exacerbated the trend toward current reporting. That emphasized timeliness, speed of drafting, and identifying facts, not making predictions. Estimative skills suffered as a result.

Meanwhile, complaints that the NIEs did *not* cover long-term social issues of national importance, such as demographics, the spread of AIDs, and similar matters, brought efforts to reorient estimates in ways that made them so general and forward-looking as to lose even more relevance to policy makers. A conscious effort was also made to open up the NIE process to a wider base of opinion, by incorporating views of scholars outside the intelligence community. As one example the NIE "Global Trends 2015" (2001) contains informed speculation on possible futures, and includes contributions from a number of academics and think tanks, but is hardly the stuff to enthuse a busy president, much less his harried National Security Council staff. In other instances the casting of a super-long-term projection has brought changes in threat criteria traditionally used for evaluation. In the estimate "Foreign Missile Developments and the Ballistic Missile Threat Through 2015" (2001), in contrast to the previous standard, the analysis emphasized the initial testing phase of a new rocket as the moment of threat, rather than deployment of a tested system in numbers sufficient to be militarily significant. Such a device can bias NIEs to favor a greater-than-expected threat.

Alternative analysis, extolled during the Clinton years, became the latest panacea within the intelligence community. The CIA created an office expressly to encourage the use of the method in the late 1990s, and its inspector general actually reported on the extent to which these methods were being utilized in May 1999. The techniques go beyond testing an analysis to determine whether different hypotheses shake its conclusions. One variant, called "linchpin analysis," seeks to find factors that might determine a given outcome, and examine the adequacy of evidence for each such variable. In another variant, a full-blown report would be written based on some alternative conclusion to ascertain whether available evidence would sustain the different judgment. So-called Red Teaming would be another variant in which analysts are enjoined to think like the adversary when making their assessments. While testing analyses is always useful—an important instrumental device in estimating—it becomes dangerous when alternatives are substituted for straight-line projections. The logic here is to reason from conclusions and the temptation is to pick among the evidence. The dangers inherent in that approach are amply demonstrated by the Team B report of 1976 and the Pentagon's al Qaeda–Saddam alliance analysis of 2002. This is another route to the greater-than-expected threat. Regrettably, the Intelligence Reform and Terrorism Prevention Act of 2004 writes into law a requirement that the intelligence community emphasize alternative analysis.

Another post–Cold War development has been the drive to make intelligence analysts less specialized. During his tenure as Clinton's first director of central intelligence, R. James Woolsey instituted a "tier" system, essentially a prioritization of intelligence issues. Top tiers would receive constant, in-depth coverage; the others much less. The concept was that specialized analytical work across the spectrum could be reduced, in view of the community's inability to know whence the next intelligence "crisis" might arise, as well as to accommodate personnel reductions of the era. Task forces would instead be created to "surge" the intelligence coverage of an area each time a crisis occurred. The effect of this approach encouraged analysts with generalized knowledge, as opposed to those deeply immersed in a particular subject. The result was the ranking of priorities, but an ancillary problem was that neophyte task forces brought analysts to a subject with only the knowledge developed in remote and possibly unrelated areas, yet outnumbering and usually outranking the specialists with detailed knowledge of the subject. In addition, a tier system is inherently reactive in dynamic terms, with the intelligence focus in many cases following disturbing developments rather than predicting them. To some extent these analytical difficulties were offset by the existence of the fusion centers working for the DCI, but there a different set of problems applied—the DCI centers drew talent away from the Directorate of Intelligence and left participating analysts less well shielded against politicized demands for reporting.

DCI Woolsey is probably best remembered for something he said, rather than for what he did. In congressional testimony at one point, Woolsey remarked that the United States might someday remember the Cold War as easier than the present, because in those (good old) days the enemy was at least known, while in the present the United States might find itself in a forest full of "snakes," that is, unknown threats. That seems to have been the experience of the 1990s—the CIA began the Clinton years preoccupied with global issues such as transnational crime and drug trafficking, moved to increasing concern regarding proliferation in the mid-to-late 1990s, and developed an overriding focus on terrorism from the late 1990s until today. The combination of the proliferation of weapons of mass destruction and terrorism is today seen as the primary intelligence problem.

For the CIA the watershed year proved to be 1998, during George J. Tenet's tenure as Director of Central Intelligence. Two events of that year set the tone for the new threat perception. One involved Pakistan's testing of a series of nuclear devices, and India's springtime response of conducting its own nuclear test series. These developments came as the biggest surprise to U.S. intelligence since Saddam Hussein's invasion of Kuwait in 1990. (Incidentally, the postmortem on this intelligence failure, conducted by a group under Admiral David Jeremiah, concluded—typically—that the CIA had lacked human intelligence sources, particularly in India, but had too much information in the system for the available analysts to review—a commentary on the tier system in action.) The second formative event involved the August 1998 simultaneous car bombings of two U.S. embassies in Africa by the al Qaeda terrorist group. In response to this latter development, the Clinton administration fired cruise missiles at terrorist training camps in Afghanistan (and, apparently in error, against a factory in Sudan), and DCI Tenet in private declared war on al Qaeda.

The September 11, 2001, Terrorist Attack, the Iraq War, and the Intelligence Reform and Terrorism Prevention Act

From 1998 on, Tenet began to talk of reinvigorating the Directorate of Operations and supported a strengthened Counterterrorist Center, even if he did reject the center's operational proposals. He did so in conjunction with national security officials of the Clinton and George W. Bush administrations. Still, for whatever reasons, the Counterterrorist Center and the CIA failed to put sufficient emphasis on indications that al Qaeda planned to operate inside the United States, and that terrorists were considering using commercial airliners as weapons, while the administration of President George W. Bush failed to take seriously those indications it did receive. As a result, on September 11, 2001, al Qaeda was able to launch a major operation on American soil. On that day, al Qaeda operatives simultaneously hijacked four airliners, two of which hit the twin towers of the World Trade Center in New York City, one the Pentagon in Washington, D.C., and the fourth crashed in Pennsylvania. The resultant controversy over the intelligence failure before September 11 led to the most massive investigations of U.S. intelligence since those of 1975, when the Church and Pike committees had reviewed all aspects of intelligence work. In this case, beginning in 2002 a joint Senate-House committee, comprising the intelligence committees of each chamber of Congress, investigated the intelligence failures. In addition, a joint congressional-presidential commission conducted an even deeper investigation in 2003–2004. (Among its other conclusions would be that the U.S. intelligence agencies had failed to collect enough human intelligence.)

These investigations were still in progress when a fresh controversy engulfed the intelligence community over its analyses of whether Iraq under dictator Saddam Hussein possessed weapons of mass destruction, or had an alliance with the al Qaeda terrorists. In attempting to build backing for an invasion of Iraq in March 2003, the Bush administration made both these claims and produced suitably alarming intelligence reports to back them. An examination of the published reports released to support the administration's military decision indicates that they either exaggerated or misconstrued the (limited) recent data; relied to a great extent on material predating the 1990–1991 Gulf War, when Iraq's capabilities of that time had been destroyed; left out or discounted data from UN disarmament teams of the 1990s, and claims by the Iraqi government itself, where these were damaging to the Bush administration's assertions; and misled the public on those disagreements which nevertheless persisted within the intelligence community. If the published versions accurately reflect the still-classified reporting, there can be no doubt that the consensus reporting embodied huge intelligence errors. A further unresolved question is whether the erroneous reports were the product of pressures overtly or subtly brought to bear by the Bush administration (politicization) or were the result of honest analytical error.

The Senate Select Committee on Intelligence (SSCI) in 2004 did examine the secret record of the NIEs and other intelligence reports, reports that remain classified at this writing. Dominated by the president's own political party, the SSCI investigation chose to exclude from its published report any assessment of the political issue: how the administration had utilized the intelligence in the debate preceding the decision to authorize war with Iraq, which bore directly on the politicization question. In its report released in 2004 the SSCI nevertheless found that the secret reporting indeed erred, had been misleading on key intelligence questions, had depended on assumptions that required analysts to prove the negative in order to conclude that the Iraqis *did not* possess given weapons, had been overly reliant on a handful of Iraqi exile sources judged to have been deliberately misleading themselves, and generally had been based upon thin data. While the SSCI failed to tell the complete story by refusing to deal with the question of whether the Iraq intelligence had been politicized, its conclusions on the NIE and other reports were devastating, and its report merged at the same time that the 9/11 Commission delivered its own recommendations for reforming U.S. intelligence. The SSCI and 9/11 Commission efforts thus dovetailed in important ways. One result was the 9/11 Commission recommendations that provided the catalyst to the enactment of the Intelligence Reform and Terrorism Prevention Act of 2004, and its inclusion of an instruction on "alternative analysis," owes much to the SSCI investigations of Iraq.

Even as this legislation was being hammered out in Congress, the Bush administration pursued its own course on intelligence. The House Permanent Select Committee on Intelligence, chaired by Representative Porter Goss (R-FL), had earlier launched a parallel investigation of the Iraq intelligence. That inquiry, however, was effectively squelched at an early stage (September 2003). Then in the summer of 2004 President Bush appointed Goss to succeed George Tenet as director of central intelligence. Bush also ordered the CIA to double the number of its case officers in the Directorate of Operations, and to increase the number of analysts as well. In addition, Bush sought to deflect the heat from some of the other Iraq investigations by forming a new presidential commission, chaired by Judge Laurence Silberman, to focus on intelligence regarding weapons of mass destruction. The commission was supposed to bring in authoritative explanations as to how the Iraq intelligence turned out the way it did while also looking at the general difficulties in collecting data on these kinds of weapons. Released in March 2005, the so-called Silberman-Robb Commission echoed the SSCI's devastating criticisms of CIA collection and analysis.

The major change wrought by the 2004 intelligence reform law involved the creation of the post of national intelligence director (DNI). The director is to operate a series of fusion centers, starting with a National Counterterrorism Center, and in effect would draft the DCI's center of that name out of the CIA. The law provides scope for a constellation of centers to form around the DNI's office—in fact encourages that consequence because the director now has a statutory responsibility to ensure quality intelligence analysis but only very limited actual control over the CIA, which retains its director of central intelligence. The Pentagon is also largely excluded from control by the 2004 law, and there are already indications that military authorities are seizing more intelligence roles and missions for themselves. For example, the military is creating an independent capability to conduct espionage operations.

The net effect of the 2004 reforms may therefore be to create an intelligence director with less power than the old one, and to turn the CIA into a mostly-espionage agency with only residual intelligence analytical capability. One of the huge advantages the United States enjoyed throughout the period since the creation of the CIA in 1947 has been the Agency's strong analytical capability. For all the intelligence disputes and even errors, analysis played an important role in helping keep the Cold War from becoming a hot one. Ironically the United States is in danger of dismantling a capability that won this war and replacing it with something much less resilient.

A New Agency: The Origins and Expansion of CIA Covert Operations

Athan Theoharis

Prior to World War II, the United States had no independent agency responsible for coordinating the collection and analysis of intelligence and for conducting other secret operations that could further the nation's security interests. The War and Navy Departments had during the 1880s established special intelligence units to collect information essential to planning military policy and anticipating possible military threats, while the State Department through its consular service collected political and economic information relevant to the nation's commercial interests and diplomacy. Given the distinctive and parochial interests of these departments, the collected information was rarely shared, and the information that each sought was primarily responsive to its department's specialized responsibilities. The political-military crisis of World War II, and then the onset of the Cold War confrontation between the United States and the Soviet Union, combined with questions that were raised by Japan's devastating surprise attack on Pearl Harbor on December 7, 1941, changed all that.

The Pearl Harbor attack demonstrated dramatically that a centralized intelligence service having broad powers would be essential if senior administration officials were to anticipate future foreign threats and then formulate an appropriate response. For, although Japanese military officials had taken precautions to preclude discovery of their planned surprise attack, U.S. intelligence agents had already intercepted Japanese diplomatic messages and had then broken the Japanese code. As a result, during the very time when critical U.S.-Japanese negotiations were being held in Washington, D.C., in the weeks before the attack, U.S. policy makers had advance knowledge of the Japanese negotiating strategy and intent to attack should these negotiations fail to meet minimal Japanese demands. Pearl Harbor, then, was not so much an intelligence failure as a failure to analyze and understand acquired intelligence. And a central cause of this failure was the lack of coordination among War, Navy, and State Department analysts and of these analysts' narrow bureaucratic perspective.

To address this problem, the Truman administration in February 1947 proposed legislation, the National Security Act of July 26, 1947, to create a centralized intelligence service, the Central Intelligence Agency (CIA). This new agency was assigned a limited role to coordinate "the intelligence activities of the several Government departments and agencies [Defense, State, Justice] in the interest of national security" and "correlate and evaluate" such intelligence to ensure that the president and senior administration policy makers would have a refined and contextualized intelligence product. Introduced as part of a bill to unify the U.S. armed services, the section of the National Security Act creating the CIA commanded minimal attention from members of Congress during the resultant congressional hearings and debate. Only two concerns were then raised about a proposal to create a centralized intelligence service. The first reflected a fear that the new agency might become a "gestapo" that would monitor domestic political activities, and further might intrude on the Federal Bureau of Investigation's domestic security responsibilities. To allay this concern, the proposed bill was amended to explicitly prohibit the CIA from any "police, subpoena, law enforcement powers, or internal security functions." The second concern centered on whether this new agency should only analyze collected information or as well collect on its own and then analyze all collected intelligence. In this case, the bill was not amended to bar the Agency from any collection role, leaving unresolved whether the CIA was to be solely an analytical agency or an agency that both collected intelligence on its own and analyzed this information in conjunction with that provided by the other established intelligence services.

Almost immediately with its creation, and expanded in subsequent years, the CIA both analyzed and collected intelligence, assigning personnel overseas and actively recruiting U.S. citizens traveling abroad and foreign sources who could obtain information about the plans and capabilities of foreign governments and foreign movements of particular interest. Regardless, the two concerns articulated during the debate preceding passage of the National Security Act indirectly document Congress's conception of the role and responsibilities of this newly created agency—an intelligence (less euphemistically, spy) agency that would enhance the ability of the president and senior administration officials to formulate the nation's foreign and military policies.

ORIGINS OF CIA COVERT OPERATIONS: NSC 4A, NSC 10/2

An important catalyst to Congress's decision of 1947 to create a permanent intelligence service stemmed from the deterioration in U.S.-Soviet relations after 1945 that gave rise to the so-called Cold War. In contravention of the agreements concluded at the Yalta Conference of February 1945 whereby Soviet officials had agreed to "free and unfettered" elections in Eastern Europe and the Balkans at an early date, such elections were both delayed and when held were neither free nor unfettered. European and Asian communists, moreover, in the postwar era were in a position to exploit the devastating economic and social consequences wrought during World War II (partly the byproduct of brutal German occupation policy) and the political vacuum created by wartime governments that either had been military allies of Nazi Germany (Italy, Bulgaria, Hungary, Rumania), had collaborated with the Axis powers (Vichy France, Croatian Ustashe), or had been occupied with their governments or colonial rulers forced into exile (Greece, Yugoslavia, Czecho-slovakia, Poland, Indochina, Indonesia, Burma, China). As a result, European and Asian communist parties and communist-led anti-Axis resistance move-ments would be in a strong position to extend their influence in the postwar period.

In response, the Truman administration adopted a policy of containment to stem feared Soviet expansion, formalized through the so-called Truman Doctrine of 1947 and the Marshall Plan of 1947–1948. Through economic and technical assistance to the governments of Greece, Turkey, France, Great Britain, and Italy, the administration sought to undercut popular support for the communist-led rebel movement in Greece, undercut neutralist sentiment in Turkey, and support the reconstruction of the war-devastated economies of western Europe. These measures were intended to undermine the political appeal and revolutionary potential of communism by promoting economic recovery. Administration officials concurrently devised other plans to neu-tralize a perceived expansionist and subversive communist threat. These ini-tiatives, however, would necessitate intervention in the internal affairs of sovereign states, and their success was dependent on ensuring that the specific role of U.S. agents not become known.

Internal deliberations among senior administration officials on how best to effect these interventionist objectives ultimately became the catalyst to the CIA's initial conduct of covert operations. For different reasons, neither State nor Defense Department officials wanted to assume direct operational re-sponsibility over proposed plans. Instead, they endorsed having CIA operatives implement "vitally needed psychological operations" insofar as CIA personnel were already in the field operating under cover. Based on his reading of the National Security Act, however, CIA general counsel Lawrence Houston at first advised DCI Roscoe Hillenkoetter that before assuming this role the CIA should obtain explicit legislative and budgetary authorization from Congress. This assessment was rejected as Agency officials subsequently concluded that the CIA could conduct covert operations under Section 102 (5) of the National Security Act, which stipulated that the Agency could "perform such other functions and duties related to intelligence affecting the national security as the National Security Council may from time to time direct."

The Agency's initial conduct of covert operations was formally authorized by National Security Council directives: NSC 4A of December 14, 1947, and NSC 10/2 of June 18, 1948. NSC 4A authorized the CIA to "initiate and conduct, within the limits of available funds, covert psychological operations designed to counteract Soviet and Soviet-inspired activities which constitute a threat to world peace and security or are designed to discredit and defeat the United States in its endeavors to promote world peace and security." NSC 10/2 provided a broader and ultimately permanent mandate authorizing the CIA to conduct covert operations "so planned and executed that any U.S. Government responsibility for them is not evident ... and that if uncovered the U.S. Government can plausibly disclaim any responsibility." The specific activities to be conducted would include "propaganda, economic warfare; preventive direct action, including sabotage, anti-sabotage, demolition and evacuation measures; subversion against hostile states, including assistance to underground resistance movements, guerrillas and refugee liberation groups, and support of indigenous anti-communist elements in threatened countries of the free world."

OFFICE OF POLICY COORDINATION AND THE CENTRAL INTELLIGENCE AGENCY ACT OF 1949

The broader and more ambitious mandate of NSC 10/2 necessitated the establishment of a special branch to conduct planned and ongoing operations, the Office of Special Projects, soon renamed the Office of Policy Coordination (OPC). Creation of the OPC, moreover, coincided with the enactment (on June 20, 1949) of the Central Intelligence Agency Act of 1949. Among other provisions, this Act exempted the Agency from congressional budgetary and accounting requirements, thereby reducing the need for Agency and administration officials to depend on special funds thus ensuring that politically risky operations could be conducted without being subject to congressional oversight. One result was that from unanticipated and reactive initiatives, conducting covert operations in time became an ongoing CIA responsibility. Indeed, during the years 1949 through 1952 (the only years for which statistics are available), OPC personnel increased ninefold from 302 to 2,812 (in addition the Agency employed 3,142 overseas contract personnel) and its budget increased twentyfold from $4.7 million to $82 million. And, whereas in 1949 OPC personnel were assigned to seven overseas stations that number increased to forty-seven by 1952.

When first instituted in 1947, CIA covert operations had been relatively limited—confined to psychological warfare operations in Central and Eastern Europe that included unattributable publications, radio broadcasts, and blackmail. Beginning in 1948, however, the number and scope of such operations exploded—and eventually included acquisition of a radio transmitter for broadcasting behind the so-called Iron Curtain (later leading to the establishment of permanent stations in Munich, Germany—Radio Free Europe in 1950 and Radio Liberty in 1951), establishment of a propaganda printing plant in Germany, assembling balloons to drop propaganda materials in Eastern Europe, funding the Christian Democratic Party during the 1948 Italian parliamentary elections (to preclude a possible Communist Party electoral victory), and funding a French non-communist trade union (to counteract the communist-controlled Confederation Generale du Travail). CIA operations also moved beyond propaganda and political action and as well sought either to destabilize or to promote popular opposition toward the recently imposed communist governments in Eastern Europe, the Balkans, and the Far East. A special Guerrilla Warfare Group was established to train and recruit anti-communist defectors and political and ethnic refugees. During the years 1948 through 1953, CIA agents funded and otherwise assisted paramilitary resistance operations in Poland, the Baltic states, Albania, Ukraine, China, the Philippines, and North Korea. These operations failed to undermine communist control (with the exception of the Philippines), in part because some were infiltrated by communist agents and all encountered the overwhelming power of the communist governments' military and police forces.

IRANIAN AND GUATEMALAN COUPS

CIA paramilitary, propaganda, and political initiatives, because covert, ironically did not shield the Truman administration from the criticisms of Republicans in Congress who charged that Truman's (and the preceding Roosevelt administration's) "softness toward communism" had brought about the "sell out and betrayal" of Eastern Europe and China. Rejecting a passive policy of containment that they claimed ceded the initiative to the Soviet Union, these critics concurrently called for the adoption of a more aggressive policy of "liberation" to free the peoples of Eastern Europe and China from communist enslavement. These themes also informed the campaign strategy and rhetoric of Republican presidential nominee Dwight Eisenhower during the 1952 election, and contributed to Republican successes in both the presidential and congressional elections that year. Committed to a bolder and more aggressive anticommunist policy, the newly elected Eisenhower administration endorsed and expanded the CIA's covert operations capabilities. The administration's focus, however, shifted from Europe and China—at the same time as in effect it abandoned any effort to liberate China and Eastern Europe (dramatized by its response to the brutal Soviet suppression of the Hungarian revolution in 1956).

Instead, the Eisenhower administration pursued a more attainable objective of containing and/or defeating radical nationalist movements that sought to overthrow conservative and pro-Western governments in the Middle East, Latin America, Africa, and Southeast Asia. In this case, it adopted the tactics employed by CIA operatives that had succeeded earlier in defeating the

Hukbalahap rebellion in the Philippines and ensured the election of Ramon Magsaysay to the Philippine presidency. CIA covert operations, now conducted through a special Directorate of Plans (subsequently renamed the Directorate of Operations), soon commanded 70–80 percent of the Agency's budget.

This expanded resort to covert operations was captured in a CIA-engineered coup to overthrow the government of Mohammed Mossadegh and restore Mohammed Reza Pahlavi as the shah of Iran.

This covert operation had its origins in political changes in Iran. In 1950 the Iranian government initiated negotiations over the terms of the British-owned Anglo-Iranian Oil Company's (AIOC) oil concession. At the time, AIOC had a lucrative contract whereby it had control over the pumping, refining, and shipment of all oil in south Iran. The company's payments for this concession, moreover, were so low that it paid more in taxes to the British government than it did to Iran. At the very time when the renewal of this contract and an alternative proposal to nationalize the Iranian oil industry were being debated in the Iranian parliament, the incumbent prime minister was assassinated on February 19, 1951. His successor, the fiery nationalist Mossadegh, immediately promoted a bill to nationalize the oil industry. The bill was approved and AIOC was nationalized on May 2, 1951.

Protesting this action, the British government organized a global boycott of Iranian oil (having been dissuaded by the Truman administration from attempting a military invasion). When Mossadegh refused to budge, a stalemate ensued. Mossadegh's position was strengthened as a consequence of the shah's unsuccessful attempt to dismiss him in mid-1952. An ensuing riot emboldened Mossadegh to issue a decree assigning to himself full powers in January 1953. Then, when the Iranian parliament rejected Mossadegh's request to appoint himself commander in chief, the prime minister dissolved the parliament on July 19, 1953, and then on August 8, 1953, opened trade negotiations with the Soviet Union.

Mossadegh's actions alarmed President Eisenhower, who was already troubled by the prime minister's mercurial temperament and who feared that he might lead Iran into the Soviet camp. These concerns had led Eisenhower, prior to Mossadegh's actions dissolving the parliament, to approve a plan on June 25, 1953, to overthrow Mossadegh, a plan drafted by CIA operative Kermit "Kim" Roosevelt and code-named Operation TPAJAX.

Entering Iran under a false passport, Roosevelt worked with four to five CIA operatives first to get the Iranian army and police to back the shah against Mossadegh, then to secure the cooperation of a prominent Iranian army commander, General Fazallah Zahedi, and finally to orchestrate pro-shah rioting in the streets of Teheran. Acting on this plan, which depended on his cooperation, the shah fired Mossadegh, appointing Zahedi as his replacement. When full-scale rioting broke out in the streets of Teheran on August 18 and 19, 1953, pro-shah tank units surrounded Mossadegh's residence, ending his career. This action triggered the shah's triumphal return from Italy on August 22, 1953, having fled there after issuing the order firing Mossadegh.

Overthrowing Mossadegh proved to be easy, and had been accomplished without revealing the CIA's role. The coup appeared to have been an internal affair, the result of the actions of conflicting Iranian factions. Its immediate result was that the shah obtained absolute power, which he held until overthrown by a popular uprising in 1979 led by militant Islamic fundamentalists. Kermit Roosevelt returned to CIA headquarters, having been promoted assistant director of the Directorate of Plans.

The Iranian coup proved to be a prelude to another, equally successful CIA-engineered coup, code-named Operation PBSUCCESS, that overthrew Guatemalan president Jacobo Arbenz Guzmán. Arbenz had won election to the Guatemalan presidency in November 1950 on a platform of agrarian and economic reform. Acting on this pledge, in February 1953 Arbenz ordered the expropriation of 400,000 acres of the 550,000 acres held by the U.S.-based United Fruit Company, which land was to be apportioned to Guatemalan peasants. Arbenz compounded this threat to U.S. economic interests by secretly purchasing 2,000 tons of arms from the Skoda arms firm of communist Czechoslovakia. These two actions, because they suggested the threat of a communist beachhead in Latin America, led President Eisenhower on August 12, 1953, to authorize the CIA to develop a plan to overthrow Arbenz.

Conceived by CIA operative Albert Haney, the resultant plan involved a two-pronged operation—first to recruit Guatemalan military officers to launch an invasion from neighboring Honduras, and then to intimidate Arbenz into resigning through psychological warfare tactics. The latter was advanced through the establishment of a CIA-funded radio station, calling itself the "Voice of Liberation" and operating out of Honduras. The former involved Haney's recruitment of a former colonel in the Guatemalan army, Carlos Castillo Armas, to lead a CIA-trained and -recruited task force of Guatemalan exiles. At the time Armas was living in exile, having attempted an unsuccessful military coup in 1949.

Under CIA direction, a 170-man army was trained and supplied in military camps in Nicaragua and the Panama Canal Zone before being transported to neighboring Honduras. The CIA-funded radio station began broadcasting on May 1, 1954, and in addition cartoons, posters, and articles based on CIA information were placed in the Latin American press calling for Arbenz's overthrow. Armas formally launched his invasion from Honduras on June 18, 1954, with air cover funded by the CIA. The Voice of Liberation hyped this military operation as the start of the liberation of Guatemala. Armas's army of exiles did not overpower the Guatemalan military. Instead, a frightened Arbenz, convinced he confronted a force commanding greater air power, panicked. Resigning on June 27, 1954, he sought asylum in the Mexican embassy, allowing Armas to march triumphantly into Guatemala City to proclaim himself president on September 1, 1954. And, although never implemented,

CIA officers when drafting plans for this operation had compiled a list of suspect Guatemalan political and trade union leaders for possible assassination.

NSC 5412

The Iranian and Guatemalan coups were strikingly successful, both in the ease by which popularly elected governments had been overthrown and by the ability of CIA officials to mask the Agency's role. The proliferation of CIA covert operations since 1948, nonetheless, with the resultant displacement of the State and Defense Departments as the agencies that assumed exclusive responsibility to implement the nation's foreign and military policies, led President Eisenhower in 1954 to institute administrative changes to ensure that CIA operations would further his own foreign policy priorities.

Eisenhower's decision was a byproduct of a broader initiative of 1953 to evaluate the operations of the federal government and to identify needed changes to reduce costs and ensure greater efficiency. This review was conducted by a commission headed by former Republican President Herbert Hoover. Owing to the sensitivity of its operations, the CIA was evaluated by a special committee, headed by General James Doolittle.

As the result of its review, the so-called Doolittle Committee extolled the value of covert operations, concluding that they were essential to repulsing the Soviet subversive threat. Given the nature and objectives of communist regimes, the committee emphasized, the United States had no alternative but to adopt measures that might seemingly violate national norms. These required "an aggressive covert psychological, political and paramilitary organization more effective, more unique, and if necessary, more ruthless than that employed by the enemy [the Soviet Union]."

At the same time, Committee members were troubled by the Agency's seemingly mindless growth and the secrecy inevitably shrouding the planning and conduct of covert operations with the attendant undermining of needed external oversight. Its recommendations underlay a decision of the National Security Council to issue a series of directives, NSC 5412, between March and December 1955. Under NSC 5412/1 of March 12, 1955, a special Planning Coordination Group (known as the 5412 Committee, subsequently renamed the 303 Committee during Lyndon Johnson's administration and then the 40 Committee under President Nixon) was established. The group was to be the "normal channel for giving policy approval for such [covert] programs as well as for securing coordination and support thereof." The group would review and approve "all compatible activities" that were proposed to destroy "international communism," with CIA officials directed to develop plans that could repulse or contain "international communist" control over "any" area of the world and also assist those leaders and groups "anywhere" in the world that could advance U.S. interests.

This administrative change was intended to subject the planning and execution of CIA covert operations to executive oversight. Such review proved necessary given the committee's endorsement and the administration's support for expansive measures to contain a perceived worldwide and subversive communist threat. NSC 5412 spelled out what was in fact an ambitious agenda—whether to "discredit the prestige and ideology of International Communism," "impair relations" between the Soviet Union and communist governments in Eastern Europe and China, "counter any threat of a party or individuals directly or indirectly responsive to Communist control," "strengthen the orientation toward peoples and nations of the free world," "increase the capacity and will of such [pro-Western] peoples and nations to resist International Communism," or "develop underground resistance and facilitate covert and guerrilla operations."

The purpose behind NSC 5412 was to ensure that the CIA would operate as a presidential agency, that its formulation and execution of covert operations would be responsive to the president's objectives. Because issued secretly and unilaterally, NSC 5412 provoked no public or congressional debate even though its proposed centralization profoundly affected constitutional principles of limited government and divided powers. The U.S. Constitution had established a system of checks and balances. Thus, while presidents had broad powers in the military-diplomatic areas as "commander in chief" and to "conduct foreign relations," these powers were counterbalanced by Congress's exclusive power to declare war, to approve appropriations, to confirm ambassadorial and departmental appointments, and to ratify treaties. Because done in secret and solely at the direction of the president, the CIA's conduct of covert operations in effect undermined Congress's powers to approve or reject proposed presidential initiatives. The system put in place by NSC 5412 ensured that risky operations and questionable tactics would not be debated as to whether they promoted the national interest or violated the nation's avowed ideals—whether to intervene in the affairs of sovereign states, emulate the tactics adopted by the Soviet Union, support or undermine particular foreign political movements and leaders, and resort to sabotage and assassination.

For, while not publicly known at the time, the Doolittle Committee had recommended a course that many in Congress and the public might have found inimical to the national interest, or in violation of the nation's principles. In stark and dramatic language, the committee articulated an alarmist rationale for CIA covert operations: "It is now clear that we are facing an implacable enemy whose avowed objective is world domination by whatever means, and at whatever cost. There are no rules in such a game. Hitherto acceptable norms of human conduct do not apply. If the United States is to survive, long-standing American concepts of 'fair play' must be reconsidered.... We must learn to subvert, sabotage, and destroy our enemies by more clever, more sophisticated, and more effective methods than those used against us. It may become necessary that the American people be made acquainted with, understand, and support this fundamentally repugnant philosophy."

SOUTH VIETNAM, LAOS, INDONESIA

The Doolittle recommendations were never made public. Administration officials at no time acquainted the American public and Congress to ensure their understanding and support for a "fundamentally repugnant philosophy." NSC 5412, however, did usher in a far-reaching expansion of CIA covert operations.

This is highlighted by CIA covert operations in South Vietnam during the years 1953–1975, which encompassed the range of activities proposed in NSC 5412. The first involved assisting the French in the waning days of their efforts to repulse a nationalist anticolonial revolution that had broken out in its former colony of Indochina in 1945. Japanese military advances during World War II had forced the French to relinquish control over Indochina, and had created a vacuum which rebel forces (the so-called Vietminh led by communist activist Ho Chi Minh) were able to exploit to declare their independence. The French sought to reestablish control and became engaged in a costly conflict with the Vietminh.

Through the CIA proprietary Civil Air Transport (CAT), CIA pilots in 1953 airlifted supplies to a French army in Laos and then in 1954 flew 684 air sorties to supply besieged French troops at Dien Bien Phu. CIA officials had concurrently offered to assist the French in organizing a more effective guerrilla operation. The French rebuffed this offer, preferring to retain direct control over military operations directed at the Vietminh. This phase ended when Dien Bien Phu fell on May 7, 1954. Reversing course, the recently elected French government of Pierre Mendes-France decided to cease military operations in Indochina and in July 1954 negotiated a military truce with the Vietminh whereby French troops would withdraw south of the seventeenth parallel (before leaving the country) and Vietminh troops to the north. The so-called Geneva Accords further provided that nationwide elections would be held in 1956 to reunite the country—with the expectation that the Vietminh would win these elections.

Not reconciled to the communization of Vietnam, the Eisenhower administration sought to establish an independent, noncommunist government in the south under the leadership of Ngo Dinh Diem, a Vietnamese nationalist then living in exile and not tainted by collaboration with the French. Not only did the U.S. government provide economic and military training assistance to Diem but the CIA, under the direction of Edward Lansdale, a former Air Force colonel who had helped orchestrate the defeat of the Huk rebellion in the Philippines, initiated a covert operation to consolidate Diem's control by assisting in building an efficient police force that could suppress the various dissident factions (including Buddhist and other religious sects opposed to the Catholic Diem) as well as communist-controlled organizations. CIA officials contracted with Michigan State University in 1955 to train Diem's security forces as part of this effort to restore order in the south and repress the fractured but potentially destabilizing anti-Diem factions. This assistance to the Diem government intensified in 1957 with the formal outbreak of civil war in the south as the North Vietnamese under Ho Chi Minh assisted in the formation of the National Liberation Front (NLF), the so-called Vietcong, when the promised elections of 1956 were not held. Then in 1964 CIA officials launched a psychological warfare program, code-named OPLAN 34, to interdict northern supply lines to the NLF rebels in the South and to capitalize on popular opposition in the north to communist rule.

Following direct U.S. military intervention in Vietnam triggered by the February 1965 attack by NLF forces on a U.S. army barrack in Pleiku that resulted in the death of nine U.S. military advisers, CIA officials intensified their efforts to shore up the Diem government. In conjunction with the U.S. military command, in 1968 CIA station chief William Colby launched a pacification program to undermine the Vietcong. Code-named Operation PHOENIX, this program sought to identify NLF leaders and their supporters in the south, who were then to be "neutralized" by South Vietnamese security forces. The program provoked public criticism following the disclosure of the numbers of those identified who were killed—according to Colby's 1971 testimony 20,587 were killed, 29,978 imprisoned, and 17,717 turned into South Vietnamese agents, suggesting that this was an assassination program.

CIA covert operations in Laos paralleled those in Vietnam, given that state's geographic proximity to Vietnam and the timing of its independence from France in 1954 (having been, along with Vietnam and Cambodia, part of the French colony of Indochina). CIA operatives not only assisted the French attack on Vietminh bases in Laos in 1953, but beginning in 1961 and intensified after 1965 they conducted a secret war in Laos. In 1961 CIA operatives assisted in establishing a Laotian faction, the pro-American Committee for the Defense of the National Interest, and funded the military operations of Colonel Phoumi Nosovan to prevent the establishment of a Marxist government under Laotian Prince Souvanna Phouma. After 1965, CIA operatives recruited and trained Meo mountain tribesman (the Hmong) to interdict North Vietnamese supply routes through Laos used by the North Vietnamese to ferry arms and troops to the NLF in South Vietnam.

NSC 5412 had defined the threat to U.S. security interests as stemming from the expansionist objectives of Soviet-directed communism. This did not mean, however, that U.S. policy makers supported covert operations only when there was evidence of direct Soviet involvement. They viewed the Soviet threat in broader terms and also sought to check the radical nationalist movements that emerged in the post–World War II era and that succeeded in obtaining their independence from European control. Administration officials had become convinced that such movements were either orchestrated by or were receiving direction from the Kremlin. Eisenhower administration officials accordingly turned to the CIA to contain these nationalist movements, as it had in its efforts to contain or defeat the communist-led movements in Laos and Vietnam. This became the basis for its policies toward the Indonesian government of Achmed Sukarno.

Indonesia was a former Dutch colony and (like Indochina) had been occupied by Japan during World War II. Declaring their independence in 1945, the Indonesians fought the returning Dutch, who eventually agreed to give up control in November 1949. In the ensuing years, Sukarno, a mercurial but charismatic nationalist, was able to gain power in part because he commanded the support of the army. His willingness to cooperate with the powerful Indonesian Communist Party, advocacy of a neutralist foreign policy of non-alignment, and radical economic policies (given Indonesia's rich oil and mineral resources) caused the Eisenhower administration to become alarmed. The administration's concern intensified when in 1955 Sukarno convened an international conference in Bandung to which he invited the leaders of recently independent African and Asian countries, but also communist China, to promote a policy of nonalignment whereby so-called Third World states would promote their interests by consciously rejecting alignment with either the United States and the Western democracies or the Soviet Union and the communist bloc.

In response, President Eisenhower authorized CIA officials to develop a plan to neutralize Sukarno. To achieve this objective, CIA officials attempted to capitalize on internal rivalries within the Indonesian military and on factional rivalries in the Indonesian parliament. Their first action was to fund the Muslim Masjumi party during 1955 parliamentary elections. This support proved unsuccessful as the Indonesian Communist Party made major electoral gains, encouraging Sukarno instead to develop closer ties with the communists. Then, in 1958 CIA operatives supported a military coup launched by disgruntled colonels to overthrow Sukarno. The coup attempt failed when the head of the army, Abdul Haris Nasution, dismissed the rebel colonels and announced that further dismissals would follow. And, while Eisenhower administration officials denied having played any role in promoting the rebellion—with President Eisenhower claiming instead at an April 30, 1958, press conference that "every rebellion that I have heard of has its soldiers of fortune"—this denial was undercut when the Indonesian air force on May 18, 1958, shot down a B-26 piloted by CIA employee Allen Pope. When captured, Pope possessed identity cards confirming his relationship with CAT (the CIA proprietary airline) and his post privileges at the U.S. Clark Air Force Base in the Philippines.

The Vietnam, Laos, and Indonesian operations were unique only in their scope and duration. They illustrate how much CIA covert operations had expanded—captured in a host of similar initiatives launched in the late 1950s and early 1960s. These included supporting Buddhist and other political dissidents in Tibet (following communist China's conquest of that country in 1950–1951), an unsuccessful attempt to recruit disgruntled Syrian military officers to overthrow the leftist Baathist government of Syria, a successful coup that overthrew the government of Jose Velasco Ibarra in Ecuador, funding the Jordanian monarch, funding the Liberal Party of Japan in that country's 1958, 1960, and 1963 parliamentary elections, and supporting a general strike in 1963 that resulted in the overthrow of the Marxist government of Cheddi Jagan in Guyana (formerly British Guiana).

BAY OF PIGS AND OPERATION MONGOOSE

Covert operations never became commonplace but increasingly dominated the CIA's activities, supplanting the Agency's initial intelligence and counterintelligence purpose. The principal requirement for launching such operations was that they would be conducted in secret, and ensure presidential deniability. In this respect, the CIA-engineered coup of April 1961 to overthrow the government of Cuban Premier Fidel Castro proved to be the striking exception. Following the disastrous failure of this operation, President Kennedy admitted having authorized the invasion—and the CIA's role. This revelation, however, did not trigger a congressional inquiry into the significance of this admission. Congress made no effort in 1961 or in succeeding years to ascertain whether such CIA-engineered covert operations were atypical or normative. Only in the mid-1970s would Congress seek to uncover and assess the White House–CIA relationship.

The decision to authorize a plan to overthrow the Castro government through the Bay of Pigs invasion of April 17, 1961, was the byproduct of the Eisenhower administration's reassessment of its decision to recognize the Castro government when it came to power on January 2, 1959, through a successful revolution against the corrupt and repressive government of Fulgencio Batista. The administration very quickly became alarmed over Castro's subsequent actions—expropriating foreign-owned land holdings and businesses,

Fidel Castro delivering a speech in 1960. (Courtesy of Photofest)

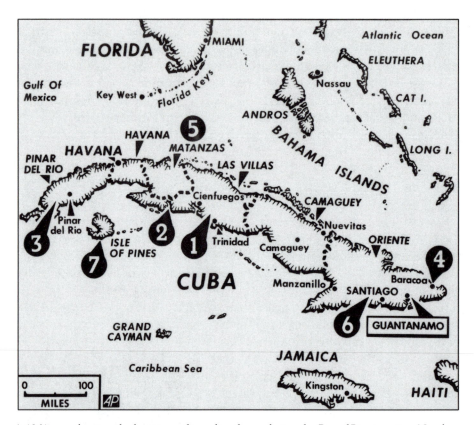

A 1961 map showing the locations of invading forces during the Bay of Pigs invasion. Numbers are irrelevant. (AP/Wide World Photos)

initiating show trials preparatory to executing Batista era officials, and concluding trade agreements with the Soviet Union under which Cuban sugar was exchanged for Soviet arms, machinery, and technical advisers. Concerned that Cuba was becoming a Soviet satellite and, further, might seek to foment revolutions elsewhere in Latin America, CIA officials in January 1960 drafted plans to neutralize Castro. This initial four-part plan included proposals either to assassinate the Cuban leader (and his brother Raul) or to orchestrate a paramilitary coup. These proposals were refined and scaled back in the succeeding months, and in March 1960 President Eisenhower authorized CIA officials to recruit and train (at a secret camp in Guatemala) Cuban exiles to invade Cuba. The plan, code-named Operation ZAPATA, was based on the premise that the landing of this paramilitary force would trigger a popular uprising and defections from the Cuban military. CIA supervisors estimated that execution of this plan to recruit and train a paramilitary force would require six to eight months, ensuring that final approval would be deferred to Eisenhower's successor. Following his election to the presidency in November

1960, John Kennedy did approve the planned invasion but on the condition that the U.S. role not become known. This led Kennedy to refuse a later CIA request (prior to the actual invasion) that he authorize air strikes to support the invading brigade. Such air support, CIA officials supervising this operation emphasized, was essential to neutralize Castro's air force. Kennedy's rejection ensured the defeat of the invasion—although the task force's landing did not trigger the promised popular uprising and military defections. Confronting a well-organized military, the landing force, Brigade 2506, suffered heavy casualties and had no choice but to surrender. Of the recruited volunteers comprising the invading party, 1,214 were captured and 1,700 were killed. The capture of these Cuban exiles forced Kennedy to repudiate his original condition and admit publicly to the U.S. role in organizing and financing this operation. The president did so to promote negotiations with the Cuban government that in effect ransomed the captured invaders—in return for which the Castro government was given medical and other nonmilitary supplies.

The Bay of Pigs debacle did not mean that the Kennedy administration abandoned a plan to overthrow Castro. Instead, the administration pressured CIA officials to intensify their efforts to achieve this objective—resulting in a covert operation code named Operation MONGOOSE, which the president approved in November 1961. On one level, CIA officials sought to destabilize the Castro government. This included seeking to contaminate Cuban sugar exports and sabotaging shipments of machinery. These efforts were supplemented by CIA initiatives to assassinate Castro, efforts that dated from 1960, intensified after 1962, and continued until 1965. Between 1960 and 1965, CIA operatives attempted at least eight times to assassinate Castro and at the same time devised plans to discredit the Cuban leader. The specific operations ranged from the criminal to the absurd. They included soliciting the assistance of Mafia dons Santos Trafficante, Sam Giancana, and John Roselli to recruit a Cuban to kill Castro; to smuggling high-powered rifles into Cuba for the use of a prospective assassin; to inserting deadly bacterial powders in a scuba diving suit to be given as a gift to Castro; to impregnating a box of cigars with a substance that would cause Castro to become disoriented; and finally to dusting Castro's shoes with thallium salts to cause his beard to fall out.

ASSASSINATION PLANNING: CONGO, DOMINICAN REPUBLIC, SOUTH VIETNAM, CHILE

The eight known CIA plots to assassinate Castro leave unresolved the question whether Presidents Kennedy and Eisenhower had been fully aware and had then authorized them. A policy of presidential deniability, combined with the subsequent discoveries that relevant records had been destroyed or that minutes of NSC meetings intentionally did not record any discussion or decision relating to a subject as sensitive as assassination planning, precludes a definitive resolution of this matter. In 1975, moreover, congressional investigators uncovered CIA memoranda that confirmed that as early as 1961 Richard Bissell, the deputy director of plans who had exercised operational responsibility for the Bay of Pigs invasion, instructed William Harvey, at the time chief of the Agency's foreign intelligence staff, to establish an "executive action capability" that was to include researching methods that could result in the assassination of foreign leaders. Bissell had earlier asked his science adviser, Joseph Scheider, to review the general "capability of the clandestine service in the field of incapacitation and elimination." The terms "executive action" and "elimination" suggest that Bissell was interested in enacting a formal program to assassinate foreign leaders. Whether or not these instructions moved beyond the planning stage, assassination planning had become a component of CIA covert operations, at least during the years 1960–1970.

The January 1960 proposal to assassinate Castro predated by eight months another such CIA plan. In August 1960, CIA officers formulated a plan to assassinate Patrice Lumumba, at the time the charismatic prime minister of the Congo. Lumumba had recently become prime minister when that former colony acquired its independence from Belgium in June 1960. His political radicalism, unpredictability, and pro-Soviet leanings immediately troubled Eisenhower administration and CIA officials. As part of a broader initiative to undermine Lumumba's government, in the summer of 1960 CIA officials proposed a series of actions to assassinate Lumumba (in contrast to Castro, Lumumba's support derived not from his leadership of a broad-based popular movement but from the force of his personality). The various proposals were never implemented—although toxic biological materials and a dart gun were procured and delivered to the CIA station chief in Leopoldville, Congo, for use by an individual recruited to implement the recommended assassination plot. Lumumba was subsequently assassinated, although not as a result of the Agency's assassination planning. Captured by rival factional leaders in December 1960, he was transferred to Congo's Katanga province in January 1961 where he was killed while in captivity.

A third instance of CIA assassination planning targeted the Dominican Republic's dictator Rafael Trujillo. Trujillo was assassinated on May 30, 1961 by Dominican military officers.

Owing to Trujillo's brutality and corruptness, both the Eisenhower and Kennedy administrations decided to prevent his continuance in power. They had become concerned that his continuance could unleash the sort of popular uprising that had led to Castro's success in Cuba. Both presidents initially sought to pressure Trujillo to institute political and economic reforms. President Kennedy, for example, lobbied Congress in 1961, at a time when sugar quota legislation was being debated, to scale back the Dominican quota and then sought to use this as leverage on the Dominican dictator. Trujillo did not budge, however.

Their frustrations with Trujillo eventually led both presidents to direct the CIA to devise a plan to effect his abdication or overthrow. Dating from the spring of 1960 through May 1961, CIA officials debated whether to deliver rifles with telescopic sights (through diplomatic pouches) to dissident Dominican military officers. This debate had been triggered by these officers' requests, who at the time did not hide their intent to assassinate Trujillo and not simply use these weapons to overthrow the dictator. A CIA memo of June 1960, in fact, records that during a meeting with Roy Rubottom, the assistant secretary of state for inter-American affairs, J. C. King, the chief of the Agency's Western Hemisphere Division, had queried Rubottom as to whether the purpose for delivering "a small number of sniper rifles or other devices" (which would include fragmentary grenades, high-powered rifles, pistols, and antitank rockets) to a proposed drop site in the Dominican Republic was "for the removal of key Trujillo people from the scene." King's memorandum on this conversation records Rubottom's response as "yes." The objective of hastening Trujillo's downfall remained a recurring theme in subsequent correspondence, although these records leave unclear whether the purpose was simply to instigate a coup and/or ensure Trujillo's assassination. Furthermore, the participants involved in these secret discussions took great care to ensure confidentiality. And although eventually delivered to the Dominican Republic, machine guns and rifles were never given to the identified conspirators—CIA officials having concluded that delivering them would be untimely, as precipitous action at this time could bring about an undesired power vacuum.

The fourth assassination plan targeted South Vietnamese President Ngo Dinh Diem. Although U.S. and CIA officials had in 1954 acted to install Diem as president and in subsequent years provided crucial assistance to sustain his presidency, by late 1963 they had become concerned that his repressive policies (particularly toward protesting Buddhist monks) could undermine popular support for a noncommunist South Vietnam. Diem's repressive tactics and unpopularity did eventually trigger a coup on November 2, 1963, led by South Vietnamese generals who captured and then killed Diem (and his brother-in-law, the interior minister).

Troubled by Diem's brutal responses to Buddhist demonstrations, including having South Vietnamese police sack sacred Buddhist temples, and the South Vietnamese president's refusal to institute reforms to address the demands of Buddhist and other embittered South Vietnamese, the Kennedy administration by the fall of 1963 considered supporting a coup to overthrow the Diem government. At the time, administration officials had received queries from senior South Vietnamese military officials who were seeking assurances of U.S. support should they launch a coup. These communications further indicated that the plotters were considering assassinating Diem. Extant CIA records do not confirm that CIA officials had directly counseled assassination, only that they recommended allowing this planning to go forward. In this case, the murky evidence concerning the role of CIA operatives suggests that no action had been taken either to further a coup or an assassination but that they were committed to a "hands off approach."

The last known assassination plot involved Chilean General Rene Schneider. In both 1964 and 1970, at the direction first of the Johnson and then of the Nixon administration, the CIA had secretly funded the nominee of the Chilean Christian Democratic Party during the 1964 and 1970 elections for the Chilean presidency. This covert assistance was intended to prevent the election of Salvador Allende, a Marxist and the Chilean Socialist Party nominee. In 1964, this assistance had succeeded. In 1970, however, Allende received a plurality of the popular vote (and had outpolled the two other candidates). By coming in first, and given past precedent, Allende would normally have been elected president by the Chilean parliament. To prevent this, the Nixon administration turned to the CIA first to ensure that the Chilean parliament would abandon precedent and not elect Allende. This tactic failed. As a second option, administration officials considered a proposed plan to foment a military coup.

Given the Chilean military's long tradition of nonintervention in politics, a plan to ensure military support for a coup could succeed only if General Schneider was displaced, given his known opposition to military intervention in civilian politics. On October 19 and 20, 1970, a group of Chilean military officers, whom CIA operatives were actively supporting, unsuccessfully attempted to kidnap Schneider. Then, on October 22, 1970, CIA officers provided arms and ammunition to these Chilean military officers, who mortally wounded the general when attempting to kidnap him that day. Extant records leave no doubt that in September 1970 President Nixon had authorized the CIA to foment a coup, but do not confirm that the president or senior CIA officials had in October 1970 authorized the supplying of arms and ammunition to assist the Chilean officers' plot to kidnap Schneider.

Schneider's death did not result in Allende's overthrow that month. CIA operatives nonetheless continued to work closely with dissident elements in Chilean society in subsequent years to sustain consumer and trucker strikes and other popular protests over Allende's economic policies of land reform and nationalization of key industries. This discontent eventually triggered riots that led Chilean military officers in September 1973 to launch a successful coup whereby Allende was overthrown and replaced by General Augusto Pinochet on September 11, 1973.

CONGRESS FOR CULTURAL FREEDOM, NATIONAL STUDENT ASSOCIATION, OPERATION CHAOS

The known instances of CIA assassination planning raise at least two questions. The first involves the specific individuals targeted under the proposed assassination plots. None posed either a direct or imminent threat to U.S. security and in fact had been targeted because of their political philosophy and advocacy, as radical nationalists, of a foreign policy that challenged the goals of U.S. administrations. Second, the CIA's assassination planning raises a moral concern and thus seemingly would at minimum require that low-level CIA officers must not on their own support foreign nationals willing to resort to assassination without both the sanction of the U.S. president and the advance knowledge of the DCI. Extant records do not confirm that presidents, and DCIs, sanctioned or knew about such plots. But this does not mean that CIA plotters were acting on their own. Under the strategy of deniability, no written records would have been created confirming the president's authorization. Furthermore, in at least one known instance—involving the question of whether President Eisenhower had during an August 1960 NSC meeting authorized a proposal to assassinate Patrice Lumumba—congressional investigators discovered in the mid-1970s that should an operation as sensitive as assassination have been discussed and approved at an NSC meeting the minutes of that meeting would purposefully not record that the matter either had been discussed or decided.

CIA covert operations raise an additional policy question insofar as some of the Agency's covert propaganda activities spilled over to influence domestic politics and public opinion. These activities included a secret program, initiated on April 7, 1950, and code-named QKOPERA, to fund the Congress for Cultural Freedom and its various foreign-language journals: *Encounter* (British), *Preuves* (French), *Tempo Presente* (Italian), *Forum* (Austrian), *Der Monat* (German), *Hiwer* (Lebanese), *Cuadenos* (Latin American), and *Chinese Quarterly* (Chinese). Through CIA funding, the congress was also able to sponsor a series of international cultural conferences (which Americans attended), art exhibits, and musical performances. The congress's publications, moreover, were widely read outside their native countries. These CIA-sponsored cultural initiatives, as an unintended result, not only counteracted Soviet cultural activities in Europe, Latin America, the Middle East, and the Far East but also influenced the views of American intellectuals, and indirectly the popular culture.

The CIA's covert propaganda initiatives were not confined to assisting favored intellectuals, or supporting what could be termed the "high culture." The Agency also helped fund the filming of George Orwell's anticommunist books *1984* and *Animal Farm*—films that were shown to American audiences and throughout the world. The CIA also helped fund a foreign-based news feature service (Forum News)—with some of its news releases picked up by American newspapers. CIA operatives recruited and paid several hundred primarily foreign freelance reporters, funded the research of American academics (primarily political scientists and historians), and subsidized the publication of over 1,000 books about the history and politics of Eastern Europe and the Soviet Union (25 percent of which were published in English, with many of these published by the U.S. publisher Praeger). Appraising this policy of subsidies, the chief of the Agency's propaganda unit in 1961 extolled the "advantage of our [CIA] direct contact with the author [of CIA funded books] is that we can acquaint him with whatever material we want him to include and that we can check the manuscript at every stage. Our control over the writer will have to be enforced . . . [and the Agency] must make sure the actual manuscript will correspond with our operational and propagandistic intention."

CIA domestic covert propaganda activities were scaled back in 1967, the result of a controversy precipitated by the publication of an article in the March 1967 issue of *Ramparts Magazine*. This article exposed one of the Agency's covert funding programs, namely that since 1952 the CIA had helped finance the international programs of an American college student organization, the National Student Association. Disclosure of the CIA's subsidization of this association publicly raised the issue of academic freedom, since the student leaders had coordinated the group's annual conference in the United States and maintained year-round contact with those student governments that elected representatives to this annual conference. President Johnson moved quickly to allay these concerns by appointing on February 15, 1967, a special commission, headed by Undersecretary of State Nicholas Katzenbach. The president, however, had then confined the commission's mandate to investigating the Agency's covert funding of American colleges through ostensibly private foundations. Consistent with this limitation, the so-called Katzenbach Commission's report, released on March 29, 1967, recommended a ban only on "any covert financial assistance or support, direct or indirect, to any of the nation's educational or private voluntary organizations."

The Katzenbach Commission's narrow mandate precluded an inquiry into the scope of the Agency's extensive covert operations—which could have a direct or indirect impact on domestic politics. In addition to the Congress for Cultural Freedom and the National Student Association, these included the Agency's covert relationship with the international division of the AFL-CIO, clandestine contacts with foreign nationals studying at American colleges and universities, interviews with and recruitment of American businessmen and professionals who traveled abroad, and interviews and solicitation of foreign diplomats and consular officials traveling through or stationed in the United States. When appointing the Katzenbach Commission, moreover, the president succeeded in undercutting support for a broader inquiry demanded by Senate majority leader Mike Mansfield. Following the *Ramparts* exposé, Mansfield had called for a review of all CIA covert funding activities within the United States. Johnson's success in averting an independent review of CIA operations, however, proved to be temporary.

On December 22, 1974, *New York Times* reporter Seymour Hersh authored a front-page article disclosing that, in violation of its 1947 charter banning any "domestic security" role, the CIA had "conducted a massive illegal domestic intelligence operation during the Nixon Administration against the anti-[Vietnam] war movement and other dissident groups in the United States." Thousand of activists were targeted, Hersh reported, with Agency operatives even employing illegal investigative methods of break-ins, wiretaps, and mail opening.

Hersh's exposé understated a more complex and massive reality, and triggered the first-ever congressional examination of the heretofore secret (and, in some cases, abusive) activities of various U.S. intelligence agencies. The resultant investigations were conducted by special congressional committees (in the Senate by the so-called Church Committee and in the House by the so-called Pike Committee, named after their respective chairmen Senator Frank Church and Congressman Otis Pike). Congress's action in creating these special committees stymied an earlier attempt by President Ford to preempt congressional action by appointing a presidential committee, headed by Vice President Nelson Rockefeller. Ford had given the commission a narrow mandate to investigate only CIA domestic operations.

For the first time, congressional investigators obtained access to formerly secret records, and thereby uncovered a history of secret abuses of power—and, most notably, that dating from 1967 (under Johnson's presidency) and expanded in 1969 (under Nixon's) CIA officials had launched a massive domestic surveillance program, code-named Operation MHCHAOS. This covert program had been initiated in response to pressure from the Johnson administration. Seeking evidence to confirm that the militant anti–Vietnam War and civil rights movements were acting in concert with the Soviet Union, communist China, or Cuba, the president had first turned to the FBI for evidence to discredit these movements. Dissatisfied with the FBI reports and seeking more convincing documentation, he turned to the CIA. The president might have anticipated that Agency officials would obtain the desired confirmation of such links from the CIA's foreign sources. CIA operatives instead infiltrated these domestic organizations and then compiled dossiers on tens of thousands of their adherents.

Conducted by employees in the Agency's counterintelligence division, Operation CHAOS failed to develop the desired evidence of such links "in terms of espionage and sabotage." DCI Helms in fact advised President Johnson on November 15, 1967, that the Agency had uncovered "no evidence of any contact between the most prominent peace movement leaders and foreign embassies in the U.S. or abroad," and had instead concluded that the movements were indigenous and their activities determined by their members' ideological opposition to the president's foreign and domestic policies. The DCI repeated this assessment in a follow-up briefing of President Nixon in 1969. Nonetheless, and despite these findings, CIA officials continued this politically sensitive domestic spying program until 1973 and discontinued it then only because of a new political risk. The changed domestic political climate triggered by press and congressional revelations involving the so-called Watergate Affair (and even more troubling, about the CIA's relations with the Nixon White House) had increased the chances that this domestic spying program could be uncovered—as indeed it was.

The Church and Pike Committees' investigations had uncovered a dark side of the CIA's history (as that of other U.S. intelligence agencies, notably the FBI), a history of abuses of power that were made possible because of the blind acceptance of the imperative need for secrecy and the lack of congressional oversight. Moreover, many in Congress demanded the enactment of legislative charters to govern the permissible operations of the U.S. intelligence agencies, thereby abandoning an earlier policy of deference to the executive branch.

The dramatic revelations of the Church and Pike Committees led both the House and the Senate to establish in 1976 permanent oversight committees to monitor the intelligence agencies. Then, in the years 1977 through 1980, Congress began to review and hold hearings on various proposed charter bills to proscribe the role of the U.S. intelligence agencies—with liberals and conservatives differing over how specific any legislative restrictions should be. Events of 1979–1980, however, proved to be the death knell for any congressional action—the events stemming from the seizure of U.S. citizens employed in the U.S. embassy in Teheran by radical Iranian students in 1979, the Soviet invasion of Afghanistan in 1979, and the election of Republican presidential nominee Ronald Reagan in 1980.

The Iran and Afghanistan crises had heightened concerns that the United States was losing the Cold War and that this was partly due to inadequate foreign intelligence—concerns that underpinned candidate Reagan's demand for increased defense spending and his call to "unleash" the intelligence agencies. In the latter case, this meant rescinding the restrictions that Presidents Ford and Carter had imposed on CIA operations in the aftermath of the 1975 congressional investigations, to enacting legislation criminalizing the public identification of CIA undercover operatives, and amending the Freedom of Information Act to exempt CIA and FBI records from that Act's disclosure requirements.

HUGHES-RYAN, ANGOLA, INTELLIGENCE OVERSIGHT ACT

Congress's effort to enact a new CIA legislative charter was formally abandoned following Ronald Reagan's election to the presidency in November 1980. Nonetheless, on December 30, 1974, and predating the establishment of the Church and Pike committees, Congress for the first time sought to institute a system of effective congressional oversight over CIA covert operations when approving the so-called Hughes-Ryan Act, Public Law 93-559 (an amendment to the Foreign Assistance Act of 1974). The Hughes-Ryan Act required presidents to issue a written finding that any major CIA covert operation "is important to the security of the United States." Such presidential findings were then to be reported "in a timely fashion" to eight congressional committees. Significantly, because aware of CIA covert operations, although not their scope or specific uses, and despite the fact that such practices were not explicitly mandated by the 1947 National Security Act, Section 102 (5) of which had unwittingly provided the loophole exploited to expand the Agency's functions to include covert operations, Congress did not in 1974 enact standards either explicitly authorizing CIA covert operations (and defining their character and purpose) or require that presidents brief Congress in advance as a condition for any such planned operations. By 1974, a consensus had evolved that covert operations furthered the nation's security interests and that their success required that they could be planned and executed in secrecy. The reporting requirement would nonetheless serve to deter covert operations that could not command public support. In addition, the written finding requirement imposed on presidents the responsibility to record their approval as to their necessity, at the same time ensuring that presidents could not after the fact evade responsibility for operations that could have adverse political consequences should they become known.

The Hughes-Ryan Act marked a potentially far-reaching change in congressional policy. Its enactment confirmed that members of Congress were no longer willing to defer unquestioningly to the president on national security matters, or to acquiesce blindly when presidents affirmed a need for absolute secrecy. This reassessment of the presidential role in conducting national security policy was first triggered by disillusionment over Presidents Johnson's and Nixon's conduct of the Vietnam War, and then by the questions about the White House–CIA relationship that surfaced in the aftermath of the Watergate Affair first during the Senate investigation of 1973 into this break-in and cover-up and then during the House impeachment inquiry of 1974. One result was support leading to the passage of a series of amendments to the 1966 Freedom of Information Act based on the principle of the public's right to know. Two further consequences were congressional decisions of 1975 first to authorize the Church and Pike Committees' investigation and then to curtail a publicly compromised CIA covert operation involving Angola, code-named IAFEATURE, that President Ford authorized on July 8, 1975.

A Portuguese colony, Angola did not command the interest of U.S. policy makers until April 1974 when a leftist military coup in Portugal led to the overthrow of Marcello Caetano, the hand-picked successor as prime minister of Portuguese dictator Antonio Salazar. The Caetano (and Salazar) governments had been engaged in a low-level military conflict with left-led revolutionary movements in Portugal's African colonies of Angola, Mozambique, and Portuguese Guinea (now Guinea-Bissau), costly policies that eventually triggered the April 1974 coup. The new military government soon decided to abandon the fight to preserve these colonies (including as well Cape Verde, Sao Tome, and Principe). In January 1975, it announced that it would withdraw from Angola, and would grant formal independence to that colony on November 11, 1975. In the interim until the formal grant of independence, the Portuguese appointed a coalition government (composed of leaders from three different Angolan revolutionary factions) until popular elections were held. Of the three factions, the movement commanding the most support was the Marxist Popular Movement for the Liberation of Angola (MPLA) led by Agostinho Neto. The MPLA, however, had previously received (and continued to receive) funding and training support from the Soviet Union and from a contingent of Cuban military advisers.

Committed to preventing the MPLA from acquiring control of Angola and seeking to capitalize on the rivalries among the three Angolan revolutionary factions, President Ford in July 1975 authorized the CIA to expend $14 million and then in August to expend an additional $11.7 million to fund the two other Angolan factions, the National Front for the Liberation of Angola (FNLA) led by Holden Roberto and the National Union for the Total Independence of Angola (UNITA) led by Jonas Savimbi. One byproduct of the CIA's assistance to these factions was that Soviet and Cuban support for the MPLA increased, changing the character of this conflict from a possible civil war between rival Angolan factions to a Cold War crisis.

Required by Hughes-Ryan, the Ford administration briefed the senior members of the eight congressional committees in July about its initial funding of this covert operation. Senator Dick Clark, at the time the chair of the African Affairs Subcommittee of the Senate Foreign Relations Committee, learned of this decision through a briefing circulated to all members of the Foreign Relations Committee. Then, prior to a planned fact-finding trip to Africa, Clark learned that this CIA covert operation had been expanded in August. Troubled by the original and expanded commitment, Clark could not at first go public owing to the nondisclosure condition of the reporting requirement. Nonetheless, he moved quickly to exploit reports on U.S. funding of the rebel forces published in the *New York Times* and *Washington Post*. The senator, in the waning days of Congress's 1975 session, introduced an amendment to the 1976 Defense Department appropriation to terminate any funding for this Angolan operation. Clark's amendment was approved by the Senate in December 1975 and by the House in January 1976.

The Ford administration's decision to fund the rebel forces in Angola highlights the limits of the Hughes-Ryan Act. Significantly, this operation was terminated by Congress only because its existence was publicly compromised, and the Act's reporting requirements had increased this possibility. Yet, Congress lacked the authority to countermand a planned covert operation and further to subject the president's rationale for proposed covert operations to critical scrutiny as to its costs and consequences. Even in a changed political atmosphere of heightened congressional assertiveness, the decision to launch covert operations remained a presidential prerogative. The Hughes-Ryan Act had simply increased the risks of conducting only those operations which, if publicly exposed, could provoke a powerful public protest. By the end of the 1970s, moreover, congressional sentiment supportive of disclosure and restraint had abated. This revised assessment led Congress to enact legislation scaling back Hughes-Ryan's reporting requirements.

The Act had required presidents to notify eight congressional committees about approved major CIA covert operations: the House and Senate armed services, foreign affairs, appropriations, and intelligence committees. In effect, a total of 163 members of Congress and senior congressional staff would become apprized of an approved major CIA covert operation. Such numbers increased the risk of a leak. Accordingly, in 1980 CIA and Carter administration officials successfully lobbied Congress to amend the 1974 requirement, scaling back required briefings to two committees (the House and Senate intelligence committees). Approved on October 14, 1980, the Intelligence Accountability Act, known as the Intelligence Oversight Act, nonetheless specified that presidential notification of the two committees of such findings was to be "timely." The Intelligence Oversight Act, moreover, did not require presidents to keep these committees "fully and currently informed" in advance of a planned operation.

IRAN-CONTRA

The Intelligence Oversight Act, nonetheless, confirmed Congress's insistence on a limited supervisory role over CIA covert operations. Although prior notification was not required, the intent of the Act reflected an expectation that delayed briefings would be exceptional, confined to unanticipated circumstances that would require immediate action. Passage of this Act, however, had coincided with Ronald Reagan's election to the presidency on a platform of "unleashing" the intelligence agencies, a platform that ensured that the new administration would pursue a more aggressive foreign policy, and would be more willing to approve controversial covert operations that could promote its ambitious foreign policy agenda. Although the focus of candidate Reagan's campaign signaled a commitment to a more militant anti-Soviet policy, the immediate crises in Afghanistan and Iran had also figured large in this call for a reassessment and informed the new administration's foreign policy planning.

The Soviet invasion of Afghanistan in December 1979 had triggered a popular rebellion centered in mountainous rural areas and commanding the support of militant Islamist fundamentalists. In addition to pressuring the Soviet leaders to abandon this military invasion (in part by suspending U.S. wheat shipments to the Soviet Union and by barring U.S. participation in the 1980 Olympic Games held in Moscow), President Carter in 1980 authorized the CIA to provide covert support (funds and weapons) to the Afghan rebels (funneled through Pakistan's intelligence service). President Reagan continued and expanded this support, to include supplying the so-called *mujahedeen* Stinger ground-to-air missiles that could help neutralize Soviet air power. Then, having failed to convince Congress to exempt CIA (and FBI) records from the mandatory review and disclosure requirements of the Freedom of Information Act, Reagan administration and CIA officials in 1984 succeeded in having Congress exempt the Agency's "operational" files from the Act's mandatory review requirements. And, in a companion action in 1984, Congress lifted the ban on U.S. financing of the anti-MPLA rebel factions in Angola with the CIA that year and then in 1986 airlifting millions of dollars in military supplies to UNITA, the major rebel group opposing the MPLA government.

This renewed interest in secrecy and support for covert operations reflected the persistence of Cold War assumptions that radical revolutionary movements were controlled by the Soviet Union, and that their success would threaten U.S. economic and strategic interests. This conception also underpinned the Reagan administration's authorization of a covert operation to overthrow the radical Sandinista government of Nicaragua.

The Sandinistas had come to power in July 1979 through an armed rebellion that had capitalized on popular opposition to the corrupt and repressive government of Anastasio Somoza. On assuming power, the Sandinistas instituted major changes in that country's domestic and foreign policies, including providing aid to a rebel movement in neighboring El Salvador. To consolidate their control in Nicaragua, the Sandinistas dissolved the Somoza-controlled National Guard, an action that ensured that disgruntled, unemployed guardsmen could form the basis for a counterrevolutionary movement, one that did emerge within a year and that sought to capitalize on opposition (by large landowners and other economic and social conservatives) to the Sandinistas' sweeping agricultural and social reforms.

Ostensibly to deter the Sandinistas' support for the rebel movement in El Salvador and concerned over their receipt of military training and support from Cuba, raising the specter of a communist beachhead in the Western Hemisphere, on November 23, 1981, President Reagan approved a National Security Decision Directive (NSDD-17) authorizing the CIA to expend $18 million to defeat the insurgency in El Salvador "by Cuba, Nicaragua, or others." Although the stated objective of this finding was to prevent the Sandinista government from assisting El Salvadoran rebels, the method that was adopted to achieve this goal was to effect the overthrow of the Sandinista government by recruiting and training the so-called Contras, primarily former Somoza national guardsmen who mounted military attacks on Sandinista forces from neighboring Honduras and Costa Rica. The CIA's covert support of the Contras first became publicly known in 1982 with other more dramatic revelations of CIA actions surfacing in 1984, provoking congressional criticism and restrictions.

The most controversial of the CIA programs became known in 1984. As part of their support for the Contras, CIA operatives had mined the Nicaraguan port of Corinto, an action that the International Court in 1984 (ruling on a Nicaraguan suit) found to be in violation of international law. Later that year, in October, American journalists obtained a copy of a CIA training manual on psychological operations and guerrilla warfare prepared by CIA contract employee "John Kirkpatrick" (a pseudonym), reporting that the manual included a section on kidnapping, terror bombing, and assassinations.

When first learning of CIA's covert operations involving the Contras, Congress on December 8, 1982, approved an amendment to the fiscal 1983 appropriation bill. The more sensational 1984 revelations led to congressional approval on October 12, 1984 of an amendment to the 1985 defense budget bill; both of these amendments became known as the Boland Amendment. The amendments themselves prohibited any direct or indirect CIA assistance to the Contras.

Because both amendments had been incorporated in an omnibus appropriation bill, President Reagan was denied the opportunity to veto the restriction on continued aid to the Contras. And, while the CIA was thereby forced to suspend its covert aid program to the Contras, the Reagan administration both sought to convince Congress to rescind this restriction and concurrently sought alternative means to sustain this counterrevolutionary movement. These efforts included soliciting funding assistance to the Contras from both wealthy right-wing American citizens and friendly foreign governments (Saudi Arabia, Brunei). Furthermore, because the Boland Amendment had specifically prohibited CIA support, administration officials assigned operational responsibility over efforts to continue support for the Contras to officials on the National Security Council staff, notably John Poindexter and Oliver North. In what proved to be a counterproductive action, NSC officials, with Oliver North playing the key role, in time devised a further plan to fund the Contras by diverting surplus funds that had been obtained through the sale of 2,008 TOW antitank and 235 HAWK antiaircraft missiles to Iran.

The Iranian phase of what became known as the Iran-Contra affair had its origins in a controversial recommendation proposed by NSC officials in the summer of 1985 to sell missiles to Iranian "moderates" who in return would assist in securing the release of American citizens (including CIA station chief William Buckley) held hostage by Lebanese militants. Iran had considerable influence over these militants and at the time was in the throes of a difficult military war with Iraq (and was desperately seeking military supplies). An additional benefit of this recommendation was that the arms sale could promote the normalization of U.S.-Iranian relations (severed with the Iranian hostage crisis of 1979–1980 and the coming to power of a militantly anti-American Islamic government). This highly sensitive covert operation (the more so because it contradicted the Reagan administration's stated policy of refusing to negotiate with terrorists) eventually did cause additional political problems for the Reagan administration because of the president's decision to flout the reporting requirements of the Intelligence Oversight Act. Owing to pressure from CIA officials who were particularly troubled by the president's failure to have earlier issued an appropriate finding for missile sales of August and November 1985, President Reagan on January 17, 1986, belatedly signed an after-the-fact finding authorizing these and future arms sales. The signed finding, moreover, stipulated that Congress not be notified of this decision.

This secret operation was publicly compromised in October–November 1986, first owing to the publication of an exposé in a Lebanese newspaper that reported the arms-for-hostages trade with Iran and then the disclosure of Attorney General Edwin Meese (following a Justice Department investigation triggered by this story) that proceeds from this arms sale had been diverted to assist the Nicaraguan Contras. The resultant controversy spawned by these twin disclosures triggered a congressional investigation in 1987, conducted jointly by the House and Senate intelligence committees, and as well a criminal investigation conducted by Independent Counsel Lawrence Walsh.

One result of the disclosure that the Reagan administration had intentionally flouted the reporting requirements of the Intelligence Oversight Act was a lengthy debate as to whether congressional oversight powers had to be clarified. A compromise between Congress and Reagan's successor, George H. W. Bush, was eventually reached. On August 15, 1991, Congress enacted Public Law 102-88, the Intelligence Authorization Act of 1991, requiring the president to "fully and currently" inform the Congress "in a timely fashion" of the authorization of covert operations. Although the 1991 law did not explicitly stipulate that such notification must be made before such operations were instituted, or empower Congress to challenge proposed covert operations, the report accompanying the bill did require that such findings were to be reported "in a few days." (In the case of the Iran-Contra affair, a presidential finding authorizing the diversion of the surplus funds to the contras was never issued and the congressional intelligence committees first learned of President Reagan's January 1986 finding relating to the Iranian program only when this operation was publicly compromised in October–November 1986.)

The Iran-Contra affair raised a second issue, one that involved the truthfulness of the testimony of administration (and CIA) officials during the congressional investigation of 1987. Because of the Meese report and other revelations that fall, the joint congressional committee investigating the Iran-Contra affair had focused on the central role of members of the National Security Council (NSC) staff in executing this covert operation, and had specifically sought to ascertain whether the activities of the NSC staff were known and authorized by President Reagan and senior CIA officials. Congressional investigators accordingly interviewed key CIA officials, inquiring specifically about their knowledge and their assistance to the former CIA and military officials and the NSC staff who had been directly involved in executing this operation. The congressional investigation, moreover, was held concurrent with a criminal inquiry launched by Independent Counsel Walsh, whose inquiry centered on whether White House, NSC, CIA, and other departmental officials had knowingly violated (or were aware of others having violated) the requirements of the Intelligence Oversight Act, the Boland

Amendment, and the Arms Export Control Act (the latter requiring that arms sales exceeding $10,000 were to be reported to Congress).

Owing to the recent death of DCI William Casey, both the congressional and criminal inquiries were unable to resolve definitively his role in the decision to divert the surplus proceeds from the arms sale to the Contras. Congressional and independent counsel investigators did question, among others, four CIA officers—Clair George, Duane Clarridge, Alan Fiers, and Joseph Fernandez. These four were pointedly questioned about their knowledge of aspects of the Iran-Contra operation. Eventually concluding (from reviews of relevant, formerly classified records and other interviews) that the four had either given false or intentionally misleading answers, the independent counsel sought and secured their indictment by a federal grand jury convened to consider criminal prosecution.

The deputy director for operations from July 1984 through December 1987, George had supervisory responsibility over both the Iranian and contra phases of the Iran-Contra operation. When questioned both by congressional investigators and then subsequently by the grand jury, George denied any personal knowledge of who had been behind the Contra resupply operation, of the true identity of a former CIA operative, and of having been in contact with retired Air Force General Richard Secord, who had been directly involved in both the Iranian and contra phases of this covert operation. George was subsequently indicted by a federal grand jury on September 6, 1991, on nine counts of perjury, false statements, and obstructing congressional and grand jury investigations. Tried in November–December 1992, he was convicted of two of the seven counts (two of the original nine counts having been dismissed, with the jury finding George not guilty of the other five). The two counts involved his false statements and perjury during congressional testimony about the role of a former CIA operative in the contra resupply operation and denial of any knowledge of North's and Secord's role in the Iranian initiative. Scheduled for sentencing in February 1993, George was pardoned by President George H. W. Bush on December 24, 1992.

The chief of the CIA's European Division from 1984 to 1986, Clarridge had helped obtain air transport for a shipment of TOW missiles to Iran in November 1985. He was indicted by a federal grand jury on November 28, 1991, on seven counts of perjury and false statements to congressional investigators pertaining to his denial of any knowledge of the purpose of this shipment. Clarridge claimed that he had thought the shipment was a "commercial operation" involving the shipment of oil drilling equipment. Clarridge's trial was scheduled to begin on March 15, 1993, but was aborted when President George H. W. Bush pardoned him on December 24, 1992.

The chief of the CIA's Central American Task Force from October 1984 through 1988, Fiers had direct knowledge of the contra resupply operation during the period of the Boland Amendment's restrictions, including of North's direction of this operation and the day-to-day involvement in this resupply operation of former CIA operatives Felix Rodriguez and Richard Gadd. Fiers was indicted on six counts of perjury and false statements to congressional investigators involving his response to questions concerning the role of the former CIA operatives in providing aid to the contras and his further denial of any knowledge of North's role in the Contra resupply operation and the diversion of funds from the Iranian arms sales to the Contras. On January 9, 1991, Fiers pled guilty to two counts of withholding information from Congress—concerning his briefing of the Senate Select Committee on Intelligence in November 1986 about his knowledge that surplus funds from the arms sales had been diverted to the Contras and further of having concealed his knowledge of North's resupply operation during testimony before the House Select Committee on Intelligence in October 1986. Sentenced on January 31, 1992, to one hundred hours of community service, Fiers was pardoned by President George H. W. Bush on December 24, 1992.

A CIA station chief in Latin America, Fernandez played a key role in the Contra resupply operation of 1985–1986. He was indicted on June 20, 1988, on five counts of obstructing the investigations of both the so-called Tower Commission (the presidential commission established to investigate the Iran-Contra affair) and the CIA's Inspector General when questioned about his relationship with North and Secord and his knowledge of and involvement in the Contra resupply operation. Fernandez was convicted on none of these counts when Attorney General Richard Thornburgh refused to release classified information sought by his defense counsel. This refusal led the presiding judge to dismiss the indictment on October 12, 1990.

The Iran-Contra affair raises, directly and indirectly, the question about Congress's oversight role relating to CIA covert operations. President Reagan's January 1986 finding and the false and perjurious statements of CIA officials when responding to congressional inquiries confirm that the president and CIA officials (despite a specific law and Congress's oversight responsibilities) disdained having to answer to Congress. Their actions denied Congress any opportunity to evaluate the wisdom and consequences of proposed covert operations. Further, in this case when members of Congress either had learned about a covert operation or had asked relevant questions, CIA officials chose not to answer truthfully.

This effort to subvert any congressional review raises important constitutional questions. In effect, some CIA covert operations amounted to acts of war, conducted without an advance congressional declaration. Furthermore, Congress's decision in 1949 to immunize CIA funding from normal budgeting and accounting procedures had effectively denied itself the opportunity to become informed about the scope and purposes of planned operations—operations that could affect the nation's economic and strategic interests. Neither of these developments had been anticipated when Congress in 1947 enacted legislation creating the CIA and then in 1949 had exempted the CIA's budget from congressional oversight. Significantly, the limited congressional response of 1991 (at a time when indictments had been handed down concerning the false and misleading testimony of CIA and senior administration officials) underscores the far-reaching impact of the Cold War on executive-legislative relations. It confirms that the evolving consensus about the Soviet threat as deriving from communism's subversive and worldwide expansionist character had led to an acceptance of both the need for secrecy and deference to the executive branch.

TERRORISM, AL QAEDA, THE KEAN COMMISSION

The collapse of communist governments in Eastern Europe and the Balkans and the dissolution of the Soviet Union in 1989–1991 formally brought to an end the crisis of the Cold War. In light of this changed international order, questions arose about the role the CIA should play in a post–Cold War world, and whether covert operations remained necessary. Quite independently of this reassessment, and at a time when one threat to U.S. security interests had ended in the late 1980s and early 1990s, a new crisis had surfaced—the threat of Islamist terrorism.

The seizure of U.S. embassy employees by militant Iranian students in 1979 and then the kidnaping of U.S. citizens in Lebanon during the 1980s also by militant Islamist fundamentalists highlighted this new threat. In the 1980s, however, administration and CIA officials viewed the terrorist problem as regional in nature—centered in the Middle East—and directed by foreign governments (Iran and Libya) and secondarily by radical Palestinians (whose terrorist activities were directed at Israeli citizens). The specific events that triggered this concern involved the hijacking of airplanes, bombings at the Rome, Italy, and Vienna, Austria, airports, the hijacking of the cruise ship *Achille Lauro*, a bombing attack on a West Berlin discotheque, a suicide bombing attack on the U.S. embassy in Beirut (Lebanon), and the suitcase bombing of Pan American flight 103 over Lockerbie, Scotland.

For U.S. policy makers, the terrorist threat assumed a quite different dimension in the 1990s when the United States became a direct target. The specific events then involved a truck bombing attack in 1996 on the Khobar Towers complex that housed American airmen stationed in Saudi Arabia, the truck bombings in 1998 of U.S. embassies in Kenya and Tanzania, and a ship bombing attack in 2000 on the U.S.S. *Cole*. These were not government-supported operations, however, and had instead been planned and executed by a terrorist network, al Qaeda, funded and directed by Saudi exile Osama bin Laden and headquartered and with training camps in Afghanistan.

To address this new terrorist threat, in 1998 President Clinton authorized (and reaffirmed in 1999) the CIA to conduct covert operations to immobilize the al Qaeda network, including the capture or killing of bin Laden. CIA operatives in response sought to recruit Pashtun tribal chiefs in southern Afghanistan and funded the military operations of a rebel force, the Northern

Alliance (then involved in a military campaign to overthrow the Taliban government of Afghanistan, a militant Islamist government that provided sanctuary and bases for al Qaeda on Afghan territory). CIA officials even considered deploying CIA officers on the ground in Afghanistan and in 2001 considered the use of armed Predators (unmanned aircraft) to "eliminate the al Qaeda threat." These operations either were not implemented or failed, including a 1998 cruise missile attack targeting an al Qaeda training camp in Afghanistan at a time when CIA intelligence had reported that bin Laden would be present at this camp.

The failure of these CIA covert operations (and as well other diplomatic and military initiatives of the Clinton and George W. Bush administrations) proved fateful. On September 11, 2001, nineteen Middle Eastern alien residents commandeered four commercial jets, flying two of them into the World Trade Center in New York City, the third into the Pentagon, and crashing the fourth in a deserted field in western Pennsylvania. This al Qaeda–directed and financed terrorist attack resulted in the deaths of 2,973 and billions of dollars in direct and indirect economic losses. In response, the Bush administration launched a military invasion of Afghanistan that succeeded in overthrowing the Taliban government and destroying al Qaeda's training camps and operational headquarters. While bin Laden and Mullah Omar (the head of the Taliban government) were not captured (at the time or later), this military operation successfully disrupted the al Qaeda terrorist network and its ability to conduct future terrorist operations.

The nation's attention at first focused on the Afghanistan military operation and on anticipating and neutralizing future terrorist attacks within the United States. In 2002, however, the House and Senate intelligence committees launched a joint investigation into why the U.S. intelligence community had failed to anticipate this devastating terrorist attack. Denied access to all relevant records, the joint committee nonetheless issued a scathing report in July 2003 criticizing, in particular, the CIA and the FBI for not having aggressively pursued information about al Qaeda's plans and for having failed to coordinate their operations or to have shared relevant information.

Continued questions about the intelligence community's shortcomings led President George W. Bush on November 18, 2002, to sign legislation creating an independent commission, the National Commission on Terrorist Attacks on the United States (known as the Kean Commission), to investigate this intelligence failure and to recommend changes to preclude future terrorist attacks. In contrast to the joint House and Senate committee's investigation, the Kean Commission did secure extensive access to relevant records and interviewed key White House officials (including Presidents Clinton and George W. Bush, Vice President Cheney, and NSC adviser Condoleezza Rice). The Kean Commission publicized its major findings in a series of public hearings in the spring of 2004 and in a final report released on July 22, 2004.

The Kean Commission's central recommendation, which directly affected the role of the CIA, involved the creation of a National Intelligence Director, whose office would be headquartered in the Executive Office of the President, and who would have budgetary and oversight authority over all fifteen U.S. intelligence agencies. In addition, the Kean Commission recommended that "Lead responsibility for directing and executing paramilitary operations, whether clandestine or covert, should shift to the Defense Department. There it should be consolidated with the capabilities for training, direction, and execution of such operations already being developed in the [Defense Department's] Special Operations Command."

The Kean Commission's recommendations shaped the resultant public and congressional debate and legislative response, culminating with President George W. Bush's signing legislation, on December 17, 2004: the Intelligence Reform and Terrorism Prevention Act. This law implemented the commission's principal recommendation and created a new office within the Executive Office of the President headed by a Director of National Intelligence. The 2004 law, however, did not strip the CIA of its covert operations function or authorize the Defense Department to assume a central role in planning and executing paramilitary (or other covert) operations.

One month earlier, on November 18, 2004, President George W. Bush ordered a special interagency task force (composed of representatives from the State, Justice, and Defense Departments and the CIA) to "see whether or not transferring paramilitary authorities in their entirety from the C.I.A. to the Department of Defense would best serve the nation or whether there are other ways to have paramilitary forces work in better coordination." This review was to be completed in ninety days, and could have stripped the CIA of its covert operations role (at least in the area of paramilitary activities). The review, Assistant Secretary of Defense Thomas O'Connell (who had supervisory responsibility for the Defense Department's special operations and low-intensity warfare) assured the *New York Times*, had "no preordained outcome." It soon became known, however, that the Defense Department was in the process of developing plans to expand its authority to organize, train, and equip elite command forces and, further, that a recently drafted Pentagon directive instructed regional military commanders to expand their intelligence gathering.

Press reports of November 2004 through February 2005 uncovered Defense Department plans to acquire an expanded intelligence gathering and special operations role. One reported that the Pentagon had already created a battlefield intelligence unit to work with the Department's Special Operations forces during planned counterterrorism missions. Another reported that under Defense Department's appropriations, approved in October 2004, the Department was authorized to pay informers and recruit foreign paramilitary soldiers for its Special Operations, thereby reducing Defense's reliance on the CIA for intelligence and covert operations. An anonymous CIA official, responding to a *New York Times* inquiry about this provision, denied that it would rival the Agency's programs. This CIA official claimed that "The fact that D.O.D. [Department of Defense] has fixed a gap in its capability is a good thing," adding that "But the C.I.A. exists to do exactly this. Just because another agency has a new authority doesn't mean we stop doing what we're doing. In fact, the president has asked us to increase our capability by 50 percent."

Following an intensive review of proposed changes to restructure the intelligence community, on June 29, 2005, President George W. Bush ordered a series of changes to ensure greater coordination among the intelligence agencies. The president, however, rejected the recommendation to transfer planning for covert operations to the recently established centers for Counterterrorism and Counterproliferation and instead retained the CIA's responsibility to coordinate and oversee spying and covert operations, re-affirming the CIA's preeminence in these areas.

Lapdog or Rogue Elephant? CIA Controversies from 1947 to 2004

Kathryn Olmsted

Americans are ambivalent about centralized power, and the Central Intelligence Agency (CIA) is no exception to this rule. From the Agency's creation in 1947, some Americans worried that a centralized intelligence agency might subvert their liberties. Throughout its history, CIA officials have tried to calm citizens' fears that the Agency might become, as some congressmen speculated at its inception, a "Gestapo." In addition, CIA officials have periodically had to defend the agency from charges that it either provided poor intelligence or that it distorted intelligence to serve political ends. These two themes—fear of the agency's extensive power and suspicion of the quality of its intelligence—have pervaded the controversies involving the agency.

These controversies have surged and receded in waves. Before the agency was created, many journalists and public officials fought hard against the creation of what they saw as a potentially dangerous force. Once it was established, however, most journalists and congressmen were—for a time, and in the interest of winning the Cold War—inclined to let the agency stay cloaked in secrecy. By the 1960s and 1970s, as the Vietnam War and then the Watergate scandal progressed, this cloak of secrecy was torn away. Concerns about the Agency's suspected role in the Watergate scandal ultimately led to the first intensive congressional investigations, which raised profound questions about secrecy and presidential power. By the 1980s and 1990s, periodic scandals erupted over agency whistleblowers, moles, and defectors. The Agency faced one of its greatest crises in this era with the Iran-Contra scandal and allegations about CIA tolerance of drug trafficking. CIA controversies continued into the twenty-first century with investigations into its failure to have predicted the September 11, 2001, terrorist attacks; inquiries into leaks of the identity of a CIA operative; and charges of distortion of intelligence before the Iraq War of 2003.

These various crises stem from the Agency's difficult task as a secret agency in a democracy. Americans' traditional suspicion of secret power at times made the CIA the source of contradictory fears. On the one hand, Americans sometimes worry that the CIA is a frighteningly competent Gestapo that reads their mail, infiltrates their organizations, ignores evidence of their sources' crimes, and—in their most paranoid moments—assassinates their president. This CIA was accused of being, in Senator Frank Church's words, a "rogue elephant on a rampage," a frightening beast uncontrolled by democratic overseers. On the other hand, Americans have at times accused CIA officials of weakness and incompetence: of failing to predict crises and, even worse, allowing themselves to be manipulated by imperial presidents. CIA controversies, in short, are a Rorschach test of Americans' conflicting attitudes about the necessity of a powerful, interventionist, and secretive government in a dangerous world.

THE CREATION OF THE AGENCY
AND THE "INTERNAL SECURITY" BAN

The first critics of the CIA emerged before its creation and articulated the issues that future skeptics expanded upon. Even before the Japanese attack on Pearl Harbor, President Franklin Roosevelt's intelligence adviser, William Donovan, urged him to create a new civilian centralized intelligence agency. But military chiefs and FBI director J. Edgar Hoover staunchly resisted this idea. The army and the navy believed that intelligence should be a province of the uniformed services, while Hoover wanted to protect the FBI's own bureaucratic turf as the only federal investigative agency. After the devastating losses at Pearl Harbor, however, Roosevelt was convinced that the nation needed more centralization of intelligence. For many Americans the shock of the Pearl Harbor attack created a sea change in their attitudes toward central intelligence: many former critics were persuaded that the United States needed one agency to coordinate intelligence gathering and analysis. "Before Pearl Harbor we did not have an intelligence service in this country comparable to that of Great Britain, or France, or Russia, or Germany, or Japan," General Hoyt Vandenberg, one of the first directors of the CIA, explained to the Senate Armed Services Committee in 1947. "We did not have one because the people of the United States would not accept it." In the wake of Pearl Harbor, there was no debate when in 1942 Roosevelt by executive order established a wartime agency, the Office of Strategic Services, and authorized it to conduct special operations at the direction of the Joint Chiefs of Staff.

In late 1944, as World War II drew to a close, Donovan drew up a plan for a permanent centralized spy agency—the first centralized intelligence agency in peacetime in American history—and presented it to President Roosevelt. Once again, the military intelligence agencies, the State Department, and the

FBI opposed this plan. A copy of Donovan's memorandum was leaked to the conservative *Chicago Tribune*, prompting adverse publicity about the proposed creation of a secretive federal bureaucracy—a "Gestapo."

"Creation of an all powerful intelligence service to spy on the post-war world and to pry into the lives of citizens at home is under consideration by the New Deal," read the lead of the *Tribune*'s story on February 9, 1945. The newspaper set forth the major themes articulated by future critics of the CIA. First, the *Tribune* and like-minded conservative congressmen worried that the creation of a peacetime spy agency would presage the dawning of a totalitarian police state in America, and that the president would use this "Gestapo" or Soviet-style secret police to spy on and punish his political enemies. "What is it they call that Russian spy system—the OGPU? It would certainly be nice to have one of those in our own country," one Republican senator commented drily. Other critics of the proposed agency feared that it could be manipulated by the president to produce intelligence designed to further his own foreign policy goals. The new spy director, the *Tribune* speculated, could "determine American foreign policy by weeding out, withholding, or coloring information gathered at his direction."

In light of the outcry provoked by the *Tribune* article, Roosevelt decided to shelve Donovan's proposed spy agency plan. When Harry Truman became president following Roosevelt's death a few months later, he was initially uninterested in reviving the idea. As the tensions between the Soviet Union and the United States increased during the early years of the cold war, however, Donovan decided to try again. In 1947, he approached Truman with a new plan for a centralized agency. Aware that Truman was particularly sensitive to concerns that the new agency might turn against Americans, he emphasized that his proposed agency would have no internal security or police functions, and in fact would not even operate within the United States.

Having learned of Donovan's renewed initiative, critics again tried to derail it by leaking the details to the *Chicago Tribune*. On June 15, 1947, the *Tribune* claimed that the CIA's predecessor, the Central Intelligence Group, was a "Gestapo" with "1500 secret agents." To allay these concerns, drafters of the section of the National Security Act of 1947 that set up the CIA specifically stated that it would "have no police subpoena, law enforcement powers, or internal security functions." Nonetheless, the National Security Act also contained an "elastic clause," which charged the CIA with performing "such other functions and duties related to intelligence affecting the national security as the National Security Council may from time to time direct." CIA officials would stretch this elastic clause in the years to come.

Prohibiting the CIA from operating in the United States, the argument went, would prevent it from violating American freedoms. This specific ban of an internal security function helped, at least in the early years, to reduce any fears that the CIA would be used against American citizens. Congress, however, had not devised a law that could prevent the other feared abuse: that

CIA officials would distort the agency's intelligence, whether to serve their own bureaucratic or foreign policy interests or promote those of their boss in the Oval Office.

THE 1950s: UNQUESTIONED SUPPORT

Owing to the crisis in U.S.-Soviet relations with the onset of the Cold War, this controversy quickly abated. Instead, with the Central Intelligence Agency Act of 1949, Congress agreed that the United States needed secret warriors as part of the cold war army—and exempted the agency's budget from normal budgetary and accounting requirements.

As the Cold War continued into the 1950s, few congressmen questioned the role of the CIA, nor did they seek to ascertain whether the Agency had expanded beyond intelligence gathering to conducting secret operations. Allen Dulles, the director of central intelligence, reported to the congressional oversight committees just once or twice a year, where he would field questions like, "The Commies still giving us a rough time, Allen?" In general, the congressional overseers decided that it was better not to know what the CIA was doing. For them, ignorance was bliss. As one overseer, Senator Leverett Saltonstall, explained: "The difficulty in connection with asking questions and obtaining information is that we might obtain information which I personally would rather not have."

The Agency in this era also had little to fear from the press. From the 1940s to the 1960s, most journalists shared in the "Cold War consensus" and believed that they needed to protect America's clandestine soldiers. Most publications willingly abided by government calls to limit coverage of CIA activities. For example, the *New York Times* recalled its reporter from Guatemala in 1954 when the agency thought that he was not sufficiently supportive of its interests there. In 1960, the *Times* again complied with administration desires and downplayed a story on the coming CIA-sponsored Bay of Pigs invasion of Cuba.

There were a few exceptions to this rule of consistent congressional and journalistic support for the CIA. In 1953, Senator Joseph McCarthy charged that the agency was infiltrated by communists, and was only narrowly dissuaded from launching a major investigation. More significantly, Democratic Senator Mike Mansfield of Montana repeatedly introduced bills throughout the 1950s requiring tighter oversight of the CIA. Although Mansfield voiced his support for the Agency, he contended that its lack of accountability might allow it to waste money, support undemocratic groups, perform poorly, and distort its intelligence reports. Mansfield had his best chance at achieving oversight in 1956, when the Senate Rules Committee voted 8–1 for his proposal. But after intense lobbying by CIA Director Allen Dulles, the Senate voted 59–27 to defeat the Montana senator's plan. Mansfield's criticisms would be revived in Congress in the 1970s, but in the 1950s his calls for independent oversight fell on deaf ears. The Cold War consensus in favor of complete secrecy for the CIA was demonstrated in a classified report drafted in 1954 for President Dwight Eisenhower, the result of an investigation into the mission and administration of the CIA chaired by General Jimmy Doolittle. As the Doolittle Committee explained, "we are facing an implacable enemy whose avowed objective is world domination . . . if the United States is to survive, long-standing American concepts of 'fair play' must be reconsidered. We must . . . learn to *subvert, sabotage and destroy our enemies by more clever, more sophisticated and more effective methods than those used against us*." When the Doolittle Report was first declassified in 1975, a Senate committee expressed shock and dismay at these words; but in 1954, the president, most members of Congress, and most journalists agreed with them.

The unquestioned support for the CIA in Congress and the press was briefly challenged in 1961, following the disastrous CIA-led and financed invasion at the Bay of Pigs. Because the Agency had played the major role in planning and carrying out the invasion, the failure of Cuban exile forces to overthrow Fidel Castro angered President John Kennedy. The president appointed retired General Maxwell Taylor to study the reasons for the failure and recommend reforms to ensure future success. At first, President Kennedy and his brother Robert, the attorney general, seemed inclined to punish the Agency for its failure in the Bay of Pigs and CIA officials' misreading of the political situation in Cuba. Indeed, both Allen Dulles and covert action chief Richard Bissell were forced to resign. But Robert Kennedy was convinced that the CIA could play a valuable role in Kennedy administration foreign policy. The president simply needed to exercise tighter control over the Agency. As a result, the CIA emerged from the crisis stronger than ever. Indeed, the Kennedys ordered the CIA to get rid of Castro by other means—by assassinating him. The plots against Castro were unknown to the public at the time, but would cause a major scandal when they were disclosed years later.

THE 1960s: A NEW ERA OF SCRUTINY

By the middle of the 1960s, public support for the CIA was beginning to erode. As President Lyndon Johnson escalated American involvement in the Vietnam War, some Americans, including members of Congress, grew more inclined to question the administration on foreign policy. This willingness to challenge the government extended to its secret agencies. In April 1966, the *New York Times* published the first mainstream press investigation of the CIA. More than twenty *Times* reporters worked on the lengthy series, which concluded that the CIA had taken on many more functions than Congress had intended and might have evolved into "a sort of Frankenstein's monster." Although *Times* editors did allow CIA officials to vet the series before publication, their action signaled nevertheless that the CIA was entering a new era of press scrutiny.

The first major revelation of CIA domestic operations came in March 1967. *Ramparts*, a left-wing magazine, reported that the agency had funded the National Student Association, a large, influential, and liberal organization for college students. Starting in the early 1950s, agency operatives had begun covertly funneling hundreds of thousands of dollars through cooperative foundations to help expand the student association. By the 1960s, the agency provided NSA leaders with scholarships, a rent-free headquarters, and draft deferments.

CIA officials since the early 1950s had supported the student association in hopes of countering Soviet propaganda. According to Tom Braden, the CIA official who conceived of the program, the Soviets were dumping up to $250 million a year into various labor, student, and peace front groups. The CIA proposed to match this propaganda with some of its own. As Braden wrote in a May 20, 1967, article in the *Saturday Evening Post*, "When an adversary attacks with his weapons disguised as good works, to choose innocence is to choose defeat."

The hysterically anticommunist Congress of the 1950s, however, would never consent to funding the left-liberal groups that Braden believed would be most effective at countering Soviet propaganda. So the CIA reached into its secret funds to aid the liberal students.

Braden wrote his article to counter what he called the "inane, misinformed twaddle" in the press following the *Ramparts* revelations. Quite unintentionally, however, he reignited the controversy by confirming the allegations and adding new groups to the list of CIA beneficiaries. Not only was the NSA funded, he explained, but Agency money was also funneled to numerous labor groups, the European group of intellectuals known as the Congress for Cultural Freedom, and the highbrow British magazine *Encounter*. Claiming that they did not know about the CIA connection, two *Encounter* editors quit in protest.

The revelations about CIA funding of domestic groups provoked a firestorm of controversy. Many Americans believed that the Agency had crossed an important line. Was the spy agency turning out to be the "Gestapo" that its early critics had feared? Some of the leaders of the CIA-funded groups had been unwitting participants in the cultural cold war, and they reacted with anger. "Now we find we were deceived, and that we were unwitting perpetrators of deception," two former leaders of the National Student Association wrote in the March 3, 1967, edition of *Commonweal*. Leaders who had known the source of their money reacted with defensive justifications and denials. The scandal as a whole gave credence to the wildest speculations about CIA domestic activities. As the editors of *Commonweal* wrote, "There is no point in complaining about a growing attachment of the New Left to 'conspiracy theories' when genuine conspiracies are popping up all around."

The *Ramparts* series marked a watershed for the CIA. Before, Agency critics in Congress, the press, and the White House had focused on making the CIA stronger and more effective. Even Senator Mansfield's oversight proposal had been presented as an opportunity to enhance the Agency's credibility. Now, for the first time, opponents were directly attacking the CIA's role and its excessive secrecy.

The Johnson administration responded to the scandal in overt and covert ways. Publicly, President Johnson expressed concern and directed Attorney General Nicholas Katzenbach to investigate. Like later presidential investigations of the CIA, his appointment of the Katzenbach Commission was an attempt to head off a full-scale congressional inquiry. The commission recommended that the CIA avoid funding private groups, but stopped short of a complete ban on such aid. Secretly, CIA operatives continued their program of discrediting, sabotaging, and harassing the young journalists who had exposed their secrets. Indeed, covert operations chief Desmond FitzGerald ordered Deputy Inspector General Edgar Applewhite to ruin *Ramparts* in any way he could. "I had all sorts of dirty tricks to hurt their circulation and financing," Applewhite told journalist Evan Thomas years later. "The people running *Ramparts* were vulnerable to blackmail. We had awful things in mind, some of which we carried off, though *Ramparts* fell of its own accord. We were not the least inhibited by the fact that the CIA had no internal security role in the United States."

OPERATION CHAOS

Many other CIA officers were not inhibited by the CIA's lack of an internal security role. Despite the ban on domestic spying, President Lyndon Johnson had in 1967 pressured the CIA to begin surveillance of radical antiwar critics of the Vietnam War. The ostensible aim of the illegal program, code named CHAOS, was to determine if communist countries were advising and supporting the protesters. CIA officers in time expanded CHAOS to include other leftist or countercultural groups with no discernible connection to Vietnam, such as the women's liberation movement.

In 1969, the newly inaugurated president, Richard Nixon, encouraged the CIA (and other U.S. intelligence agencies) to continue spying on the antiwar movement and to coordinate their domestic spying efforts. This Nixon-era initiative culminated in the "Huston Plan." One of Nixon's aides, Tom Charles Huston, came up with this plan to lift restrictions on domestic intelligence operations, such as mail-opening and wiretapping programs, and create an interagency committee to coordinate the newly aggressive efforts. As Theodore White aptly described the plan, it would have allowed federal agents to reach "all the way to every mailbox, every college campus, every telephone, every home."

The specific catalyst to the Huston plan was Nixon administration officials' concern that FBI Director J. Edgar Hoover would no longer perform illegal investigations. In Huston's view, Hoover had recently grown "bull-headed as hell" and "old and worried about his legend." Huston and CIA officials were also concerned about the FBI's failure to coordinate its efforts with the

Sam Papich, J. Edgar Hoover, and Richard Helms. (Courtesy of the National Archives)

Agency. In fact, Hoover had completely broken off relations with the CIA in 1970 in a fit of pique over the Thomas Riha affair. When Riha, a Russian history professor at the University of Colorado, disappeared in 1969, FBI officials suspected that he had defected to the Soviet Union, but they did not tell the CIA about their suspicions. An FBI agent in Denver, however, decided on his own to alert the Agency. Learning of this breach of security, Hoover demanded that CIA officials name the FBI agent. When they refused, Hoover cut off all contact with the Agency. Intended to circumvent Hoover's restrictions, the Huston Plan was an ingenious scheme by the Nixon White House to expand domestic spying without implicating the president. But the FBI director, ever the wily bureaucrat, scuttled the "Huston Plan" when he demanded that the president formally authorize in writing these "clearly illegal" activities. Although the Huston Plan was never implemented, CHAOS continued until it was exposed in 1974.

THE KENNEDY ASSASSINATION AND CIA CONSPIRACY THEORIES

Operation CHAOS revealed the anxiety of Johnson and Nixon administration officials about increasing public skepticism of their foreign and domestic policy initiatives. A new politics emerged during the 1960s, giving rise to questions about the wisdom of the containment policy and demands that Congress focus on promoting freedom and equality at home. In this new era of scrutiny, some citizens began to suspect CIA collusion in the most momentous of crimes: the murder of President John F. Kennedy.

Immediately after the assassination of President Kennedy, some Americans began to suspect a conspiracy. Dallas police had arrested Lee Harvey Oswald on the afternoon of November 22, 1963, and charged him with killing the president. Oswald was a loner with a bizarre past: a former Marine, he had defected to the Soviet Union in 1959, only to return to the United States two years and a half years later proclaiming his disillusionment with Soviet-style communism. In the summer of 1963, Oswald had told acquaintances of his admiration for Cuba's communist leader, Fidel Castro, and had joined an anti-Castro organization, he said, in order to infiltrate it.

Just two days after his arrest, Oswald was shot and killed by Dallas strip club owner Jack Ruby, who claimed he shot the alleged assassin because of his own uncontrollable grief over the president's murder. Ruby's silencing of Oswald immediately struck many Americans as evidence of a potential conspiracy behind the assassination. Indeed, a poll taken the week after the assassination showed that only 29 percent of Americans believed that Oswald had acted alone.

To answer questions about the assassination, President Lyndon Johnson appointed a commission headed by Chief Justice Earl Warren. Former CIA chief Allen Dulles sat on the Warren Commission and withheld much pertinent information from his fellow members about the CIA's various plans to assassinate Castro. Because Oswald was an avid fan of Castro, the Kennedy administration's plots against Castro's life—and Oswald's possible knowledge of these plots—could have been seen as key pieces of evidence pointing to his possible motive. Denied access to evidence of the Castro plots, the Warren Commission never investigated Oswald's alleged anger over them. Instead, the Warren Report portrayed Oswald as a crazed sociopath with no discernible motive. By withholding the discussion of the Castro plots from the Warren Commission, CIA officials and the Johnson administration prevented the American public from fully understanding this cataclysmic event during the 1960s.

The Warren report did briefly dampen conspiracy fears when it proclaimed in 1964 that Oswald had acted alone. Soon after the Warren report's release, 87 percent of Americans told pollsters they believed its conclusion. But some still had their doubts. In 1966 and 1967, several books questioned the commission's work. Mark Lane's *Rush to Judgment*, Edward Jay Epstein's *Inquest*, Sylvia Meagher's *Accessories After the Fact*, and Josiah Thompson's *Six Seconds in Dallas* all raised the possibility of a conspiracy in the assassination. Lane's and Epstein's books sat atop the *New York Times* bestseller lists for months.

In 1967, a conspiracy theory about the CIA's involvement in the JFK assassination gained notoriety when New Orleans District Attorney Jim Garrison began an investigation. By May of that year—just two months after the *Ramparts* revelations about CIA funding of the National Student Association made the headlines—Garrison stated publicly what he had hinted privately for months: that the CIA and anti-Castro Cubans were behind the assassination. Garrison charged that the CIA was hiding evidence that Oswald was working for the Agency just days before the assassination. He believed that Bay of Pigs veterans—in other words, former CIA agents—were angry with Kennedy for canceling air strikes during the Cuban invasion. This decision had doomed the invasion, Garrison said, and prompted the Cubans to plot their revenge. In New Orleans, he contended, these former CIA agents had arranged to use Oswald as a patsy in their plot to kill the president. After the assassination, the CIA and FBI together had worked to cover up the truth. To expose the web of deceit, he accused a local businessman, Clay Shaw, of being part of the conspiracy and put him on trial.

Garrison was appealing to a grass-roots fear of federal power, and particularly of secret federal power. He exploited some Americans' concerns that the federal government might have evolved into a true Frankenstein's monster beyond democratic control. In the late 1960s journalists dismissively reported that conspiracy "buffs" who supported Garrison's investigation were skeptical of all governmental pronouncements. A fusion of activists from the left and the right, these conspiracists had come to believe that the assassination was symbolic of the frightening power of the secret government. If they did not expose the CIA's role, they believed, American democracy would be at risk.

Garrison's investigation ended in farce when a jury cleared Shaw after just forty-five minutes of deliberation. The establishment press ridiculed his efforts and his ham-handed efforts at bribing witnesses. His inquiry collapsed. However, the flamboyant and unscrupulous prosecutor had succeeded in shifting conspiracists' attention, as historian Robert Goldberg has said, "from the mechanics of the shooting to the questions, why and who benefited?" Over the years, dozens of books would elaborate on Garrison's theory and introduce new accusations. A House committee in the 1970s investigated the conspiracy theories before concluding that, indeed, there was a second gunman and a shadowy conspiracy behind the assassination. Garrison himself was immortalized in the 1991 movie *JFK*, which portrayed him as a lone American standing up against a secret government conspiracy.

In response to the movie *JFK*, Congress set up an Assassination Records Review Board to examine the remaining classified files on the assassination and to declassify as many as it could. After six years of work, the panel released almost four million pages of previously sealed documents. The review board reaffirmed the lone gunman theory, but chided the government for its "penchant for secrecy" that had helped to keep the conspiracy theories alive.

THE CIA AND WATERGATE

In the 1970s, the CIA entered a new era of controversies. The Agency, once a revered institution of Cold War America, faced not only charges of conspiracy, but questions about its competence, abuses of power, and secrecy. Some experts believed that the agency would not survive the decade. The storm of controversy began with the Watergate break-in.

On June 17, 1972, Washington metropolitan police caught five well-dressed burglars breaking into the headquarters of the Democratic National Committee in the Watergate office complex. In their pockets and briefcases, the men had sequential hundred-dollar bills, high-tech surveillance equipment, and sophisticated burglary tools. (Despite their evident experience with break-ins, however, the burglars had made some elementary mistakes, such as taping open the bolt of the stairwell door, that led to their discovery by a private security guard and Washington metropolitan police.) When the men were arraigned in court that morning, one of the burglars, James McCord, told the judge that he was a security consultant. The judge then asked McCord the name of his former employer. McCord whispered: "CIA." Indeed, McCord was a nineteen-year veteran of the agency, and was currently employed by President Nixon's reelection committee. In addition, the other men arrested had worked for the Agency in Cuba. When police subsequently identified two Nixon aides as supervisors of the break-in, one of them, E. Howard Hunt, was also an Agency veteran, while the other, G. Gordon Liddy, was a former FBI agent and was currently employed by the Nixon reelection committee.

The CIA connections of the Watergate burglars caused some conspiracy theorists in later years to charge that the Agency actually planned President Nixon's downfall. Two prominent books in 1980s speculated that the break-in was actually part of a CIA "secret agenda" or "silent coup" against the Nixon White House. More important, the question of the CIA's possible role provided the catalyst to congressional inquiries into the role and operation of the agency.

The Watergate break-in was just one of several illegal Nixon White House operations to spy on and discredit the president's enemies. In 1971, Nixon aides had established a secret unit called the "plumbers" to find and punish the source of leaks of the classified Defense Department history of U.S. involvement in Vietnam—the so-called Pentagon Papers. The president was angry about this leak to the *New York Times*. One of the plumbers' first duties was to find information to discredit Daniel Ellsberg, the former analyst who had leaked the Pentagon Papers to the *New York Times*. Ellsberg had formerly worked on this top-secret study of the Vietnam War, which revealed the lies of the Johnson administration about the war. Outraged by the deceptions he had documented and having concluded that the Nixon administration would not abandon this policy, Ellsberg in 1971 decided to leak the classified study to the public. The Nixon administration prosecuted Ellsberg for disclosing government secrets, but President Nixon also wanted to find secret information about the analyst in order to destroy his public image. Led by Hunt and Liddy, the plumbers tried to "neutralize" Ellsberg by breaking into his psychiatrist's office in Los Angeles with the intent to leak derogatory information to the press.

As a former Agency employee, Hunt contacted the CIA to elicit support for his secret operation. He asked for, and received, cameras, bugging equipment, and disguises. The CIA also gave him a psychological profile of Ellsberg. In addition, in a separate operation, the CIA gave Hunt secret documents relating to the assassination of President Ngo Diem in Vietnam. Hunt wanted the documents so that he could alter them to make it appear that the Kennedy administration had ordered Diem's murder. He also turned to former Agency men when he needed burglars for the break-ins at Ellsberg's psychiatrist's office (who were later recruited for the Watergate break-in).

Contrary to the "silent coup" allegations, the CIA was not the driving force behind the Watergate break-in. It was complicit only in helping Hunt to conduct his illegal burglaries. In addition, CIA officials had responded to President Nixon's request to expand Operation CHAOS, the Johnson-era domestic surveillance program of American radicals. The investigation of the Watergate burglary would provide the opening wedge for the subsequent revelation of these illegal activities.

President Nixon, moreover, unsuccessfully sought to curb the FBI's investigation of the burglary at its inception. During a June 23, 1972, meeting with his chief of staff, Bob Haldeman, the president discussed how to stop the inquiry. Secret Oval Office machines recorded the conversation, and this particular tape later became known as the "smoking gun." On the tape, Nixon can be heard discussing with Haldeman how to force the top two men at the CIA, director Richard Helms and his deputy, Vernon Walters, to order the FBI to stop its investigation on grounds of national security. "We protected Helms from one hell of a lot of things," Nixon says, somewhat mysteriously. As a result, he concludes, Helms should agree to participate in the plot. If the true story of Watergate gets out, Nixon instructs his aide, "it's going to make the CIA look bad, it's going to make Hunt look bad, and it's likely to blow the whole Bay of Pigs, which we think would be very unfortunate for the CIA."

In the short term, Helms and Walters agreed to play along. Walters told the acting director of the FBI, L. Patrick Gray, to limit the Watergate inquiry because it might disclose national security secrets. But Walters quickly began to worry about implicating the CIA in the cover-up. He told the Nixon aide in charge of the cover-up, White House counsel John Dean, "I am prepared to resign before I do anything that would implicate the agency in this matter." Nixon was sufficiently angered by the CIA's reluctance to assist the cover-up that he forced Helms to resign and, as a consolation, named him ambassador to Iran.

Nixon's efforts to enlist the CIA in the cover-up ultimately sealed his doom. James McCord, the head burglar and a key figure in the cover-up, began to worry that the White House was planning to blame all the illegalities of the Nixon administration on a rogue CIA. In December 1972, McCord sent a secret letter to a White House aide. "If Helms goes and the Watergate operation is laid at CIA's feet, where it does not belong, every tree in the forest will fall," McCord warned. "It will be a scorched desert."

McCord was not making idle threats. He, Hunt, Liddy, and the four other burglars were indicted for burglary, conspiracy, and illegal wiretapping. All but McCord and Liddy pleaded guilty. After a short trial, on January 30, 1973, the jury found both men guilty. Before setting their sentences, however, the judge in the case, John Sirica, publicly expressed his doubts that the conspiracy was limited to the seven men indicted. "I am still not satisfied that all the pertinent facts that might be available—I say *might* be available—have been produced before an American jury," he said. Faced with the possibility of a lengthy sentence, McCord decided to tell the judge everything he knew about the cover-up. In his letter to the judge, McCord reported that the defendants had been pressured to plead guilty, that witnesses had perjured themselves during the trial, and that the conspiracy extended beyond the seven men indicted. Moreover, he said, "The Watergate operation was not a CIA operation. The Cubans may have been misled by others into believing that it was a CIA operation. I know for a fact that it was not." McCord's letter to Sirica started the unraveling of the Watergate cover-up.

Throughout the summer of 1973, a special Senate investigating committee chaired by folksy Sam Ervin of North Carolina held hearings on the Watergate conspiracy. All of the major players in the scandal testified during televised hearings: McCord, Liddy, Hunt, and the president's top aides. The most sensational testimony came from the president's counsel, John Dean, who decided to cooperate with the prosecutors and investigators. Dean directly implicated the president in the Watergate cover-up. Although Dean could not at first prove his allegations, presidential aide Alexander Butterfield then revealed the existence of the oval office taping system. The Senate and a special prosecutor subpoenaed the tapes, and the Supreme Court directed the president to release them in July 1974. The "smoking gun" tape, with its proof of Nixon's role in the cover-up and his tantalizing suggestion of CIA involvement, thereupon became public knowledge.

As McCord had predicted, most trees in the Nixon administration did fall; the president and many of his top aides were forced to resign. But the CIA also paid a price. Many members of Congress, who for years had allowed the CIA to escape close scrutiny, were incensed by the CIA's apparent role in the Watergate cover-up. The Watergate transcripts, in particular, whetted the curiosity of members of Congress. What did the president mean when he said he protected the CIA from "one hell of a lot of things"? Why did he say an inquiry would "blow the whole Bay of Pigs"? Were there more CIA skeletons in the closet—and if so, should they be exposed?

The congressional overseers were in the mood to launch an investigation. The tinder was ready. The final spark came from the press.

THE POST-WATERGATE INVESTIGATIONS
AND THE "YEAR OF INTELLIGENCE"

The fall of 1974 marked one of the lowest points of public trust in government. After Nixon resigned, President Gerald Ford confirmed many Americans' suspicion of their institutions when he issued a full and complete pardon to his predecessor. Later that week, on September 8, 1974, *New York Times* investigative reporter Seymour Hersh revealed that the CIA had misled Congress about its role in the overthrow of Chile's elected president, Salvador Allende. In top-secret testimony to a House Foreign Affairs subcommittee, CIA chief William Colby had revealed that the Nixon administration had spent millions over the past three years to destabilize the Allende regime. Colby's testimony, Hersh explained, "indicates that high officials in the State Department and White House repeatedly and deliberately misled the public and the Congress about the extent of United States involvement" in Chile. Furious, Congress quickly passed a bill that revamped and expanded the oversight system. The Hughes-Ryan amendment to the Foreign Assistance Act of 1974 required the CIA to brief eight congressional subcommittees in advance of any covert operations. In addition, the law required the president to sign a "finding" that each covert action was necessary to the national security, and to report this finding to Congress. The Hughes-Ryan amendment was an example of a new assertiveness by Congress, which had recently restricted funds for the war in Southeast Asia and tried to limit presidential war powers with the War Powers Act of 1973. In the post-Watergate atmosphere, the shell-shocked Ford administration quietly accepted this dramatic expansion of congressional power over the CIA.

Hersh's most explosive scoop about the CIA was still to come. Throughout the fall of 1974, Hersh had heard rumors of a massive trove of documents about illegal and improper Agency activities. The internal report on these activities, christened the "family jewels" by CIA officers, ran to 693 pages. It had been commissioned by James Schlesinger, an outsider whom Nixon had appointed director of central intelligence after Richard Helms had disappointed him. During his brief and contentious tenure, Schlesinger had been appalled to discover the CIA's assistance to E. Howard Hunt in the operation to discredit Ellsberg. Determined not to be surprised again, Schlesinger ordered CIA employees to report all questionable Agency activities to him.

Conscience-stricken CIA operatives eagerly took up the challenge. Schlesinger received a report documenting CIA involvement in drug testing on unwitting Americans, assassination plots, and mail opening programs. Most explosively, the "family jewels" told of Operation CHAOS, the domestic spying operation started by the Johnson administration and expanded by the Nixon administration. This latter program was soon discovered by Hersh, and resulted in a dramatic exposé.

The *New York Times* displayed Hersh's scoop prominently across its front page on December 22, 1974: "HUGE C.I.A. OPERATION REPORTED IN U.S. AGAINST ANTIWAR FORCES, OTHER DISSIDENTS IN NIXON YEARS," the headline read. The lead captured Hersh's major accusation that the CIA had conducted a "massive, illegal domestic intelligence operation." CIA officials responded by disputing that the project was "massive," but the new DCI, William Colby, publicly confirmed the story's major points.

To restore the Agency's credibility and to avert a more damaging congressional inquiry, President Ford appointed an executive commission headed by Vice President Nelson Rockefeller to investigate the domestic spying charges. Undeterred by the presidential commission, the new, post-Watergate Congress voted to investigate the secret government. The Senate created a special investigating committee in late January 1975, while the House followed suit in February.

President Ford's purpose in creating the Rockefeller Commission was to head off major reforms. Ford administration officials wrote in internal memos that they planned to use the commission to limit damage to the CIA and, as deputy chief of staff Richard Cheney wrote, to avoid "congressional efforts to further encroach on the executive branch." But the panel surprised everyone by making a few revelations in its final report, released five months later. First, the commission disclosed the Agency's drug tests on unsuspecting Americans from 1953 to 1966. One unwitting subject, Frank Olson, had jumped—or been pushed—to his death after the Agency had slipped LSD into his drink. His grieving family became the focus of many negative stories about the CIA.

Second, the commission inadvertently helped to revive conspiracy theories about the JFK assassination. Ironically, the commission members had the opposite intention: they tried to debunk prevalent conspiracy theories by addressing them directly. One eighteen-page section of the commission's report examined new conspiracy theories alleging CIA complicity in the assassination and found them to be completely without foundation. However, when the commission refused to make public its research into the CIA's plots against Castro, some critics charged that the commission was just another government cover-up.

The Rockefeller Commission had not fulfilled its goal of quieting calls for reform. Both congressional investigating committees were more determined than ever to launch aggressive inquiries into controversial CIA actions, to draft a new charter for the Agency, and even to consider its abolition. The most extensive investigations of CIA activities in history were about to begin.

FRANK CHURCH AND THE "ROGUE ELEPHANT"

Liberal Democrat Frank Church chaired the distinguished Senate panel charged with investigating the CIA. A former choirboy from Idaho, Church was appalled by the allegations of CIA domestic spying. He was even more upset, however, by new allegations first aired on CBS News in February 1975, as the senator was just beginning to assemble a staff. CBS correspondent Daniel Schorr reported that President Ford was worried that congressional investigators might discover some literal skeletons in the CIA closet: assassination plots against foreign leaders. President Ford himself was the indirect and inadvertent source for Schorr's story. During a meeting with *New York Times* editors, the president had explained that he did not want Congress discovering certain CIA actions. "Like what?" one of the editors had asked. "Like assassinations!" the president had blurted out. Then, in horror, he added: "That's off the record!" The *Times* agreed to suppress the story. But someone at the meeting leaked it to Schorr.

Allegations about CIA murder plots had appeared in the press before. But the earlier stories had been confined to alleged plots against Castro, and in any case had never been confirmed. Once Schorr began investigating the story, he sought an appointment with CIA director Colby, and then surprised him with the Ford story. "Has the CIA ever killed anyone in this country?" he asked cleverly. Colby fell into the reporter's trap and responded too narrowly: "Not in this country!" Colby refused to discuss specific cases, but Schorr thought he now had enough information to report the allegations on television.

The charges of assassination plots proved to be a nightmare for CIA officials, but they also posed problems for the Church Committee. Once the murders became "Topic A" of the press coverage of the CIA scandals, as Daniel Schorr described them, then the senators were forced to devote much of their limited time and resources to investigating them. The Church Committee never proved that the CIA actually killed a foreign leader. But this was not, as Schorr said, for want of trying. The committee documented at least eight attempts against Castro's life, including many joint ventures with the mafia. In addition, the committee found that the CIA had tried to kill Patrice Lumumba of the Congo and Rafael Trujillo of the Dominican Republic, but both of these men were ultimately killed by rival groups. The committee determined that U.S. leaders had encouraged the coup against President Ngo Diem of South Vietnam, but had not ordered his murder. Finally, the committee added one more case study to its final report on alleged assassination plots against foreign leaders. Rene Schneider had been the head of the Chilean armed forces during the CIA-sponsored coup attempt against Salvador Allende, the democratically elected president of Chile, in 1970. As a strong supporter of the democratic process in Chile, Schneider stood in the way of the CIA's plans for overturning the election. The Church Committee found that the CIA at first supported, then allegedly withdrew support from, a plan to kidnap the general. When the coup plotters went ahead and kidnapped Schneider, he was killed when he tried to defend himself. The CIA objected to the committee's decision to include Schneider's murder in the list of agency assassination plots. But, as Church argued, "the possibility that he

Chairman Frank Church (D-ID), of the Senate Intelligence Committee, displays a poison dart gun on September 17, 1975, as Co-Chairman John G. Tower (R-TX) looks on during the panel's probe of the Central Intelligence Agency at a Washington hearing. (AP/Wide World Photos)

would be killed should have been recognized as a foreseeable risk of the kidnapping."

The media devoted most of its attention to the sensational issue of CIA assassination plots. As a result, many reporters neglected the Church Committee's solid efforts to investigate the agency's mail-opening programs, its domestic spying, and its role in the overthrow of Allende's elected government. The committee documented 900 major covert operations and several thousand minor ones conducted by the Agency since 1961. It also revealed that the CIA had collected 1.5 million names of "subversive" Americans in a database as a result of its massive mail-opening program, while Operation CHAOS had prompted the creation of files on 7,200 citizens. All of the committee's reports would form an extensive documentary foundation for future historians. The reports became the bible of conspiracy theorists, who digitized them two decades later and placed them on the Internet.

The committee never resolved the thorny issue of those responsible for the plots. Most of the members seemed to believe that Presidents Eisenhower, Kennedy, Johnson, and Nixon had at least tacitly, if not explicitly, approved the attempted murders. However, Church, a strong supporter of the two Democratic presidents under study, persisted in blaming the plots on the CIA. The Agency, he said, was a "rogue elephant on a rampage." For proof, he pointed to the lack of documentary evidence that any president had ever approved an assassination. Former CIA director Richard Helms countered that it was absurd to expect to find such evidence. "I can't imagine anybody wanting something in writing saying I have just charged Mr. Jones to go out and shoot Mr. Smith," he testified. The Agency, he insisted, had simply carried out the wishes of the executive.

OTIS PIKE AND THE IMPERIAL PRESIDENCY

The special investigating committee in the House took on a different agenda and came up with radically different conclusions. Otis Pike, a moderate Democrat from New York, chaired a polarized House panel, which included conservative Republicans and some of the most liberal members of the House. Determined not to duplicate the Church Committee's work, Pike decided to focus his committee's efforts on the CIA's overall performance, rather than limiting his inquiry to Agency abuses.

Because the Pike Committee took a more systemic approach to investigating the Agency, its conclusions were even more devastating than those of the Church Committee. The Pike Committee asserted that auditors had little control over the CIA budget; as a result, the committee concluded, the agency was fraught with waste and fraud. Even more distressing, the committee concluded that CIA analysts seldom predicted major crises—in other words, the agency failed to perform its major intelligence function. The Pike Committee, for example, discovered that the CIA had no advance knowledge of the Egyptian attack on Israel in 1973, and had in fact insisted that there would be no war just hours before the Egyptian attack. CIA intelligence in this case, an Agency postmortem concluded, was "quite simply, obviously, and starkly wrong."

Finally, the Pike Committee charged that many CIA covert actions were at best amoral and at worst harmed American interests in the long term. Pike insisted, however, that an imperial president, not a rogue agency, was responsible for these actions. As the committee's final report concluded: "All evidence in hand suggests that the CIA, far from being out of control, has been utterly responsive to the instructions of the President and the Assistant to the President for National Security Affairs."

The Pike Committee report was potentially dangerous for the Agency, but the committee's own mistakes and a clever counteroffensive by CIA officials and the Ford administration succeeded in containing the damage. The Ford White House had formed a special ad hoc group to battle the investigating committees. These executive staffers worked with CIA consultant Mitchell Rogovin to orchestrate press and public opposition to more disclosures. Rogovin received a boost from an unexpected source. In early 1975, a disillusioned former CIA officer who had worked in Latin America, Philip Agee, published a book and magazine article that named every CIA asset and source he could remember from his ten years with the Agency. Agee's deliberate decision to endanger the lives of these agents prompted outrage in Congress, the media, and the public. In the winter 1975 issue of his magazine, *Counterspy*, Agee named the CIA station chief in Lima, Peru. This agency officer,

Richard Welch, had since moved to Athens, Greece. On December 12, 1975, Welch was assassinated by Greek terrorists angry over American support for Greece's authoritarian government.

Although the Church and Pike Committees had never identified any undercover operative, let alone Welch, agency officials and the Ford administration implied that the congressional investigators were responsible for his death. Rogovin later claimed credit for orchestrating the outrage over Welch's death, saying that the White House had publicized Welch's murder and "waved it around like a bloody shirt."

Two months after the anger provoked by Welch's killing, the Pike Committee encountered another destructive controversy with the leak of its final report. President Ford had refused to allow the publication of the report, which was highly critical of the Agency, on the grounds that it damaged national security and endangered individual CIA agents. When the House voted to uphold the president, someone leaked the report to CBS's Daniel Schorr, who arranged to have the report published by Clay Felker, publisher of the *Village Voice*. The *Voice* put out the report as a special edition on February 11, 1976, with a headline in red capital letters: "THE CIA REPORT THE PRESIDENT DOESN'T WANT YOU TO READ." The resultant controversy over the leak overshadowed the substance of the report, which condemned the Agency for wasting money and failing to predict six recent world crises, including the 1973 Middle East war. The Pike Committee—the most significant challenger to the CIA's authority in its history—collapsed in acrimony as the House Ethics Committee launched an investigation into the source of the leak.

In the end, the "year of intelligence" led to few real reforms. The great goal of the investigators and reformers had been to have Congress enact a new charter for the CIA that would spell out the agency's duties beyond the vague phrases of the 1947 and 1949 acts. One proposed charter bill was more than 200 pages long. It would have prohibited the CIA from undertaking many covert operations, including the overthrow of democratically elected leaders, the use of biological or chemical weapons, the creation of floods and epidemics, and support for terrorists. The bill never became law. Liberals and conservatives differed over whether charter legislation should spell out restrictions on CIA activities—restrictions opposed both by the White House and CIA officials. A changed international climate and the election of Ronald Reagan to the presidency in 1980 finally killed this effort to enact a new legislative charter.

When Jimmy Carter assumed the presidency in 1977, he acted to restrain the CIA by executive order. During his campaign for the presidency Carter had called for intelligence reform, and his vice president, Walter Mondale, was one of the Church Committee's most aggressive members. In 1978 President Carter issued an executive order that restricted CIA spying on American citizens at home and abroad. The order required that the Agency obtain warrants from the attorney general for some types of surveillance of American citizens. In 1981 President Ronald Reagan loosened the fetters placed on the CIA. Reagan replaced Carter's order with his own, E.O. 12333, which allowed some CIA domestic spying, surveillance of Americans abroad, and some covert operations in the United States.

As a result of the intelligence investigations, the Senate did establish a permanent intelligence committee in May 1976, and the House created its oversight committee in July 1977. But this reform, called a "sham" by one Pike Committee member, merely laid the foundation for a reduction in the number of committees charged with intelligence oversight. In 1980, Congress passed a new law, the Intelligence Oversight Act, requiring the president to brief only the two intelligence committees about approved CIA covert operations, rather than eight committees required by the Hughes-Ryan amendment. Although the CIA was required to report more activities to the committees, the number of congressional overseers was cut dramatically by the 1980 law. Bowing to the reality of presidential reluctance to inform congressional committees in advance of covert operations, the Intelligence Oversight Act required the president only to keep the two intelligence committees "fully and currently informed" of intelligence activities. These briefings were supposed to be given in advance of the covert operations, but the 1980 act further allowed the president in some cases to restrict prior notice to just eight leaders (the majority and minority leaders of each house and the ranking majority and minority members of both intelligence committees).

The other major law passed in response to the post-Watergate intelligence revelations aimed to increase, rather than to reduce, governmental secrecy. The Intelligence Identities Protection Act of 1982, proposed as a means to halt Philip Agee's activities, made it a crime to reveal the names of CIA covert operatives. Supported overwhelmingly in Congress, the bill was approved by the Senate by a vote of 81 to 4.

WATCHDOGS AND WHISTLE-BLOWERS

The Church and Pike investigations were not the only controversies that the CIA faced during the year of intelligence. In that atmosphere of suspicion and exposé, other congressmen and journalists sought to publicize covert actions. In addition, some disgruntled ex-employees chose to blow the whistle on what they saw as CIA abuses and crimes.

In March 1975, columnist Jack Anderson revealed that the CIA had spent hundreds of millions of dollars in a failed attempt to raise a sunken Soviet submarine from the bottom of the Pacific Ocean. The operation, dubbed "Project Jennifer," was aimed at recovering Soviet codebooks and nuclear missiles. As part of the project, the agency had paid reclusive billionaire Howard Hughes to build an enormous salvage ship, the *Glomar Explorer*, and pretend that it was trying to harvest minerals from the ocean floor. In breaking the story, Anderson defied a plea from CIA director William Colby to suppress it. Colby, however, had persuaded the *Los Angeles Times*, *Time* magazine, and even CIA nemesis Seymour Hersh to spike the story in the interests of national security. One of the targets of the CIA's domestic spying program, Anderson refused to stay "on our side," as Colby called it, and went ahead with the story. As a result, the agency dropped its plans for another attempt at recovering the sub.

Some congressmen also refused to stay on the CIA's team. As one result of the Hughes-Ryan amendment, many more members of the House and Senate knew about the CIA's covert actions around the world. The law, however, did not provide a way for them to register their opposition to these actions. Under the law, the CIA director had to brief selected congressmen about covert actions, but these overseers were not allowed to disclose this secret information to anyone outside the oversight committees. They had knowledge, but no power. Senator Dick Clark of Iowa faced this problem after he received CIA briefings on its aid for one of the warring factions in Angola. In that African nation, three groups were fighting for control of the newly independent country. Although the State Department favored a diplomatic solution to the war, President Ford opted to spend $14 million on arms and CIA assistance for one faction.

Senator Clark harbored serious doubts about the wisdom of the covert action. Indeed, his doubts were shared by many State Department and Agency employees, including the CIA officer in charge of the intervention in Angola, John Stockwell. But the senator was bound to secrecy. Finally, after Seymour Hersh revealed some aspects of the Angola operation in the *New York Times*, the senator decided to seek a congressional ban on aid to Angola. Congress voted to support the so-called Clark amendment and, for the first time, to force the CIA to halt a covert action.

Not only journalists and congressmen but former Agency employees themselves also began to expose Agency activities in the mid-1970s. The trend of angry memoirs by ex-CIA officers began in 1974, when Victor Marchetti collaborated with former State Department analyst John Marks to write *The CIA and the Cult of Intelligence*. Like all Agency employees, Marchetti had signed a contract stating that he could not reveal any information he learned at the agency. Having grown disillusioned by Vietnam, he decided to write a book exposing the "cult" of secrecy at Langley. Backed by the Nixon administration, the CIA hauled Marchetti into court for breach of contract. Following a nearly two-year battle, he was forced to delete 168 passages from his book. His publisher made the deletions, but left white spaces where the deleted text would have been. The effect was to highlight the agency's censorship.

The Marchetti court battle started a continuing controversy over the Agency's right to censor its ex-agents. The CIA claimed that it needed to protect national security secrets, while Marchetti and other former operatives insisted that the censorship impeded free speech rights and the public's right to know.

The next whistle-blower took a much more extreme stance than Marchetti. Philip Agee had become so disillusioned by his experiences as a CIA officer in Latin America that he decided to expose Agency operations and workers. By publishing his book in Britain, and thereby avoiding American courts, Agee succeeded in revealing the names of Agency fronts, contacts, and officers. Some at the CIA viewed Agee as the first Agency defector.

Most Agency apostates, however, had the more narrow and pragmatic goal of exposing specific agency operations with the hope of improving and strengthening the intelligence community. For example, former CIA analyst Sam Adams stirred controversy in May 1975 when he published an explosive article in *Harper's*. Adams told the story of his bureaucratic battle with the Pentagon over the estimated strength of the Vietcong. As the CIA analyst assigned to examine the state of enemy morale, Adams had concluded that the Agency's official estimate of 270,000 Vietcong had been too low by at least 200,000 men. The implications of his analysis were stunning: if the enemy was much stronger than previously assumed, then the war might be unwinnable. In his article in *Harper's* Adams described how the military and the top CIA brass had refused to consider his new information because the Johnson administration did not want to hear the bad news. His exposé was a classic example of what critics of the CIA had feared from the start: that Agency officials would tailor intelligence to fit the political needs of the current president. This would not be the last time the CIA faced this charge.

Ex-agent exposés did not end with the "year of intelligence." In 1978, John Stockwell, the chief organizer of the CIA covert action in Angola, published an angry account of this operation, charging that the then secretary of state Henry Kissinger's escalation of the conflict had provoked Soviet and Cuban intervention and helped to plunge the African nation into chaos. Stockwell believed that the CIA had degenerated into the type of Gestapo feared by critics from the beginning. "Eventually, like any secret police, they became abusive of people: they drugged American citizens, opened private mail; infiltrated the media with secret propaganda and disinformation; lied to our elected representatives; and set themselves above the law and the Constitution." In contrast, Frank Snepp, a former CIA officer in Saigon, wrote in his 1977 memoir that he supported the Agency and its goals, but contended that it had badly bungled the evacuation of Saigon at the end of the Vietnam War. In his bitter account of the conflict, *Decent Interval*, Snepp charged that senior CIA and State Department officials had condemned many of their agents to certain death by their blindness and stupidity in the last months of the war.

Like all Agency employees, Snepp had signed a secrecy agreement pledging not to publish any CIA-related information without the prior approval of Agency officials. However, he did not submit his manuscript to Agency censors before publication, arguing that he disclosed no classified information and that the CIA enforced such prepublication agreements selectively. For example, the CIA had not protested when former DCI William Colby published his largely positive memoirs without submitting his manuscript for Agency review. The Justice Department conceded that Snepp's book contained no classified information, but still sued him to enforce the secrecy contract and seize his profits.

Snepp's case went to the Supreme Court in 1980 and established a precedent for future agency whistle-blowers. By a 6–3 vote, the court agreed with the Agency and ruled that Snepp had violated his secrecy contract. As a result of the decision, Snepp had to turn over all of his book profits to the government, Stockwell negotiated an agreement to pay the CIA any future profits from his book, and the CIA won the right to censor all future books by former Agency workers. After the Snepp decision, the next published CIA apostate, Ralph McGehee, worked with the CIA to get approval for his blistering critique of the Agency, *Deadly Deceits: My Twenty-Five Years in the CIA*. He spent years negotiating with the Agency, and publicly decried CIA efforts to reclassify information in his manuscript that had been previously released. McGehee ultimately published his book in 1983. But the Snepp decision and a changing political climate combined to make *Deadly Deceits* the last of the major exposés of the era.

INTERNAL CONFLICTS: TEAM B, THE HELMS PERJURY CASE, AND THE NOSENKO AFFAIR

As it fell to its nadir in public respect, the CIA faced assaults from the right as well as the left. Beginning in 1974, conservatives who opposed the Nixon-Ford administration's policy of détente with the Soviet Union complained that CIA analysts had underestimated the Soviet threat. By 1975, these hard-liners won support from the President's Foreign Intelligence Advisory Board (PFIAB). The chair of this panel persuaded President Ford to set up a team of outside experts to prepare a new estimate of Soviet intentions and capabilities. This outside panel participated in a system of "competitive analysis" with CIA analysts, or Team A; the outsiders were dubbed Team B.

Headed by conservative Harvard historian Richard Pipes, Team B grimly reported that the Soviets were seeking to win a nuclear war with the United States. Succumbing to pressure from Team B and its supporters, the CIA analysts on Team A increased their projections of Soviet military expenditures and achievements. The dueling panels of analysts attracted media attention when someone—apparently a Team B member—leaked the dispute to the press. Some members of Congress contended that the entire Team B exercise was designed to create the illusion of a stronger Soviet Union and thus justify greater military expenditures. The subsequent collapse of the Soviet Union showed that the CIA analysts were closer to the truth than their outside auditors. Team B members angrily denied the charges that their estimates were politically motivated, and began to impose their stamp on the CIA and the Pentagon when Ronald Reagan became president.

Other internal CIA conflicts escaped the confines of Langley and emerged in the headlines in the late 1970s. One of the most disturbing controversies for some Agency veterans was the perjury conviction of former CIA director Richard Helms. During the internal accounting of errors that produced the "family jewels," someone within the Agency reported to the CIA's inspector general that Helms had lied to two congressional committees in 1973 about the CIA's involvement in overthrowing Allende's government in Chile. After an internal review, the new CIA director, William Colby, referred the matter to the Justice Department for possible prosecution, and a grand jury began hearing evidence in December 1974. Some Helms supporters in the Agency never forgave Colby for this, seeing the referral as a betrayal of a fellow secret agent. In 1977, faced with prosecution for perjury, Helms worked out a plea agreement with Justice Department prosecutors. He pleaded no contest to two misdemeanor charges of failing to testify "fully and completely" to Congress. A federal district court judge imposed a two-year suspended sentence and a fine of $2,000. After leaving the courthouse, Helms (whose attorney announced that his client would "wear this conviction like a badge of honor") attended a luncheon for retired CIA officers, who quickly donated the $2,000 to pay his fine. The case exemplified the tension between the dedication of CIA officials to keep secrets and their obligation to tell the truth to democracy's watchdogs.

Another CIA conflict became public in late 1970s. In his 1978 book *Legend*, Edward Jay Epstein recounted the long, bitter battle within the Agency over the legitimacy of one of most important Soviet defectors ever. In 1964, KGB officer Yuri Nosenko had disappeared from his hotel in Geneva. A few weeks later, he resurfaced in Washington, D.C., where American officials announced that he had defected to the West. News stories at the time described Nosenko's defection as a significant intelligence coup. Unknown to the public at the time, Nosenko did have important information to relay to the CIA. He had reviewed the KGB's file on Lee Harvey Oswald after the Kennedy assassination, he claimed, and he could unequivocally assure the Americans that the Soviets had no connection with President Kennedy's murder. He offered to testify before the Warren Commission, which was in the process of investigating the assassination.

Quickly, however, the CIA counterintelligence chief, James Angleton, and his staff suspected that the timing of Nosenko's defection was a little too convenient. These counterintelligence officials concluded that Nosenko was a false defector sent by the Soviets to spread disinformation in the West. In particular, they distrusted the former KGB officer because some of his information conflicted with that provided by another Soviet defector, Anatoliy Golitsyn, who was an Angleton favorite. A low-level, unstable former KGB analyst, Golitsyn insisted that the Soviets had inserted a mole into the top levels of the CIA. The mole, he maintained, was just one part of the KGB's "monster plot" to infiltrate and take over the CIA. When Nosenko disputed this, Angleton was convinced he was still under Moscow's control.

To test Nosenko's truthfulness, the CIA imprisoned him in a tiny room in a Virginia safe house for three years. Agency officers interrogated him, injected him with drugs, and tried everything short of torture to force him to change his story. Nosenko, however, continued to insist that he was a genuine defector. In 1968, an internal CIA report concluded that Nosenko was indeed telling the truth, and that Golitsyn was the unreliable informant. DCI Richard Helms, who despite the report still had private doubts about Nosenko, released the prisoner and employed him as a CIA consultant.

James Angleton continued to suspect Nosenko, and he launched a massive hunt within the Agency for the "Soviet mole" allegedly carrying out the monster plot. Angleton's obsession with the "mole" ruined the careers of some top CIA officers. In addition, Angleton refused to accept the legitimacy of future genuine KGB defectors who disagreed with Golitsyn's charges.

The Nosenko case tore the CIA apart and prompted the counterintelligence division to waste years chasing illusory leads. One of Angleton's opponents, William Colby, became CIA chief in 1973 and began pressing for Angleton's retirement. When Seymour Hersh revealed Operation CHAOS, which Angleton's office had directed, Colby at last had an excuse to fire the controversial counterintelligence chief in late 1974. In 1977, President Carter's CIA director, Stansfield Turner, launched a new investigation that vindicated Nosenko. Angleton nevertheless continued to keep the controversy alive, leaking his version of the story to Epstein and other writers. Following Angleton's death in 1987, two prominent books examined the scandal and determined that Nosenko was telling the truth; diehard Angleton supporters continued to insist on the existence of the "mole" and the "monster plot" into the 1990s.

THE "YEAR OF THE SPY"

As Americans began to learn about the divisive mole hunt in the CIA, two more spy cases in the 1980s demonstrated that the Agency continued to have serious problems in its counterintelligence division. Nineteen eighty-five started out well for the CIA with the defection of Vitaly Yurchenko, the highest-ranking KGB officer ever to switch allegiance to the West. The defection was first reported as a great coup for the CIA. For three months, Yurchenko poured out volumes of intelligence to his Agency debriefers. As the former chief of KGB operations in North America, Yurchenko had extensive knowledge of Soviet activities in Canada and the United States. But Yurchenko grew depressed during his months in Washington. When his former girlfriend, who was married to a Soviet diplomat in Canada, refused to join him, he reconsidered his defection. On a fall night in 1985, as he and his

CIA handler ate dinner in a Georgetown restaurant, he asked his guard if he would be shot if he suddenly bolted. "We don't treat defectors that way," the CIA man protested. Yurchenko then calmly walked out of the restaurant and proceeded to the Soviet embassy, where he announced his decision to re-defect. He subsequently maintained in Soviet press conferences that he had been drugged and kidnapped by the Americans. While few people believed that story, the CIA's loss of Yurchenko was seen as a major counterintelligence failure.

Yet the Yurchenko case was a relative triumph compared to the disaster of the Edward Lee Howard affair. The Howard case had been smoldering for two years before Yurchenko's defection. In 1983, the Agency had assigned Howard to its Moscow station. As part of his training process, he learned many of the secrets of the CIA in Moscow, including clues to the identities of Russians who were secretly working for the Agency. Shortly before he left for Moscow, however, Howard failed a polygraph test. The test administrators detected signs of drug use, petty theft, and deception. Rather than working with Howard, Agency officials took the highly unusual step of firing him on the spot. Over the next two years, Howard was repeatedly drunk, made threats, took mysterious trips to Europe, and even confessed to his Agency contacts that he was thinking of selling secrets. Yet CIA officials tried to hush up the case, and did not alert the FBI to Howard's threats. Then, when Yurchenko defected, the Russian told the CIA about an Agency man who was selling secrets to the KGB. The CIA knew instantly from the description that Yurchenko was talking about Howard. Since the FBI was listening in on Yurchenko's sessions, the CIA could no longer cover up the story of its first-ever defector to the Soviets. FBI agents began watching Howard. In a tale more worthy of the Keystone Kops than James Bond, however, FBI agents were not looking when Howard escaped from his New Mexico home and fled to Moscow.

Howard and Yurchenko were the CIA's contributions to the "year of the spy," as the press dubbed 1985. That year, National Security Agency analyst Ronald W. Pelton and former naval intelligence officer John A. Walker, Jr., and his family were apprehended for spying for the Soviets. The media portrayed the U.S. intelligence community as riddled with spies. In 1988, the House Intelligence Committee investigated the various counterintelligence failures, and proclaimed that "something is fundamentally wrong" with U.S. counterespionage efforts. The debate continued to rage within the Agency over the causes of these failures. Some blamed Angleton for his devastating and ineffective mole hunt; others said that it was Colby's dismissal and discrediting of Angleton that had weakened the Agency from within.

Ironically, the most dangerous mole in the CIA's history, Aldrich Ames, began his espionage activities during 1985, yet was not exposed during the "year of the spy." As the CIA's chief of Soviet counterintelligence in 1985, Ames knew the names of all the Soviets who were secretly working for the CIA. He was in an ideal position to sell these names to the KGB. Angry, unstable, and in chronic need of money, that April Ames boldly entered the Soviet embassy in Washington and delivered a letter describing some Soviets who had offered to spy for the CIA. The delighted KGB paid him $50,000. Two months later, he turned over the names of more than ten Soviets working for the CIA and FBI in return for $2 million. Some of these CIA sources were killed; others vanished.

As their assets disappeared, CIA officials realized that the Agency had been penetrated and launched an internal investigation to uncover the mole. Nevertheless, they failed to uncover Ames's espionage activities for nine years. When he was arrested in 1994, members of Congress and the media asked in astonishment how the Agency could have missed all of the warning signs. Ames drank heavily, received poor job evaluations, parked his Jaguar in the CIA parking lot, and paid cash for a half-million dollar house. Yet Agency officials resisted for years recognizing that one of their own had changed sides. Finally, in 1993 CIA officials turned the case over to the FBI, which suc-ceeded in catching Ames a year later. In return for cooperating with CIA debriefers, Ames received a life sentence rather than facing certain execution.

The Ames case, with its revelations of treachery and incompetence, de-moralized the Agency. DCI James Woolsey ordered three different investi-gations into the causes of the fiasco, but still could not save his job, resigning at the end of 1994. Both the Senate and House Intelligence Committees issued detailed reports that, in the words of the Senate report, criticized the CIA's "gross negligence" in the case.

THE CIA AND IRAN-CONTRA

While CIA officials struggled to find the elusive mole in the late 1980s, its new, aggressive director, William Casey, involved it in a presidential scandal as momentous as Watergate—and potentially even more dangerous for the Agency's survival. By the end of the 1980s, the CIA would be accused of the worst crimes of its history: subverting the Constitution and tolerating drug trafficking in American cities.

When he assumed the presidency in 1981, Ronald Reagan promised to unleash the agency, which he charged had been hobbled by the reforms enacted in the aftermath of the Church Committee exposés. To signal a new direction for the CIA, he appointed as DCI a man who shared his views: his campaign manager, William Casey.

Casey had a distinguished record serving in the OSS during World War II, but for the past forty years had worked in the business world. His gruff, aggressive attitude prompted criticism from liberals from the start, as did rumors that he had struck a secret deal with the Iranian government to keep American hostages in Iran until after the 1980 election. Those rumors were never proved. But Casey did embark on other documented illegal activities— activities whose exposure would lead to one of the CIA's worst crises.

The scandal eventually known as the Iran-Contra affair started with CIA involvement in Nicaragua. In 1979, Nicaraguan revolutionaries, called the Sandinistas, had overthrown the dictator of that country, longtime U.S. ally Anastasio Somoza. The Carter administration reluctantly decided to recognize the new government. But to Ronald Reagan, Nicaragua under the Sandinistas was a "second Cuba," a Soviet foothold on the American continent. Casey shared Reagan's opinion. In 1981, Casey proposed and Reagan approved an order authorizing the Agency to create and fund a small army of former Somoza supporters, called the Contras.

Under the Intelligence Oversight Act of 1980, Casey was required to notify both the Senate and the House Intelligence Committees of any major covert actions by the CIA. Casey convinced these committees to support this secret war in Nicaragua by saying that the purpose was not to overthrow the Sandinistas but to stop Nicaraguan arms shipments to the rebels in neighboring El Salvador. Congress agreed to fund the war on this premise.

With the CIA money flowing in, the Contra ranks grew from 500 to 3,000 men in three years. Because their force was too small to confront the Sandinistas on the battlefield, they began a guerrilla war of terrorism. They blew up oil supplies, assassinated Sandinista officials, and launched terrorist attacks against peasant communities. The Contras' terrorist tactics made them increasingly unpopular among members of the two intelligence committees. These congressmen were also disturbed that the Contras did not seem to be intercepting any arms from Nicaragua to El Salvador, which was the ostensible reason they were receiving CIA money.

Congress began to restrict funding for the Contra war in 1982. Massachusetts Democrat Edward Boland, chair of the House Intelligence Committee, wanted to cut off all funding for the Contras. But the Senate Intelligence Committee, chaired by Arizona Republican Barry Goldwater, wanted to continue the funding. The two committees finally arrived at a compromise. The CIA would get its money for Nicaragua, but it could not use that money to overthrow the Sandinistas. This was the first of the later famous Boland amendments; it specifically prohibited the CIA from spending money "for the purpose of overthrowing the government of Nicaragua." All of the Boland amendments limited the ways that U.S. money could be spent in Nicaragua. President Reagan signed all of the Boland amendments, and, by doing so, had to accept their legitimacy.

Because the Contras failed to collect a large following or achieve many results in the coming year, the CIA made a crucial decision to intervene directly in the war. CIA boats sailed into Nicaraguan harbors and blew up oil tanks. Agency helicopters engaged in gun battles with the Sandinistas. Then, in 1984, CIA operatives began to mine the Nicaraguan harbors. These mines could have destroyed any number of Russian, British, and Latin American ships delivering food and fuel to Nicaragua. The Nicaraguan war was turning from a proxy war into a war in which the CIA was directly involved. To make matters worse, the intelligence committees charged that they had not been notified of the mining, as required by law. Casey had included one obscure sentence about the mining in an eighty-one-page briefing, which congressmen did not believe was sufficient. Senator Goldwater, normally a strong CIA supporter, wrote Casey that he was "pissed off" about the deception.

The mining of the harbors proved to be the last straw for Congress. Members of the Senate Intelligence Committee, despite their sympathy for the Contras and their hatred for the Sandinistas, were furious that the CIA was engaging in acts of war that could have created a serious international incident, if not brought the United States to the brink of war. The angry Congressmen passed the most stringent Boland amendment, which prohibited the CIA, the Defense Department, "or any other agency or entity of the United States involved in intelligence activities" from helping the Contras. President Reagan signed this new law, as he had signed the previous Boland amendments. The elected representatives of the American people had decided to stop U.S. funding of the Contra war, and the president had signaled his agreement when he signed the law.

Casey and other Reagan administration officials, however, had decided to try to find a way around this restriction. The DCI, assisted by senior White House officials, came up with several creative schemes of dubious legality. First, he arranged for private donors to open their checkbooks for the Nicaraguan rebels. Next, he asked the State Department to ask other countries to give money to the Contras. Opponents later charged that this violated the Boland amendment, which prohibited any U.S. agency, including the State Department, from helping the Contras. Critics also worried that the United States had promised something to these other countries in return for contributions—a quid pro quo.

For Casey, getting the money was only part of the problem. He also needed someone in the U.S. government to coordinate the Contra war effort. But the Boland amendments had legally banned the CIA or "any other agency or entity involved in intelligence activities" from having anything to do with the Contras, directly or indirectly. Congressman Boland had worked hard to make the language airtight. Casey and other senior Reagan White House officials, however, contended that the law did not ban aid by the National Security Council. Later, when the scandal broke, critics charged that this distinction drawn by Casey and other Reagan aides was simply legalistic pretense.

To run the Contra war, Casey chose a young go-getter assigned to the staff of the National Security Council (NSC), Marine lieutenant colonel Oliver North. North not only helped to raise money for the Contras, but also helped them to spend it: advising them on which weapons to buy, organizing supply systems, and recommending strategy. He soon could not keep up with all these responsibilities. He asked a retired general, Richard Secord, to help him buy guns for the Contras. Secord created a conglomerate that purchased guns, and then sold them to the Contras at a substantial mark-up that averaged

217

29 percent. Secord called his secret conglomerate "the Enterprise." The Enterprise was, as Senator Daniel Inouye (D-HI) subsequently remarked, "a shadowy government with its own air force, its own navy, its own fund-raising mechanism, and the ability to pursue its own ideas of the national interest, free from all checks and balances and free from the law itself." Meanwhile, North asked another retired general to help him raise money from private American donors, such as beer tycoon Joseph Coors.

Despite all of the money from other countries and from private donors, the Contras still could not win significant military victories. North decided that another source of outside revenue was needed for his favorite cause. Then he got the "neat idea" to combine the Contra project with the other major project he had been handling for the White House since 1985: the Iranian arms-for-hostages deal.

The arms-for-hostages swaps arose out of President Reagan's deep concern about American hostages whom Middle Eastern terrorists, suspected of being funded by Ayatollah Khomeini's government in Iran, had seized in Lebanon. In the early 1980s, pro-Iranian radical groups in Beirut kidnapped seven American men individually and held them hostage. One of the hostages was of special concern to President Reagan and CIA director Casey: CIA officer William Buckley, the station chief in Beirut. In public, the president had insisted that he would never negotiate with terrorists. But in 1985, after meeting with the family of one of these hostages, Reagan began to reassess his resolve against dealing with terrorists. Visibly shaken after an emotional meeting with this hostage's family, Reagan began to ask his aides daily what they were doing to secure the release of the hostages.

Knowing of his boss's concern about the hostages, Reagan's national security adviser at the time, Robert McFarlane, was intrigued when an ex-Israeli spy walked into his office one day and said he knew a man who might be able to free the hostages. That man, an Iranian named Manucher Ghorbanifar, reportedly had great contacts with "moderates" in the Islamic government in Tehran. Ghorbanifar claimed to have influence over the Iranians, who in turn had influence over the kidnappers in Beirut.

McFarlane obtained President Reagan's approval to meet with Ghorbanifar, and soon began working out a deal with him. Iran wanted missiles and spare parts for its ongoing war with Iraq. The United States, in turn, wanted the release of the hostages, and also to make contact with individuals who Ghorbanifar claimed were moderates in the Iranian government. There were three sticking points to making a deal, though. First, any deal would violate the Reagan administration's highly publicized crusade to protest and prevent the sale of arms to Iran. The State Department, moreover, had accused Khomeini's government of supporting terrorism and pressured other countries to stop selling arms to the ayatollah. Second, under the Arms Export Control Act, the Reagan administration would be required to notify Congress of the sales. Finally, the arms-for-hostages plan also violated the government's publicly stated opposition to dealing with terrorists. Essentially, an arms deal would be a bribe to the kidnappers.

Because of these problems, the constitutionally appointed guardians of the nation's foreign policy, Secretary of State George Schultz and Secretary of Defense Caspar Weinberger, strongly opposed the plan. Both Shultz and Weinberger dismissed the idea as ridiculous. Their opposition did not stop McFarlane and North, who convinced the president to overrule these two cabinet officials. Reagan verbally approved the first arms-for-hostages trade, which resulted in the release of only one hostage. Ghorbanifar suggested a second trade, and the president again agreed. During the second deal, North called on Duane Clarridge, the CIA's chief of the European Division, for help with logistics. Clarridge arranged to have the missiles shipped by airline secretly owned by the CIA and obtained clearances from foreign governments for the flight. When deputy CIA director John McMahon heard about the CIA's involvement, he was furious. "We can't do that without a finding!" he shouted. He insisted that the CIA counsel draw up a finding for the president to sign, retroactively approving the CIA's role in the arms transfer. The president signed on January 17, 1986. Not only was the finding retroactive, but it included an extraordinary clause: "Because of the extreme sensitivity of these operations, . . . I direct the Director of Central Intelligence not to brief the Congress . . . until such time as I may direct otherwise." By failing to notify Congress, Reagan flouted the reporting requirement of the Intelligence Oversight Act of 1980.

Because the arms-for-hostages swaps violated the Arms Export Control Act and the Intelligence Oversight Act, Casey acted to avoid a direct role for the Agency in the deals. To do so, he relied on North and the National Security Council staff, as he had done with the illegal war in Nicaragua. In the end, the United States and Iran made five arms-for-hostages deals. The terrorists released three hostages in exchange for arms, but also seized two new hostages.

Because Casey put North in charge of both of the illegal operations, it did not take North long to figure out that he could combine them. The Contras needed money; the Iranian arms deals generated profits. By early 1986, North was using the Enterprise to divert the profits from the Iranian arms sale to the Contras in Nicaragua.

By coincidence, both the Iranian and Contra ends of Oliver North's illegal operations were exposed within two weeks of each other. The first exposure came as a result of developments in Nicaragua. On October 5, 1986, the Sandinistas shot down one of the Enterprise's planes, capturing one of the crew, Eugene Hasenfus, a former CIA agent. Members of Congress immediately demanded an investigation into whether this was a CIA operation and thus a violation of the Boland amendment. Later that same month, in an apparent attempt to embarrass the Reagan administration, some agents of the Iranian government leaked the story of the U.S.-Iranian arms deals to *al Shiraa*, a Lebanese newspaper.

In response to these revelations, Attorney General Ed Meese launched an internal inquiry. Afraid of repeating Richard Nixon's mistakes during Watergate, Meese wanted to avoid any charges of a cover-up. Meese, not the press, uncovered the diversion of funds from the arms deals to the Contras, and he announced it in a news conference in November 1986. Meese's announcement triggered a flurry of investigations into the Iran-Contra affair. All of the investigations—whether conducted by a special presidential commission, a special prosecutor, Congress, or the press—focused on whether the president knew about the diversion. None were able to uncover written evidence that he did—foreclosing any calls for Reagan's impeachment.

Although the president survived the investigations of the Iran-Contra affair, the CIA's image was badly tarnished. DCI Casey had "tried to insulate himself and the CIA" from the crimes of Iran-Contra, Independent Counsel Lawrence Walsh wrote in his final report. Walsh did uncover evidence that Casey had participated in the illegal activities and tried to conceal them from Congress. Casey, however, had died by the time of Walsh's report. Walsh, however, eventually charged four CIA officials for crimes in the scandal. Former covert operations chief Clair George, and Duane Clarridge, former chief of the European division of the CIA, were indicted for perjury; Costa Rica station chief Joseph Fernandez was indicted for conspiracy, obstruction, and perjury; and Alan Fiers, CIA chief of the Central American Task Force, was charged with two counts of withholding information from Congress. Fernandez's case was dismissed before trial, Fiers pleaded guilty, and George was convicted. While Clarridge's trial was pending, President George H. W. Bush pardoned Clarridge, Fiers, George, and other Iran-Contra figures in December 1992, prior to leaving office with his defeat in his bid for reelection.

Walsh found no documentary evidence that Casey knew about the most troubling aspect of Iran-Contra: North's decision to raise funds for the private army of Contras by diverting the surplus funds obtained through selling arms to Iran. During his congressional testimony, North claimed that Casey knew about and approved the diversion of funds, and—in an account hotly disputed by Casey's relatives—author Bob Woodward claimed that during a deathbed interview with Casey the director had confirmed to him that he knew about the diversion.

North even alleged that Casey had discussed the idea of using secret, illegal weapons sales to finance private covert operations—and thus fund a secret foreign policy out of the view of Congress. In North's words, Casey wanted an "off-the-shelf, self-sustaining stand-alone entity"—a CIA outside of the CIA—that could carry out the DCI's whims without the knowledge of any overseers. Casey was not alive to answer these accusations. The independent counsel, moreover, concluded that North was not a very credible witness on this point.

While unable to prove that Casey knew about the diversion of funds, Walsh offered a devastating assessment of the CIA's role in Iran-Contra. "The objectivity, professionalism, and integrity of the Central Intelligence Agency were compromised by Casey's attitude and behavior," his final report starkly concluded.

DARK ALLIANCE: THE CIA AND DRUGS

The damage the CIA sustained from the Iran-Contra affair went far beyond the prosecutions of a few officials. The scandal seriously eroded the Agency's credibility as the nation moved into the post–Cold War era. The CIA's involvement in Nicaragua also provided fodder for critics who charged that the Agency at best tolerated—and at worst encouraged—drug trafficking by its clients.

As early as 1985, Senator John Kerry of Massachusetts began hearing allegations that the Contras were selling drugs. Following the exposure of the Iran-Contra scandal, Kerry chaired a major investigation into the links between drug dealers and the Contras. His committee also examined the response of U.S. officials to these links. In December 1988, the Kerry committee issued a report containing 1,100 pages of exhibits and testimony documenting the Contras' involvement in drug trafficking. As this report stated, "it is clear that individuals who provided support for the Contras were involved in drug trafficking, the supply network of the Contras was used by drug trafficking organizations, and elements of the Contras themselves knowingly received financial and material assistance from drug traffickers." The committee also concluded that several U.S. agencies, including the CIA, knew about the trafficking but had failed to stop it.

The Kerry Committee report received little coverage in the press at the time. Its charges were given new life eight years later in an unlikely venue. In August 1996, the *San Jose Mercury News* published a story by Pulitzer Prize–winning reporter Gary Webb alleging that a California drug ring had funneled millions of dollars to the Contras. Headlined "Dark Alliance," the story charged that the crack cocaine explosion in African American ghettoes had its roots in these drug dealers' earlier attempts to raise money for the CIA's army in Nicaragua.

Webb never suggested that the CIA had deliberately sought to sell drugs to African Americans as a way to raise money. He did, however, imply that CIA officials had looked the other way when they realized the Contras were selling drugs and had done so because of their strong support for the Contras' cause. Although Webb had not claimed a CIA conspiracy, many readers interpreted his reporting that way. Webb's story, despite its appearance in a regional newspaper, quickly spread throughout the world via the Internet. Although located in the heart of Silicon Valley, the *Mercury News* was an industry leader in placing and promoting stories on the World Wide Web. Soon the story was getting hundreds of thousands of hits a day as readers around the country learned about the allegations.

To quell these rumors, DCI John Deutch attended a town hall meeting in Watts—an unprecedented act for a CIA chief. Raising his voice to be heard above the boos and catcalls, Deutch insisted that the CIA never ignored evidence of drug trafficking by its clients. The several hundred residents who attended the meeting were not appeased, nor were many other African Americans. As many African Americans embraced the story and asserted that it proved a government conspiracy against blacks, some of the most prestigious newspapers in the country attacked Webb's reporting and depicted the entire controversy as evidence of "black paranoia." In the end, the *Mercury News* conceded that the story was flawed and reassigned Webb, who quit in disgust. An internal CIA investigation later confirmed that some Agency officials had, in fact, ignored evidence that some Contras had been selling drugs.

THE FAILURE OF INTELLIGENCE BEFORE 9/11

The accusations about the CIA and drugs reflected a consistent theme of public suspicion of the power of the CIA. The second continuing controversy involving the Agency—concern over its susceptibility to White House manipulation—also continued into the 1990s and beyond. In 1991, during Senate confirmation hearings of Robert Gates, President George Bush's nominee as CIA director, a brief stir erupted when some Agency veterans charged that Gates had a tendency to slant intelligence to please his White House patrons. After some contentious testimony, the Senate confirmed Gates, and this controversy died quickly.

This was not the case, though, with the controversies concerning the terrorist attack of September 11 and the intelligence cited to justify Iraq war. Immediately after the terrorist attacks on the World Trade Center and the Pentagon in September 2001, some congressmen demanded to know what had gone wrong. Why had the CIA and FBI failed to anticipate and thwart September 11? As in the case of the Iran-Contra affair—and the intelligence failure of Pearl Harbor—in 2002 Congress appointed a joint House-Senate committee to investigate this matter. Headed by Democratic Senator Bob Graham and Republican Congressman Porter Goss, the joint committee encountered problems that would have been familiar to veteran Church and Pike committee members. Former Ford administration staff members Dick Cheney and Donald Rumsfeld, now vice president and secretary of defense, employed the same tactics that they had used against the inquisitive congressmen in 1975: stonewalling, delaying, and attempting to discredit the investigators. The committee came under siege when, like the Pike Committee, it was accused of a leak. CNN reported that the National Security Agency had intercepted a clear warning of the attacks the day before they occurred, but had failed to translate the intercept in time. The FBI launched an investigation to identify the source of this leak, and the committee was temporarily diverted from its task.

Despite White House opposition, the congressional committee eventually released a comprehensive and scathing report in July 2003 that identified the failures of both the CIA and the FBI. In its final report the committee concluded "the intelligence community failed to capitalize on both the individual and collective significance of available information that appears relevant to the events of September 11. As a result, the community missed opportunities to disrupt the September 11 plot by denying entry to or detaining would-be hijackers, to at least try to unravel the plot through surveillance and other investigative work within the United States; and, finally, to generate a heightened state of alert and thus harden the homeland against attack." Although the FBI came in for the most criticism, the committee also criticized the CIA for missing "repeated opportunities" to alert the FBI that two known terrorists "could well be in the United States." These two men, Khalid al Mihdhar and Nawaf al Hazmi, who lived in San Diego and had numerous contacts with an FBI informant, were among the nineteen hijackers on September 11. The failures of the CIA and FBI to share information was a "systemic weakness" of the structure of the U.S. intelligence community, the committee concluded. To solve this problem, the members recommended separating the jobs of CIA director and overall intelligence chief by creating a new cabinet-level position of Director of National Intelligence.

The joint committee also decried the Bush administration's decision to censor its final report, including a twenty-eight-page section that described the links between the Saudi Arabian government and the hijackers in San Diego. The report claimed that two Saudi citizens, Omar al-Bayoumi and Osama Bassnan, were "probably" Saudi intelligence agents operating in San Diego. While no clear evidence had been uncovered confirming that Bassnan, described as an "associate" of al-Bayoumi, knew the hijackers, al-Bayoumi had befriended them and loaned them money. The committee members protested the deletions, although subsequent leaks to reporters revealed the general outlines of the censored pages. The committee, moreover, demanded a further investigation of the possible Saudi role in the 9/11 attacks. Bush administration officials dismissed that section of the report as speculative and refused to declassify it, even after Saudi officials called for its release.

The joint committee's inquiry did not end the controversy. Families of the September 11 victims persisted in demanding the establishment of an independent, blue-ribbon investigating commission with broad power to discover the truth. President Bush at first resisted the creation of such a commission, charging that it would be a distraction for national security officials. Persistent lobbying by the 9/11 families forced him to accede to the creation of such a panel in November 2002. The commission nonetheless got off to a controversial start. The president first appointed former secretary of state Henry Kissinger as chair. But Kissinger and his vice chair, former Democratic Senator George Mitchell, resigned rather than disclose the names of their business clients. (The 9/11 families had suggested that these business ties might lead to

CIA Director George Tenet makes his opening statement at the start of his testimony before the commission investigating the September 11 attacks, April 14, 2004, on Capitol Hill in Washington. (AP/Wide World Photos)

conflicts of interest.) President Bush then appointed former New Jersey governor Thomas Kean as chair, while the congressional Democrats named as vice chair former congressman Lee Hamilton, a veteran of the Iran-Contra investigation. Launching their inquiry, the investigators once again charged that the administration was frustrating and delaying their progress, and Kean publicly criticized the administration for withholding documents.

The commission's public hearings sparked fireworks in March 2004 when former White House counterterrorism chief Richard Clarke criticized the Bush administration for giving a low priority to fighting terrorism. Clarke further testified that the invasion of Iraq actually undermined the war on terror by diverting needed resources and serving to inflame anti-Americanism throughout the world. Clarke and the Kean Commission staff reports also criticized CIA director George Tenet for having been reluctant to assassinate al Qaeda leader Osama bin Laden before the attacks occurred. CIA officials told the commission that the White House had never clearly authorized an assassination except during a "credible capture operation," and that in any event bin Laden's death might not have prevented the September 11 attacks.

Bush administration officials also blamed the CIA and other intelligence agencies for having failed to prevent the attacks. In her April 2004 testimony before the 9/11 commission, National Security Adviser Condoleezza Rice claimed that the intelligence community had given "frustratingly vague" warnings before September 11. The commission, however, thereupon revealed that President Bush had received on August 6, 2001, PDB (President's Daily Brief) from the CIA titled "Bin Laden Determined to Attack Inside the United States." Rice contended in response that the memo contained only "historical" information.

The 9/11 Commission released its eagerly awaited final report on July 22, 2004, an event that was covered live on national radio and television. The report was highly critical of the CIA and proposed several structural reforms. Besides echoing the joint congressional committee's recommendation of a new, cabinet-level director of national intelligence, the commission urged that Congress restructure and strengthen its intelligence oversight system. The bipartisan commission, however, avoided blaming either the Clinton or Bush administrations for failing to anticipate the 9/11 attacks.

In a special lame-duck session in December 2004, Congress overwhelmingly passed an intelligence reform bill that implemented many of the recommendations of the 9/11 Commission, including the creation of a Director of National Intelligence, separate from the CIA director. The National Intelligence Director would serve as head of all fifteen intelligence agencies and control most of their budgets. The law also established a new national counterterrorism center within the Executive Office of the President to coordinate information sharing among intelligence agencies. Its supporters called the law the most important intelligence reform since the dawn of the Cold War. "Just as the National Security Act of 1947 was passed to prevent another Pearl Harbor, the Intelligence Reform Act will help us prevent another 9/11," Senator Susan Collins of Maine opined. Critics, however, said that the law would do little more than add another layer of bureaucracy to the nation's intelligence community.

THE "SIXTEEN WORDS" AND INTELLIGENCE MANIPULATION

Concurrent with the Kean Commission's inquiries into the failure of the U.S. intelligence agencies to have anticipated the terrorist attack, some members of Congress demanded a separate investigation into the quality and the use by the White House of intelligence cited in justification of President Bush's decision to invade Iraq in March 2003. The Bush administration had maintained before the invasion that an attack on Iraq was necessary because Iraqi leader Saddam Hussein possessed massive quantities of weapons of mass destruction (biological and chemical weapons and an ongoing nuclear weapons program)—and had cited CIA reports to that effect. No such weapons were uncovered, however, in the aftermath of the successful invasion. The failure to find the weapons raised key questions about the CIA: had it been incompetent, or had it been manipulated by a pro-war White House?

In his January 28, 2003, State of the Union address, President Bush made several claims that were later proven to be incorrect. Most notably, Bush claimed that Saddam Hussein had been linked with the terrorist group al Qaeda and that Iraq had tried to buy nuclear material from Niger. Bush explained, "the British government has learned that Saddam Hussein recently sought significant quantities of uranium from Africa." The sixteen-word sentence had the intended powerful effect, for it implied that the Iraqi government was building a nuclear bomb. But on March 7, Mohamed ElBaradei, the director general of the International Atomic Energy Agency, told the United Nations Security Council that this charge was based on forged documents. One IAEA official told Seymour Hersh, "These documents are so bad that I cannot imagine that they came from a serious intelligence agency. It depresses me, given the low quality of the documents, that it was not stopped. At the level it reached, I would have expected more checking." Still, President Bush cited Iraq's alleged weapons of mass destruction program as the main reason for invading Iraq on March 20.

The forgery issue erupted into the headlines in July 2003. Joseph Wilson, a retired diplomat who had served in the first Bush and the Clinton administrations, wrote an opinion piece for the July 6 *New York Times* saying that he had investigated the Niger claims at the request of the CIA in the summer of 2002, and had found them to be baseless. His report, he added, was known to the White House. Wilson further charged that the Bush administration had "twisted" intelligence "to exaggerate the Iraqi threat."

Wilson paid for his criticism of the president. On July 14, syndicated columnist Robert Novak wrote that "two senior [Bush] administration officials" had told him that Wilson had been recommended for the Niger investigation by his wife, Valerie Plame, a CIA operative. Wilson angrily responded that the naming of his wife endangered her life and violated the Intelligence Identities Protection Act of 1982. He believed that her name had been deliberately leaked in an attempt to silence him and other whistle-blowers from the intelligence community. Then, on September 28, the *Washington Post* reported that "two top White House officials" had called "at least six" journalists and tried to get them to disclose Plame's identity. "Clearly, it was meant purely and simply for revenge," a senior administration official told the *Post.* Pressured by CIA officials concerned over the compromising of a valued operative, the Justice Department belatedly launched a probe of the leak of Plame's name. In December, Attorney General John Ashcroft recused himself from the case to avoid the appearance of a conflict of interest. He appointed a special prosecutor, U.S. Attorney Patrick J. Fitzgerald. The investigation continued through 2005, with Fitzgerald questioning, among others, the president, vice president, White House aide Karl Rove, and vice president's Chief of Staff I. Lewis Libby, Jr. In August 2004, Fitzgerald pressured *Time* reporter Matthew Cooper and *New York Times* reporter Judith Miller with jail time, unless they testified about their sources.

In response to pressure from members of Congress (and to the intiation of an investigation by the Senate Select Committee on Intelligence), President Bush finally agreed to appoint a special commission headed by Judge Laurence Silberman and former senator Charles Robb to investigate the reasons for the poor intelligence on Iraq. The announcement did not mollify the critics for two reasons. First, the commission got off to a slow start and failed to schedule any public hearings before the November 2004 election. Second, Bush named as cochair of the panel a former federal judge who was viewed by critics as a Republican partisan inclined to cover up the abuses of Republican presidents. During the George H. W. Bush administration, Silberman had been one of two judges on the three-member appellate court who voted to toss out the Iran-Contra convictions of Oliver North and John Poindexter on technicalities. Silberman's control of the panel would ensure that there would be "no real investigation," Democratic Senator Harry Reid charged. "This is going to be Judge Silberman, in an aggressive way, making sure that nothing gets out of hand. He is there to protect the President, not to get fair information."

Attempting to tamp the furor over the revelations about the false claims in the president's State of the Union address, DCI George Tenet publicly took the blame for the false charges that Iraq had sought to buy nuclear materials from Niger, saying that he had failed to insist on the deletion of the sentence relating to Niger. Some members of Congress were outraged. "That the CIA knew the uranium allegation was patently false and allowed the president of the United States to stand before Congress and the American people and use it as a reason to go to war is absolutely shocking," said Congresswoman Ellen Tauscher (D-CA). In June 2004, Tenet suddenly resigned as CIA chief. Although Tenet insisted that he wanted only to spend more time with his family, many journalists and public officials suggested that he had been designated to take the blame for the intelligence failures both before 9/11 and before the Iraq war.

Other critics, though, attributed the faulty intelligence directly to the White House. Disgruntled CIA officers began telling reporters and congressmen that the White House had pressured the Agency to tell it what it wanted to hear. In fact, when the CIA had failed to uncover evidence either of Saddam's alleged weapons of mass destruction or of links between Iraq and al Qaeda, Defense Department officials had set up a separate team of intelligence analysts to find such proof. In an episode reminiscent of the notorious "Team B" controversy of the 1970s, this Defense Department group had tried to undercut the more cautious CIA analysts. In its final report, the 9/11 Commission agreed that Iraq did not contribute in any way to the 9/11 attacks, but stopped short of blaming the CIA or the Bush administration for claiming a false link between Iraq and the terrorists.

The Senate Intelligence Committee, in a separate investigation, was more willing to point fingers, and its majority report released in July 2004 put the blame for the poor intelligence squarely on the CIA. The committee further declared that Congress never would have endorsed the invasion had members known that Iraq had no weapons of mass destruction. Committee chair Pat Roberts said the CIA conclusions had been wrong and based on "unreasonable and largely unsupported" intelligence. This, perhaps, was the greatest failure of the CIA in its history: a failure to give reliable intelligence to national policy makers as they debated war. "Mistakes leading up to the war in Iraq rank among the most devastating losses and intelligence failures in the history of the nation," said intelligence committee member Jay Rockefeller.

The intelligence committee's report raised two important questions. First, had CIA officials ignored evidence that the cited intelligence was faulty—in other words, did they turn a blind eye to information that contradicted the case for war? The other key question went to the heart of the CIA's perpetual dilemma: in their assessment of Iraq's nuclear capabilities, had CIA analysts been manipulated by the president? The members of the Senate Intelligence Committee answered this question along partisan lines. Republicans insisted that President Bush was misled by a rogue CIA, while Democrats claimed that the Agency was manipulated by a rogue president. The Senate committee vowed to investigate the question further.

President Bush's choice of successor to George Tenet as CIA chief only worsened the fears of some Agency employees that the White House was trying to manipulate the nation's intelligence. The president nominated a former CIA officer and the current chair of the House Intelligence Committee, Porter Goss, to take over the top job at the Agency and restore its credibility. Goss encountered some opposition in the Senate because of fears that he would be too partisan. Then, soon after his confirmation, he ignited a new controversy when he informed Agency employees in a memo that their job was to "support the administration and its policies in our work." The statement was a stark reminder of the possibility that the nation's intelligence could be politicized. As Goss settled in at the Agency, several top officials resigned, including deputy director John McLaughlin, the two top leaders of the clandestine service, and counterterrorism expert Michael Scheuer, who had published a book charging the Bush administration with losing the war on terror. Some CIA officers said anonymously that Goss was destroying morale at the Agency by purging anyone viewed as insufficiently supportive of Bush.

The debate over intelligence manipulation continued into 2005 as both sides claimed to find more evidence to support their arguments. In April, the Silberman-Robb Commission reported that U.S. intelligence agencies had been "dead wrong" in their assessments of Iraqi weapons of mass destruction. This, the panel concluded, was the CIA's fault; the White House had not pressured the analysts to change their conclusions.

The administration's critics proclaimed the panel to be a whitewash. They cited a newly surfaced British document, called the Downing Street memo, as proof that the White House had manipulated intelligence. According to these top-secret minutes, the primary intelligence adviser to British Prime Minister Tony Blair told Blair in July 2002 that U.S. intelligence was being "fixed" to justify war with Iraq. Congressman John Conyers (D-MI) gathered the signatures of a half million Americans and one hundred members of Congress demanding that President Bush answer questions about the memo. The president had no response to the explosive revelations in the document, while his spokesman reiterated that the president had never "fixed" intelligence.

Soon after the publication of the Downing Street memo, the Valerie Plame case again burst into headlines. In July 2005 special prosecutor Patrick Fitzgerald threatened two reporters (Judith Miller of the New York Times and Mathew Cooper of Time) with jail unless they revealed who had outed Plame.

Both Miller and Cooper were among a handful of reporters who had talked with Bush administration officials about Plame's identity. Unlike Novak, Miller had not published a story (although Cooper had), and both could offer testimony about the role of senior Bush administration officials. Insisting that she would not betray a confidential source, Miller dramatically went to jail rather than testify to the grand jury investigating the case. Even after *Time* executives (collapsing under pressure) released Cooper's notes for his story, Cooper planned not to testify but changed his mind after his source called him at the last minute and told Cooper that he was free to name him. On October 28, 2005, a federal grand jury returned a five-count indictment of Libby: one count of obstruction of justice; two counts of false statements; and two counts of perjury.

The controversy over the nonexistent "weapons of mass destruction" was one more example of a recurrent American nightmare involving the CIA. Just as the *Chicago Tribune* had suggested back in 1947, many Americans worried that a centralized intelligence service could be misused and exploited for political purposes by the current occupants of the White House.

CONCLUSION

In 1947, as Congress considered its creation, many critics worried that the CIA might become a "Gestapo." By 2004, some Americans were convinced that it had become one. Over the years, investigations and exposés had revealed evidence of real CIA conspiracies. As a result, some Americans were inclined to believe the worst conspiracy theories about the allegedly all-powerful Agency. At the same time, other CIA critics charged that the Agency was dangerously weak. In this scenario, the Agency was incompetent at predicting events and subject to presidential manipulation.

Although a consensus had emerged on the need for a centralized intelligence agency that could analyze intelligence and conduct secret operations, many citizens remained concerned about the potential dangers of such an agency. Americans, moreover, seemed unable to make up their minds whether their foreign intelligence agency was a rogue elephant or a tool of the imperial president. They could agree that both options were equally frightening.

---------------------☆ **6** ☆---------------------

Biographies of Important CIA Administrators

Richard Immerman with Kathryn Olmsted, John Prados, and Athan Theoharis

Because so many significant and colorful individuals have contributed to the history of the Central Intelligence Agency (CIA), and because the history of the Agency has contributed so fundamentally to the history of modern America and indeed the world, the list of biographies to include in this volume is potentially endless. To make the list manageable, the authors established criteria, and opted for these criteria to be narrow.

For one, CIA officers brought to the Agency a variety of experiences and skills. Some were former Office of Strategic Services officers (the World War II intelligence service) who continued their espionage work after 1947 with the creation of the CIA. Others transferred from the military and brought skills in paramilitary operations. Others were recruited either because of their language skills, scientific training, or expertise about the history, culture, and politics of diverse foreign states or geographic regions. Others were independently wealthy and attracted to a career in governmental service.

The primary criterion, the one that forms the backbone of the list, however, was leadership of the CIA and its predecessors. Hence the biographies span the years from William Donovan of the Office of Strategic Services (OSS) to Sidney Souers of the Central Intelligence Group (CIG) to Porter Goss, the current director of the Central Intelligence Agency (CIA). Those in the CIA who held pivotal leadership roles below the level of director also met this criterion, but only if they left an indelible mark. Thus the list includes biographies of such CIA notables as James Jesus Angleton, Ray Cline, and Richard Bissell.

We limited the number of case officers, station chiefs, or contract agents to those who were involved in particularly pivotal or controversial events in the CIA's evolution. Examples of those who fit this criterion are Francis Gary Powers because of the U-2 incident, David Phillips because of his role in

TABLE 6.1

Director	Tenure
Sidney W. Souers	January 23, 1946–June 10, 1946
Hoyt S. Vandenberg*	June 10, 1946–May 1, 1947
Roscoe H. Hillenkoetter	May 1, 1947–October 7, 1950
Walter Bedell Smith	October 7, 1950–February 9, 1953
Allen W. Dulles	February 26, 1953–November 29, 1961
John A. McCone	November 29, 1961–April 28, 1965
William F. Raborn, Jr.	April 28, 1965–June 30, 1966
Richard M. Helms	June 30, 1966–February 2, 1973
James R. Schlesinger	February 2, 1973–July 2, 1973
William E. Colby	September 4, 1973–January 30, 1976
George H. W. Bush	January 30, 1976–January 20, 1977
Stansfield Turner	March 9, 1977–January 20, 1981
William J. Casey	January 28, 1981–January 29, 1987
William H. Webster	May 26, 1987–August 31, 1991
Robert M. Gates	November 6, 1991–January 20, 1993
R. James Woolsey	February 5, 1993–January 10, 1995
John M. Deutch	May 10, 1995–December 15, 1996
George J. Tenet	July 11, 1997–July 11, 2004
John E. McLaughlin (acting)	July 11, 2004–September 24, 2004
Porter J. Goss	September 24, 2004–Present

*Director of the Central Intelligence Group, the precursor to the Central Intelligence Agency (CIA) established in 1947.

founding the Association of Former Intelligence Officers, George Carver because of Vietnam, and Edward Lansdale for his role in MONGOOSE as well as Vietnam. Similarly, we include individuals who served as fundamental building blocks to constructing the CIA's structure. Lawrence Houston was responsible for much of the Agency's enabling legislations; Sherman Kent set the standards for the production of National Estimates; Walter Pforzheimer was the Agency's historian as well as legislative counsel. Kent and Pforzheimer also represent the disproportionate number of Yale graduates who were so instrumental during the CIA's early years.

A final criterion was the notoriety, typically unwelcome, identified with certain CIA personnel because they were complicit, directly or indirectly, in some well-known operation, or they published a book or article that provoked public controversy in ways that affected the Agency's reputation. Frequently an individual, such as E. Howard Hunt, did both; his involvement in the Bay of Pigs invasion and then the White House Plumbers and Watergate Affair raised questions about the CIA's role and relationship with the White House. Philip Agee serves as a different kind of example. There was little particularly special about Agee's career in the CIA. But after he left the Agency he was celebrated—or castigated—for exposing the Agency's "dirty tricks" in his writings. Indeed, because many believe that his publicizing the names of CIA agents led to the assassination of Richard Welch, the CIA's station chief in Athens, Greece, Agee is commonly linked with the enactment of the Intelligence Identities Protection Act of 1982. For that reason his biography is included. On the list also is Aldrich Ames; he represents those CIA agents who committed treason. In sum, except for the directors of the Central Intelligence Agency, the biographies in this volume are intended to be representative, not inclusive.

SAMUEL A. ADAMS

Born in Connecticut in 1934, Samuel Adams received his B.A. in European history and his law degree from Harvard University. In 1963, he joined the CIA as an intelligence analyst, soon winning commendations for his analyses of the Congo. Assigned to the Vietnam desk in 1965, Adams was directed to estimate the number of Vietcong guerrillas in South Vietnam. (CIA and military analysts had earlier estimated that there were approximately 270,000 communist guerrillas in that country.) Basing his assessment on documents captured from the enemy, Adams soon concluded that previous estimates had undercounted the communists by hundreds of thousands. The implications were astounding. As Adams later wrote, "If the Vietcong Army suddenly doubled in size, our whole statistical system would collapse. We'd be fighting a war twice as big as the one we thought we were fighting." If the enemy was so strong, then the war might be unwinnable.

Adams's superiors, however, first ignored, then challenged his conclusions. After reviewing the numbers, they decided to keep the original estimate. The so-called Tet Offensive of January 1968, when North Vietnamese and Vietcong troops attacked and for a time controlled major cities in the South— which Adams described as "the biggest surprise to American intelligence since Pearl Harbor"—required a reassessment of the original estimates. Agency officials accordingly revisited the numbers controversy, and ultimately accepted Adams's estimates. By then, however, Adams had grown more disaffected and disillusioned. Fearing that he was about to be fired and that the documents proving his case would be destroyed, he secretly removed the papers on the enemy estimates and buried them in a Virginia wood.

Adams first went public with his disagreements with the Agency in 1973, during testimony in the trial of Daniel Ellsberg and Anthony Russo. Ellsberg and Russo had been indicted for their role in leaking the so-called Pentagon Papers to the media in 1971. Adams resigned from the CIA soon after his testimony and two years later began to draw media attention to his allegations.

In "Vietnam Cover-Up: Playing War with Numbers," published in *Harper's* magazine in 1975, Adams detailed his war of numbers with the Agency and then publicly accused CIA officials of a "conspiracy against its own intelligence." That same year he also testified before the House Select Committee on Intelligence, chaired by Congressman Otis Pike. Adams spent the next five years researching a book on the controversy—research that convinced him that military officers had pressured the CIA to ignore his conclusions.

Adams's editor for the *Harper's* article, George Crile, later moved to CBS News. In 1980, Crile solicited Adams's assistance to put together a Vietnam documentary, "The Uncounted Enemy," which aired on January 22, 1982. The program alleged that General William Westmoreland, the supreme commander in Vietnam, had engaged in a conspiracy to force the CIA to change its estimates.

Westmoreland sued Adams and CBS for libel. As the jury began deliberations following an eighteen-week trial, Westmoreland settled out of court. The general received no money, but both he and CBS issued a public statement expressing their respect for each other.

Adams subsequently wrote his memoir on the affair, published posthumously as *War of Numbers* in 1994. In 1988, he died in his Vermont home of an apparent heart attack.

PHILIP AGEE

Born in 1935 into a wealthy, privileged family, Philip Agee grew up in a conservative environment and received a Catholic education (graduating from Notre Dame University and serving as an altar boy as a youth). He joined the CIA during the 1950s after graduating from college, enlisting in what he then considered a global crusade against communism. As a CIA officer during the years 1960 to 1966, while stationed in South America he recruited agents, bugged phones, penetrated communist embassies, and performed many other sensitive assignments.

By the mid-1960s, however, Agee began to grow disillusioned with the Agency, having concluded that the CIA's mission was to protect greedy, corrupt South American elites. He nonetheless continued working for the CIA, serving in 1967 and 1968 as a special consultant for the Olympic Games held in 1968 in Mexico City. But his political radicalization prompted him to make a final break after the Games were over. At first, he started a small manufacturing business in Mexico. By 1970, he had decided to expose the CIA. Over the next four years, living in Cuba and in Paris, France, Agee researched and then published a book criticizing CIA operations in Latin America. Convinced that CIA agents were shadowing him as he wrote the book, he even believed that Agency operatives planted a bug in his typewriter.

Published in 1975, Agee's book, *Inside the Company: A CIA Diary*, became an instant sensation. In it, he detailed Agency operations in Latin America during the 1960s and his own ideological journey, ending his book with an appendix naming every CIA agent or asset he could remember. The only way to stop the CIA from oppressing poor Latin Americans, he argued, was to expose the people who worked for it. Agee also served as an adviser to a new magazine, *Counterspy*, that published articles critical of CIA operations and also the names of CIA agents around the world. "The most effective and important systematic efforts to counter the CIA that can be undertaken right now," Agee wrote, "are . . . the identification, exposure and neutralization of its people working abroad."

A few opponents of the CIA agreed with Agee. Most, however, were appalled by his brazen decision to endanger the lives of those with whom he had worked. Such CIA critics as Senator Frank Church, who in 1975 chaired a special Senate committee's massive investigation of Agency abuses, condemned Agee for putting the lives of agents at risk. Senator Church, and others, maintained that Agee's tactics would only serve to discredit those who wanted to reform the CIA.

Church's fears were realized. On December 23, 1975, terrorists in Athens, Greece shot and killed the CIA station chief there, Richard Welch. *Counterspy* had named Welch in its winter 1975 issue, although it had incorrectly identified him as an agent in Peru.

Welch had not been named by either the Church Committee or the House Committee chaired by Otis Pike, neither of which ever disclosed the name of any undercover agent. But defenders of the Agency in Congress and the White House exploited his assassination to discredit congressional investigators and their proposed reforms, with President Ford calling for an end to this "self-flagellation." Buckling to these criticisms, the House in January 1976 voted not to release the reports of the Pike Committee. Welch's body was flown home to a somber, heroic welcoming ceremony at Andrews Air Force base and burial at Arlington National Cemetery, a privilege normally reserved for those who had served in the military. CIA Counsel Mitchell Rogovin later conceded that the Agency saw the advantage in lauding Welch and had waved his assassination "around like a bloody shirt."

Agee, however, remained unapologetic. The identification of Welch, he maintained, was not an invitation to kill him but rather "an invitation to return to Langley." He continued to insist that naming CIA agents and operatives was the only way to stop the Agency from oppressing poor people around the world.

In 1978, Agee helped found the magazine *Covert Action Information Bulletin*. It aimed to reveal CIA operations and agents around the world. He also published a book called *Dirty Work: The CIA in Western Europe*, which exposed American operatives in Europe. CIA officials claimed that Agee's books and articles had compromised many agents and operations. At the U.S. government's request, five successive NATO countries expelled Agee, and his U.S. passport was revoked. In addition, in 1982 Congress enacted the Intelligence Identities Protection Act, which made it a crime to reveal the identity of U.S. undercover agents.

Agee continued to write and speak out against the CIA from his home in Cuba. In 1987, he published his autobiography *On the Run*. In the 1990s, the *Los Angeles Times* published the allegations of a Cuban defector that Agee had received money from Cuban intelligence and the KGB. The charge implied that Agee had been working as a paid agent of the communists almost from the beginning. Agee denied this charge, attributing it to a CIA disinformation campaign.

By then an admirer of the Cuban Revolution, Agee started a travel agency in Cuba in 2000 and urged American citizens to visit Cuba in defiance of the U.S. government's travel ban.

ALDRICH AMES

Born in 1941, Aldrich "Rick" Ames spent the first years of his life in rural Wisconsin before attending and graduating from the University of Chicago. When he was ten years old, his father, Carleton, went to work for the CIA as a clandestine officer in Burma. Rick Ames first began working at the Agency in the summers as a teenager. During college he worked as a CIA clerk. After graduation, he became a covert operative.

Ames made a poor spy from the start. At his first post in Ankara, Turkey, he earned poor evaluations from his superiors. Reassigned to CIA headquarters in Virginia, his personnel file was filled with reports criticizing his repeated drunkenness, sloppiness, and breaches of security. He next served at the CIA office in New York from 1976 to 1981 with his principal assignment to recruit communist agents who worked at the United Nations. Although earning generally favorable work evaluations there, his supervisors nonetheless continued to cite problems with his procrastination and inattention to detail.

Posted to Mexico City in 1981, Ames's drinking worsened and his marriage fell apart. Against Agency policy, he became romantically involved with one of his intelligence recruits, Rosario Casas Dupuy, Colombia's cultural attaché to Mexico. He eventually married her and, in 1983, despite his poor record, was put in charge of Soviet counterintelligence in Mexico. His job, at least as he characterized it, involved long drinking sessions with his opposite number in the KGB. During these afternoons in Mexico City bars, Ames befriended the KGB officer and became more disaffected from the Agency.

Ames subsequently decided to become a spy for the Soviet Union. His ultimate motive, however, was monetary. His new wife, Rosario, was reportedly disappointed in his meager CIA salary. "I felt embarrassed and potentially humiliated to be in a situation in which I had sort of lost control of the household budget, and getting from one paycheck to the next was getting increasingly difficult," Ames later admitted. Transferred to CIA headquarters in Langley, Virginia, in 1983, Ames, despite his checkered record, was put in charge of Soviet counterintelligence, where he learned the names of the CIA's agents inside the Soviet Union. Realizing the value of this information to the Soviets, he decided to sell CIA secrets to the KGB.

In April 1985, Ames boldly walked into the Soviet embassy in Washington and handed a note addressed to the chief KGB officer in the embassy. In it, he identified the few Russians who were secretly working for the CIA. He later claimed that he was fairly sure—although not completely certain—that the men were actually double agents working for the KGB, and therefore he was not giving the Soviets anything that they did not already have. "I suspected," he later said, "that their cooperation was not genuine, that their true loyalty was to the KGB, and therefore, I could cause them no harm." For this information, he asked for, and received, $50,000. The Soviets instantly realized Ames's potential: he was an American Kim Philby.

One month later, Ames gave the Soviets an intelligence bonanza: the names of more than ten agents who were working for either the CIA or the FBI in Russia. Some had been working for the United States secretly for decades. A congressional investigation later described this as a "crippling blow to the CIA's Soviet operations." Learning the names of these sources, the Soviets arrested and executed several of them. In all, Ames is blamed for the deaths of more than ten agents and the exposure of more than 100. Ames later said that he did not fully understand why he had given these names to the KGB. But he realized that he had already "crossed a line I could never step back." The grateful Soviets ultimately paid him more than $2 million, and deposited $2 million more in foreign bank accounts.

Over the next nine years, Ames conveyed secret information to the Soviets in return for large monetary payments. His lifestyle suddenly improved: he paid cash for a luxurious house; he bought a Jaguar that cost him more than his yearly salary. All this time, some of the CIA's best agents in the Soviet Union were disappearing. An internal CIA investigation was launched to uncover this security breach. For years, however, Agency officials refused to believe that one of their own could be capable of treachery.

Ames's spying continued for nine years. During this time, he served in the Rome station from 1986 to 1989, where he supervised CIA surveillance of Soviet operations, among other duties. He regularly removed bags full of top-secret documents from his office and passed them on to the Soviets. He also researched and responded to specific KGB questions about CIA sources in the Eastern bloc.

Ames returned to Langley in 1989, and despite his notorious alcohol abuse, sloppiness, and poor performance and evaluations, he was assigned to a variety of jobs related to Soviet counterintelligence over the next two years until 1991, when he was assigned to the Agency's Counternarcotics Center.

The CIA's rather lackluster investigation of the disappearance of its Soviet agents had continued for years. At first, CIA and FBI officials believed that their sources might have been compromised by CIA defector Edward Lee Howard. Then, when a former Marine guard at the U.S. embassy in Moscow,

Clayton Lonetree, confessed in 1986 to having spied for the KGB, the investigators blamed him for the blown cases. A KGB disinformation campaign did all that it could to encourage these misperceptions.

By 1991, however, CIA investigators finally focused on Ames and launched an inquiry into his background and finances. But when he passed a routine polygraph test, the investigators lowered their guard and placed the Ames investigation on hold. Gradually, though, a joint CIA-FBI investigative team zeroed in on Ames, and by October 1992 he had become their prime suspect. The FBI assumed control over the case in 1993 and extensively monitored Ames and his wife.

Ames was arrested by FBI agents on February 21, 1994, apprehending the most damaging turncoat in the CIA's history. Congress subsequently launched an investigation of the Ames case. After chronicling the "numerous and egregious failures" of the Agency's handling of the case, the congressional investigators concluded: "The system which permitted Ames' prolonged betrayal must be changed. The country cannot afford such calamities in the future."

In return for his cooperation in describing what information he had given to the Soviets, Ames escaped execution, and his wife received only a five-year prison sentence for helping him. Ames was sentenced to life in prison without possibility of parole.

JAMES JESUS ANGLETON

A controversial figure in the history of the CIA, James Jesus Angleton was born in Boise, Idaho, in December 1917, of his father's whirlwind courtship of a Mexican girl in Nogales, Arizona, where James Hugh Angleton had been with General John J. Pershing, chasing the Mexican rebel Pancho Villa. "Hugh" Angleton became a crack salesman for the National Cash Register Company and eventually its European representative. James Jesus, the eldest of four children (two boys, two girls) grew up in Arizona, close to the Mexican side of the family, and in Rome. His middle name was in honor of the maternal grandfather. Angleton himself did not like to use it.

Angleton showed an early literary bent, becoming fascinated by Italian literature, especially Dante. After a brief run at a British school, Malvern College, Angleton entered Yale, from which he graduated in 1941. He began writing poetry (few samples of which can be found) and joined with a roommate to found a literary journal, *Furioso*. The magazine published their own work along with poems by such luminaries as e.e. cummings, Ezra Pound, and William Carlos Williams. Angleton became personal friends with cummings. Angleton married Cicely d'Autremont, a Vassar student. Theirs would be a difficult marriage. He went on to Harvard for graduate work in law and business. Norman H. Pearson, a former Yale professor and chief of the OSS Counterintelligence Branch (X-2) in London, talent-spotted Angleton, who by the summer of 1943 had joined the agency, soon to be assigned to X-2 in London.

Angleton took naturally to the work of counterintelligence. OSS chief William Donovan once called him the wartime Agency's most professional counterintelligence officer. Angleton's background and language abilities led to his assignment to Italy late in 1944, where he systematized the work, including compiling a manual on the enemy intelligence organization and networks. Angleton rose to major in the OSS and head of X-2 operations in Italy. He stayed on in Milan after the end of World War II with the SSU, CIG, and the CIA, recruiting certain agents he ran personally. When the CIA intervened in the 1948 Italian elections with a political action campaign, Angleton was a primary actor in this operation. In the course of his Italian tours Angleton reportedly brought in many Soviet documents, including code materials. He was then assigned to CIA headquarters as a staff assistant for collection to the head of the Agency's Office of Special Operations.

During this period the Washington representative of the British Secret Intelligence Service was Harold "Kim" Philby, Angleton's friend from London OSS days. They developed a custom of frequent lunches together. Angleton never recognized Philby for the Russian spy he turned out to be, a major failure by any index of counterspy performance. However, the Philby story played out for more than a decade, not to be fully established until 1962, when Philby defected to the U.S.S.R. During that time Angleton, reassigned to Staff C, the CIA counterintelligence unit, worked to transform it into the Counterintelligence Staff, which he headed from 1954 on, gradually solidifying his leadership, becoming unassailable in CIA counterintelligence. He survived attempts to reorganize CIA counterintelligence in 1958 and 1967. When the Philby failure became public it did not prove too damaging.

Privately this experience convinced Angleton that he could never again permit himself to be fooled. As the head of the Counterintelligence Staff, Angleton came to wield considerable power within the CIA. He once wiretapped a party given by a Treasury Department official simply to amuse DCI Allen Dulles with the gossip. Angleton became arbiter on all agency espionage activities, vetting them to prevent infiltration by Soviet spies. In the cause of counterintelligence his staff conducted a mail-opening operation, code-named HTLINGUAL, that tampered with U.S. mails for two decades. He also established himself as the primary conduit between the CIA and Israeli intelligence. Angleton exercised a political role as well. When Mary Meyer, a friend and wife of a CIA colleague, was murdered in 1964, Angleton seized her diaries for alleged security reasons, though their political sensitivity lay in what they might say about John F. Kennedy, to whom she had been mistress. In 1967, when the CIA came under fire for revelations in *Ramparts* magazine of its role in funding the National Student Association through private foundations, Angleton conducted the counterinvestigation of the journalists. And from the Johnson to the Nixon administrations, Angleton's staff ran Operation CHAOS, monitoring and preparing dossiers on opponents of the Vietnam War.

Angleton's activities directly impacted on the CIA when data from Polish and Soviet defectors in the early 1960s dovetailed with his own suspicions about the possibility that a Russian spy, or "mole," had infiltrated the agency. His suspicions not only led to the hostile interrogation of a further defector bearing different information, but resulted in the virtual gutting of the CIA's Soviet Bloc Division, many of whose senior officers one by one came under attack as the alleged mole. By the end of the decade Soviet operations had ground to a halt, half a dozen careers lay in ruins, and Angleton had found no mole. Similar suspicions led Angleton to intervene in specific cases with the security services of France, Norway, Great Britain, and Canada with disastrous results. At one point suspicions rose so high that another CIA officer compiled the same sort of bill of particulars to portray Angleton himself as the Soviet mole. The evident effects of these activities eventually divided the CIA itself between a "fundamentalist" faction that believed in Angleton's mole thesis and the rest who did not. The controversy provoked internal reviews and even an investigation by the CIA Inspector General. The Angleton debacle also affected later CIA counterintelligence failures since Agency officials subsequently bent over backwards to avoid a repetition of this disaster.

A further example of Angleton's conspiratorial worldview, fueled by one of his defectors, involved his belief in a Russian master plan to deceive the West on all fronts and that, consequently, the Sino-Soviet split was a deliberate illusion. This particular Angleton theory did not convince all CIA analysts, but did impede a proper appreciation of world developments by the agency and extended the time necessary for the CIA to reach appropriate conclusions regarding the nature of Soviet versus Chinese communism and the end of Moscow's monolithic control.

When William Colby became DCI he refused to believe Angleton's conspiracy theories. Colby cut back the size and power of the Counterintelligence Staff as a first step. When he learned of Angleton's links to Israeli intelligence and channels for communication independent of official Agency lines, he asked for the counterspy's resignation. The counterspy rejected Colby's offer of a consulting contract to write papers for the Agency. The Angleton firing became yet another issue aired in the "Year of Intelligence," 1975. At the time the public made much of Angleton's passion for raising orchids and hobby of fly-fishing.

Israel has erected two monuments to honor James Angleton and the CIA awarded Angleton its Distinguished Intelligence Medal. A favorite of Allen Dulles, Angleton helped write the eulogy at his funeral, at which he was a pallbearer. In retirement, Angleton helped collect money for Richard Helms's 1978 legal defense fund and focused on his hobbies. In his last public interview, in April 1987, he claimed that five leads to Soviet moles had been left hanging when he was forced out of the CIA. Angleton died of lung cancer a month later.

C. TRACY BARNES

Born in 1911, C. Tracy Barnes attended Yale University and Harvard Law School. His career in intelligence began during World War II, when he served in the U.S. Army Air Forces. He also worked for the Special Operations Branch of the Office of Strategic Services (OSS), participating in several parachute operations behind enemy lines in France, and assisting Allen Dulles in Bern, Switzerland. After pursuing a law career in the same firm as Frank Wisner, he relocated to Washington, D.C., in 1950, serving as both counsel to the undersecretary of the army and deputy director of the Psychological Strategy Board (PSB).

In 1952 Barnes joined the CIA and immediately became head of its recently established psychological and paramilitary staff within the Directorate of Operations, headed by Allen Dulles. In this capacity he contributed to the planning and implementation of PBSUCCESS, the covert operation that overthrew the Arbenz government of Guatemala in 1954. He held a variety of positions during the subsequent decade: chief of the CIA base in Frankfurt, Germany from 1954 to 1956; London station chief from 1957 to 1959; and assistant to the Deputy Director for Plans from 1960 to 1961.

Working closely with Richard Bissell, Barnes played a key role in planning the Bay of Pigs covert operation to overthrow the Castro government in Cuba in April 1961. As was the case with many agency luminaries at the time, his career suffered from the operation's failure. Barnes did nevertheless become head of the Domestic Operations Division before retiring from the Agency in 1968. He died on February 19, 1972.

MILTON A. BEARDEN

A swashbuckling field operator, Milton A. Bearden rose to become one of the DO's "barons" during the heady last days of the Cold War. Spanning three continents, Bearden's career encapsulated the high points of the post-Vietnam CIA experience. He is best known as chief of station in Islamabad, Pakistan, during the final three years of the Soviet intervention in Afghanistan, when Bearden served as commander of the CIA secret war with the Afghan *muja-hedeen.*

After Bearden's birth in Oklahoma in 1938, his father moved the family to Washington state (where he worked at Hanford for the Manhattan Project) and afterward to Texas. After college the young Bearden spent four years in the Air Force before joining the CIA in 1964. Bearden's CIA assignments mirrored his languages—German and Chinese—and he went first to Bonn as a case officer in West Germany in 1965, and then to Hong Kong in 1968.

Focused on data to help win in Vietnam while at the CIA's China listening post, Bearden was next posted to Geneva, where he watched the International Red Cross and other negotiations run in tandem with the Paris Peace Talks aimed at ending the Vietnam conflict. He returned to the United States in 1975, spent a year at Langley, then served another tour in Hong Kong before being posted to Dallas, Texas, as chief of a CIA domestic contact office there.

DDO Clair George reassigned Bearden from Texas to Lagos, Nigeria, and then to the Sudan, where Bearden served as chief of station at Khartoum from 1983 to 1985. While at Khartoum Bearden met DCI William J. Casey during one of his world tours. Casey brought Bearden back to Langley. The CIA officer turned down an offer to lead Casey's Nicaragua operation, and instead became deputy chief of the Soviet/East European Division. In that capacity he participated in the interrogation of Vitali Yurchenko, and supervised agency officer Aldrich Ames. After another officer, CIA trainee Edward L. Howard, himself defected to Moscow, Bearden put both himself and Ames on a list of potential suspects who had known something about Soviet operations that had been broken by Russian security services and were therefore under counterintelligence investigation. In the meanwhile, Bearden, because of differences with his division chief, in the summer of 1986 sought a field assignment as chief of station in Islamabad, Pakistan.

For three years in Islamabad, Bearden presided over the denouement of the secret war in Afghanistan. He adjudicated disputes among the Afghan *mujahedeen* over the allocation of U.S. weapons and money, managed the introduction of "Stinger" antiaircraft missiles into the war, and handled CIA relations with the Pakistani government, the primary actors in the secret war. Bearden violated CIA standing orders at one point to enter Afghanistan and have his picture taken in-country. When the Russians evacuated in 1989 he returned to Afghanistan and had his picture taken standing on the same bridge over which Soviet tanks and trucks had rolled to leave that nation.

Bearden returned to Langley in the summer of 1989 as chief of the Soviet/East European Division at a key moment in history. He was in Berlin when East Berliners pulled down the Berlin Wall, and in Washington when the abortive coup against Gorbachev spelled the end of the USSR. Later Bearden went back to Bonn, capping his thirty-year CIA career as chief of one of the agency's most important stations.

Bearden continued to worry about Soviet agents at work inside the CIA, recounting in his memoirs numerous instances where he had worked at this issue. The matter of the "Soviet mole" became probably the most controversial of Bearden's career due to charges that he had warned Ames of CIA surveillance against him. Bearden's memoir is completely silent on this matter. Reprimanded by DCI R. James Woolsey in September 1994 for his role in the Ames case, the very next day Bearden was presented the Distinguished Intelligence Medal for his role in the Afghan covert operation.

Following his retirement in January 1995, Bearden registered as a lobbyist for Sudanese business interests.

RICHARD MERVIN BISSELL, JR.

Born on September 18, 1909, Richard Mervin Bissell, Jr., received his Ph.D. in economics from Yale in 1932, after which he taught at the university until 1941. He spent the war years in Washington as the chief economic analyst for the Department of Commerce and then as an executive in the War Shipping Administration. In 1948 he became a member of the Economic Cooperation Administration (ECA), the organization that oversaw the implementation of the European Recovery Plan (the Marshall Plan). In 1950 he encouraged the ECA to use its programs to strengthen anti-Soviet defenses. Bissell became acting administrator of the ECA in 1951 and sought to align ECA programs more closely with the Truman administration's Cold War military policies. He oversaw the ECA's inclusion into the Mutual Security Administration.

After a short stint with the Ford Foundation, Bissell, who was a close acquaintance of many within the leadership of the still-fledgling CIA, joined the Agency. He immediately became DCI Allen W. Dulles's special assistant for planning and coordination, contributing to the covert operation that succeeded in overthrowing the Arbenz government in Guatemala. By the end of 1954 Dulles had placed Bissell in charge of the project to develop the Agency's U-2 spy plane project. Known for his impressive mind and energy, Bissell's reputation soared with the U-2's success and in 1958 he became the head of CORONA, the Agency's satellite surveillance program. The next year Dulles appointed him Deputy Director for Plans. He took command of the CIA's covert operations, which soon meant responsibility for the organization, planning, and implementation of the Bay of Pigs invasion of April 1961. Until the failure of this covert operation, Bissell was believed to be the presumptive successor to Dulles as DCI. But Bissell was closely identified with the fiasco, and as a result it became only a question of time before he left the Agency; he resigned in 1962. He then worked as a consultant for several Cold War defense projects and companies and was president of the Institute for Defense Analysis from 1962 to 1964. Although he eventually became an executive with United Aircraft Corporation, Bissell continued to consult on defense projects for the remainder of his life. He died on February 7, 1994.

J. COFER BLACK

Born in 1950 in Stamford, Connecticut, J. Cofer Black received B.A. (in 1973) and M.A. (in 1974) degrees in international relations from the University of Southern California. Following graduation in 1974, he accepted an appointment with the CIA and over the next twenty-eight years served in the field in six foreign tours, and then held administrative positions at CIA headquarters until resigning in 2002 to become Coordinator for Counter-terrorism in the Department of State with the rank of Ambassador at Large.

Black's leadership abilities as a field officer, including serving as station chief in Khartoum, Sudan, led to his promotion first to Task Force Chief in the Near East and South Asia Division in 1995 and then to Deputy Chief of the Latin America Division in June 1998. In June 1999 Black left this latter post to become Director of the Counterterrorist Center, heading the Center until December 2002 when he became State Department Counterterror-ism Coordinator. As State Department Coordinator, Black coordinated U.S. counterterrorism efforts with foreign countries (thus the ambassadorial rank) and planned the Department's Antiterrorism Training Program.

Black's tenure as Director of the CIA's Counterterrorist Center came at a critical time and provoked controversy, the latter triggered by inquiries launched by the House and Senate Intelligence Committees in 2002–2003 and then by the Kean Commission in 2003–2004 into the role of the U.S. intelligence agencies prior to the September 11, 2001, terrorist attack. Black had become director at a time of heightened concern about Osama bin La-den's and al Qaeda's roles in the terrorist attacks on U.S. embassies in Kenya and Tanzania in 1998 and then the U.S.S. *Cole* in 2000. In response, CIA officers had sought to contain or apprehend bin Laden and dismantle the al Qaeda terrorist network by attempting to recruit Afghan tribal leaders and fund the Northern Alliance's efforts to overthrow the Taliban government in Afghanistan (given bin Laden's and al Qaeda's use of Afghanistan as a base to train terrorists and launch terrorist operations). Under Black, these efforts intensified, although Agency officials were unable to develop a successful plan or to recruit sources to infiltrate bin Laden's al Qaeda network. The Coun-terterrorist Center, more importantly, failed to coordinate the counter-terrorism activities of the U.S. intelligence agencies. CIA officers had learned in January and then March 2000 that Khalid al Mihdhar and Nawaf al Hazmi (Saudi nationals who had volunteered in 1999 to participate in the planned al Qaeda "planes" operation and on September 11, 2001, were members of the team that flew American Airlines flight 77 into the Pentagon) had attended a terrorist planning meeting in Kuala Lumpur, Malaysia, and that both had obtained U.S. visas and in 2000 had either flown to Los Angeles or intended to enter New York. This discovery was not relayed either to the State De-partment or to the FBI, resulting in the State Department's failure to list al Mihdhar and al Hazmi on its TIPOFF watch list (to deny entry to the United States) and the FBI's failure to locate and apprehend these two men who in 2000–2001 were residing in San Diego, California. This failure enabled al Mihdhar to reenter the United States in July 2001 (having left the United States in June 2000) and did not alert FBI counterterrorism agents of the need to locate the two men or press one of the Bureau's counterterrorism in-formants in San Diego for information about their activities. In their final reports, the House and Senate Intelligence Committees and the Kean Commission cited this failure of coordination, the failure to assess the significance of the August 2001 arrest of Zacarias Moussaoui, and the possible use of airplanes as weapons to justify their recommendations to reorganize the U.S. intelligence community by creating a Director of National Intelligence and a National Counterterrorism Center, both to be headquartered in the Executive Office of the President. These recommendations were implemented in legislation enacted by Congress, and signed into law by President George W. Bush on December 17, 2004, the Intelligence Reform and Terrorism Prevention Act.

WILLIAM FRANCIS BUCKLEY

Born on May 30, 1928, in Medford, Massachusetts, William Buckley joined the U.S. Army following graduation from high school in 1947. After serving as a company commander during the Korean war, Buckley enrolled at Boston University, where he earned a B.A. in political science. Resuming his military career, he served in the special forces in Vietnam and as an advisor to the South Vietnamese Army during the 1960s and in 1969 was promoted to lieutenant colonel.

Buckley worked for the CIA in two stints: from 1955 to 1957, and again from 1965 until his death in June 1985. During his service as CIA station chief in Beirut, Lebanon, he was taken hostage in 1984 by members of the militant Islamic group Hezbollah. Held prisoner for fifteen months, he ultimately died under torture.

Buckley was one of seven American hostages at the heart of what became the arms-for-hostages scandal of the mid-1980s, known as the Iran-Contra affair. President Reagan and his senior aides in 1985–1986 entered into negotiations with individuals associated with the Iranian government, a government which was the prime supporter of Hezbollah. At first this initiative was only supposed to involve one transaction: in return for the sale of missiles the Iranians would arrange to have all seven hostages released. After the initial shipment of arms was delivered, however, the Iranians contended that they could only get one hostage released. National Security Adviser Robert McFarlane requested Buckley. At that point, the Iranians informed him that Buckley was "too ill" to be moved. In fact, he had died three months earlier. The arms trades continued, and their profits (the surplus over the amount paid by the Iranians) were eventually diverted to the so-called contras in Nicaragua. When publicly exposed in November 1986, the secret arms-for-hostages deal and the secret funding of the Nicaraguan contras became known as the Iran-Contra scandal.

Buckley's body was eventually recovered and in 1991 was returned to the United States for official burial in Arlington National Cemetery.

GEORGE H. W. BUSH

Born on June 12, 1924, George Herbert Walker Bush enlisted in the armed services on his eighteenth birthday in 1942, serving as a Navy pilot in the Pacific during World War II, where he was awarded the Distinguished Flying Cross for bravery in action. As did many other World War II veterans, Bush enrolled as an older (and married) student at Yale College earning a B.A. degree in 1948 and distinguished himself in the classroom (Phi Beta Kappa) and on the athletic field (captaining the baseball team). After graduating from Yale, Bush embarked on a career in the Texas oil industry. A successful businessman, he entered Republican politics, winning election in 1966 and then reelection in 1968 to Congress from a conservative district in Houston, although failing in 1964 and 1970 attempts to win election to the U.S. Senate. President Nixon, however, rewarded Bush for his political loyalty first by appointing him U.S. Ambassador to the United Nations in December 1970, then Chairman of the Republican National Committee in 1973, and then Chief of the U.S. Liaison office in the People's Republic of China in 1974. In January 1976, Bush won Senate confirmation as Director of Central Intelligence, serving in this post until resigning following Jimmy Carter's election to the presidency in November 1976. An unsuccessful candidate for the Republican presidential nomination in 1980, Bush accepted the vice presidential nomination and served as Ronald Reagan's vice president until 1988. In 1988, he was elected president but was defeated in his bid for re-election by Bill Clinton in 1992.

Bush's tenure as DCI came during a tumultuous period in U.S. politics and for the CIA. In the aftermath of the Watergate break-in scandal, members of Congress abandoned an earlier deference to the presidency and the intelligence community, establishing in 1975 special committees (the Pike and Church Committees) to investigate for the first time the U.S. intelligence agencies, including the CIA. Obtaining access to formerly secret CIA records, the two committees in public hearings and published reports exposed the CIA's past abuses of power and questionable operations, including assassination planning. These revelations triggered demands for greater openness, enhanced congressional oversight, and the enactment of legislative charters, which both created morale problems within the Agency and concerns within the Ford Administration over their effect on presidential powers. Capitalizing on the December 1975 assassination of Richard Welch, the CIA station chief in Athens, Greece, whose cover had been publicly compromised, administration officials and congressional leaders succeeded in limiting this challenge and reasserting presidential authority. In addition, in November 1975, Ford had dismissed James Schlesinger as Defense Secretary and advised DCI Colby of his intention to replace him as part of a reorganization of the national security structure, nominating Bush as Colby's successor. Senator Church led opposition to Bush's nomination, claiming it was political, but was unsuccessful in defeating Senate confirmation. Nonetheless, the administration and the new DCI had to operate within tighter constraints as both the House and Senate in 1976 established permanent oversight committees and in succeeding years (1977–1980) held extensive hearings on proposed legislative charters.

Conversely, the Agency was buffeted from the right over its analysis of Soviet defense spending and strategic plans. The President's Foreign Intelligence Advisory Board, for example, endorsed a "competitive analysis" system to evaluate whether CIA analysts had underestimated Soviet defense spending. Bowing to these pressures, in June 1976 Bush appointed an independent panel of outside experts, led by Harvard professor Richard Pipes, to evaluate Soviet strategic forces and objectives. The report of this so-called Team B was completed on December 2, 1976. By then Ford had been defeated and President-elect Jimmy Carter did not feel bound by this conservative analysis. The creation of Team B, however, was a further blow to Agency morale. Following Carter's election, Bush sought to continue as DCI but the president-elect informed him of his intention to select his own DCI. Bush resigned.

Bush was subsequently honored for his service as DCI less because of his relative importance than for political reasons. In 1999, Congress enacted legislation naming CIA headquarters in Langley, Virginia, the George Bush Center for Intelligence. At the ceremony dedicating the renamed building, the head of the Directorate of Operations announced the establishment of a special George Bush Chair for Leadership to be awarded to one of the Directorate's best senior officers.

GEORGE A. CARVER

A key CIA officer during the Vietnam war, George Carver was an actor in almost every key episode of the Vietnam conflict from 1960 through 1975, and his influence at the CIA helped establish institutions that remain today. One colleague said of the short, slight officer, "Carver can do more, with less evidence, than any other man I've known." Carver himself admitted, when testifying at a trial in the 1980s, that in certain of his cables from Vietnam he had exercised "a degree of poetic license."

Though born in Louisville, Kentucky, in 1928, Carver grew up in China, where his parents were missionaries and his father eventually headed the English department at the University of Shanghai. Though too young for World War II service, Carver nevertheless lived the war—as a child in the International Settlement of Shanghai and then at the Shanghai American School. After the war Carver attended Yale College, where he graduated in 1950. He went on to Oxford and earned a doctorate with a thesis on Thomas

Hobbes. Carver was a champion debater at Yale and a member of Phi Beta Kappa; at both schools he crewed, his team won a championship for Oxford at a meet with Cambridge.

Carver joined the CIA in 1953 and served in the Directorate of Plans as a case officer in the Far East Division. He married Ruth Hughes in 1957 and with her had four sons and one daughter. Carver went to Saigon with cover as an economist with the Agency for International Development. He became friends with William E. Colby, successively deputy, then station chief in Saigon, who used Carver as chief liaison with the coup plotters in 1960, a fact discovered by Saigon's intelligence. The Ngo Dinh Diem government threatened to arrest Carver and induced the CIA to evacuate George Carver from the country. His cover blown in the Saigon press, Carver transitioned from operations work to intelligence analysis, where he was especially influential.

In 1963, during the summer of maneuvering that preceded the coup against Diem, Carver authored a CIA paper that maintained that the overthrow of Diem would be the best hope for maintaining U.S. interests in Vietnam. He also wrote the draft of NIE 53-63, which held that Diem was in trouble, leading DCI John McCone to interfere with analytic conclusions (he did not believe Carver's conclusions) with deleterious consequences for the United States.

When Admiral Raborn became DCI in 1965–1966 he determined to appoint a special officer to handle Vietnam matters, including all analytical and many operational matters. George Carver very shortly became the second person appointed Special Assistant for Vietnam Affairs (SAVA), a position he held through the end of the Vietnam war. As SAVA Carver supported the creation of the Phoenix program, had an important role in the elaboration of criteria for pacification progress, and provided the Nixon administration reassuring intelligence to back its invasions of Cambodia and Laos and its mining of Haiphong harbor. In one important exception, in March 1968 Carver had briefed President Johnson's "Wise Men" on adverse trends in Vietnam, which led them to recommend the end of escalation and search for opening peace talks with the North Vietnamese. On this occasion, the deputy SAVA strongly encouraged Carver not to sugar-coat the message he was taking to the advisory group.

Carver's best known capitulation involved the "Order of Battle Dispute" of the mid-1960s, when the CIA came into conflict with the U.S. military command in Vietnam over the size of the North Vietnamese and Viet Cong forces they faced in the field. Carver led CIA delegations at conferences in Washington, and again in Saigon, at which he effectively undercut the CIA position and let the military estimate prevail. Only a few months later, in the Tet Offensive of January 1968, the adversary attacked with huge forces and sustained losses that should have knocked them out of the fight, except that their force level really was closer to the abandoned CIA estimate than the one

Carver had accepted. This episode became the focus of a controversial CBS television documentary which led to the 1982 lawsuit *Westmoreland v. CBS*. Carver testified at the trial.

In 1973, when William Colby became DCI, he reorganized the system for the creation of national intelligence estimates and vested this power in a group of National Intelligence Officers, each of whom held the same sway on some issue area as SAVA had had on Vietnam. Colby made Carver the informal chairman of this group, which evolved into the National Intelligence Council that still exists today. This group either failed or succeeded (by Carver's account) to anticipate the Yom Kippur war in the Middle East that year.

DCI George Bush sent Carver to West Germany in the summer of 1976 as his representative in the federal republic. In that capacity Carver monitored the CIA station as well as intelligence liaison with the Germans. He held the job for three years until he retired in 1979. In 1980–1981 he served on the intelligence panel of President-elect Ronald Reagan's transition team. Carver went into private consulting and became a fellow with the Center for Strategic and International Studies in Washington. He died in 1994 after suffering a heart attack while driving home from the airport.

WILLIAM JOSEPH CASEY

Born on March 13, 1913, William Joseph Casey attended Fordham University and St. John's University Law School in New York City prior to serving in the U.S. Navy during World War II. He soon joined the Office of Strategic Services (OSS) and established the OSS headquarters secretariat, which functioned as the OSS Director's personal staff. In this capacity, Casey was assigned the task of organizing its London base. He served as chief of the Secret Intelligence Branch in the European Theater during the final two years of the war and oversaw 102 intelligence missions in Germany. Casey resigned his commission on V-J Day and went to work for the Research Institute of America until 1950. He also served on the Economic Cooperation Administration (ECA) in Paris during 1948 and taught, practiced, and published books on business and tax law until the early 1960s, during which time he amassed considerable wealth.

In 1966 Casey was an unsuccessful candidate for election to the House of Representatives as a Republican. His active participation in Richard Nixon's successful 1968 presidential campaign, however, led to his appointment as Chairman of the Securities and Exchange Commission in 1971. He became the State Department's Undersecretary for Economic Affairs in 1973, and in 1974 Gerald Ford named him president and chairman of the Export-Import Bank. In 1976 Ford appointed Casey to the President's Foreign Intelligence Advisory Board. He then served as Ronald Reagan's campaign manager in 1980. Following his election to the presidency, Reagan in 1981 named Casey Director of Central Intelligence.

Under Casey's directorship, the CIA actively pursued numerous covert operations. These included massive assistance to the *mujahedeen* resistance in Afghanistan and to the so-called contras in Nicaragua, and, to a lesser extent, the Polish Solidarity movement. Casey personally became a lightning rod for the many critics of President Reagan's aggressively anti-Soviet policies, and numerous politicians called for his dismissal when it was learned that he had failed to disclose all the names of his legal clients and had not registered as an agent of the foreign governments that he had represented. Likewise called into question were his evasive and mumbling responses when testifying to congressional oversight committees, his appointments of subordinates, his business dealings with companies with which the CIA held contracts, and his role in the 1980 presidential campaign. The controversies surrounding Casey intensified during President Reagan's second term with revelations in November 1986 and in succeeding months relating to the so-called Iran-Contra affair, in which the administration had secretly sold HAWK and TOW missiles to Iranian moderates to ensure the release of American hostages and had then diverted the surplus funds from these arms sales to Nicaraguan counter-revolutionaries. Casey had lied when first testifying to Congress about his involvement in the Iran-Contra affair. He suffered a debilitating stroke in December 1986 before the Senate could further investigate his testimony. He resigned his position as Director of Central Intelligence in January 1987 after undergoing an operation to remove a brain tumor. Casey died shortly thereafter, on May 6, 1987, taking details of the scandal with him to his grave.

DUANE R. CLARRIDGE

Born on April 16, 1932, in Nashua, New Hampshire, Duane "Dewey" Clarridge received a B.A. in history from Brown University in 1953 and an M.A. in international relations from Columbia University in 1955. Following graduation, he was appointed a CIA officer and subsequently rose to leadership positions in the Agency, only to retire in 1987 under a cloud of suspicion arising from his actions and congressional testimony involving the Iran-Contra scandal.

Following a promising career in the field, in 1981 Clarridge was promoted to chief of the Directorate of Operations (DO) Latin American Division, where he supervised CIA efforts in support of the Nicaraguan contras. He left this post in October 1984 to become chief of the DO's European Division, retaining this position until February 1986, when he became director of the recently created Counterterrorist Center. The center would be responsible for coordinating counterterrorism activities within the Agency and among the fourteen other U.S. intelligence agencies.

Clarridge's actions as chief of the European Division proved to be controversial. Having retained close contact with National Security Council aide Oliver North after his stint in the Latin American Division, in November

1985 Clarridge helped North secure an airplane to transport eighteen HAWK missiles from Israel through Portugal to Iran. These missiles were part of the covert and highly sensitive arms-for-hostages deal that became the heart of the Iran-Contra scandal. This shipment proved to be particularly controversial in that it had predated President Reagan's issuance in January 1986 of a Finding (required under the 1980 Intelligence Oversight Act) authorizing the arms-for-hostages deal. As such, his role in arranging this shipment became a key issue during the inquiries launched in 1987 by the so-called Tower Commission, by a joint House and Senate committee, and during the criminal investigation by Independent Counsel Lawrence Walsh. During testimony before the Tower Commission and the joint committee, Clarridge denied knowing that the shipment involved HAWK missiles, claiming that he had thought it involved oil drilling equipment and was a "commercial enterprise." On November 26, 1991, a federal grand jury returned a seven-count indictment that Clarridge's testimony was either perjurious or false. Clarridge's trial on these charges was scheduled to begin on March 15, 1993, but he escaped prosecution when President George H. W. Bush (in the waning days of his presidency) pardoned him on December 24, 1992.

Prior to his indictment, Clarridge had been reprimanded and reduced in rank for "provid[ing] assistance to NSC [National Security Council] staff in connection with [shipping arms to Iran]...without proper authorization." DCI Webster had found Clarridge "culpable in respect to his testimony before Congress" and for "fail[ing] to keep his senior officers [in the CIA] properly apprised and to obtain appropriate authorization." Webster's reprimand triggered Clarridge's resignation.

The Independent Counsel's investigation of Clarridge's role had the further consequence of uncovering special CIA records procedures. The Counsel had learned that Clarridge's sensitive communications of November 1985 to CIA headquarters involving this shipment had been sent as "privacy channels"—a special procedure that was to be employed to ensure that such communications would be held temporarily until the reported information was no longer needed and then destroyed. In this instance, however, Clarridge had retained copies of these communications in a "shadow file" in his office. Then, when the Iran-Contra scandal became public, Clarridge, who by then had left the European Division to head the Counterterrorist Center, contacted his former secretary and had her forward this file to him. When the Independent Counsel learned of Clarridge's possession of this file, he discovered that one of the cables relating to this shipment was "missing," and suspected that it had been destroyed.

RAY STEINER CLINE

Ray Cline numbers among the relatively small cadre of CIA officers who worked both as an analyst in the Directorate of Intelligence and in the field for the Directorate of Operations. He is among an even smaller elite who served in the analytic mecca of the Office of National Estimates.

A complicated man, Cline constantly engaged in rather fine-tuned calculations of the odds in his favor. This comes through repeatedly. Richard Helms writes "In time I became aware of what I can best define as Ray's hand in my pocket." A subordinate who worked under him at State Department intelligence added that whenever Cline said something, it was time to stop and figure out his angle. An analyst who spent a decade in intelligence until leaving in disgust during the Vietnam war, and who worked in the Office of Current Intelligence that Cline once headed, confirms his antipathy for both DCIs Richard Helms and William Raborn.

Ray Steiner Cline was born in Anderson, Indiana, a town outside Indianapolis, in June 1918. A high school football star, he attended Harvard College on scholarship, graduated in 1939, completed a year of graduate work at Oxford in 1939–1940 and was selected in 1941 for the prestigious Society of Fellows at Harvard. After the Pearl Harbor attack, Cline volunteered for government service. Assigned to naval communications as a civilian he became a cryptologist and served from August 1942 until June 1943. He then shifted to the OSS, where he worked through the remainder of World War II with the current intelligence staff of the Research and Analysis Branch. Cline ended up heading the staff. After the war Cline worked briefly for the Operations Division of the Army General Staff, then at the Office of the Chief of Military History, where he wrote *Washington Command Post*, a volume of the Army's official history of World War II that focused on the War Plans Division, the heart of the U.S. military staff system at the high command level at that time. He then completed work for his doctorate, which he received from Harvard in 1949.

At that time Cline joined the CIA, working in the Office of Reports and Estimates for its Global Survey Division, producing an early version of what became the "Central Intelligence Bulletin." He then moved to the newly-formed Office of National Estimates (ONE), as a drafting officer on the National Intelligence Estimates. In October 1951 Cline went to London as a liaison officer with British intelligence to establish an exchange of NIEs for Joint Intelligence Committee appreciations. He returned to ONE in November 1954 to handle a special staff that focused on Soviet estimates. Reassigned to the Office of Current Intelligence in 1955, Cline headed a staff that produced intelligence on both Russia and China.

When Allen Dulles made a world tour in 1956 Cline served as his escort officer and began to see the operations side of the agency. A year later he convinced Dulles to override Frank Wisner's control of appointments and assign him as chief of station in Taiwan. On Taiwan Cline's greatest achievement was to become a drinking buddy of Chinese Nationalist leader General Chiang Ching-kuo, son of the Taiwanese ruler and leader of the Nationalist government's intelligence services. From this developed the Nationalist government's operations on the mainland, a Nationalist U-2 squadron executing missions in behalf of the CIA, Nationalist pilots and experts aiding CIA operations in South Vietnam.

After four years in Taiwan Cline returned to Washington as Deputy Director for Intelligence (DDI). In this capacity he played an important role during the Cuban Missile Crisis, being among the first to bring U-2 photographic evidence to the attention of President John F. Kennedy and national security adviser McGeorge Bundy. Cline's support of DCI John McCone during this period cemented relations between the two men.

Unlike his predecessor Robert Amory, who was officially unaware of the Bay of Pigs project, Cline was kept in the picture on Project MONGOOSE and other covert activities in Cuba. Cline's DI also had an important analytic input on the Vietnam war.

Cline numbered among those having little regard for DCI William F. Raborn, and was reportedly the source for some of the leaks of the time showcasing Raborn's inexperience or lack of knowledge. If so, the consequences of getting rid of Raborn proved to be personally disastrous for Cline, since Richard Helms became the head of the CIA. Significantly, Cline's reassignment, to chief of station in Bonn, then-West Germany, dated from exactly when Helms arrived at the top floor of CIA headquarters. Cline left so abruptly that President Lyndon Johnson joked at a dinner one night that Cline was "running out" on him. Typically, the CIA man not only wrote Johnson a letter protesting that he did indeed support administration policy, but had that letter sent to LBJ through political maven Tommy "The Cork" Corcoran, to whom he knew the president would pay attention. Cline remained in Germany for over three years.

In late 1969 Cline took over the Bureau for Intelligence and Research (INR) at the State Department. Almost immediately he became embroiled in an ongoing dispute over Soviet strategic nuclear forces. When White House manipulation of intelligence forced DCI Helms to delete a key paragraph from a National Intelligence Estimate (NIE) that forecast that the Soviets were not seeking a nuclear first-strike capability against the United States, Cline dissented to the NIE, inserting the identical language as an INR footnote. Cline also objected to Henry Kissinger's imposing "holds" on Soviet nuclear data at the National Security Council, preventing the circulation of this intelligence to avoid the growth of opposition to his arms control policies. He resigned in 1973, reportedly disgusted at Kissinger, by that time the secretary of state. Cline testified at hearings of the Pike committee in 1975 on the data "holds" and other intelligence issues. In 1977 hearings on the CIA's use of journalism and journalists, Cline testified that "the First Amendment is only an amendment."

Cline moved on to an analyst's job at the Center for Strategic and International Studies, then part of Georgetown University, successfully getting CSIS to subsidize the writing of his book *Secrets, Spies, and Scholars*. In 1979 he published a CSIS monograph, *Taiwan: Pawn in the China Game*. Cline got into the Soviet-sponsorship-of-terrorism sweepstakes of the 1980s with a shorter monograph on that subject. The columnist Jack Anderson reported that he participated in the ultra-conservative World Anti-Communist League, attending several of its conferences.

During the 1980 presidential election Cline worked for Ronald Reagan's campaign. He was implicated, according to Carter official Jody Powell, with other former CIA and FBI employees in a political intelligence operation that purloined briefing data and debate preparation materials from the Carter campaign. As CSIS executive director Cline had by then begun a "Free China" project that has been described as a latter-day China Lobby. In the next years he founded a think tank–advocacy group called the Global Strategy Council. China expert and former CIA colleague James Lilley tells a story of one of Cline's public pronouncements, favoring continued U.S. relations with Taiwan, disrupting a diplomatic meeting between President Reagan and Chinese leader Deng Xiaoping. Cline also became involved with figures including General John Singlaub and Barbara Studley, arms dealers in the Iran-Contra Affair. Congressional investigators of Iran-Contra took a lengthy deposition from Cline. That his involvement was merely peripheral is indicated by the refusal of Iran-Contra special prosecutor Lawrence Walsh to take any action on this case. In his final years Cline suffered from Alzheimer's Disease. He passed away at home in March 1996.

CHARLES GALLIGAN COGAN

"Chuck" Cogan is emblematic of the best and the brightest in the Directorate of Operations. Tall, slim, and a dapper dresser, he impressed journalist Bob Woodward as "Mr. Hathaway Shirt" and another journalist, George Crile, as one of an "old school" elite among the DO.

Born in 1928, Charles Cogan graduated magna cum laude from Harvard College in 1949 with a deep interest in things French, a taste for poetry, Shakespeare, and theater. Starting out as a journalist, with his high point a stint with *Look* magazine, he served with the Army Signal Corps during the Korean war from 1951 to 1953. He then briefly returned to journalism in Richmond, Virginia, before joining the CIA late in 1954, briefly serving at headquarters and spending his entire thirty-seven-year career with the DO.

Assigned to India during the early part of the Tibetan covert operation, Cogan focused on Indian political matters and subsequently returned to India for a second tour in 1960. Showing his predilection for cultural features of the societies of countries where he served, as well as a certain athleticism, Cogan played polo and participated in an Indian pig-sticking competition. The athleticism helped later in Jordan, where Cogan hunted with King Hussein. Cogan was subsequently assigned as deputy chief of station in the Congo at the height of the Katangan rebellion. In the Congo he helped save a fellow

CIA officer badly burned in a plane crash in the bush. Sent to the Sudan, Cogan left to become chief of station in Morocco.

The Moroccan interlude began Cogan's shift back toward Near East and South Asian affairs. After a brief detachment to the National War College for the advanced course taught there, during which Cogan's field trip was to Afghanistan, he was assigned as chief of station in Amman, Jordan. He then returned to Langley as the DO's division chief for the Near East and South Asia (NESA), a post he held during the critical years of 1979 to 1984. During a period in which U.S. foreign policy became preoccupied with Middle Eastern questions, Cogan manned the helm of the CIA division principally concerned with this area.

The principal problem during this period was the Iran hostage crisis. Cogan was the CIA officer who retained primary contact with the military joint task force responsible for planning hostage rescue operations both for the first, abortive mission, code-named "Rice Bowl," and the later, never-executed version, "Honey Badger." Cogan reportedly handed over a half million dollars to a former Iranian admiral during the last months of 1979 in an operation intended to support a coup against the fundamentalists of Ayatollah Khomeini, an initiative that was broken up by the Iranian security services.

Those same months saw the inception of the CIA covert operation in Afghanistan, on which for four years Cogan served as the Agency's expert in presentations to Congress on funds for and tactics in the war against the Soviets. Cogan apparently had friendly relations with Saudi ambassador Prince Bandar and helped create links between Bandar and CIA director William J. Casey, which the latter used to secure funding for the Afghan war and to solicit Saudi contributions to the Reagan administration's covert operation in Nicaragua. Cogan's reported opposition to expanding the Afghan war from a harassment effort against Soviet occupiers to a full-fledged attempt to defeat the U.S.S.R. in Afghanistan helped lead to his leaving NESA.

Cogan was NESA chief in 1983, at the time of the bombings of both the U.S. embassy in Beirut which resulted in the deaths of CIA officers, and of the U.S. Marine barracks in Beirut. He was reportedly less impressed than Director Casey at reports passed on by Israeli intelligence attributing the bombings to Syria. The CIA went ahead with a plot against a Syrian-backed fundamentalist leader in Lebanon that led to the bloody car bombing of a Beirut apartment building that completely missed its target. The embassy and barracks bombings have long been linked to Iranian-backed fundamentalist groups.

During this period the NESA division also issued a notice that an Iranian arms dealer, Manucher Ghorbanifar, had peddled false intelligence and was not to be trusted. Despite such warnings, White House operatives used Ghorbanifar in the series of shady dealings that became known as the Iran-Contra affair. Cogan would subsequently be deposed by the congressional joint committee investigating this scandal.

Cogan left NESA to accept an assignment as chief of station in Paris, one of the CIA's top overseas positions. In 1989 he became the Agency's officer-in-residence at Harvard's Kennedy School of Government, one of a handful of CIA officers given Agency sanction to teach and comment on intelligence subjects in academia. Retiring in 1991, Cogan was appointed a fellow of Harvard's Olin Center, where he continued to write and lecture on French history and Franco-American relations, including publishing a biography of Charles de Gaulle. Cogan is a 1989 recipient of the Distinguished Intelligence Medal and twice winner of the Intelligence Medal of Merit.

WILLIAM EGAN COLBY

Among the most controversial figures to serve as Director of Central Intelligence, William E. Colby also played an important role in bringing the CIA into the modern age of intelligence. Colby established the system the CIA—and now the Director of National Intelligence—uses to create National Intelligence Estimates, brought online the type of remote sensing technologies with real-time readouts that remain the standard today, reenergized the CIA's Directorate of Operations, and led the agency into the era of formal congressional oversight. Colby also led the CIA during the congressional investigations of the Church and Pike Committees in 1975–1976, and for this and for allegedly giving up Richard Helms to Justice Department investigators he was widely criticized by Agency officers.

Born in St. Paul, Minnesota, on January 4, 1920, William E. Colby was the son of an Army officer and educator. He grew up at Fort Benning, Tianjin, China, and Burlington, Vermont. Colby graduated from Princeton College in 1940, and briefly attended Columbia Law School until World War II brought him to volunteer for officer training in the U.S. Army. Colby trained as an artillery officer and paratrooper but responded to a recruiting pitch from representatives of the Office of Strategic Services, beginning his lifetime association with intelligence work. In the summer of 1943 Colby joined the OSS, which trained him as a "Jedburgh" commando. He led a mission to work with the Resistance in central France in the summer of 1944 following the Normandy invasion, and an OSS Operational Group fighting in Norway in 1945. His OSS unit actually took the surrender of thousands of German soldiers in the Norwegian city of Trondheim.

Following the war Colby married Barbara Heinzen, with whom he had five children, finished Columbia law school in 1947, and joined the law firm headed by former OSS chief William J. Donovan. In the late 1940s he joined the National Labor Relations Board as a lawyer. With the onset of the Korean War in 1950 his former OSS commander recruited Colby into the CIA, where he resumed an intelligence career that endured through retirement. Colby first worked on Soviet operations for the Office of Policy Coordination, as a desk officer within its Scandinavian Branch, then as chief of station in Stockholm.

There, and in Denmark and Norway, Colby helped set up networks of agents who agreed to stay behind if the Soviet Union conquered their countries in a war, forming the nucleus of a new espionage and resistance movement. In 1953 he moved to Italy and headed political action operations for the CIA station in Rome. Colby spearheaded efforts to blunt the impact of the Italian Communist Party, leading to anticommunist success in 1958 elections.

Colby's fluency in French led to his assignment to Saigon in early 1959 as deputy chief of station. The following year he won promotion to head the station, leading the CIA effort in South Vietnam during the first years of the Vietnam war. He began efforts to infiltrate commandos into North Vietnam, started unconventional warfare projects in the Central Highlands, and presided over a significant expansion of the CIA program in the country. This marked the beginning of more than a decade in which Colby was closely identified with the CIA in Vietnam. In fact, DCI John McCone later termed Colby as his main man on Vietnam. Colby returned to Washington as deputy chief of the Far East Division of the Directorate of Plans under Desmond FitzGerald. He succeeded FitzGerald as division chief in early 1963 and held that post for five years at the height of the Vietnam war. Colby was also responsible for CIA operations in Laos, Thailand, Indonesia, and Taiwan during that time.

Designated to lead the agency's Soviet Division, Colby was preparing to assume that post in early 1968 when President Lyndon Johnson requested his services back in Vietnam as deputy chief of the major U.S. pacification entity, the organization known as Civil Operations and Rural Development Support (CORDS). He succeeded Robert Komer as CORDS director in the fall of 1968 and held the personal rank of ambassador. At CORDS Colby was responsible for a program that dogged him ever after: the "Phoenix" program, which aimed at neutralizing the guerrilla infrastructure run in South Vietnam by the National Liberation Front. Charges that Phoenix was an assassination program led to multiple investigations and congressional hearings at which Colby defended himself as well as he could, but ultimately without convincing Americans that these activities were innocent.

Faced with the health problems of one of his children, Colby returned to Washington in mid-1971, where he assumed the post of executive director–comptroller of the Agency. In this capacity he became the point man under DCIs Richard Helms and James R. Schlesinger for the CIA's responses to various investigations of Agency involvement in the Watergate affair. In 1973 Colby briefly served as CIA deputy director for operations, the top post in the clandestine service, until in May he was appointed Director of Central Intelligence. Colby's confirmation hearings again became a venue for airing charges regarding the Phoenix program. He nonetheless won confirmation and was sworn in on September 4, 1973.

Colby represented the classical CIA, endowed with all the operational experience that service in that period afforded. It became his fate to lead the

257

agency at a time of political upheaval in America, however, and he could not keep the CIA out of trouble that began with Watergate and only worsened. In late 1974 press revelations that the CIA had engaged in prohibited domestic spying on the antiwar movement triggered the Church and Pike investigations, and Colby trod the delicate waters of trying simultaneously to satisfy the Ford administration, which strove to limit the investigations, and the congressional investigators. Colby feared that an uncooperative CIA could be swept away in this climate of inquiry, but White House and State Department officials were enraged at Colby's actions. During these tense months his marriage fell apart and he ultimately was remarried to Susan Shelton, a congressional staffer whom he had met on one of his frequent forays to Capitol Hill. President Ford fired Colby in November 1975, replacing him as DCI by George H. W. Bush.

Within the CIA, during these same months Colby's leadership was challenged by officers disgruntled by his decision to hand information over to the Justice Department regarding his predecessor, Richard M. Helms, who was revealed to have lied under oath during congressional testimony regarding CIA covert actions in Chile. In fact, Colby's own hand had been forced by CIA officers who threatened to go to the Justice Department themselves, and the Agency stood under a legal obligation to provide such information. Colby's reputation was nonetheless marred by the Helms affair, and even after his death former CIA officers never forgave him for his role in what ultimately became a legal prosecution of Helms.

In retirement Colby acted as a consultant, did law work, and was politically active on arms control and disarmament issues. He died under tragic circumstances in 1996, disappearing from a canoe on the Chesapeake Bay. It is a measure of the controversy surrounding Colby that during the days that passed before his body was recovered the wildest speculations circulated, everything from murder to a contrived defection to Russia being advanced as explanations for his disappearance. His death was, however, an innocent one. The controversy surrounding Colby has prevented observers from recognizing the full importance of this director's role in the history of the CIA.

JOHN M. DEUTCH

Born on July 27, 1938, in Brussels, Belgium, John Deutch received a B.A. in history and economics from Amherst College in 1961 and a Ph.D. in physical chemistry from MIT in 1965. In 1961, he accepted an appointment as a systems analyst in the Defense Department, as one of Secretary of Defense McNamara's so-called whiz kids, leaving in 1962 to attend graduate school at MIT. After obtaining his Ph.D. Deutch accepted an appointment as assistant professor of chemistry at Princeton University in 1966, leaving in 1970 to accept an appointment as professor of chemistry at MIT Deutch returned to government service in 1977 as deputy secretary of energy, leaving this post in 1980 to return once again to MIT as dean of the chemistry department. In 1993, he accepted appointment as undersecretary of defense for acquisitions and technology and was promoted in 1994 to deputy secretary of defense. Following James Woolsey's resignation as DCI, Deutch was confirmed as director of central intelligence in May 1995, serving until December 1996 when he resigned in response to President Clinton's decision to reorganize the national security bureaucracy and appoint a new DCI. Deutch returned to MIT as institute professor, served on various corporate boards, and in October 2003 was an invited member of a panel on "Intelligence and the War on Terror" convened by the Kean Commission.

Deutch's appointment as DCI came in the wake of the Aldrich Ames spy scandal and questions about the Agency's earlier relationships with brutal Guatemalan military officers. As DCI, he instituted tighter management procedures and launched a housecleaning of the Directorate of Operations (DO), including dismissing senior DO officers. His actions and critical comments about DO officers (including an injudicious comment to *New York Times* reporter Tim Weiner that "compared to uniformed officers, they [DO officers] certainly are not as competent or as understanding of what their relative role is and what their responsibilities are") created both tensions within the Agency and a morale problem that ultimately undermined President Clinton's support. Following his resignation, moreover, an internal CIA investigation was launched over his actions as DCI when transferring classified information to his personal computer at his home in violation of CIA security procedures. In August 1999, DCI Tenet suspended Deutch's security clearance, a decision triggered by the revelations concerning his handling of classified information. The timing of this discovery in the midst of the controversy surrounding the Wen Ho Lee case also led Justice Department officials to launch a criminal investigation. Although Deutch was not implicated in espionage or in compromising national secrets, he was subject to prosecution. President Clinton (on the last day of his presidency) foreclosed any such action by pardoning him on January 20, 2001.

WILLIAM JOSEPH DONOVAN

Born on January 1, 1883, William "Wild Bill" Joseph Donovan graduated from Columbia University in 1905 and received his law degree from the same institution two years later. Prior to America's entrance into World War I, he practiced law in Buffalo, New York, and served with a cavalry unit of the New York National Guard along the U.S.-Mexican Border. With U.S. involvement in World War I, Donovan served with the 165th Infantry Regiment of the 42nd Infantry Division in France, earning the Medal of Honor, Distinguished Service Medal, and Distinguished Service Cross. He completed his military career having attained the rank of colonel.

During the interwar years Donovan returned to his corporate law practice, and in 1929 founded his own Wall Street firm. He also served as U.S. District Attorney for Western New York and as assistant U.S. Attorney General during the Coolidge administration. In 1940 President Franklin D. Roosevelt sent Donovan to England to investigate that nation's ability to survive a war with Germany. While abroad Donovan also studied the political and military situation in the Mediterranean. In mid-1941 he recommended that Roosevelt establish a "Service of Strategic Information." FDR responded by appointing Donovan as his chief intelligence officer, or Coordinator of Information (COI), in July 1941. In June 1942 the president replaced the COI with the Office of Strategic Services (OSS), which came under the jurisdiction of the Joint Chiefs of Staff, and appointed Donovan to head this new agency.

Following the Allied triumph and the deterioration of relations with the Soviets, Donovan assisted the U.S. prosecution team at the Nuremberg Trials, although he participated in the process only indirectly. Earlier, at President Roosevelt's request, Donovan drafted a proposal in November 1944 to create a permanent centralized intelligence agency. His proposal encountered considerable resistance, primarily from the established intelligence bureaucrats (in naval and military intelligence, the State Department, and the FBI). His memorandum was leaked to the *Chicago Tribune*; the article describing this proposal was headlined "New Deal Gestapo." Following the Japanese surrender in August 1945, formally ending military conflict, President Truman dissolved the OSS in September 1945. In time, the new security crisis of the Cold War led President Truman to propose legislation to Congress: the National Security Act, which contained a provision creating the Central Intelligence Agency (CIA). This legislation was approved in July 1947. Donovan was personally disappointed that President Harry S. Truman did not select him to direct the CIA. He had by then returned to his law firm. In 1953, however, President Dwight D. Eisenhower appointed him ambassador to Thailand. During his year in that country, Donovan increased the number of American advisors in Thailand in an attempt to thwart communist activities in Southeast Asia. It was his final government service. Donovan died on February 8, 1959.

ALLEN WELSH DULLES

The grandson of William Foster, secretary of state under President Benjamin Harrison, Allen Welsh Dulles was born on April 7, 1893, and began his professional career in 1916 as a secretary in the American Embassy in Vienna. The following year he relocated to the embassy in Bern, Switzerland, where he worked in intelligence. As a member of the American delegation to the Paris Peace Conference in 1919, Dulles helped to establish the borders of the newly established country of Czechoslovakia as part of an initiative intended to provide a framework for peace and stability in central Europe. After serving in the American embassy in Berlin and subsequently with the American

Commission in Constantinople, he returned to the United States in 1922, where he took on the responsibility of chief of the State Department's Near Eastern Affairs Division. He also attended the Geneva conferences of 1925–1926, the Three Power Naval Conference of 1927, and the Geneva conferences of 1932–1933. Dulles left the State Department to practice law with Sullivan & Cromwell in New York, whose managing partner was his brother John Foster Dulles, during the second half of the 1920s and throughout the 1930s. During World War II, he joined the Office of Strategic Services (OSS), and in November 1942 he became head of the OSS office in Bern, Switzerland, where he remained throughout the war, organizing intelligence-gathering operations in Nazi-occupied Europe.

After the war Dulles served as president of the Council on Foreign Relations and advised CIG director Hoyt S. Vandenberg and then DCI Roscoe H. Hillenkoetter. Along with William H. Jackson and Mathias Correa, he participated in a National Security Council–ordered examination of the effectiveness of the American intelligence system. The so-called Jackson-Correa-Dulles committee submitted its report in 1949. The next year DCI Walter Bedell Smith asked Dulles to implement the report's recommendations, and in 1951 he became deputy director of the Office of Special Operations and the Office of Policy Coordination (OPC); he eventually combined both groups into the Directorate of Plans.

Dulles became deputy director of the CIA in 1951 and the agency's third director two years later in the administration of Dwight D. Eisenhower. He worked closely with his brother, President Eisenhower's secretary of state, to improve coordination between the CIA and the State Department. As DCI Allen Dulles took great interest in covert and intelligence operations, many claim at the expense of improving the agency's intelligence-gathering and collecting capabilities. During his tenure the CIA carried out coups in Iran, Guatemala, and Indonesia, and authorized a series of questionable covert operations in the Congo, Japan, Laos, and Vietnam. To improve the Agency's intelligence-collection capabilities vis-à-vis the Soviets, given the difficulty of recruiting Soviet sources, Dulles sought to exploit new technologies. Under his directorship, the Agency developed the U-2 spy plane and a satellite surveillance program (Corona). Dulles's term as the longest-serving Director of Central Intelligence ended in 1961, when he resigned after the disastrous results of the Bay of Pigs invasion of April 1961, for which the Agency received paramount blame. He continued nevertheless to serve the government in various capacities, including membership on the commission that investigated the assassination of President John F. Kennedy. He died on January 29, 1969.

DESMOND FITZGERALD

A swashbuckling covert operator with the Central Intelligence Agency, Desmond FitzGerald rose to become Deputy Director for Plans (DDP), the senior official in the clandestine service, from 1965 to 1967. FitzGerald's strong suit from the beginning of his CIA career was covert action, and the operations directorate under his leadership reflected that interest.

Born in New York City on June 16, 1910, FitzGerald was the son of a prominent stockbroker. Educated at St. Mark's School, Harvard College, and Harvard Law School, FitzGerald knew many of the top-drawer elite of his generation, and built up those connections even further. He married Marietta Peabody, granddaughter of the founder of the exclusive school Groton, and daughter of a Radcliffe founder. Possessing the gentility and culture of the affluent eastern establishment, FitzGerald passed the New York State bar in 1937, joining the law firm Spence, Hopkins, Walser, Hotchkiss, & Angell. When World War II came he enlisted in the army and was sent to the China-Burma-India theater, where he attained the rank of major and served as an adviser to the Chinese Nationalist 6th Army in Burma. After the war he returned to his New York law firm as a partner and briefly involved himself in Republican politics, but soon jumped at the chance when a lawyer friend, Frank Wisner, offered him a job with the Office of Policy Coordination (OPC), which Wisner was going to Washington to lead. He divorced Marietta, who went on to wed a British diplomat. FitzGerald married Barbara Green Lawrence in 1948.

Fitgerald's OPC assignment, as executive officer of the Far East Division under Colonel Richard Stilwell, put him on the cutting edge of the biggest U.S. covert operations program of the era, the effort to combat the People's Republic of China, which OPC waged from Japan, South Korea, Taiwan, Hong Kong, and Burma. FitzGerald especially favored the latter component, featuring a couple of abortive attacks into China by Chinese Nationalist forces supported by the CIA. The Burma operation later soured as the Chinese Nationalists began fighting the Burmese government and dealing in drugs to enrich themselves. FitzGerald also sparkplugged the very active program of covert operations carried out against mainland China from Taiwan.

FitzGerald remained deputy chief of the Far East Division of the reorganized CIA when the CIA attempted to defuse the Burma situation by repatriating the Nationalists to Taiwan. Only a fraction of the Chinese participated. The Chinese presence in upper Burma (now Myanmar) has been entrenched ever since. Among covert actions waged by the Far East Division during this period were strong paramilitary operations during the Korean war, a political action in the Philippines leading to the election of Ramon Magsaysay in 1953 (the original claim to fame of the CIA's Edward Lansdale), airlift and other activities in French Indochina, political action activities in Japan to sustain the power of the Liberal Democratic Party, and continuing China operations.

Aware that he had had no experience in the field, FitzGerald angled for such an assignment, and in 1954 Frank Wisner helped arrange a posting as chief of the China Command, created as a sort of Asian theater-level echelon to impose unified leadership of all activities aimed at the People's Republic of

China. The CIA's station chiefs, however, worked hard to deal directly with headquarters, leaving China Command a sinecure until its elimination in 1956. FitzGerald returned to Washington as chief of the Psychological and Paramilitary Operations Staff of the Directorate of Plans (DDP), CIA's clandestine service. In mid-1958 he returned to the DDP Far East Division as its chief. In this capacity FitzGerald presided over the height of the Tibet paramilitary operation and the inception of the secret war in Laos, along with the growth of a substantial covert action program in South Vietnam.

When John McCone was appointed director of central intelligence in November 1961, FitzGerald served as the escort officer for the DCI's extensive tour of U.S. installations and CIA stations worldwide. It did not hurt in his selection for this task that he was friends with President John F. Kennedy—indeed some at CIA thought him related to the Fitzgerald side of the Kennedy family. This familiarity may have contributed to his appointment in January 1963 as chief of Task Force W, the CIA unit responsible for operations against Cuba once Project MONGOOSE was reorganized in the wake of the Cuban Missile Crisis. FitzGerald shepherded a new covert action plan to approval in June 1963. He met personally in Europe with one of the CIA's principal agents in efforts to assassinate Fidel Castro in November 1963. But the Cuba project was reoriented after embarrassing leaks resulting from Cuban exile activities. FitzGerald's unit became the DDP's Special Affairs Staff. From that post he won promotion to chief of the Western Hemisphere Division in 1964. President Johnson's selection of Richard Helms as deputy director of central intelligence in April 1965 opened up the post of deputy director for plans to which FitzGerald was appointed.

FitzGerald presided over CIA covert actions in the Congo and Portugese Africa, the continuation of the Tibet affair, and security operations in Argentina, Bolivia, and elsewhere. His most important activities, however, included the CIA's secret war in Laos and numerous activities alongside U.S. combat forces in South Vietnam. He told journalist Stewart Alsop this story about Vietnam intelligence: FitzGerald was periodically summoned to the office of Secretary of Defense Robert S. McNamara to brief him on the situation. McNamara once admitted that making sense of events, despite all his numbers, remained difficult. Des replied that making decisions had to pass beyond facts and figures to rely upon instinct, and that his instinct was that the United States faced a tough fight in Vietnam. Alsop recounts that McNamara gave FitzGerald a "long incredulous stare" and never again asked him to brief on Vietnam.

FitzGerald was known for keeping himself fit and remained an avid tennis player. It therefore shocked many people when he collapsed on the court while playing tennis at his country home near The Plains, Virginia, on July 23, 1967. On September 13 President Johnson posthumously awarded FitzGerald the National Security Medal, the nation's highest honor for intelligence service, for "exceptional competence and stimulating leadership [that] won the confidence of his associates and established a standard of excellence to guide and inspire others."

ROBERT M. GATES

Former Director of Central Intelligence Robert Michael Gates served as an intelligence officer on the National Security Council staffs of Richard M. Nixon and Gerald R. Ford, a special assistant to the national security adviser under Jimmy Carter, the deputy director for central intelligence under Ronald Reagan, and the deputy national security adviser, and then director of central intelligence, for George H. W. Bush. Gates is also the only professional intelligence analyst—as opposed to clandestine services operator—to have attained the highest position in the U.S. intelligence community.

Robert Gates enrolled as a history major at the College of William and Mary, where he obtained a Bachelor's degree in 1965. He focused on the Soviet Union for the Master's Degree he earned a year later from Indiana University. Recruited to the CIA while at Indiana, he arranged to join the Agency after fulfilling his military service in the Air Force. A man of the plains—he had been born in Wichita, Kansas, in 1943—he returned to them as a young officer at Whiteman Air Force Base in Missouri from October 1966 until January 1968. As an intelligence analyst for the Air Force, Gates was then seconded to the CIA as an analyst with the Office of Current Intelligence (focusing on the Soviet Union). His work on the Soviets in the Middle East proved distinguished enough that in June 1971 he was selected as an intelligence analyst to support the U.S. delegation to Strategic Army Limitation Talks being held between the United States and U.S.S.R. He then worked under Fritz Ermarth as assistant national intelligence officer for Soviet strategic programs, notably writing the draft of a special national intelligence estimate that was published in September 1973. Gates completed his academic training with a Ph.D. in Soviet Studies from Georgetown granted in 1974.

Gates first worked at the White House during the summer before Richard Nixon's resignation. He eventually became an NSC staffer for Soviet matters. Gates had the unique perspective of a CIA officer who knew how policy was made in Washington and not just in the country that he watched. That would have consequences later. At the end of the Ford administration Gates returned to Langley, where he served on a liaison staff bringing intelligence material to policy shops like the NSC staff. He served in this role until President Carter's National Security aide, Zbigniew Brzezinski brought him back to the White House as a special assistant, a job he held for two and a half years. Toward the end of 1979 he served for a few months at Langley as director of a center at the Office of Strategic Research. DCI Stansfield Turner then appointed Gates his executive assistant. He served Admiral Turner for eight months, starting in February 1980. When the Carter administration ended Gates had become the national intelligence officer for the Soviet Union in his own right.

The intelligence transition team formed to assist the changeover from Carter's administration to that of Ronald Reagan was particularly ideological and thus would seemingly get rid of anyone at the upper reaches of the Turner CIA. Gates, however, was left alone when William J. Casey succeeded Turner as DCI. Indeed, in some ways his role was enhanced as Gates directed an executive staff for the DCI and the DDCI, particularly in support of Admiral Bobby Inman, whom Gates had known and liked for some years. He soon solidified his standing with DCI Casey. In January 1982 Gates was appointed deputy director for intelligence, leading the analytical side of the CIA for over four years. A further token of Casey's esteem would be Gates's ex officio assignment, beginning in September 1983, as chairman of the National Intelligence Council, responsible for the drafting of all National Intelligence Estimates (NIE) in behalf of the DCI. In April 1986 Gates was promoted to deputy director of central intelligence.

The immensely controversial Iran-Contra affair threatened to halt Gates's career even as it seemed to enhance it. This happened after Director Casey collapsed on the job at the end of 1986. President Reagan then nominated Gates to succeed Casey in February 1987 but the nomination failed due to questions about Gates's role in Iran-Contra. These questions centered on his handling of a 1985 NIE that seemed intended to suggest the possibility of fresh diplomatic dealings with Islamic fundamentalists in Iran; his knowledge of the sales of U.S. weapons to Iran; whether he had been warned of, and the use he made of knowledge about, certain bank accounts used to funnel the surplus funds from arms sales to Iran to the Nicaraguan contra rebels; his knowledge of the activities of White House staffer Oliver North; and, lastly, his role in preparing DCI Casey for the false testimony he gave Congress toward the end of 1986. Because these issues threatened to create a firestorm at any Gates nomination hearing, Gates withdrew himself from consideration as DCI in early March 1987. Nevertheless Gates served as acting DCI from the end of 1986 through May 1987, when William Webster took over as director of central intelligence.

Following his election to the presidency in November 1988, George H. W. Bush appointed Gates deputy national security adviser under Brent Scowcroft in January 1989. Gates remained in the White House for over two years, during which time first the Soviet empire in Eastern Europe, and then the Soviet Union itself, successively collapsed, ending the Cold War. Gates and Scowcroft have been criticized for their early hesitation in believing in these events and for having failed to position the United States to deal with them effectively. For its part, the CIA has been criticized for "missing" the fall of the Soviet Union (somewhat unfairly since Agency analysts had reported all along on the weakening of Gorbachev and the disastrous Soviet economy). Shortly before the fall of the Soviet Union, in June 1991, Robert Gates achieved the distinction of being nominated to become director of central intelligence for the second time. He remains the sole figure in CIA history to receive multiple nominations for DCI.

Gates's nomination hearings laid bare a multitude of charges regarding intelligence analysis at the CIA since the early 1980s. In many ways these hearings became the most extensive inquiry into U.S. intelligence since the Church and Pike committee investigations of 1975. Gates had held major responsibility for that analysis, and during his confirmation hearings was tarred by both serving and retired CIA officers for having politicized intelligence reporting. His involvement in Iran-Contra was again resuscitated. Among other charges relating to intelligence analysis aired at the hearings were CIA reporting on the 1981 plot to assassinate Pope John Paul II, allegations of Soviet state support for terrorism, CIA reporting on Nicaragua and Afghanistan, the Soviet strategic defense initiative, and specific weapons issues. Gates was able to refute the charges and won confirmation. He was sworn in as DCI on November 12, 1991.

Given his confirmation controversies, as DCI Gates proved somewhat cautious in his handling of the NIE process. His innovations were in the nature of changing direction and atmosphere. During his tenure Gates started the CIA on its climb out from the Cold War. He initiated a series of what became the equivalent of "summit" conferences between the heads of U.S. and Russian intelligence, which would have been unheard of during the Cold War. Gates also promised new openness and the declassification of a variety of CIA Cold War records, including those for over a dozen significant covert action programs. Some declassifications did occur, though much of the Gates promise remains unfulfilled to this day. Even the DCI proved unable to shake the CIA out of its cult of secrecy.

Gates retired in January 1993 to become a consultant and to write his memoir. He later assumed the directorship of the George H. W. Bush Presidential Library and then became president of Texas A&M University. In early 2005 Gates refused the invitation of the second President George Bush to become the nation's first director of national intelligence. He is a holder of the National Security Medal, a three-time winner of the Distinguished Intelligence Medal, and twice winner of the Central Intelligence Medal.

CLAIR ELROY GEORGE

An officer whose career illustrates the pitfalls of intelligence work, Clair E. George spent thirty-three years with the Central Intelligence Agency. His tragedy lay in remaining wedded to an outmoded concept of CIA secrecy at a time when standards of information and accountability had changed in the United States. With Richard M. Helms, George holds the distinction of being the most senior CIA officer convicted of criminal offenses stemming from agency operations. Unlike Helms, who pleaded nolo contendere to an indictment, George was convicted by a jury in the second of two trials.

Born in Beaver Falls, a suburb of Pittsburgh, on August 3, 1930, George was the son of an agricultural chemist and a mother who later became administrative assistant to the mayor. A red-headed fireball, high school debater, and drum player, George also took on a night job at a steel mill after the death of his father. A political science major at the University of Pennsylvania, he headed the local chapter of the Skull and Bones Society and became vice president of his fraternity. Accepted to Columbia Law School in 1952, he instead enlisted in the U.S. Army. George received Chinese language training at the Army Language School at Monterey, California, and then was assigned to the Counterintelligence Corps in Japan and Okinawa. He joined the CIA in 1955.

George's initial Agency assignment was to Hong Kong in August 1956. There he used his Chinese to debrief defectors and deal with agents. He acquired the reputation of a good recruiter and street man. Returning to headquarters in 1960, he met and married fellow Agency officer Mary C. Atkinson. They had two daughters. From 1961 to 1964 George was assigned to Paris. He then became chief of station in Bamako, Mali, for two years starting in July 1964. When his recruiting efforts were uncovered by local security services, George left the country before being declared persona non grata, preserving his Agency cover. George was then reassigned to a subordinate position in the much larger CIA station in New Delhi. In 1971 he became the chief of operations-external for the DO's Soviet Division, supervising all agency operations against Soviet personnel that took place outside Russia and the Soviet Bloc.

In early 1975 George received what had until then been regarded as a plum assignment, chief of station in Beirut. He arrived that summer, two months after the Lebanese civil war had broken out. Very shortly it became apparent that the Agency could barely function in Beirut. That December CIA station chief Richard Welch was assassinated in Athens and George volunteered to replace him but did not arrive in Greece until the summer of 1976. George effectively exchanged one of the most dangerous jobs in the CIA for another one almost as dangerous. He served in Athens for three years.

By 1979 George had become a well-regarded senior officer and was promoted to head the Africa Division of the Directorate of Operations. He held this position through 1981, when he became associate deputy director for operations, in line for the top DO position. Though an admirer of DCI William J. Casey, George was frustrated by Casey's penchant for dealing directly with subordinate officers, cutting the DDO and ADDO out of the loop.

Possibly aware of George's unhappiness at the DO, in 1982 Director Casey made George the CIA's senior liaison officer to Congress. George, who could be charming but permitted himself rages when he thought it useful, proved a disaster in the congressional liaison role. When the CIA mined Nicaraguan harbors in 1984, an open violation of international law, George went along with Casey, barely raising the matter with the congressional intelligence oversight committees, which became hugely controversial almost immediately. He later claimed it had been the State Department's responsibility to tell Congress of this action because it had been thought up (by a CIA officer) in an interagency committee the department chaired.

In July 1984 Director Casey moved George into the position of deputy director for operations. Within months of taking over this position George installed a taping system that enabled him to make recordings and transcriptions of his secure telephone calls with CIA field stations. George became the top overseer of a huge array of operations, which during this period included secret wars against the Soviets in Afghanistan, Nicaragua, Angola, Ethiopia, and Cambodia; additional headaches in Lebanon, where CIA station chief William Buckley was kidnapped and murdered; and a huge counterespionage scandal in 1985, the "Year of the Spy," when a wide variety of American spies serving the Russians, Chinese, and Israelis were exposed. Unknown to George, that very year CIA officer Aldrich Ames began his own spying for the Russians. It was also the year of the (possibly false) Soviet defector Yuri Yurchenko (who fled back to Russia), in whose debriefing Ames had participated.

The Iran-Contra affair, and especially the Nicaraguan end of it, created George's criminal problems. Director Casey, along with NSC staffer Oliver North and other operatives, carried on an off-the-books covert operation in Nicaragua beginning in 1984 that was subsequently partly financed after 1985 by surplus funds obtained from arms sales to fundamentalist Iran. The Nicaraguan government shooting down of a supply plane on October 5, 1986, along with revelations in Lebanese newspapers that occurred almost simultaneously, began to unravel both ends of this operation. During the years 1985 to 1986, CIA officers had facilitated arms shipments to Iran, helped with contacts with former military and Agency operatives, furnished intelligence to operatives in Nicaragua, and taken a number of other measures to help facilitate the Iran-Contra activities. Agency officials had done so even though the Agency dating from 1984 was prohibited by law from acting against Nicaragua. George testified falsely under oath in October and December 1986 before several congressional committees regarding his and the Agency's knowledge of, and participation in, these activities. He had also assisted Director Casey in the preparation of false testimony that the DCI presented that November. After a special prosecutor, Judge Lawrence E. Walsh, began to investigate these events, George again provided false testimony to a grand jury.

In 1991 George was indicted on eight criminal counts of providing false testimony to Congress, and two counts of perjury before a federal grand jury. A trial on these charges in the spring and summer of 1992 ended in a hung jury. Tried a second time, George was found guilty on December 9, 1992. Within weeks of that verdict, however, President George H. W. Bush issued presidential pardons for George, two other CIA officers, former Secretary of

Defense Caspar Weinberger, and former Assistant Secretary of State Elliott Abrams. Clair George has since lived quietly in retirement.

PORTER J. GOSS

Born in Waterbury, Connecticut, in 1938, Porter Goss majored in classics and Greek at Yale University. After graduating in 1960, he served in the U.S. Army before joining the CIA in 1962. Stationed in Miami, he helped manage Cuban exiles who opposed the revolutionary regime of Fidel Castro.

Goss worked as a covert operative for ten years, serving in Latin America, the Caribbean, and Europe. His health seriously weakened by a severe bacterial infection he had contracted in London in 1970, Goss resigned from the Agency in 1972.

Moving to an island off southwestern Florida, Goss began a successful second career as a small businessman. He founded and published a small-town newspaper and invested in real estate. Elected to the city council of Sanibel, Florida, in 1974, he served in that position until 1982. In 1983, Florida Governor Bob Graham appointed him to the Lee County Commission.

A conservative Republican, Goss was elected to Congress in 1988 and eventually served on the House Permanent Select Committee on Intelligence, becoming chair of that committee in 1997. Some critics of the CIA considered him a lax overseer, citing his reluctance to investigate what he dismissed as the "wild and unsubstantiated allegations" that a White House official had leaked the name of CIA operative Valerie Plame to syndicated columnist Robert Novak in July 2003. These critics argued that Plame's name had been intentionally leaked to discredit her husband, Joseph Wilson, who had recently published a critical op-ed column in the *New York Times* refuting a key rationale offered by President Bush for going to war with Iraq. "Somebody sends me a blue dress and some DNA, I'll have an investigation," Goss glibly remarked, in a sarcastic reference to the earlier scandal involving President Clinton and White House intern Monica Lewinsky.

Following George Tenet's resignation as DCI, President George W. Bush nominated Goss as his successor in August 2004—at a time of a critical public and congressional debate over the CIA's seeming failure to have anticipated the terrorist attack of September 11, 2001. Propelled by the findings first of a joint House-Senate intelligence committee investigation of 2002–2003 and then by public hearings and the final report of the so-called Kean Commission in 2004, many called for a reorganization of the U.S. intelligence community through the creation of a new office headquartered in the Executive Office of the President and led by a national intelligence director.

Goss's nomination as DCI was immediately questioned by some Democrats, citing his earlier ties to the CIA and his recent partisan comments about Democratic presidential nominee John Kerry. They questioned whether Goss possessed the independence to head an agency at a time of doubt about its subservience to the president and when reform of the intelligence community was being debated. Nevertheless, his nomination was approved by the Senate Intelligence Committee by a 12–4 vote and by the full Senate by a vote of 77–17.

Goss's confirmation did not end the controversy provoked by his appointment, or the questions about the future direction and status of the CIA. Soon after taking office in September 2004, he caused a stir when he told CIA staff that their job was to "support the administration and its policies in our work." His statement revived concerns that the nation's intelligence would be politicized. As Goss settled in at the Agency, several top CIA officials resigned, including Deputy Director John McLaughlin, the two top leaders of the clandestine service, and terrorism expert Michael Scheurer, who had recently published a book charging the Bush Administration with having lost the war on terror. Some anonymous CIA officers protested that Goss was destroying Agency morale by purging anyone viewed as insufficiently supportive of President Bush. And, with the passage of the Intelligence Reform and Terrorism Prevention Act in December 2004, creating the new post of National Intelligence Director and a presidentially mandated inquiry into the conduct of paramilitary operations, Goss's status, and that of the Agency, was placed in limbo.

RICHARD McGARRAH HELMS

Born on March 30, 1913, Richard McGarrah Helms graduated from Williams College in 1935, after which he began a professional career as a journalist. Commissioned as a lieutenant in the U.S. Navy during World War II, he was stationed in New York City, where he worked in antisubmarine operations for the Eastern Sea Frontier. Shortly thereafter he joined the Office of Strategic Services (OSS) and served in the Secret Intelligence Branch. Assigned to a variety of European cities, he participated in spy activities against Nazi Germany. With the end of the war he remained in Germany, working for the Strategic Services Unit.

Upon the creation of the Central Intelligence Group in 1946, the Strategic Services Unit was redesignated the Office of Special Operations (OSO). Discharged by the navy as a lieutenant commander, Helms returned to Washington, D.C., where he became chief of Foreign Division M, which oversaw intelligence activities in Germany, Austria, and Switzerland. Having by then joined the CIA, in November 1951 he became deputy assistant director for operations of the OSO and was promoted to assistant director the following summer. At this time CIA officials combined the OSO and the Office of Policy Coordination (OPC) to create the CIA Clandestine Service. Distrustful of covert operations and wary of the planned Bay of Pigs invasion, Helms did not participate in that operation's planning or execution. When the invasion failed and his rival Richard Bissell resigned as chief of the clandestine service, Helms filled this vacant position.

Helms was appointed deputy director of the Central Intelligence Agency in 1965, and upon DCI William F. Raborny's resignation the following year, he became the new director during the administration of Lyndon Johnson. His time was dominated by the Vietnam War and by pressure from Presidents Johnson and Nixon to develop evidence linking anti-Vietnam War protestors with international communism. On President Nixon's and National Security Advisor Henry Kissinger's insistence, he oversaw the CIA's failed attempt in 1970 to prevent the election of Salvator Allende to head the government in Chile. His actions ultimately made him vulnerable to criminal prosecution when he sought to evade congressional inquiries involving U.S. policy in Chile. The extent to which he and the CIA were complicit in Allende's subsequent overthrow and assassination remains contested. President Nixon, who never took Helms into his confidence and relied on Kissinger as his primary source of intelligence, opted not to reappoint him CIA director as the Watergate scandal intensified. Stepping down as DCI, Helms was appointed U.S. ambassador to Iran in 1973, where he served for the next three years. His 1973 testimony before the Senate Foreign Relations Committee, in which he claimed that the CIA did not initiate covert operations to subvert the Chilean government, led to his indictment for perjury. Helms pleaded guilty and received a two-year suspended sentence and a $2,000 fine. He died on October 23, 2002.

ROSCOE HENRY HILLENKOETTER

Born on May 8, 1897, Roscoe Hillenkoetter graduated from the U.S. Naval Academy in 1919, serving briefly with the Atlantic Fleet during World War I. He joined the Office of Naval Intelligence (ONI) in 1933, receiving an assignment to the American embassy in Paris. Serving as an assistant naval attaché to the embassy until 1935, Hillenkoetter completed a tour of duty aboard the U.S.S. *Maryland*, and he then returned to the Paris embassy. He also acted as assistant naval attaché to Madrid and Lisbon and assisted in the evacuation of Americans from Spain during the Spanish Civil War. After the German occupation of Paris in June 1940, Hillenkoetter moved to Vichy, France, and aided the French underground. He observed German military actions in North Africa and was subsequently wounded during the Japanese attack on Pearl Harbor of December 1941 when his ship, the U.S.S. *West Virginia*, was sunk. Hillenkoetter served as Admiral Chester W. Nimitz's chief intelligence officer in the Pacific Theater from September 1942 until March 1943, and he took command of the U.S.S. *Dixie* prior to receiving a land assignment with the Bureau of Naval Personnel in 1944.

Immediately following the war Hillenkoetter served as the commander of the U.S.S. *Missouri*, but in 1946 he returned to his prewar post as naval attaché in Paris. In May 1947 he became the director of the Central Intelligence Group (CIG) and then in September 1947 the first director of the Central Intelligence Agency (CIA) created under legislation approved by

Congress in July of that same year. In 1949 Congress passed the Central Intelligence Agency Act exempting CIA appropriations from budgetary and accounting requirements, and inadvertently serving as a spur to Hillenkoetter and Truman (and subsequent) administration officials to rely on the CIA to plan and implement worldwide covert operations. Hillenkoetter, however, personally opposed paramilitary operations and the overthrow of democratically elected governments. He also struggled to manage the Office of Research and Estimates (ORE) so that it would better provide the president with essential information and assist him with decisions regarding national security. His efforts had mixed success.

Indeed, during his tenure as DCI Hillenkoetter had numerous detractors who claimed that he was unable to manage the intelligence community. He was blamed for the CIA's failure to have anticipated the Bogotá Riots of 1948, for the incorrect estimation of the Soviet Union's nuclear capabilities (with the Soviets' successful explosion of an atomic bomb in August 1949), and for not predicting North Korea's attack on South Korea in June 1950. Hillenkoetter continued as the head of CIA until 1950, when he was replaced by Walter Bedell Smith. He was then appointed the commander of the U.S. Navy's Seventh Task Force during the Korean War. After his retirement from active service as a vice admiral in 1957, Hillenkoetter worked for a series of private businesses. He died on June 18, 1982.

LAWRENCE R. HOUSTON

Born on January 4, 1913, in St. Louis, Missouri, Lawrence Houston graduated from Harvard College in 1935 and the University of Virginia Law School in 1939. Following U.S. involvement in World War II, Houston accepted an appointment in the Office of Strategic Services, serving in the Middle Eastern theater as a deputy chief stationed in Cairo, Egypt. Houston continued work in intelligence after the war when he accepted an appointment as general counsel for the Central Intelligence Group (an interagency organization established under President Truman's January 1946 executive order) As counsel, Houston helped draft the legislation (the National Security Act of 1947) creating the CIA. Houston continued as CIA general counsel serving from 1947 until his retirement in June 1973.

As CIA counsel, Houston played a crucial role in defining the Agency's authority and the expansion of its responsibilities, whether by helping draft legislation (the Central Intelligence Agency Act of 1949) that defined the status of CIA employees and that exempted the Agency from normal budgetary and accounting requirements, by issuing internal rulings interpreting provisions of the 1947 and 1949 laws to authorize the Agency to conduct covert operations and prepare national estimates, or defining when and under what circumstances the Agency should inform the Congress and other federal officials about the activities of its employees. In November 1947, for example, he initially advised DCI Hillenkoetter that prior congressional approval and funding would be required should the CIA conduct covert operations. Encountering opposition to such a formal request, he concluded that such operations could be conducted if requested by the National Security Council under the "other functions and duties" section of the 1947 Act. Then, in September 1949, he advised Hillenkoetter that the 1947 Act had created an independent CIA with the National Security Council's role only that of providing the "broadest type of guidance." In July–September 1950, moreover, he advised DCI Smith that the CIA had the authority to develop national estimates and need not await guidance and direction from the Departments of Defense and State. Houston also drafted in 1950 the rules governing the Agency's contracts with Air America, hiding the Agency's ownership of this airline, and in 1955 the guidelines and performance specifications for the production of the U-2 spy plane. In 1962 Houston helped negotiate a trade to exchange captured Soviet spy Rudolf Abel for Francis Gary Powers, the pilot of the U-2 plane shot down by the Soviets.

Ironically, one of Houston's last rulings as general counsel in 1972 symbolized the loss of the Agency's theretofore independence from any external oversight. In August 1972, James McCord (a former CIA counterintelligence officer who, as chief security officer for President Nixon's reelection committee, had been apprehended six weeks earlier in the Watergate break-in) advised DCI Helms by letter of his concerns that Nixon campaign officials might attempt to implicate the CIA in this break-in. Houston advised Helms that he need not inform FBI and Justice Department investigators of this (and other) McCord letters. In addition, in October 1972 Houston decided not to share McCord's letters with government prosecutors who were preparing for the trial of the seven indicted Watergate burglars. Congressional investigators subsequently learned of McCord's letters and Houston's rulings, and sharply questioned the CIA counsel about his actions—reflecting what became a departure from an earlier deference to the Agency and blind acceptance of claims for absolute secrecy.

Following his retirement in 1973, Houston continued to reside in Washington, D.C., until his death on August 15, 1995.

EVERETT HOWARD HUNT

Born on October 9, 1918, E. Howard Hunt served in both the Navy and the U.S. Army Air Forces during World War II, assisting in the production of military training films. At the start of the war, Hunt worked as a *Life* magazine war correspondent. Commissioned as a second lieutenant in the Air Corps, he eventually joined the Office of Strategic Services (OSS), where he worked in Detachment 202, the OSS Operational Group in China. In 1948 Hunt became a member of the Economic Cooperation Administration (ECA, the agency that oversaw the administration of the Marshall Plan) and served in Europe in 1948–1949.

Hunt joined the Central Intelligence Agency when his tenure with the ECA concluded in 1949. He served as the station chief in Mexico City from 1950 to 1952 and became deputy chief the following year after the formation of the CIA Clandestine Service. Hunt relocated to Washington, D.C., in 1953 to act as the Clandestine Service's chief of the Southeast Europe Division. Upon the CIA's authorization to initiate PBSUCCESS, a covert operation to overthrow the Arbenz government in Guatemala, Hunt switched to the Western Hemisphere Division, where he worked under Tracy Barnes. Along with David Atlee Phillips, Hunt was responsible for preparing and implementing the political and propaganda aspects of the Guatemala coup. In 1954 Hunt was transferred to Tokyo, where he served as chief of covert operations for the North Asia Command. From 1956 until the spring of 1960, Hunt was station chief in Montevideo, Uruguay, leaving this post to assist in the planning of the Bay of Pigs invasion of April 1961. Working with anti-Castro Cuban exiles, Hunt sought to create a government that could be installed in Cuba under a plan whereby the landing party would trigger a popular uprising and lead to the overthrow of the Castro government.

Following the operation's dismal failure, Hunt served as assistant to the CIA Director, Allen Dulles, and then joined the Domestic Operations Division. He spent a year in Madrid and then joined the Western European Division of the Clandestine Service in 1966. In 1971 he joined the Nixon White House, serving as a consultant on intelligence matters. In this capacity, he initiated an investigation intended to document the Kennedy administration's involvement in the escalation of the Vietnam War and responsibility for the assassination of South Vietnamese president Diem in early November 1963. He also worked with the White House Special Investigative Unit (the so-called Plumbers) where he recruited four Cuban Americans to participate in a 1971 break-in of the office of Daniel Ellsberg's psychiatrist (at the time of the Pentagon Papers crisis). In preparation for this break-in, Hunt contacted his former CIA colleagues for technical assistance (camera, false documents) and to prepare a psychological profile on Ellsberg. Then, in 1972, he recruited these same Cuban Americans to participate in a planned break-in to the headquarters of the Democratic National Committee in the Watergate office and apartment complex. Arrested for his role in this break-in, Hunt eventually pled guilty to burglary, conspiracy, and bugging charges. For his role, Hunt was sentenced to thirty-three months in prison. Hunt's role in the Ellsberg and Watergate break-ins caused some to question the CIA's relationship with the White House and the Agency's possible involvement in the Watergate affair, concerns that underpinned the Church and the Pike Committees' investigations of 1975. Throughout his career with the CIA and afterward Hunt was a prolific author of both fiction and nonfiction.

WILLIAM H. JACKSON

A lawyer and banker born in Nashville, Tennessee, in 1901, William H. Jackson graduated from Princeton College in 1924 and earned his law degree from Harvard. Hired by the firm Cadwalader, Wickersham, & Taft, Jackson worked there for two years before moving to the Wall Street law firm of Carter, Ledyard, & Milburn, where he became a partner in 1934. There he was instrumental in talent spotting, in the sense that he forged networks for a number of young lawyers who later became spies, notably Frank Wisner and Tracy Barnes, who also worked for Carter, Ledyard. Jackson introduced those men to Allen W. Dulles, who had earlier worked at a different Wall Street firm, Sullivan & Cromwell.

With the advent of World War II Jackson joined the U.S. Army Air Force, was commissioned a captain, and attended air intelligence school at Harrisburg, Pennsylvania. In 1943 he was assigned to U.S. headquarters in London, England, where he played a role in liaison work between U.S. military commanders and the Office of Strategic Services. Promoted to colonel, Jackson later dabbled in psychological warfare activities with U.S. military radio broadcasts and joined the intelligence staff (G-2) of the Twelfth Army Group of General Omar Bradley. He ended the war as Bradley's deputy assistant chief of staff for intelligence. In this role he coordinated intelligence activities between the OSS, represented in Europe by Colonel David Bruce, and in France, where the OSS chief was William J. Casey. His active duty ended in August 1945.

After the war Jackson returned to Carter, Ledyard, but then joined the banking firm J. H. Whitney and Company in 1947. In February 1948 Secretary of Defense James Forrestal commissioned Allen Dulles to conduct the first major outside review of U.S. government organization for intelligence. Dulles, at the time president of the Council on Foreign Relations, recruited Council members Jackson and Mathias F. Correa as the principals on this policy review. They met for almost a year at the Whitney Company offices. The Dulles-Jackson-Correa report of early 1949 furnished a blueprint for the evolution of U.S. intelligence, advocating, among other things, a strong program of covert action and a consolidation of disparate offices into coherent directorates. The report's recommendations were embodied in a presidential decision document, NSC-50, in 1949.

In 1950 General Walter Bedell Smith became the Director of Central Intelligence. As Dwight Eisenhower's chief of staff during World War II, he had dealt with Jackson and thought him well qualified to help implement the strictures of NSC-50. Smith brought Jackson on as Deputy Director of Central Intelligence (DDCI) on October 7, 1950. As DDCI William H. Jackson played an important role in Smith's decision to consolidate the Office of Policy Coordination (OPC) and the Office of Special Operations (OSO) into a single Directorate of Plans. Jackson and Smith were instrumental in recruiting another wartime colleague, Gordon Gray, to head the Psychological Strategy Board.

Jackson also helped form the "Princeton Group," a board of senior outside consultants that helped the Agency, especially its intelligence estimators, as a sounding board. Another of Jackson's innovations is the MIT Center for International Studies (CENIS), formed on the Agency's behalf by Max Millikan, whom Jackson recruited to the Directorate of Intelligence and who created CENIS as a sort of agency think tank.

Jackson carried out management studies of both OPC and OSO, and he helped establish a unified Directorate of Intelligence within the CIA. He soon found parts of the OPC and OSO especially resistant to his inquiries even though they were headed by friends (Frank Wisner). Having originally agreed to serve as DDCI only temporarily, Jackson left his post on August 3, 1951. He remained a special assistant and consultant to the DCI, however, and continued to perform chores for both DCIs Smith and Allen Dulles, Smith's successor, through 1956.

President Dwight D. Eisenhower reportedly offered Jackson the DCI position. He turned it down. Jackson nevertheless agreed to chair the President's Commission on International Information Activities. This unit recommended the abolition of the Psychological Strategy Board (PSB) and a reorganization of the National Security Council to include a new Operations Coordinating Board (OCB), which absorbed many former PSB functions. Jackson served as a consultant to Secretary of State John Foster Dulles in 1955, and a Special Assistant to President Eisenhower in 1956–1957, doing a number of chores in the security field, including acting as national security adviser for a time. He died in 1971.

Lyman Kirkpatrick once evaluated Jackson as a better intelligence officer than Allen W. Dulles. Others believe his drinking got the better of him, and that he deteriorated in effectiveness. President Eisenhower's reliance upon Jackson, however, indicates that he continued to be perceived as a valued official.

SHERMAN KENT

Sherman Kent stands among the greats of the Central Intelligence Agency. Kent innovated and regularized the process for creating National Intelligence Estimates (NIEs), the premier product of the U.S. intelligence community. Sidney Graybeal, another respected analyst, believes that no one—not even Allen Dulles—did more to make intelligence a respected profession than Kent. Deputy and successor John Huizenga, however, observes that Kent was an interesting fellow of surprisingly narrow intellectual interests, strongly oriented to the military side and often leaving political-military issues poorly covered.

Born in Chicago in 1903, Kent graduated from Yale in 1926 and returned to obtain a doctorate in history in 1933. Kent began teaching history at Yale in 1928 and continued through World War II. With the outbreak of war he joined the Office of the Coordinator of Information under William J. Donovan, which soon became the OSS. Kent became a key analyst in OSS's Research and Analysis Branch, head of its Africa section from 1941 to 1943, and its Europe-Africa Division from 1943 through the end of the war. The unit produced reports that proved critical to the U.S. invasion of French North Africa in 1942. In 1944–1945 Kent assisted in the developing investigation of the U.S. Strategic Bombing Survey. When OSS disbanded, Kent shepherded the rump Research & Analysis Branch to its new home at the State Department, where it became the Office of Research and Intelligence (OIR). He served as a consultant to the National War College and director of OIR through 1946.

When Kent left government he spent nine months on a Guggenheim fellowship writing the book *Strategic Intelligence for American World Policy* which became the basic text for the estimative trade in intelligence. It remains a classic in this field.

Kent returned to teaching history as a full professor at Yale, but was called back to government when William L. Langer, his former boss at OSS, went to the CIA to establish the Directorate of Intelligence. Langer received orders from DCI Walter Bedell Smith to create a procedure for estimating, and prevailed upon Kent to set one up. Kent established the Board of National Estimates (BNE), a corporate unit of senior intelligence analysts who managed the papers based upon contributions from the CIA and other intelligence agencies, which would then be compiled and boiled down into drafts by a subordinate Office of National Estimates.

Kent led the Board of National Estimates for eighteen years. During that time he created estimative language, a language of probability, a customary method of considering evidence, a standard procedure for accommodating the views of other intelligence agencies and departments, and procedures for checking and approving the NIEs. There were numerous disputes over NIEs during Kent's tenure, most famously including those on the Bomber Gap, Missile Gap, Vietnam, the Soviet ABM, and threats in the Taiwan Straits. Kent's methods permitted analysts to grasp these issues and debate them in a coherent fashion. Presented the President's Award for Distinguished Federal Service in 1967, he retired a year later. Kent eventually contracted Parkinson's Disease and passed away in March 1986. The CIA continues to honor him, naming its in-house unit for developing analytical techniques the Sherman Kent Center for Intelligence Analysis.

WILLIAM L. LANGER

Born on March 6, 1896, in Bolton, Massachusetts, William Langer graduated from Harvard College in 1915 with a B.A. in modern languages. Langer taught German at Worcester Academy for two years while taking courses in international relations at Clark University. Following U.S. involvement in World War I, he enlisted in the military in December 1917 serving in France in a chemical warfare unit. Rather than resuming teaching after the war,

Langer enrolled in graduate studies in European history at Harvard University, receiving his Ph.D. in 1923. After teaching at Clark University for four years, Langer returned to Harvard in 1927 as an assistant professor, where he taught modern European history, gaining promotion to associate professor in 1931 and then professor in 1936 (as the Archibald Coolidge Chair). Langer published widely in European diplomatic history, attaining the reputation as one of the nation's preeminent scholars in this field and also, from 1925 to 1936, single-handedly reviewed hundreds of books for *Foreign Affairs*, also serving on this periodical's editorial board from 1950 until his death in 1977.

With the establishment of the Office of Coordinator of Information (COI) in July 1941, Langer took a leave from Harvard to serve as its deputy chief, continuing in this role until September 1942 when he became chief of the Research and Analysis Branch of the Office of Strategic Services—COI's successor. In April 1946 he accepted another government appointment as special assistant to the secretary of state for research and intelligence. In addition to administering this office, Langer worked closely with representatives from the Navy and War Departments in defining the structure, responsibilities, and budgetary authority of the Central Intelligence Group (the interagency liaison organization established by President Truman in January 1946). Temporarily leaving the State Department to resume teaching at Harvard, Langer took another leave from the university and in November 1950 accepted appointment in the CIA as assistant director for national estimates in the Office of National Estimates. This newly established office was part of the reorganization of the Agency instituted that month by DCI Smith. In this capacity, Langer recruited (whether from the military, academe, or the private sector) individuals having expertise in the fields of "strategy, political science, economics, and other social sciences." His efforts enhanced the Agency's intelligence estimates and standing in assisting the president in formulating policy and preparing for the possibility of war. Langer permanently abandoned government service in 1952 (although he did accept a part-time appointment in 1961 to the President's Foreign Intelligence Advisory Board) to return to Harvard, where he taught diplomatic history until his retirement. In addition to his teaching responsibilities at Harvard, Langer helped establish at the University a Middle Eastern Studies Center in 1954 and in 1955 became director of Harvard's Russian Research Center. (Significantly, the Russian Research Center served as an invaluable resource for the CIA, its faculty both identifying and encouraging students to become CIA officers and suggesting research projects of particular interest to CIA analysts.) Langer died on December 26, 1977.

EDWARD GEARY LANSDALE

Born on February 6, 1908, Edward Lansdale served in both the Office of Strategic Services (OSS) and Army Intelligence during World War II. His principal duties were to conduct research for military intelligence and train agents in California and New York. After the war, he attained the rank of major and became chief of the Intelligence Division of G-2, Armed Forces/ Western Pacific, serving as deputy chief of G-2 in the Philippines until 1948. In 1947 Lansdale was promoted to captain in the Air Force, and the following year he became an instructor at the Air Force Strategic Intelligence School in Denver, Colorado. He then joined the Central Intelligence Agency, where he served in the Far East Division of the Office of Policy Coordination (the Agency's covert action branch). As a CIA officer he conducted extensive research on psychological warfare, arguing that the struggle against communism would be won by winning "the hearts and minds" of the populations of Third World countries. Conventional warfare alone would not suffice. In September 1950 he returned to the Philippines as a member of the Joint U.S. Military Advisory Group.

From 1951 to 1954, Lansdale served as the chief of the CIA's Manila Station where he devised counterinsurgency techniques to combat guerilla forces. He also emphasized the need for governments in developing countries to utilize positive propaganda and social services to obtain popular support. His actions succeeded in ending the guerrilla campaign of the Hukbalahap against the Philippine government. A fervent supporter of Ramon Magsaysay, the Philippine defense minister, Lansdale devised means by which fair elections could be conducted (through thumbprinting and voter identification).

Following the French defeat at Dien Bien Phu in May 1954 and as part of a policy of establishing an independent anticommunist government in South Vietnam, President Dwight D. Eisenhower ordered Lansdale to Vietnam, where it was hoped he could repeat his successes in the Philippines. Lansdale and several Filipino advisors created the Freedom Company of the Philippines, an organization that was funded by the CIA. Lansdale pledged full support to South Vietnam's Prime Minister Ngo Dinh Diem, helped to orchestrate the defeat of various religious sects, contributed to writing the constitution of the Republic of Vietnam, trained Diem's presidential guard, and created the Vietnamese Veterans Organization, a political support group for Diem. Relocated to the Pentagon in 1956, Lansdale served as assistant to the secretary of defense for special operations. He returned to Vietnam in 1960, and in January 1961 warned the Kennedy Administration that U.S. assistance to South Vietnam was insufficient.

President Kennedy subsequently expanded counterinsurgency operations and authorized an increase in aid to the government of South Vietnam. The president concurrently appointed Lansdale chief of operations for Operation MONGOOSE in November 1961, an authorized covert operation to promote the overthrow of the Castro government in Cuba. Not reconciled to the failure of the Bay of Pigs invasion, the administration remained committed to Castro's overthrow and hoped that MONGOOSE would be more successful. Lansdale worked in conjunction with both the State and Defense Departments, and though he wanted the operation to be political in nature, one in which anti-Castro Cubans would be placed in Cuba, he did not rule out the possibility of assassinating Castro and Communist Cuban leaders. This plan was eventually scrapped in the aftermath of the Cuban Missile Crisis of October 1962. Lansdale retired form the Air Force the following year, having attained the rank of general. From 1965 to 1968 he was the special assistant to the American Ambassador in Vietnam. In this capacity he attempted to increase political support for the Saigon government, but his efforts proved to be futile. He died on February 23, 1987.

VICTOR L. MARCHETTI

Victor Marchetti served in the U.S. Army in Germany in the early 1950s, during which time he studied Russian and was posted to the East German border. He returned to the United States to major in history and Russian studies at Pennsylvania State University and then joined the CIA in 1955, serving as a Soviet military specialist. His responsibility was to help prepare the National Intelligence Estimates on Soviet military capabilities. He soon became one of the government's top experts on Soviet military aid to Third World countries.

In 1966, Marchetti began working as a staff officer in the Office of the Director of the CIA, where he learned about the Agency's internal organization and budget. Over time, he became disillusioned with the Agency over what he believed to be its emphasis on covert action at the expense of intelligence analysis.

Following his resignation in 1969, Marchetti published a novel about the CIA, *The Rope Dancer*, in 1971. Despite his claim to have written pure fiction, the novel revealed so many details about the CIA that Agency officials sought and won a federal court ruling to censor his future writings. As other CIA employees, Marchetti had signed an agreement when becoming an agent not to reveal any classified information without the Agency's consent.

The novel's publication introduced Marchetti to many other CIA critics, who encouraged him to disclose more about the Agency's operations. Convinced that the CIA would never reform itself and that Congress lacked the will to enact reforms, Marchetti and former State Department analyst John Marks coauthored *The CIA and the Cult of Intelligence*. In their book, they argued that "a cult of intelligence" at CIA headquarters in Langley, Virginia, prevented the Agency from carrying out its prime functions of intelligence collection and analysis. "[T]he true purpose of intelligence collection—to monitor efficiently the threatening moves of international adversaries—has been distorted by the need to nourish a collective clandestine ego," Marchetti and Marks contended.

Forced to submit his manuscript for CIA review, Marchetti became outraged when Agency officials demanded hundreds of deletions. He and Marks launched what became a two-year court battle to publish the complete manuscript uncensored. An appeals court sided with the Agency, however, and the Supreme Court refused to hear the case. In the end, *The CIA and the Cult of Intelligence* was published in 1974 with 168 deletions. Marchetti's publisher left white spaces where the deleted text would have been. The effect was to highlight the scope of the Agency's censorship.

The judicial battle over Marchetti's book initiated what became a long controversy over the Agency's right to censor its ex-agents. CIA officials claimed that prepublication review was needed to protect the nation's secrets, while Marchetti (and others) insisted that this requirement undermined First Amendment rights and the public's right to know. This issue was finally settled in 1983 when the Supreme Court affirmed the Agency's right in the *Snepp* case.

JOHN A. McCONE

The only Californian to have served as Director of Central Intelligence, John Alex McCone led the CIA through the Cuban Missile Crisis and into the Vietnam war. Though coming into the agency from the outside, with no formal background in intelligence work, McCone is almost universally considered one of the greats as Director of Central Intelligence.

Born on January 4, 1902, McCone grew up in San Francisco and graduated with an engineering degree from the University of California in 1922. A staunch Republican and a convert to Catholicism, McCone was a committed Roman Catholic.

McCone's first job was as a welder, a boiler-maker for the Llewelyn Iron Works in Los Angeles. He quickly thrust his way into management and by 1933 was executive vice president of the company, which had in the meantime merged into the Consolidated Steel Company. McCone left altogether in 1937 to form with Stephen Bechtel the Bechtel-McCone Corporation, the Bechtel conglomerate of today, active in utilities, oil, and construction. The company soon became active in South America and the Middle East. McCone let Bechtel buy him out, then started the California Shipbuilding Corporation, which acquired special significance when the U.S. military in World War II required a huge expansion in shipbuilding. McCone's company built 467 ships for the government. His company also operated an aircraft modification center in Alabama for the Army Air Force. Following the war he became a shipping magnate, managing the Joshua Hendry Corporation, which had a fleet of tankers and dry cargo ships particularly active in the Pacific and Far East, plus steelworks at home.

Known as a technologist of his day, McCone's first government service was as a member of the commission appointed by President Harry Truman and chaired by Thomas K. Finletter to examine whether there should be an independent air force. Its 1948 report, "Survival in the Air Age," recommended in the affirmative. McCone briefly assisted the first Secretary of Defense, James V. Forrestal, and then in 1950 agreed to serve as undersecretary of the air force, a position he retained for about a year. In 1958 President Dwight D. Eisenhower brought McCone back to Washington as chair of the Atomic Energy Commission, serving through the end of the administration. Though some reports credit McCone with achievements in nuclear test ban agreements with the U.S.S.R., and nuclear cooperation with Western Europe, in fact inside the Eisenhower administration McCone opposed measures of arms control and any relaxation of nuclear export restrictions, such as were necessary to help Euratom, or the British and French nuclear weapons programs.

When President John F. Kennedy asked McCone in the fall of 1961 to become Director of Central Intelligence, the total of McCone's exposure to the subject amounted to analyses of the Soviet threat given to the Finletter Commission, or prevalent during the era of an alleged missile gap. McCone returned to government with a highly negative view of the Soviets. He was sworn in as a recess appointee as DCI on September 27, 1961, and confirmed by the Senate on January 31, 1962.

As DCI McCone began a reorganization of the CIA. McCone endorsed splitting off certain functions from the DDP, but his actual initiatives proved much less onerous. He also created a National Intelligence Programs Evaluation unit that facilitated community control, and the Directorate for Research (DDR), a major science unit at the CIA, leadership of which he first offered to Richard Bissell and then to Pete Scoville. The latter soon became displeased because McCone gave him science and technology responsibilities without actually consolidating the units in the field under his control. Scoville resigned in 1963, after which the desired consolidation in fact occurred, creating the Directorate for Science and Research, led by Albert Wheelon.

McCone's most celebrated moment as DCI came during the Cuban Missile Crisis. He disputed SNIEs prepared by Sherman Kent's Board of National Estimates, which took a relaxed view of the Soviet military buildup in Cuba. When McCone saw evidence of Soviet surface-to-air missile sites being built, he argued that these were intended to protect a more critical installation such as long-range missile bases. McCone proved right, his analysts wrong. On the other hand, during President Kennedy's deliberations over how to respond, McCone favored forceful options like surgical airstrikes and an invasion, which very likely would have led to war. (In covert actions against Cuba, McCone also favored the vigorous prosecution of the MONGOOSE project.)

McCone has been credited with opposing any U.S. initiative in Vietnam to get rid of Saigon leader Ngo Dinh Diem. McCone was unable to keep the Agency insulated from this activity and CIA officers were in fact so closely involved with various coup forces that attribution could not be avoided. As with Cuba, McCone favored escalatory options, and at one point elaborated an extensive program of CIA covert actions to contribute to the war, effectively ending the handover of CIA paramilitary activities in Vietnam that had begun toward the end of 1963. McCone's advocacy included OPLAN 34-A and bombing of North Vietnam in ROLLING THUNDER. His advice in early 1965 was that the United States should either get out of Vietnam or escalate strongly.

McCone's Cuba and Vietnam roles suggest that he conceived of the DCI's role as including giving policy advice. He also favored preemptive attacks on Chinese nuclear weapons facilities and so advised President Johnson.

McCone sought to curry favor with presidents. He personally delivered JFK's intelligence briefings, and thought nothing of making Kennedy a gift of a rosary that had been in his family for a years. After Lyndon Johnson succeeded Kennedy as president, the extent of McCone's contact with the White House diminished. This greatly upset the DCI, who made his displeasure known. When McCone resigned as DCI in April 1965 he told a CIA subordinate, "When I cannot get the president to read my reports, then it's time to go." Learning of McCone's concern, President Johnson instructed the White House staff to look into the number of his contacts with McCone; the inquiry showed the president had met with the DCI at least 89 times. McCone was awarded the National Security Medal upon leaving the Johnson administration.

McCone returned to his business interests. A few months later he was asked by the governor of California to chair the commission of inquiry that investigated the causes of the Watts riots in Los Angeles. One business interest eventually brought McCone back into the orbit of the CIA. McCone had become a director of the International Telephone and Telegraph Corporation (ITT), which engaged in payoffs and aspects of a political action program in Chile that paralleled similar efforts by the CIA. In 1973 McCone was called before the Senate Foreign Relations Committee to explain this activity. In 1975–1976 he defended the CIA and the intelligence community against various allegations made in the course of the Church and Pike Committee investigations. In 1987 President Ronald Reagan awarded McCone the Presidential Medal of Freedom. He lived in San Marino, California, until 1979 and after that in Pebble Beach. He died of cardiac arrest on February 14, 1991.

WALTER L. PFORZHEIMER

Born on August 15, 1914, in Purchase, New York, Walter Pforzheimer graduated from Yale College in 1935 and Yale Law School in 1938, during which time he became a trustee of the Yale Library Associates (a position which proved beneficial later). Following U.S. involvement in World War II, Pforzheimer enlisted in the military in 1942 and was stationed at the Army Air Force intelligence headquarters in Europe. Before beginning his military service, however, he exploited his contacts as a Yale library trustee to launder money to fund a sensitive Office of Strategic Services operation—under cover that the money was being spent on the university's collections. Pforzheimer did not abandon intelligence work with the end of World War II, accepting in 1946 appointment as chief of the legislative liaison division of the Central Intelligence Group (CIG). In this capacity, he helped draft that section of the National Security Act of 1947 creating a permanent centralized intelligence service, the CIA, and then lobbied Congress for its passage. He then drafted the memoranda dissolving the CIG and transferring its personnel, property, and records to the CIA.

Pforzheimer continued as legislative counsel and congressional liaison for the CIA after 1947. As counsel, he helped draft the Agency's founding guidelines (NSCID 1 and NSCID 3), outlining the duties and responsibilities of the newly created Agency and then the guidelines outlining the Agency's covert operations role (NSC 10/2). He also lobbied Congress to ensure passage of the Central Intelligence Agency Act of 1949 exempting the Agency from normal budgetary and accounting requirements. As the Agency's congressional liaison, Pforzheimer succeeded in limiting congressional oversight and also in rebuffing Senator Joseph McCarthy's threatened plan to investigate the Agency. When DCI Dulles created the Historical Intelligence Collection in 1956, he appointed Pforzheimer as the first curator. Under Pforzheimer's leadership, the Agency's collection of books on intelligence grew to 22,000 volumes, an invaluable resource and the largest such collection in the world. Retiring in 1974, Pforzheimer continued to reside in Washington, D.C., retaining his contacts with Agency personnel and serving as teacher and mentor to young intelligence officers. Informally, he was recognized as the Agency's institutional memory. Indeed, in recognition of his loyalty and long and distinguished service, the CIA's house organ, *Studies in Intelligence*, awards an annual prize in his name to the best intelligence-related article submitted by an undergraduate or graduate student, while in 1997, at the dinner commemorating the Agency's 50th anniversary, Pforzheimer was honored as a "Trailblazer." He died on February 10, 2003.

DAVID ATLEE PHILLIPS

Born on October 31, 1922, David Atlee Phillips served in the United States Army Air Forces during World War II. With the end of the war Phillips pursued a career as an actor, radio announcer, and writer. He lived and studied in Chile for several years, and, as a result of this foreign experience, was hired by the CIA as a contact agent in 1950. Initially serving as a part-time operative in the CIA Clandestine Service, he eventually became a case officer. In 1954 he and E. Howard Hunt worked on the propaganda aspects of the operation to overthrow Guatemala's president, Jacobo Arbenz. After the operation, he became a full-time employee of the Agency, and until 1955 served as a specialist in psychological warfare.

First assigned to Cuba, Phillips was relocated to Lebanon in 1957, where he posed as an American businessman for the following year and a half. He left the Agency at the end of 1958 to pursue business interests in Cuba. Rejoining the CIA in 1960, he assisted in the Bay of Pigs invasion by reprising the role he had played in Guatemala, in this case establishing a covert radio station on Swan Island. With the failure of the Cuba operation, Phillips transferred to Mexico City and functioned as a senior covert action officer. From 1965 to 1967 Phillips was the station chief in Santo Domingo, Dominican Republic. The following year he relocated to CIA headquarters and served as chief of the Cuban Operations Group of the Clandestine Service's Western Hemisphere Division. During the first few years of the 1970s, Phillips held a variety of positions within the Agency, including chief of station in Brazil and Venezuela, and chief of the Western Hemisphere Division. He retired from the CIA in 1975 at the time of the Church and Pike Committees' highly critical investigations of the CIA (and other U.S. intelligence agencies). Working with former CIA officers Ray Cline and Harry Rositzke, Phillips founded the Association of Former Intelligence Officers. Under his direction, the Association sought to rebut criticisms of the Agency's abuses of power publicized by the Church and Pike Committees. Two years later he published an acclaimed memoir of his service, *The Night Watch*. Phillips died on July 7, 1988.

VALERIE PLAME

Born on April 19, 1963, Valerie Plame came from a military family. Her father, Samuel Plame, was an Air Force officer who served in the National Security Agency for three years. After graduating from Pennsylvania State University, she sought employment with the CIA primarily because of her facility with languages, her love of travel, and her sense of public duty.

Because she was a covert operative, little is known about her CIA career. Plame did serve in the CIA's station in Athens, Greece, and had attended the London School of Economics and the College of Europe in Bruges. When living in Brussels, Belgium, she told friends that she worked as an energy analyst for Brewster Jennings & Associates. The company was a CIA front, and Plame was an operative with "non-official cover"—in other words, a spy who pretended to work for a private business. Spies with nonofficial cover have no diplomatic immunity and are vulnerable to retaliation—even assassination—by foreign governments.

In 1997, Plame moved back to Washington, D.C., in part because the Agency feared that her identity might have been revealed to the Russians by the CIA's most notorious traitor, Aldrich Ames. She soon met and married her second husband, former Ambassador Joseph Wilson. A career foreign service officer and former ambassador to Gabon (who had also served in Niger and Iraq), Wilson at the time served on the National Security Council staff of President Bill Clinton.

In 2002, Plame was assigned to the CIA's Weapons Intelligence, Non-Proliferation and Arms Control Center. She was part of a CIA team investigating whether Iraq under Saddam Hussein had bought uranium yellowcake from Niger in order to develop nuclear weapons. When Agency officials decided to send an experienced investigator to look into this matter that year, Plame suggested her husband for the job (given his earlier diplomatic assignment and contacts in that country).

Returning from his visit to Niger, Wilson concluded that the yellowcake charges were probably unfounded. He reported his doubts to the CIA and the White House. Nonetheless, in his State of the Union address of January 2003, when he laid out his case for war with Iraq, President George W. Bush stated flatly that Iraq possessed massive amounts of chemical and biological weapons, was trying to develop nuclear weapons, and had tried to buy yellowcake from Niger. The last statement was later shown to have been based on faked documents.

Convinced that the Bush administration had deliberately ignored his conclusions and had manipulated intelligence to justify its decision to invade Iraq, on July 6, 2003, Wilson published an op-ed column in the *New York Times* describing in detail his investigation of the Niger claim and his conclusion that this rumor was unfounded. If the Bush administration had purposely ignored his report because it did not support the case for war, Wilson wrote, then "a legitimate argument can be made that we went to war under false pretenses."

Eight days later, conservative columnist Robert Novak published a column that created a firestorm. Novak wrote that "two senior [Bush] administration officials" had told him that Wilson had been sent to Niger at the request of his wife, whom Novak then named and described as "an Agency operative on weapons of mass destruction." Other columnists and reporters speculated that these "senior officials" had purposely leaked Plame's name in an attempt to seek retribution against her husband. Because Novak's column had identified Plame's name, the unnamed administration officials who had provided this information had potentially violated the prohibition of the Intelligence Identities Protection Act of 1982 (enacted in response to Phillip Agee's purposeful naming of names). The 1982 Act had made it a crime to publish the name of an intelligence agent under cover. Wilson charged publicly that the leaking of his wife's name endangered her life and called for a Justice Department investigation (as did senior CIA officials).

After other journalists revealed that two Bush administration officials had called "at least six" reporters and tried to get them to print Plame's name and under pressure from the CIA over the compromising of one of its valued operatives, the Justice department belatedly launched an inquiry. Attorney General John Ashcroft recused himself from the case because of the appearance of a conflict of interest. U.S. Attorney Patrick J. Fitzgerald was appointed lead investigator and in succeeding months questioned under oath, among others, several senior White House officials, including I. Lewis Libby, Jr., chief of staff to Vice President Cheney, and White House aide Karl Rove. In February 2005,

Fitzgerald threatened two reporters (Cooper and Judith Miller of the *New York Times*) for contempt for their refusal to reveal to a grand jury the names of the White House officials who had told them of Plame's identity. Miller was cited for contempt, imprisoned for eighty-five days, and eventually testified. On October 28, 2005, a federal grand jury indicted Libby on five counts of obstruction of justice, perjury, and false statements.

FRANCIS GARY POWERS

Francis Gary Powers was born in Jenkins, Kentucky, on August 17, 1929. After graduating from Milligan College in eastern Tennessee, he joined the U.S. Air Force and was commissioned as a second lieutenant in 1952. His piloting skills led to his assignment to the top secret Strategic Air Command. In 1956 the CIA recruited him for its U-2 spy plane program. Resigning his Air Force commission so that he could serve under cover as a civilian employee of the Lockheed Aircraft Corporation, he completed the U-2 training program and was stationed in Turkey. He served with "Detachment 10-10," a unit that functioned as an undercover arm of the Weather Observational Squadron of the National Advisory Committee for Aeronautics (NACA), the precursor of the National Aeronautics and Space Administration (NASA). As a pilot of the U-2, Powers completed flights over the Soviet Union from 1956 to 1960.

While flying a U-2 over Soviet territory on May 1, 1960, Powers's plane was shot down over Sverdlovsk by a surface-to-air missile. He was subsequently detained in Moscow's Lubyanka Prison. Because his plane failed to self-destruct, Soviet officials were able to discover the purpose of Powers's photoreconnaissance mission, one that violated Soviet air space. Eisenhower administration officials at first publicly claimed that a NACA weather observation plane had inadvertently strayed into Soviet territory. Producing evidence of the plane and the captured Powers, an angered Soviet Premier Nikita Khrushchev exploited the incident to abruptly withdraw from the planned Paris summit meeting on nuclear control. After a short, highly publicized trial, Powers received a sentence of ten years in prison. On February 10, 1962, however, he was exchanged for Rudolf Ivanovich Abel, a Soviet intelligence officer whom the FBI had recently apprehended. Powers died in a helicopter crash fifteen years later on August 1, 1977.

WILLIAM F. RABORN, JR.

Vice Admiral Raborn was an unusual pick for director of Central Intelligence as much as he had been an unlikely sailor. Born in 1906 in a landlocked town in Texas and raised in Oklahoma, William Francis "Red" Raborn, Jr., always wanted to be a sailor. He got his wish with an appointment to the U.S.

Naval Academy at Annapolis. After graduating from the Naval Academy in 1928, Raborn served in battleships and destroyers until the mid-1930s, when he qualified for flight training and became a pilot. Aboard aircraft carriers and cruisers prior to World War II and as an aviation instructor early in the war, Raborn helped develop the flying techniques that sustained the U.S. Navy through the conflict. He fought in the Pacific starting in 1943 as executive officer of the aircraft carrier *Hancock*. Raborn participated in the naval campaigns of the Philippines, the South China Sea, Iwo Jima, Okinawa, and raids on the Japanese home islands.

He won the Silver Star off Okinawa, on April 7, 1945, when the *Hancock* was hit by Japanese bombs and was saved by his damage control efforts. Almost a decade later, on May 26, 1954, Raborn led a similar effort that saved a ship he himself commanded, the attack carrier *Bennington*, when he sustained a series of explosions while conducting air operations.

At the time of the *Bennington* incident Raborn was just a month past a two-year tour he had served in the Navy's Guided Missiles Division. He soon returned to that duty as rear admiral, in charge of the Navy's crash program to develop underwater-fired ballistic missiles along with new nuclear submarines to carry them. This became a wildly successful program, leading to an entirely new category of strategic nuclear weapons, all innovated in the very short interval before July 1960, when the first of these submarines proved the concept by firing two intermediate-range missiles from under the sea. In making this Polaris missile program work Raborn had had to adopt radical methods of parallel development programs as well as a new kind of budgeting technique designed to identify costs for building blocks whose prices were yet unknown. Considered a research and development expert after the Polaris experience, Raborn next served as the deputy chief of naval operations for development.

Due to the exigencies of obtaining funding for military development programs Raborn had had to develop very good relations with Congress. The budget techniques he had pioneered for the Polaris program became a key antecedent for the planned program budgeting system put into place throughout the Department of Defense (and later throughout the U.S. government) by Secretary of Defense Robert S. McNamara during the Kennedy administration.

Retiring in 1963, Raborn became an executive at the Aerojet-General Corporation. In his quest for a replacement for John McCone as Director of Central Intelligence in April 1965 President Lyndon Johnson wanted someone who had friendly relations with Congress. Quietly asking around, Johnson was given Raborn's name. Raborn was happy to serve.

Within hours of Raborn's becoming DCI the United States became embroiled in military intervention in the Dominican Republic. President Johnson's asserted reasons, to forestall a communist takeover in Santo Domingo, weakened considerably as fissures appeared in intelligence the CIA furnished the White House. Though Raborn had had no role in the Dominican affair, in the president's eyes he inevitably became linked with the CIA reporting. In fact Raborn had set up a Dominican intelligence task force within CIA, and handled himself pretty well during the crisis, but nothing he did satisfied the president.

President Johnson was aware that Raborn had no intelligence background whatsoever and had compensated by appointing Richard M. Helms as his deputy. He specifically told the admiral at their first meeting that if he wanted to see the DCI, he would call Raborn. The admiral was in time reduced to almost pathetic moves in his efforts to attract the president's attention. On one occasion Raborn clipped together a set of four or five assorted CIA reports about Vietnam and sent them to the White House as examples of what the agency was capable of doing. Apprised of complaints around Washington alleging a leadership problem at CIA, Raborn in March 1966 sent a letter defending himself to presidential aide Bill Moyers.

President Johnson made his momentous decision to commit American ground troops to major combat in South Vietnam on Raborn's watch. In point of fact the CIA delivered an important series of Special National Intelligence Estimates (SNIEs) during this period. The president did pay attention to the CIA's warnings about actions that might provoke China or Russia, but he seemed to give little weight to SNIE conclusions that Hanoi would not be dissuaded by U.S. intervention.

Raborn considered himself a quick study and was very operationally minded. Colleagues recall that in meetings where they would lay out some problem, before they could finish explaining, the admiral would invariably pick up the phone to call someone to supply the answer. Caught unawares, those people almost never had the answers sought. Ironically, with congressional relations considered his strong suit, Raborn insisted that Richard Helms accompany him each time he testified on Capitol Hill, while he delegated completely to Helms the task of briefing congressmen who requested it. Raborn initially started his directorship by holding a series of get-acquainted Sunday brunches but gave up as the awkwardness of the practice became plain.

Raborn did accomplish some things during his tenure as DCI. He installed a variant of his budgeting method which greatly facilitated the Agency's ability to plan multiyear budget programs. He also ordered a study of intelligence objectives for ten to fifteen years into the future as an aid to future planning. Raborn set up planning, budgeting, and evaluation groups within each CIA directorate. He proved especially instrumental in hammering out working arrangements between the CIA, the Department of Defense, and the newly formed National Reconnaissance Office. The DCI also ordered the creation of a special Vietnam task force to handle war issues that became the foundation for the office of the Special Assistant for Vietnam Affairs (SAVA). Finally, Raborn supported initiatives to create a twenty-four-hour Operations Center at the CIA.

On June 8, 1966, Raborn advised President Johnson of his intention to leave the CIA. He recommended Richard Helms as his replacement, and Vice Admiral Rufus L. Taylor for DDCI. Raborn left the agency at the end of June to return to the Aerojet-General company, where he worked until 1969. He then opened his own consulting firm, which he operated until 1986. Raborn died in Washington in March 1990.

KERMIT ROOSEVELT

The grandson of President Theodore Roosevelt, Kermit Roosevelt was born on February 16, 1916. In 1941, Roosevelt joined the Office of the Coordinator of Information (predecessor of the Office of Strategic Services, OSS) and worked in the OSS Secret Intelligence Branch during his five years with the service. He joined the Central Intelligence Agency shortly after its creation in 1947 as a special assistant in political operations to the CIA Clandestine Service chief. Roosevelt oversaw the installation of Gamal Abdel Nasser to power in Egypt after the 1952 coup deposed King Farouk. In 1953 he organized and carried out TPAJAX, the CIA's covert operation in Iran in which Roosevelt and other CIA operatives cooperated with Britain's Secret Intelligence Service (SIS) to overthrow Prime Minister Mohammed Mossadegh and return Shah Mohammed Reza Pahlavi to the Peacock Throne. After nearly a decade's worth of service as a Near East specialist, Roosevelt left the CIA in 1957 to pursue a career in public relations. He died on June 8, 2000.

JAMES R. SCHLESINGER

Born on February 15, 1929, in New York City, James Schlesinger received his B.A. in 1950, M.A. in 1952, and Ph.D. in economics in 1956 from Harvard University. In 1955, before completing his doctorate, he accepted an appointment as assistant professor of economics at the University of Virginia, where he taught until 1963 when he became the director of strategic studies at the RAND Corporation. Schlesinger resigned from RAND in 1969 to become Assistant Director of the Bureau of the Budget in the Nixon Administration, serving until 1971 when President Nixon appointed him Chairman of the Atomic Energy Commission. Schlesinger resigned this position in February 1973 when President Nixon nominated him as Director of Central Intelligence. Schlesinger's brief career as DCI ended on May 10, 1973 when President Nixon nominated him as Secretary of Defense. Confirmed by the Senate on July 2, Schlesinger served until November 2, 1975 when President Ford dismissed him over differences concerning the Defense Department's budget and as part of his restructuring of national security operations (including dismissing DCI Colby and nominating George H. W. Bush as his successor). Following Jimmy Carter's election to the presidency, in January 1977 Schlesinger agreed to serve as the president's special adviser on energy policy until, with the creation of the Department of Energy, he became the first Secretary of Energy in October 1977 and served in this position until July 1979. Thereafter, Schlesinger followed closely and was consulted frequently on national security policy, served on various corporate boards, in October 2003 testified as a member of the "Intelligence and the War on Terror" panel convened by the Kean Commission, and in 2004 headed a special commission investigating the Abu Ghraib prison scandal.

Schlesinger's brief tenure as DCI coincided with the onset of public and congressional inquiries into the Watergate break-in scandal and related questions about the CIA's relationship with the Nixon White House, the Watergate burglars, and a suspected cover-up. As DCI, Schlesinger instituted far-reaching personnel changes, firing or pushing into early retirement 1,500 employees (most in the Agency's operations division) and dismantled the Office of National Estimates. In addition, he ordered a special internal inquiry into any illegal activities conducted by CIA personnel. The resultant report, informally known as "The Family Jewels," proved to be one catalyst to subsequent media exposés and to the 1975 inquiries into the Agency's abuses of power launched by the Church and Pike Committees.

WALTER BEDELL SMITH

Walter Bedell "Beetle" Smith was born on October 5, 1895, and began a military career in 1910 when he enlisted in the Indiana National Guard. Commissioned a second lieutenant after enrolling in the Army Reserve Officer Training Corps (ROTC) in 1917, Smith served in Europe during World War I. Smith was wounded in France during the war, and was eventually promoted to first lieutenant. Smith continued in the military after the war, joining the War Department Bureau of Military Intelligence. During the interwar years Smith furthered his military education by attending the Infantry School at Fort Benning, Georgia, the Command and General Staff School at Fort Leavenworth, Kansas, and the Army War College. By 1939 he had attained the rank of major and was employed by the War Department General Staff.

In 1941, by then a lieutenant colonel, Smith was appointed secretary of the General Staff. He became secretary of both the newly created Joint Chiefs of Staff and then of the U.S.-British Combined Chiefs of Staff. In September 1942 General Dwight D. Eisenhower appointed him chief of staff and he served in that capacity during the North African Campaign. He eventually became chief of staff of the Supreme Headquarters, Allied Expeditionary Force (SHAEF). In this position he oversaw all operations in the European Theater, and in 1945 the Army promoted him to the rank of lieutenant general. From 1946 until 1949 Smith served as President Harry Truman's ambassador to the Soviet Union. While commanding the First Army at Governor's Island, NY, in March 1949, Smith earned his fourth star.

The following year Smith succeeded the beleaguered Roscoe Hillenkoetter as director of the Central Intelligence Agency. Disappointed that he would never serve as Army chief of staff, he threw his considerable energy into fundamentally restructuring the agency to increase its effectiveness. Smith placed the Office of Policy Coordination (OPC, the Agency's quasi-independent covert action arm) under the Agency's direct control, created the Office of National Estimates and the Board of National Estimates, and named Allen Dulles, who had served in the Office of Strategic Services (OSS), as deputy director. With Dulles's help, he created the CIA Clandestine Service, although he personally was not enthusiastic about covert operations. Smith left the agency in 1953 when President Eisenhower appointed him undersecretary of state. When the next year Secretary of State John Foster Dulles abruptly left the Geneva conference convened to address the status of Korea (following the armistice agreement of 1953) and Indochina (in response to the French decision to withdraw militarily from Indochina) in the midst of allied disharmony, Smith became America's chief delegate. Later that year he retired to private business. He died on August 9, 1961.

FRANK SNEPP

Born in 1943 in Kinston, North Carolina, Frank Snepp grew up in a genteel Southern family. He later claimed that his North Carolina upbringing prepared him for the lies and dissimulations of an Agency career. "Growing up in a culture that can blithely portray a war to preserve slavery as a crusade to protect states' rights is a wonderful preparation for a career of endless charade," he wrote in his 1999 memoir, *Irreparable Harm*. After receiving his B.A. from Columbia University in 1965, he enrolled in Columbia's School of International Affairs and was there recruited by the CIA. In 1969, he was assigned to "the steaming chaos of wartime Saigon."

As the chief strategic analyst in the CIA's Saigon station, Snepp earned the confidence of U.S. Ambassador to South Vietnam Graham Martin and station chief Tom Polgar. By the early 1970s, however, he began to have doubts about the wisdom of American intervention in Vietnam. He suppressed these concerns and continued to win promotions for his work.

As the North Vietnamese Army closed in on Saigon in 1975, Snepp watched with horror as Martin and Polgar refused to anticipate what Snepp saw as an inevitable communist victory. Then, when North Vietnamese troops surrounded the Saigon embassy, CIA operatives failed to destroy many secret documents or even draw up a list of Agency sources to be evacuated. When Southern resistance collapsed, U.S. intelligence and military personnel were airlifted out of Saigon. Snepp was one of the last CIA employees to board a helicopter on the roof of the U.S. embassy on April 29, 1975, and abandon Saigon. In despair, he looked out of the window and saw "thousands of Vietnamese jammed in the streets below, gazing skyward for the help that would never come."

Snepp returned to the United States deeply angry with the U.S. officials who had failed to plan properly for the evacuation. He first requested an internal CIA investigation into why so many friends and assets had been left behind, but discovered a lack of enthusiasm for such a project. Accordingly, he resigned and wrote a personal account of the evacuation, *Decent Interval: An Insider's Account of Saigon's Indecent End.* His book sharply criticized Ambassador Martin, Secretary of State Henry Kissinger, and senior CIA officials. "[I]n terms of squandered lives, blown secrets and the betrayal of agents, friends and collaborators," Snepp wrote, "our handling of the evacuation [of Saigon] was an institutional disgrace. Not since the abortive Bay of Pigs invasion of 1961 had the agency put so much on the line, and lost it through stupidity and mismanagement."

In 1978, the Justice Department filed a civil suit against Snepp, claiming that when publishing his book he had violated the secrecy agreement he had signed when he began work for the CIA. In response, Snepp contended that the book was not subject to pre publication censorship because it contained no classified information. He further maintained that the agreement itself violated his First Amendment rights. While conceding that Snepp had not revealed anything classified, CIA officials nonetheless argued that he had forfeited his First Amendment rights when he signed the pre publication agreement as a condition for his employment. By a 6–3 vote, the Supreme Court ruled against Snepp.

The *Snepp* decision had a chilling effect on other disaffected CIA agents, and few critical memoirs appeared in the following years. Because of this ruling, Snepp was forced to repay the CIA the $118,000 in royalties he had earned from *Decent Interval.* Snepp subsequently had a successful career in investigative journalism, working at various times for *20/20, Nightline,* and *World News Tonight with Peter Jennings,* among other television and radio shows.

SIDNEY W. SOUERS

Sidney Souers was born on March 30, 1892, and began his professional career as a businessman in New Orleans, Louisiana. In 1929 Souers joined the U.S. Naval Reserve as a lieutenant commander. In 1932 he became senior intelligence officer in St. Louis, Missouri, where he engaged in military investigations and began to lay the foundations for an intelligence organization. Souers was placed on active duty in 1940, and during World War II served as an intelligence officer in Puerto Rico, where he devised countermeasures for antisubmarine warfare. Souers eventually earned the rank of rear admiral. During the final two years of the war, he served as assistant director, and then deputy chief, of the Office of Naval Intelligence (ONI) in Washington, D.C.

After the war Souers was a pivotal advocate for a unified intelligence system. The influential (Ferdinand) Eberstadt Report incorporated the proposal, and President Harry Truman accepted it as the basis for legislation that Congress enacted in 1947 authorizing the creation of the Central Intelligence Agency. In the interim, the president in 1946 appointed Souers director of the Central Intelligence Group, the precursor to the CIA. As the first director of central intelligence, he laid the foundations for the organization of the CIA. Leaving after only six months of service, Souers accepted President Truman's request of May 1947 to create an intelligence organization for the Atomic Energy Commission. He subsequently became executive secretary of the National Security Council (also established by the 1947 National Security Act), where he remained until 1950, when he returned to his business pursuits. Souers nonetheless continued to serve as consultant to the president on security matters until Dwight D. Eisenhower took office in 1953. He spent the remainder of his life in private business until his death on January 14, 1973.

GEORGE J. TENET

But for the questions that arose regarding CIA's performance in the period prior to the U.S. invasion of Iraq in 2003, and its warnings, or lack thereof, before the terrorist attacks of September 11, 2001, George J. Tenet might have gone down in history as the greatest Director of Central Intelligence. He was certainly one of the longest-serving—upon his July 2004 retirement Tenet was just a few months away from passing Allen W. Dulles (1953–1961), who continues to hold that record. This is especially remarkable for a man who came from outside the professional ranks of either analysts or clandestine service.

Tenet's rise can be seen as the triumph of the system of legislative oversight of intelligence in the United States, for his roots lay in the Congress and its staffs, not in the field of intelligence operations. Born in January 1953 in Flushing, New York, he graduated from Benjamin Cardozo High School in Bayside, Queens. Of Greek-American parentage, Tenet's father came to the United States before the Great Depression, and his mother escaped from Albania in a submarine just before the communist takeover. Tenet arrived in Washington in the early 1970s to attend Georgetown School of Foreign Service, where he received his Bachelor of Arts degree in 1976. He then returned to New York and studied at Columbia University's School of International Affairs (SIA, now the School of International and Public Affairs), from which he obtained a Master's degree in 1978.

In 1982 Tenet joined the staff of Pennsylvania Republican Senator H. John Heinz. Several years later he moved to the staff of Vermont Democrat Senator Patrick J. Leahy, who made George Tenet his staff representative on the Senate Select Committee on Intelligence. The New Yorker's work among the staff delegates proved so highly regarded that in 1988 he was asked to head the SSCI staff as a whole, which he did for five years. The high point undoubtedly was the wide inquiry that took place during Robert M. Gates's confirmation hearings as DCI. On that occasion SSCI chairman Senator David Boren (D-OK) placed Tenet in charge.

In 1993 National Security Adviser Anthony Lake asked Tenet to join the NSC staff as a director for intelligence programs. This request was unusual since NSC intelligence staffers were invariably intelligence officers detached from their agencies. Tenet, however, was regarded as so well versed in the intelligence community's programs that he could effectively ride herd on them for the White House. Before long he became senior director for these matters on the NSC staff.

Tenet proved adept at serving many masters. For example, when the United States reached a diplomatic agreement with North Korea that promised to halt that country's quest for nuclear weapons contingent on certain Western, Japanese, and South Korean aid, and congressional support for the unpopular North Korean regime was at a premium, Tenet stepped forward to volunteer weekly reports from the NSC staff to reassure doubters on Capitol Hill. He simultaneously satisfied the CIA that he was not giving away the store, and President William J. Clinton that he was preserving White House prerogatives.

In 1995 Clinton selected Tenet as Deputy Director of Central Intelligence under DCI John Deutch. Tenet quickly gained Deutch's confidence. Deutch liked to tell the story of how Tenet saved him from an embarrassing episode with foreign officials—shepherding them out of the room on the excuse he had top secret information to impart to the DCI, then telling Deutch he had left the fly down on his pants. During his confirmation as DDCI Tenet described his aims for the intelligence community as improving its relations with Congress, providing "actionable" intelligence, reengineering the intelligence community, revitalizing the Directorate of Operations, and reinvigorating the CIA counterintelligence effort.

Deutch left the agency in December 1996, leaving George Tenet as acting DCI. President Clinton first nominated Anthony Lake to succeed Deutch, but differences over the handling of Bosnia policy threatened the confirmation and Lake withdrew. Clinton thereupon selected Tenet as Director of Central Intelligence. Confirmed easily, Tenet was sworn in on July 11, 1997. His aims remained essentially the same as they had been two years before. He has been credited with restoring a sense of purpose, bringing the Agency out of its post–Cold War doldrums.

Director Tenet did indeed succeed at many things. He improved the CIA's relationship with its congressional overseers, introduced more DCI "fusion" centers, and continued some declassification initiatives begun under Robert M. Gates. But Tenet also absorbed many of the values of the intelligence elite. Though the DCI loved history, under his direction the CIA remained recalcitrant about declassifying documents regarding the John F. Kennedy assassination, CIA activities in Chile in the 1970s, and the Agency's relationships with Nazis after World War II. In each case acts of Congress or presidential decisions forced these documents into the open. The CIA declassification program essentially released little more than old intelligence estimates about the Soviet Union.

An extraordinary development on Tenet's watch was the DCI's evolution into a regular diplomatic player. He gained such confidence on both the Israeli and Palestinian sides of the Intifada that both began to rely upon him as an arbiter and go-between. Tenet and the CIA became active participants in building confidence between the sides by helping coordinate their security efforts and hosting meetings between their chiefs of security services. About the time of the Wye negotiation the Israelis presumed upon their favorable relationship with the United States to demand the release of convicted spy Jonathan J. Pollard. When Secretary of State Madeleine Albright told Tenet of this he complained that any such release would send the signal that the right friends could make all the difference to any spy. Albright agreed. Tenet went to President Clinton and threatened to resign were Pollard released. Clinton records that he did not want to release Pollard himself and "Tenet's comments closed the door."

As early as 1998 Tenet agitated, in public speeches and private initiatives, for increasing the CIA's clandestine service and revitalizing its Directorate of Operations. Yet that same year the Agency's budgeters cut funds from the program of the Counterterrorist Center. Tenet restored the money when he heard about it, and he lobbied Congress for budgets that provided organic growth in the DO, rather than supplemental funds that could not be used to plan a program. This success proved limited. In 2002 Director Tenet reported that it would take five years or more to rebuild the DO, suggesting that little progress had in fact been made.

In the wake of the 1998 al Qaeda terrorist strikes on American embassies in Africa, DCI Tenet's directive to the intelligence community effectively declared war on the terrorists, but again little seemed to flow from the action. None of the plans crafted by the Counterterrorist Center (CTC) to go after al Qaeda leaders was actually implemented. Officers at CTC record that the intelligence on each occasion was discounted as not "actionable." Tenet had failed in at least one of the areas, promoting "responsible risk-taking," where he had promised reform as early as 1995.

President George W. Bush invited Tenet to stay on as DCI when he entered office in January 2001. Tenet's links with the Bush White House were as close as those he had had with Clinton. This later put the CIA into a very uncomfortable situation when the Bush administration wanted to go after Saddam Hussein of Iraq. Tenet's quip that the intelligence on Saddam's possession of weapons of mass destruction was a "slam dunk" in terms of its quality proved to be clearly off base, and in fact had been based on little concrete evidence at all, as subsequent investigations established beyond doubt. Critics inside the CIA during Tenet's last years maintained that he had in fact become too close to the White House. That was certainly the case when, in the summer of

2003, Tenet stepped in to take for the CIA the blame that belonged to Bush's NSC staff and political advisers for manipulating intelligence to support the Iraq war.

The Iraq intelligence failure was just one of a number of similar incidents that occurred on Tenet's watch. Anomalies occurred across the board, from the rather light touch the CIA applied to John Deutch, who was shown to have taken home secret documents and unsecured computers that held classified information; to the tragic shooting down of American missionaries in a plane over Peru in a CIA-sponsored antidrug project; to the map error in 1999 that led to the U.S. bombing of the Chinese embassy in Yugoslavia. Tenet was also accused in the late 1990s of having given up on a covert operation against Saddam Hussein by Iraqi dissidents, charges that may have contributed to his coddling of the Iraqi opposition when they supplied the CIA with phony claims about Saddam's weapons. Another "slam dunk" error similar to his claim in 2002 that Iraq possessed weapons of mass destruction came in August 1998, when Tenet professed CIA certainty that a Sudanese chemical plant was used to fabricate chemical weapons, a plant subsequently shown to have no such role, and thus not the immediate candidate for the U.S. military retaliation aimed at al Qaeda after the embassy bombings. In the early summer of 1998 the CIA also failed to have predicted the successful Indian nuclear weapons tests. The overarching error, however, remained the CIA's failure either to combat al Qaeda effectively in the years leading up to September 11, or to provide effective warning of those plots themselves.

The degree of Tenet's personal responsibility for these various events will determine how he is finally evaluated as DCI. The evaluation may well be a positive one, much as Allen Dulles is remembered as the CIA's great spy master, and not for the debacle at the Bay of Pigs.

STANSFIELD TURNER

Born in Highland Park, Illinois, in December 1923, Stansfield Turner had originally attended Amherst College (1941–1943), but then won an appointment to the U.S. Naval Academy. His Annapolis studies came during a period of foreshortened training that prevailed in World War II. Turner graduated as a midshipman in June 1946, having played on the football team and won a Rhodes Scholarship. Future president Jimmy Carter had been a member of the same class at Annapolis. Once elected president in 1976, Carter remembered Turner, who by then was a full admiral stationed in Naples as the commander in chief of the Southern Region of the North Atlantic Treaty Organization. By his own account Turner considered that he had been shunted aside and ruled out for the top navy job, and was thinking of retirement when, on February 2, 1977, he received a telephone call to meet with the president the next day. Thinking that President Carter was considering some military job, Turner was instead offered the position of Director of

Central Intelligence. Announced on February 8, Turner achieved easy confirmation and was sworn in on March 9.

Stansfield Turner had had a distinguished navy career. He served in destroyers before becoming a Rhodes Scholar at Oxford, where he studied economics, politics, and history and received a Master's Degree in 1950. He subsequently commanded a minesweeper, a destroyer, and a guided missile cruiser. Promoted to rear admiral, Turner commanded a carrier task group with the Sixth Fleet in the Mediterranean. A strong supporter of the reformist chief of naval operations, Admiral Elmo R. "Bud" Zumwalt, Turner believed that this support had marked him as a troublemaker among more conservative navy circles. For Zumwalt Admiral Turner directed the systems analysis division on the naval staff. Then promoted to vice admiral, Turner became president of the Naval War College, where he introduced serious study programs between 1972 and 1974, and then commanded the Second Fleet.

As had happened under DCI Raborn, Turner initially selected an intelligence professional as deputy director of central intelligence. Through the summer of 1977 that individual was E. Henry ("Hank") Knocke, and afterwards Frank C. Carlucci, a diplomat and widely experienced government official who had once worked with the CIA in Africa. Turner got on quite well with Carter and remained as DCI throughout the Carter administration. The director initially met with the president every week, then every couple of weeks, and finally only occasionally.

Turner's tenure at the CIA proved stormy. He angered rank-and-file agency officers by drafting a series of naval officers whom he trusted. This "Navy mafia" may have given Turner a cadre of loyal subordinates but to Agency people it indicated his distrust.

A series of gaffes also did little to improve Turner's standing among the intelligence officers. In one instance Turner, while vacationing on a Caribbean island, sent out an all-stations cable to CIA posts around the world reminding them of the need to give their all. Officers unable to take vacations were not pleased. Some took to calling him "Standstill Burner."

By far the most damaging incident for Agency morale involved his implementation of a so-called Reduction in Force (RIF) carried out in 1977–1978. The execution of this move proved ham-handed, with pink slips simply inserted into officers' mailboxes, although the move may have been made deliberately by opponents of the RIF to make the DCI look bad. A management study under Turner's predecessor as DCI, George H. W. Bush, had concluded that the Directorate of Operations contained 1,350 personnel slots more than required, and recommended these be eliminated over a five-year period. Director Turner had also concluded that overstaffing existed, basing this conclusion on three kinds of evidence: the subject kept coming up in informal talk sessions he had with mid-career officers; the CIA kept having to use senior officers in subordinate positions as there were no available slots at their grade levels; and Turner himself received such a plethora of responses when he asked questions that it seemed there were people around with nothing better to do. Determined to correct the situation, he decided to do so over a shorter period (two years), and to make a smaller overall reduction, totaling 820 positions. This was accomplished primarily by personnel attrition, slowing hiring while older officers retired, died, or left the CIA. Only 147 officers were forced into retirement, and just 17 were actually fired. Nonetheless, he was publicly accused of having fired anywhere between 820 and 2,000 people. The retirees, moreover, had been selected purely based upon efficiency reports, resulting in some inequities that flowed from the standard kinds of personal conflicts that exist in any large bureaucracy, and some of these actions were reversed in court cases or by administrative review. Most of the RIF, Turner pointed out, consisted of trimming fat at management levels in headquarters, not cutting back the clandestine service in the field.

Turner's other management reforms included consolidating CIA personnel services, setting up a single office in place of separate ones for each Agency directorate. Turner also reorganized the agency's analytical component, retitling it the National Foreign Assessment Center (NFAC) rather than the Directorate of Intelligence (an action reversed by his successor), and creating offices that dealt with substantive (functional) areas rather than geographic regions. He replaced Sayre Stevens, a CIA professional, with Robert Bowie, a former diplomat and Harvard academic, at the head of NFAC. Turner also installed an outsider to head the DO, John McMahon, whose background was in technical collection. The alternation between functional versus regional staffs at the DI has continued within CIA since Turner's watch.

Turner took seriously his role as DCI. He considered himself the leader of the full U.S. intelligence community, relying upon Knocke, and then Carlucci, as the primary managers for the CIA itself. Under Turner the Intelligence Community Staff, headed by another admiral, Daniel Murphy, acquired additional importance. Decades later, after the September 11, 2001, terrorist attacks made community reorganization a front-burner issue, Turner became a strong supporter of the concept of creating the post of Director of National Intelligence (DNI), a measure actually adopted in legislation enacted in December 2004.

The most serious international intelligence issue during Turner's tenure involved the fall of the Shah of Iran and the subsequent Iranian hostage crisis. The Agency's shortsighted analysis of the shah's strength during the months before his fall in 1978 was called into question; later weaknesses in the CIA's intelligence preparations for a mission to rescue American diplomats held hostage in Iran, which failed in April 1980, also adversely affected the CIA. It is not clear whether Turner, had he taken a more hands-on role as CIA director, could have changed any of these outcomes. In any case the Iran failure colored the entire perception of CIA performance during the Carter administration.

Turner, moreover, came to the CIA at a time when highly conservative critiques of intelligence predictions on Soviet nuclear forces were rampant in Washington. Turner imposed some discipline on the National Intelligence Estimates but did not turn them away from certain deep pessimisms regarding Soviet strategic forces. In 1994, when many of the Soviet NIEs of Turner's time were declassified, he told a conference held to mark the event: "Our estimate, in my view, in spite of having a great deal of very good information, was not a help to the president. What it should have said to him, in my view was simply two words: too much. We and the Soviets both had too much nuclear firepower to need any more."

Turner suffered critical injuries, and his wife Eli Karen was killed, in January 2000 while visiting Costa Rica, when the plane in which they were traveling crashed upon take-off. Turner subsequently recovered and continues to work as a consultant and commentator.

HOYT SANFORD VANDENBERG

Born on January 24, 1899, Hoyt Vandenberg graduated from West Point in 1923, and then attended the Advanced Flying School at Kelly Field, Texas. He completed the Air Corps Tactical School at Maxwell Field, Alabama, in 1935, the Command and General Staff School at Fort Leavenworth, Kansas, in 1936, and the United States Army War College at Carlisle Barracks, Pennsylvania, in 1939. With his completion of the War College curriculum and promotion to the rank of major, Vandenberg went to work for the Plans Division in the Office of the Chief of the Air Corps. After America's entry into World War II he was promoted to colonel in January 1942 and, due to his pivotal role in the expansion of the Army Air Forces, earned the Distinguished Service Medal. He was a member of General Henry H. Arnold's staff and chief of staff to General James Doolittle of the Twelfth Air Force.

Stationed in both England and North Africa during the war, Vandenberg flew twenty-six combat missions over North Africa and Italy. His flight career ended in the summer of 1943 when he became a deputy chief of the Air Staff in Washington, D.C. Vandenberg was also a member of Ambassador Averell Harriman's October 1943 diplomatic mission to the Soviet Union, and attended the wartime summit conferences in Quebec, Tehran, and Cairo. Three months prior to the D-day landings in Normandy, Vandenberg returned to England as deputy commander of the Allied Expeditionary Air Forces. In August 1944 he commanded the Ninth Air Force, and the following summer was promoted to assistant chief of staff for operations of the Army Air Forces, ultimately finishing the war as a lieutenant general.

General Dwight D. Eisenhower named Vandenberg chief of Army Intelligence in January 1946. He served in this capacity until June 1946 when President Harry Truman appointed him director of the Central Intelligence Group (CIG), serving in this post until May 1, 1947. As director, he increased the agency's funding and promoted independent intelligence research and analysis. During his tenure the CIG took over intelligence-gathering operations in Latin America from the Federal Bureau of Investigation (FBI). But his loyalty always remained with the Air Force, which became an independent branch of America's military in 1947. In 1948, by then a general and enjoying the political benefits attendant to being the nephew of Michigan's powerful Senator Arthur Vandenberg, he became the Air Force's second Chief of Staff. Vandenberg retired in 1953 and died on April 2, 1954 as a result of complications from prostate cancer.

WILLIAM H. WEBSTER

Born on March 6, 1924, in St. Louis, Missouri, William Webster served in the navy during World War II, following which he graduated from Amherst College in 1947. Returning to St. Louis to attend Washington University Law School, Webster graduated in 1949 and remained in that city to practice law from 1949 through 1969, interrupted temporarily first by naval service during the Korean war (reaching the rank of lieutenant) and then a brief stint in 1960–1961 as U.S. attorney for the eastern district of Missouri. Appointed by President Nixon as judge of the U.S. District Court in the eastern district of Missouri in 1970, Webster served until elevated by President Nixon to the U.S. Court of Appeals for the Eighth District in 1973. Webster left the bench when President Carter nominated him as FBI director, assuming this post on February 23, 1978. He resigned from this position on March 3, 1987, following his nomination by President Reagan as Director of Central Intelligence. Webster served as DCI until retiring in May 1991.

Webster's tenure as DCI came at a critical period in the Agency's history. First, he assumed office at the beginning of a series of congressional and criminal inquiries into the Iran-Contra scandal, investigations that examined, among other questions, the role of Agency officials in a covert operation that involved the sale of arms to Iran and the diversion of some of the proceeds from these sales to the Nicaraguan contras. Because of questions about the legality of this operation (in violation of the Intelligence Oversight Act, the Arms Export Control Act, and the so-called Boland amendment) and then the truthfulness of CIA officials in their responses to questions of congressional investigators (as well as the so-called Tower Commission), an independent counsel, Lawrence Walsh, was appointed to consider criminal prosecution. A federal grand jury eventually indicted four CIA officers (Clair George, Duane Clarridge, Alan Fiers, and Joseph Fernandez) for perjurious testimony and false statements to congressional investigators and to the Tower Commission when denying knowledge of aspects of this covert operation. Second, Webster's tenure coincided with the collapse of communist governments in Eastern Europe and the Balkans and the eventual dissolution of the Soviet Union in the years 1989–1991. Questions were raised about the Agency's failure to have anticipated the scope and rapidity of the collapse of Soviet communism and about the Agency's role in a post–Cold War world. Third, Webster assumed office at a time of heightened interest about a new international threat, that of terrorism, and the objectives of the Iraqi government of Saddam Hussein (the latter culminating in the Iraqi invasion of Kuwait in August 1990). The concern about terrorism had led to the creation in 1986 of a Counterterrorist Center within the Agency to coordinate counterterrorism operations within the Agency and among all fifteen U.S. intelligence agencies. In contrast to the late 1990s and early 2000s, however, the terrorist threat was then seen as being regional in character, mainly in the Middle East, and directed by governments (Iran, Libya) or Palestinian militants. The catalysts to this heightened interest included the kidnaping of American citizens in the Middle East (notably, the CIA station chief in Lebanon, William Buckley), terrorist attacks at a West Berlin discotheque and airports in Rome, Italy, and Vienna, Austria, and discovery that the Libyan government was constructing a chemical weapons plant.

RICHARD S. WELCH

Colleagues remember Richard Welch as impatient with bureaucracy and capable of tweaking the system almost outrageously when he thought it obtuse. Blind in one eye, he nevertheless received a perfect score on his CIA medical exam—because the optometrist had used an eye chart bearing a Roman history text from Gibbon that Welch happened to have memorized. (Welch's blindness had been the result of an accident at home with an ice-pick, back in the days when refrigerators had to be packed with ice.)

Born in Hartford, Connecticut, in December 1929, Welch was the son of a soldier and businessman. He attended a private high school in Providence, Rhode Island, that taught classics and then followed his father to Harvard College from which he graduated in Greek studies, magna cum laude, in 1951. Welch entered the CIA directly out of college with his first overseas assignment in Athens. He served there from 1952 to 1957, earning a commendation from DCI Allen Dulles. After a headquarters tour Welch was assigned to Cyprus in 1960, serving four years, in the course of which his first marriage broke up. On that tour he promised to produce a thousand reports before leaving, and reached exactly that number just as he boarded his departing flight. During a subsequent assignment to Guatemala City in 1966–1967 Welch met Maria Christina Hartleleben, personal secretary to the Guatemalan foreign minister, and they married on his birthday in 1967. Welch was then posted as chief of station in Georgetown, Guyana, during 1968–1969, for which he won the Intelligence Medal of Merit. Following another headquarters tour he went to Peru in 1972 as station chief in Lima, the post he held until reassigned to head the CIA station in Athens in 1975. At that time he was promoted to a supergrade position (GS-17) at the CIA.

Welch survived a bad bout with hepatitis in 1974 only to succumb to an assassin's bullet in Athens. His death was doubly ironic since the poor security situation in South America had led CIA officials, in 1974, to move the regular meeting among regional chiefs of station to Camp Peary, where the CIA officers were given refresher training in weapons and defensive tactics. As chief of station in Athens, however, Welch evidently did not practice the tradecraft he had been taught. He lived in the home used by his predecessor even though the address of the home, owned by the U.S. government, had been identified and was even included on tours of the city. He also failed to vary his route to work each day despite having been warned by CIA headquarters to exercise greater caution. Three masked men awaited Welch when he and his wife returned from the embassy Christmas party on December 23, 1975. Welch died from a bullet fired from a .45-caliber gun.

Welch's most important contribution derived from the impact of his death, manipulated by the Ford administration to strike back at investigators questioning U.S. intelligence activity. This effort succeeded as the House voted on January 28, 1976, to bar the release of the Pike Committee's final reports until first reviewed and cleared by the Ford administration. Welch's murder also became a major justification for the later enactment in 1982 of the Intelligence Identities Protection Act. When lobbying Congress to enact this measure, Ford (and later Carter and Reagan) administration spokespersons, then-CIA director William E. Colby, CIA spokesman Angus Thuermer, and other CIA employees had in 1976 and in succeeding years repeatedly charged that Welch lost his life because he had been "fingered" by an anti-CIA crusading magazine in the U.S. called *Counterspy*. The law subsequently provoked a quite different controversy in 2003–2005 when employed to investigate the leak of CIA operative Valerie Plame's name by "senior" Bush administration officials to syndicated columnist Robert Novak in July 2003, in apparent violation of the 1982 Act.

In fact, however, no part of the tangled web of charges about Welch's murder are accurate: Welch had already been revealed before his name appeared in *Counterspy*. The Peruvian press had published his name fully a year earlier, and his name plus identification had been published in the *Athens News* about a month before his death. Welch's colleagues, moreover, believed that the *Athens News* got the information not from any anti-CIA group but from the KYP, the Greek intelligence service, which at that time had bad blood with the Agency. Welch knew his identity had been compromised in the Greek press and still did not alter his security arrangements. At the other end of this issue were the killers, activist members of the Greek group November 17. They remained free for many years, using the same .45-caliber pistol to kill other foreign diplomats, attachés, and Greek politicians, until arrested in 2002–2003. During their trial, members of the November 17 group admitted to murdering Welch, but claimed to have learned of his identity independently of his name appearing in *Counterspy*, in fact declaring that they had never heard of the magazine.

FRANK GARDINER WISNER

Born on June 23, 1909, Frank Wisner attended the University of Virginia, where he received both B.A. and LL.B. degrees. He then practiced law on Wall Street. Joining the U.S. Naval Reserves in 1941, he was assigned to the Office of Naval Intelligence (ONI) immediately before the Japanese attack on Pearl Harbor and then in 1943 to the Office of Strategic Services (OSS). In December 1943 Wisner was assigned to work in Cairo, but he soon transferred to the Secret Intelligence Branch in Istanbul the following June. Wisner succeeded in reestablishing an OSS network in Istanbul after it had been infiltrated by the Germans. In September 1944 he took command of the OSS team in Bucharest and worked to evacuate downed Allied airmen. With the Soviet Union's military advance into Romania in the closing months of World War II, Wisner's agents successfully penetrated the Romanian Communist Party and the Soviet Army headquarters in Bucharest. Wisner remained in the city until March 1945, at which time he transferred to Wiesbaden, West Germany. There he served as OSS liaison to the Gehlen Organization, a branch of the German military intelligence that had agents in Eastern Europe and the Soviet Union. Although President Truman had disbanded the OSS in September 1945, Wisner remained in Germany as a member of the Strategic Services Unit.

Wisner returned to his law practice in 1946, but remained active in international affairs through his membership in the Council on Foreign Relations. In 1947 he became deputy assistant secretary of state for occupied countries. He left the State Department the following year and became chief of the Office of Policy Coordination of the newly created Central Intelligence Agency. Although formally directed by the State Department, the OPC in fact operated as the CIA's covert arm. Under Wisner's direction, the OPC rapidly expanded its personnel, budget, and conduct of covert operations in Central and Eastern Europe. As a result of DCI Smith's reorganization of the CIA, OPC and the Office of Special Operations were combined in 1952, creating the Directorate of Plans. Wisner became the Directorate's deputy to Allen Dulles, and was promoted to Director of this division when Dulles became DCI in 1953. He then played pivotal roles in planning and implementing covert operations in 1953 and 1954 in Iran and Guatemala, although his contribution to the Guatemalan operation was less extensive or direct.

Wisner was deeply involved in establishing the U-2 spy plane program run by Richard Bissell. He was devastated when the Soviets crushed the 1956 revolution in Hungary, and, after suffering mental and physical breakdowns in both 1957 and 1958, spent six months in the Shepherd Pratt Hospital. CIA

Director Allen Dulles named Wisner chief of the CIA's London Station, but he still suffered from mental illness. Wisner committed suicide on October 29, 1965, four years after retiring from the CIA.

R. JAMES WOOLSEY

Born on September 21, 1941, in Tulsa, Oklahoma, James Woolsey received a B.A. from Stanford in 1963, M.A. from Oxford University in 1965 (attending as a Rhodes Scholar), and law degree from Yale University in 1968. While fulfilling his military service, in 1969–1970 he served as an adviser to the U.S. delegation to the Strategic Arms Limitations Talks (SALT I) held in Helsinki, Finland and Vienna, Austria. After completing military service, he became counsel to the U.S. Senate Armed Services Committee in 1970, leaving to become a partner in the Washington, D.C., law firm, Shea and Gardner. Following Jimmy Carter's election to the presidency in 1976, Woolsey served as undersecretary of the navy from 1977 through 1979, resigning to resume practicing law with Shea and Gardner. While retaining his law practice, he accepted part-time assignments first as delegate at large to the U.S.-Soviet Strategic Arms Reduction Talks (START) and the Nuclear and Space Arms Talks in Geneva, Switzerland, in 1983–1986 (during the Reagan administration) and then as ambassador to the Negotiations on Conventional Armed Forces in Europe held in Vienna, Austria, in 1989–1991 (during the George H. W. Bush administration). In 1991, Woolsey headed a thirteen-member panel, appointed by Defense Secretary Cheney, to evaluate and recommend changes to "streamline, consolidate, reduce or enhance" the National Reconnaissance Office's imagery collection capabilities. He was appointed Director of Central Intelligence by President Clinton in January 1993, serving in this post until 1995, having resigned in December 1994 owing to a conflict with Congress over the Aldrich Ames spy scandal and lacking White House support.

Woolsey's tenure as DCI was shaped by the need to define the Agency's role in a post–Cold War world and, as well, to address the problem for U.S. security posed by efforts of nonnuclear states (India, Pakistan, Iraq, Iran, Libya, North Korea) to develop intermediate-range missiles and nuclear weapons. Woolsey specifically endorsed the need to improve recruitment of human spies and enhance technical intelligence capabilities. His efforts were aborted by the Aldrich Ames spy scandal and the questions this raised about CIA cooperation with the FBI, as well as the seeming shoddiness of the Agency's counterintelligence operations. Following his resignation, Woolsey returned to the private sector, where he served on various corporate boards but retained a keen interest in intelligence questions, both as a trustee of the Center for Strategic and International Studies and as a member in 1999–2000 of the National Commission on Terrorism.

Chronology of Key Events

Athan Theoharis

June 21, 1940

President Roosevelt issues an executive directive creating a special FBI division, the Special Intelligence Service, to conduct foreign intelligence (economic, political, and industrial) in Latin and South America. When preparing the budget for fiscal 1947, President Truman terminates funding for SIS, funding only its dissolution and transfer of its records to the CIA.

July 3, 1940

President Roosevelt sends Wall Street attorney William Donovan to London, requesting that he report back on "fifth column" activities in Europe and the British ability to withstand an imminent German invasion.

July 11, 1941

President Roosevelt issues an executive order establishing the Office of Coordinator of Information (COI) with authority to collect, analyze, and correlate all information which "may bear upon national security," issue publications designated "propaganda," and to provide "such supplementary activities as may facilitate the securing of information important for national security not now available to the Government." The president appoints Donovan to head this office.

October 10, 1941

COI Director Donovan creates a special section to take charge of espionage, sabotage, subversive activities, and guerrilla units.

December 7, 1941

Japan attacks U.S. military and naval installations in Pearl Harbor, Hawaii, sinking or destroying 19 ships and 188 planes and killing 2,335 soldiers and sailors. Despite U.S. success in deciphering sensitive Japanese communications, the attack was a surprise. This major intelligence failure—to appreciate Japanese military capabilities and to ensure advance warning of the attack—precipitated a postwar demand to enhance U.S. intelligence analyses and coordination.

February 25, 1942

Delimitation agreement assigns to FBI's Special Intelligence Service collection responsibilities for all of Latin America (excepting Panama, which was assigned to the army) to obtain "primarily through undercover operations supplemented when necessary by open operations, economic, political, industrial, financial and subversive information" and in addition information concerning "movements, organizations, and individuals whose activities are prejudicial to the interests of the United States."

June 13, 1942

President Roosevelt issues an executive order creating the Office of Strategic Services (OSS) to be headed by Donovan, in the process disbanding the COI and transferring COI's propaganda activities to the newly established Office of War Information. The OSS is empowered to collect and analyze "strategic information" and to "plan and operate such special services as may be directed by the United States Joint Chiefs of Staff" but was excluded from any intelligence or counterintelligence role in the Western Hemisphere.

December 22, 1942

The Joint Chiefs of Staff abolish the Joint Psychological Warfare Committee and direct the OSS to conduct intelligence and psychological warfare activities "necessary for the planning and execution of military programs for psychological warfare, and for the preparation of assigned portions of intelligence digests and such other data and visual presentation as may be requested." OSS activities, however, are to be confined to sabotage, espionage, and counterespionage in enemy-occupied or controlled territory, guerrilla warfare, underground groups, and contacts with foreign nationals in the United States.

February 1, 1943

The Army's Signals Security Agency (a forerunner to the National Security Agency) creates a special unit to attempt to decipher intercepted Soviet consular messages. In 1946 this highly secret project, subsequently code-named Venona, succeeds in breaking the Soviet code. Military intelligence officials brief the CIA in August 1952 about this interception program, seeking the Agency's assistance to identify Soviet intelligence officials cited in the intercepted consular messages.

November 18, 1944

OSS Director Donovan recommends to President Roosevelt the creation of a permanent centralized intelligence agency reporting directly to the president to set objectives and coordinate intelligence essential to planning and executing "national policy and strategy" and further to establish a board, to "advise and assist" this centralized agency, to be composed of the secretaries of war, navy, and state, and such other individuals whom the president might appoint. Donovan's memorandum is leaked to the *Chicago Tribune* and *Washington Times-Herald*, which in front-page stories of February 9, 1945, characterized the proposed agency as a "New Deal Gestapo."

September 20, 1945

President Truman issues Executive Order 9621 dissolving the OSS as of October 1, 1945, and transferring its personnel, facilities, and records to the State and War Departments. On the same day, President Truman directs Secretary of State James Byrnes to take the lead in "developing a comprehensive and coordinated foreign intelligence program for all Federal agencies."

September 1945

Congress approves a joint resolution to establish a select joint committee to investigate the Pearl Harbor attack. Chaired by Senator Alben Barkley, the special committee conducts hearings between November 1945 and May 1946 that focus on the U.S. success in deciphering coded Japanese communications prior to the attack. The hearings and reports, totalling thirty-nine volumes, are published in July 1946, triggering a series of critical studies on this intelligence breakthrough and the Roosevelt administration's failure to have anticipated the Japanese attack on Pearl Harbor.

January 22, 1946

President Truman issues an executive order establishing a National Intelligence Authority (NIA) composed of the secretaries of state, war, and navy and presidential representative William Leahy. The NIA is directed to "plan, develop and coordinate . . . all Federal intelligence activities." The presidential directive also establishes a Central Intelligence Group (CIG), headed at first by Rear Admiral Sidney Souers and then by Air Force General Hoyt Vandenberg, with its staff composed of intelligence officers loaned by other U.S. intelligence agencies (war, navy, state, justice). Directed to coordinate intelligence, the CIG had no independent budget, no authority to collect intelligence, and no authority to coordinate the activities of the various departments having intelligence responsibilities.

July 26, 1947

Congress enacts the National Security Act of 1947, which, in addition to unifying the armed services, authorizes the creation of a Central Intelligence Agency (CIA) to "coordinate" the intelligence activities of the various U.S. intelligence agencies; to correlate, evaluate, and disseminate "intelligence relating to national security"; and to "perform such other functions and duties relating to intelligence affecting the national security as the National Security Council may from time to time direct." The Act specifically bars the CIA from any "police, subpoena, law enforcement, or internal security functions."

September 18, 1947

The Central Intelligence Agency is formally established, headed by Admiral Roscoe Hillenkoetter.

December 12, 1947

The National Security Council issues NSC 1, spelling out the "duties and responsibilities" of the CIA to ensure better coordination and to preclude duplication of services and functions among the U.S. intelligence agencies. The CIA director is authorized to "make such surveys and inspections of departmental intelligence" to fulfill his responsibilities to the National Security Council and to coordinate intelligence activities.

December 17, 1947

The National Security Council issues NSC 4-A, authorizing the CIA to conduct "covert psychological operations designed to counteract Soviet and Soviet-inspired activities" that could threaten world peace and security or U.S. actions to promote world peace and security.

February 12, 1948

The National Security Council issues NSC 7, authorizing the CIA to establish liaison relations with "business concerns, other non-governmental organizations and individuals as sources of foreign intelligence information."

March 22, 1948

CIA Director Hillenkoetter creates a special group within the CIA, the Office of Special Operations, to conduct espionage and counterespionage operations and, on September 1, 1948, a companion Office of Policy Coordination (OPC) to conduct "covert psychological operation activities of the United States." In time, the OPC also performed sabotage and economic warfare (for example, subsidizing the Christian Democratic Party during 1948 elections in Italy, the formation of a French anticommunist trade union, and guerrilla operations in Eastern Europe and China).

June 18, 1948

The National Security Council issues NSC 10/2, expanding the CIA's authority to "plan and conduct covert operations" in "coordination with the Joint Chiefs of Staff." The CIA director is to ensure that covert operations were planned and conducted in accordance with U.S. foreign and military policy goals and other overt activities.

July 20–25, 1948

New York Times military correspondent Hanson Baldwin authors a five-part series on the CIA (headlined "Intelligence") emphasizing the continuing bureaucratic rivalries that undermined the new Agency's ability to correlate intelligence activities and ensure a rationalized intelligence product. Baldwin endorses the need for "secret operations" but emphasizes that they should be overseen by a special Congressional committee.

September 14, 1948

CIA Director Hillenkoetter assumes personal control over the budget and operations of the OPC to ensure that this Office operates "independently of other [CIA] components" for reasons of security and "flexibility of operations."

January 1, 1949

The so-called Dulles-Jackson-Correa task force recommends to the National Security Council that the CIA be reorganized to ensure a more efficient, better coordinated intelligence system. CIA Director Walter Bedell Smith's subsequent reorganization is based on these recommendations.

March 23, 1949

President Truman issues a directive creating an Interdepartmental Intelligence Conference (IIC) and an Interdepartmental Committee on Internal

Security (ICIS). The IIC would be responsible for "coordination of the investigation" of all domestic espionage, counterespionage, subversive, and "other related intelligence matters affecting the internal security," while the ICIS would handle other internal security matters. The CIA is excluded from both groups and could be represented only upon invitation and then as an "ad hoc" member.

June 20, 1949

Congress enacts the Central Intelligence Agency Act of 1949, spelling out the authority and responsibilities of the Agency, the Agency's employment and personnel policy (including exempting Agency personnel from civil service hiring and firing procedures and permitting Agency officials to bring into the United States up to 100 aliens annually without following immigration procedures), and exempting the Agency from normal congressional budgetary and accounting requirements. The Agency is permitted to expend funds "without regard to the provisions of law and regulations relating to the expenditure of Government funds," its confidential expenditures to "be accounted for solely on the certification of the [CIA] Director," and need not publish or disclose the "organization, functions, names, official titles, salaries or number of personnel employed."

October 4, 1949

The OPC begins covert funding of the private airline corporation Civil Air Transport in Asia; in March 1950 this airline is purchased to be used for CIA covert operations in Asia until going out of business in 1968.

April 7, 1950

The National Security Council approves NSC 68, recommending a substantial increase in defense and foreign aid spending to meet the worldwide military and subversive threat posed by an expansionist Kremlin, the "improvement and intensification of intelligence activities," and the "steady development of the moral and material strength of the free world and its projection into the Soviet world in such a way as to bring about an internal change in the Soviet system."

April 7, 1950

CIA officials secretly fund the Congress for Cultural Freedom, a cultural organization headquartered in Paris, France, and run by Michael Josselson. This program is code-named QKOPERA.

April 8, 1950

Soviet fighter jets shoot down a U.S. Navy patrol aircraft over the Baltic Sea, highlighting the Soviet Union's adoption of a more aggressive air defense policy and necessitating the development of a high-altitude plane that would not be vulnerable to Soviet interception and radar at altitudes over 70,000 feet—the catalyst to the development of the U-2 spy plane.

November 13, 1950

CIA Director Smith creates the Office of National Estimates and the Office of Research Reports to enhance the CIA's research and analytical capabilities to prepare reports essential to the president's foreign and military policies.

April 4, 1951

The NSC authorizes a special subcommittee, the Psychological Strategy Board, to determine the "desirability and feasibility" of proposed covert programs and of major covert projects.

October 23, 1951

The National Security Council issues NSC 10/5 to intensify the "scope and pace of [CIA] covert operations" in order to create "maximum strain on the Soviet structure and power, including the relationship between the USSR, its satellites [in Eastern Europe and the Balkans] and Communist China" which would include developing "underground resistance and facilitate covert and guerrilla operations in strategic areas."

May 1952

CIA officials establish a special relationship with the Special Operations Division of the Army Biological Laboratory at Ft. Detrick, MD, code-named Project MCNAOMI, to develop bacteriological warfare materials and delivery systems (various toxins and chemical drugs).

July 1, 1952

The chief of the CIA's Special Security Division recommends a mail cover program to monitor all mail transiting through New York City to and from the Soviet Union. On May 19, 1954, CIA Director Dulles briefs Postmaster General Arthur Summerfield about this program, which had been initiated on December 8, 1952, on approval from Chief Postal Inspector Clifton Garner. Code-named HTLINGUAL, this program is expanded by 1955 to a mail-opening program until its formal suspension in February 1973. Similar mail-opening programs are instituted in San Francisco (between 1969 and 1971), New Orleans (for three weeks in 1957), and Hawaii (in late 1954 and late 1955).

Spring 1953

CIA Director Dulles approves Operation GOLD, a covert program to construct a tunnel under Berlin, Germany, to tap Soviet military communications. Soviet officials discover this operation in April 1956.

April 13, 1953

CIA Director Dulles approves a proposal to develop "a capability in the covert use of biological and chemical materials" to support "present or future clandestine operations" for both defensive and offensive purposes. Code-named MKULTRA, this program led to CIA cooperation with universities and private contractors for research into mind-altering drugs.

June 25, 1953

Eisenhower administration officials approve Operation TPAJAX, a CIA covert operation to overthrow Iranian Prime Minister Mohammed Mossadegh and restore Mohammed Reza Pahlavi as Shah of Iran. On August 19, 1953, CIA officer Kermit Roosevelt orchestrates a successful coup and the shah returns to Iran on August 22.

August 12, 1953

The National Security Council authorizes a CIA covert operation to overthrow the Guatemalan government of President Jacobo Arbenz. On December 9, 1953, CIA Director Dulles approves a general plan, code-named PBSUCCESS, to achieve this goal, finalized on April 17, 1954. Responding to a CIA-supported military invasion from Honduras of June 18, 1954, led by Castillo-Armas, Arbenz resigns on June 27, 1954, with Armas assuming the presidency on September 1, 1954.

November 27, 1953

Dr. Frank Olson, a civilian employee of the U.S. Army, commits suicide by jumping from a New York City hotel, an unwitting victim of an experiment in the use of LSD conducted under the CIA's MKULTRA program.

June 1954

Responding to pressure from CIA Director Dulles, *New York Times* executive Julius Adler directs reporter Sydney Gruson to remain in Mexico City, precluding him from filing a story on the planning of a CIA-led coup to overthrow the Guatemalan government of Jacobo Arbenz.

July 26, 1954

President Eisenhower appoints retired Air Force General James Doolittle to head a four-person review of the CIA's personnel, recruiting, cost, and covert operations. Doolittle's report, submitted to the president on September 30, 1954, outlines the rationale and necessity of ongoing worldwide CIA covert operations and is the catalyst to NSC 5412/1 and to the reorganization of the CIA.

November 1954

Edwin Land (the inventor of the Polaroid camera) and MIT President James Killian discuss with President Eisenhower the feasibility of high altitude reconnaissance. President Eisenhower subsequently approves a plan to have the CIA develop what becomes the U-2 spy plane. Formally approved on November 23, 1954, this CIA project is code-named IDEALIST and headed by Richard Bissell.

January 14, 1955

Senator Mike Mansfield introduces a resolution to create a joint congressional oversight committee to monitor CIA activities and require the CIA to keep this joint committee "fully and currently informed with respect to its activities." Opposed by members of the Senate Armed Services Committee and the Eisenhower administration, the Mansfield resolution is rejected by the Senate on April 11, 1956, by a vote of 27–59.

March 12, 1955

The National Security Council issues NSC 5412, authorizing the CIA to conduct "espionage and counterespionage operations abroad" to include exploiting, impairing, and creating "troublesome problems" for the Soviet Union and communist satellite states, to counter "any threat of a party or individual directly or indirectly responsive to Communist control," and to "develop underground resistance and facilitate covert and guerrilla operations." All such operations were to be planned and executed in a manner ensuring that the U.S. role not become "evident" to enable government officials to "plausibly" deny any responsibility. A special NSC Planning and Coordinating Group is created to approve "all compatible activities" necessary to destroy "international communism."

February 6, 1956

President Eisenhower issues Executive Order 10656, creating an advisory body, the President's Board of Consultants on Foreign Intelligence Activities. Composed of private citizens, the board advises the president on intelligence matters but has no authority over the CIA or other U.S. intelligence agencies.

April 1956

CIA officials obtain from Israeli security the text of Soviet Premier Nikita Khruschev's secret February 1956 speech at the Twentieth Congress of the Soviet Communist Party denouncing Stalinism and Stalin's crimes.

June 20, 1956

After successful testing, the first U-2 plane overflies Soviet satellites Poland and East Germany, following which President Eisenhower on June 21 approves overflight of Soviet territory on the assurances that such flights would not be detected and that a crashed U-2 could not be traced back to the United States. The first U-2 overflight of the Soviet Union is conducted on July 4, 1956.

September 22, 1957

The National Security Council approves a covert operation to support noncommunist rebel forces to destabilize the Indonesian government of Achmed Sukarno.

October 4, 1957

The Soviet Union launches the space satellite Sputnik. On November 7, 1957, a special presidential commission, headed by H. Rowan Gaither, concludes that the Soviets had emphasized missile development and estimates that the Soviets would have in place 100 intercontinental missiles carrying megaton nuclear warheads. The report led critics of the Eisenhower administration's fiscal conservatism to decry a resulting "missile gap."

January 1958

FBI officials solicit Postal Service assistance for a mail cover program involving mail to and from the Soviet Union. Post office officials advise the FBI of the CIA's ongoing mail cover program. In February 1958 CIA officials agree to provide copies of all intercepted correspondence to the FBI under a pro-gram code-named HUNTER.

February 7, 1958

President Eisenhower authorizes a satellite reconnaissance program, code-named CORONA, to be run by the CIA (under direction of Richard Bissell) to overfly the Soviet Union and film Soviet military installations and missile deployment.

May 18, 1958

The Indonesian military shoots down a B-26, piloted by CIA employee Allen Pope, that provided air support for a CIA planned coup to overthrow the Sukarno government.

November 3, 1959

The cornerstone of CIA headquarters in Langley, Virginia, is laid, con-struction having begun in October 1957. The completed headquarters is of-ficially dedicated on November 28, 1961.

December 11, 1959

CIA Western Hemisphere Division Chief J. C. King recommends four operations to CIA Director Dulles to overthrow Cuban President Fidel Castro, the fourth of which involved assassinating Castro. In March 1960 Dulles briefs the NSC 5412 Committee on the proposed operation. The Eisenhower and Kennedy administrations are supportive of a coup to overthrow Castro, al-though the record is murky as to whether both presidents and even CIA directors were briefed on all CIA assassination plots against Castro. Between July 1960 and June 1965, CIA employees plotted eight times to assassinate Castro and his brother Raul—plots that involved the use of high-powered rifles, poison pills, and deadly bacterial powder and included the recruitment of Mafia personnel John Roselli, Sam Giancana, and Santos Trafficante.

March 17, 1960

President Eisenhower approves the CIA plan to finance the recruitment and training of Cuban emigrés for a covert operation to overthrow Cuban President Castro. Because the plan was not completed during Eisenhower's presidency, CIA Director Dulles briefs President-elect Kennedy on this planned coup on November 27, 1960. Kennedy approves the final plan on April 4, 1961, with the actual coup attempted with the Bay of Pigs invasion of April 17, 1961.

April 1960

President Eisenhower approves a contingency plan (recommended on April 14) authorizing the overthrow of the government of Dominican Republic President Rafael Trujillo "as soon as a suitable successor regime can be induced to take over with the assurance of U.S. political, economic, and—if necessary—military support." In response, CIA officials develop a covert operation of encouraging Dominican dissidents to overthrow Trujillo. On May 30, 1961, Dominican dissidents assassinate Trujillo.

May 1, 1960

The Soviet Union shoots down a U-2 plane flown over Soviet territory by Francis Gary Powers. This operation led to the cancellation of the U.S.-Soviet summit conference planned to begin on May 16 when on May 11 President Eisenhower accepted responsibility for this violation of Soviet territorial sovereignty. U-2 overflights of the Soviet Union are ended, replaced by satellite coverage. The U-2, however, continues to be used for intelligence missions, including during the Bay of Pigs invasion in 1961, the Cuban Missile Crisis in 1962, and the Vietnam war.

August 12, 1960

Soviet Colonel Oleg Penkovsky first contacts the U.S. embassy in Moscow to volunteer to provide information about Soviet military activities. CIA officials accept his offer, resulting in the acquisition of information about Soviet rocket and missile technology and Soviet intelligence plans and personnel. Penkovsky was subsequently arrested by Soviet officials on October 12, 1962, tried, and executed for treason on May 16, 1963.

August 18, 1960

The first CIA reconnaissance satellite (DISCOVERER XII) is launched to photograph first the Soviet Union and then China, the Middle East, and Southeast Asia under the code-named CORONA program. This project continues until 1972 when it is replaced by a more sophisticated satellite reconnaissance system.

August 18, 1960

At a National Security Council meeting, President Eisenhower authorizes a plan to assassinate Congolese Premier Patrice Lumumba. Between August 26 and November 11, 1960, CIA officers unsuccessfully attempt a number of times to assassinate Lumumba, who is independently killed in January 1961 during a coup launched by Congolese military officers.

April 7, 1961

In response to pressure from *New York Times* executives Orvil Dryfoos and Turner Catledge, reporter Tad Szulc's story on the planned Bay of Pigs invasion (subsequently conducted on April 17) is edited to delete references to an "imminent" invasion and any CIA role.

April 22, 1961

Following the Bay of Pigs fiasco, President Kennedy directs General Maxwell Taylor to evaluate U.S. military, paramilitary, and guerrilla activities with special attention to Cuba. Maxwell's review is predicated on the need to overthrow Castro. In November 1961 a formal CIA program, Operation MONGOOSE, is approved to overthrow or remove Castro.

May 4, 1961

President Kennedy issues Executive Order 10938, establishing the President's Foreign Intelligence Advisory Board.

December 15, 1961

Soviet intelligence officer Anatoliy Golitsyn defects, providing sensitive information about Soviet intelligence and counterintelligence operations. His charges contribute to a break in U.S.-French liaison relations and compromise CIA-FBI relations over questions about his reliability and about another Soviet defector, Yuriy Nosenko.

April 2, 1962

CIA officials recommend funding the Chilean Christian Democratic Party and the Chilean Radical Party to avert the possible electoral victory of a Marxist political movement headed by Salvador Allende. The CIA provides $100,000 to these parties in 1962–1963 for municipal elections and $3 million in 1964 to Chilean Christian Democratic presidential candidate Eduardo Frei.

May 29, 1962

Soviet Marshal Sergei Biryuzov obtains approval of Cuban President Castro and Cuban Defense Minister Raul Castro to install Soviet missiles in Cuba. This agreement is formalized in a draft treaty initialed by Raul Castro during a July 1962 visit to Moscow. Soviet military officers and technicians arrive in Cuba on July 10 and 12, with the first Soviet missiles arriving on September 8 and the initial shipment of nuclear warheads on October 4.

June 1962

KGB agent Yuri Nosenko contacts the CIA station chief in Greece to offer to serve as an agent in place but not to defect. In January 1964, however, Nosenko proposes to defect immediately and claims to have had responsibility for the KGB file on Lee Harvey Oswald. Owing to suspicions about his reliability, Nosenko is placed in confinement from April 1964 until March 1969 and is subject to harsh interrogation by FBI and CIA officials. The Nosenko affair became a source of FBI-CIA conflict and created morale problems within the CIA's security division over suspicions about possible Soviet moles.

October 14, 1962

U-2 flights over San Critobal, Cuba, confirm that Soviet personnel were installing intermediate-range surface-to-surface missiles in Cuba. Briefed the next day, President Kennedy, after five days of debate and deliberation, announces his decision to institute a strict quarantine of all offensive military equipment under shipment to Cuba—the so-called Cuban Missile Crisis.

November 1, 1963

A coup launched by South Vietnamese military officers overthrows and assassinates South Vietnamese President Ngo Dinh Diem. Prior to this coup, President Kennedy deliberated authorizing the CIA to encourage South Vietnamese military officers to overthrow President Diem and his brother-in-law, Interior Minister Ngo Dinh Nhu.

November 22, 1963

President Kennedy is assassinated in Dallas, Texas, triggering a series of investigations (notably by the so-called Warren Commission and a special House Committee) as well as publications on who assassinated the president. Various conspiracy theories were propounded, some popularized in Oliver Stone's movie *JFK*, including that the CIA was involved.

September 3, 1965

New York Times executive Turner Catledge launches a major *Times* inquiry into the CIA's activities, policies, and objectives. Learning of this planned series, senior CIA officials become concerned that its publication might threaten the "safety of the nation" by undermining the Agency's reputation and unsuccessfully enlisted the Johnson administration's assistance to prevent publication.

January 24, 1966

Senator Eugene McCarthy introduces a resolution calling for a Senate Foreign Relations Committee investigation of all U.S. intelligence agencies. McCarthy's resolution is amended to add three members from the Senate Foreign Relations Committee to the existing oversight committee. On July 14, 1966, by a vote of 61–28, the resolution is referred to the Armed Services Committee (where it was never reported out for a floor vote).

April 1966

Ramparts magazine reports that Michigan State University, under a $25 million contract with the CIA, secretly trained South Vietnamese police officers from 1955–1959.

April 25–29, 1966

The *New York Times* publishes a five-part series on the CIA, raising questions about the Agency's role, authority, and accountability.

February 1967

In its March issue *Ramparts* magazine reports that since 1952 the CIA had covertly funded the National Student Association's overseas programs. The disclosure, because it raised questions of academic freedom as well as about the Agency's involvement in domestic politics, triggers a demand for an investigation. In response, on February 15, 1967, President Johnson appoints a three-member commission headed by Undersecretary of State Nicholas Katzenbach (and including CIA Director Richard Helms and Secretary of Health, Education, and Welfare John Gardner), which in its report of March 29, 1967, recommends a ban against any direct or indirect funding of any of the nation's educational or private voluntary organizations.

March 3, 1967

Syndicated columnist Drew Pearson reports that former Attorney General Robert Kennedy "may have approved an assassination plot [against Cuban President Castro] which then possibly backfired against his late brother" that involved CIA recruitment of "underworld figures." Pearson's column led President Johnson to solicit a report from CIA Director Helms on any CIA attempts to assassinate Castro, South Vietnamese President Diem, and Dominican Republic President Trujillo. On May 10, 1967, Helms briefs Johnson on CIA assassination planning involving these named individuals.

August 15, 1967

In response to pressure from President Johnson, CIA officials institute a program, code-named Operation MHCHAOS, to infiltrate domestic civil rights and antiwar organizations to evaluate suspected Soviet, Chinese, and Cuban links and/or attempts to exploit these movements "in terms of espionage and subversion." CIA officials institute two other programs that year, Projects MERRIMACK and RESISTANCE, to obtain intelligence about the plans and proposed demonstrations of radical activists involving CIA installations, recruiters, or contractors. CIA officials discontinue Operation CHAOS in 1973.

February 26, 1970

CIA Director Helms writes FBI Director J. Edgar Hoover about the actions taken by CIA officers in their inquiry into the disappearance of University of Colorado history professor Thomas Riha. Helms's letter led Hoover on March 31, 1970, to sever CIA-FBI liaison relations unless specifically authorized by FBI headquarters and barred FBI assistance to the CIA through wiretaps, break-ins, and mail covers.

March 25, 1970

The National Security Council's 40 Committee authorizes the CIA to fund a Chilean coalition to prevent the election of Salvadore Allende as president of Chile and to solicit funding assistance from the International Telephone and Telegraph Corporation (ITT). ITT and the CIA eventually provide $775,000 to support the candidacy of Christian Democrat presidential nominee Jorge Allesandri.

June 5, 1970

President Nixon authorizes the heads of U.S. intelligence agencies to evaluate their agencies' collection capabilities. A special interagency task force is created to conduct this inquiry under the direction of White House aide Tom Charles Huston. Its report and recommendations are completed by June 25, 1970. Based on these recommendations, on July 14, 1970, Huston authorizes the heads of all U.S. intelligence agencies to resort to "clearly illegal" investigative techniques (wiretaps, bugs, break-ins, mail opening, interception of international messages), lowers the age of recruited informers to 18, and creates a special interagency group to ensure better coordination subject to White House direction. This so-called Huston Plan is recalled on July 27, 1970.

September 15, 1970

President Nixon authorizes the CIA to fund up to $10 million to prevent Salvadore Allende's election to the Chilean presidency. This unsuccessful covert operation led CIA officials in succeeding years, first to neutralize Chilean General Rene Schneider, and then to destabilize the Chilean economy and thereby increase popular opposition to the Allende government. In a September 11, 1973, coup General Augusto Pinochet successfully overthrows the Allende government.

September 3, 1971

White House aides E. Howard Hunt and G. Gordon Liddy seek CIA technical assistance (disguises, alias identification, cameras, and a psychological profile of Daniel Ellsberg) and then, with the help of three Cuban Americans, break into the offices of Dr. Louis Fielding (Ellsberg's psychiatrist).

June 17, 1972

Washington, D.C., police arrest five men in the headquarters of the Democratic National Committee in the Watergate complex—James McCord (the chief security officer of the Committee to Re-Elect the President and a former CIA officer) and four Cuban Americans (who had been recruited by the CIA for the Bay of Pigs operation). The resultant FBI investigation uncovers the role of E. Howard Hunt (a former CIA officer who had played a key role in recruiting Cuban emigrés for the Bay of Pigs operation) as an organizer of the break-in.

June 23, 1972

During a meeting in the Oval Office, President Nixon pressures CIA officials to intercede to limit the FBI's investigation into the sources of the funding of the Watergate break-in, ostensibly to avoid compromising CIA financing operations. CIA officials rebuff this request.

February 7, 1973

During hearings conducted by the Senate Foreign Relations Committee into the role of ITT and the CIA in Chile, CIA Director Helms falsely testifies when questioned about the CIA's role in the overthrow of the Allende government. Subsequently indicted and convicted of perjury, Helms is fined $2,000 and receives a suspended sentence of two years in prison.

December 17, 1974

CIA Director William Colby informs James Angleton of his decision to remove him as head of the CIA's Counterintelligence Staff. Angleton resigns, effective December 31, 1974.

December 22, 1974

New York Times reporter Seymour Hersh discloses that during the "Nixon years" the CIA had massively and illegally compiled dossiers on 10,000 anti–Vietnam War and other dissident activists.

December 30, 1974

Congress approves the Hughes-Ryan Act (an amendment to the Foreign Assistance Act) requiring the president to authorize in writing all covert operations as "important to the national security of the United States" and to report "in a timely fashion a description and scope" of such covert operations to eight specified congressional committees (the House and Senate appropriations, armed services, foreign affairs, and intelligence committees).

January 4, 1975

President Ford issues Executive Order 11928, creating a special presidential commission headed by Vice President Nelson Rockefeller to investigate CIA domestic activities. The commission's report is publicly released on June 10, 1975.

January 27, 1975

The Senate approves S. Res. 21 (introduced by Senator John Pastore on January 21, 1975) establishing a special Senate committee to investigate U.S. intelligence agencies, including whether the CIA had conducted illegal domestic surveillance, CIA coordination with other U.S. intelligence agencies, the "nature and extent" of executive oversight over the CIA (and the other intelligence agencies), and the "extent and necessity of CIA overt and covert" intelligence activities. This is the first intensive congressional investigation of the CIA since the Agency's creation in 1947.

February 19, 1975

The House establishes a special committee, chaired first by Lucian Nedzi and then by Otis Pike, to investigate the U.S. intelligence agencies. On

January 29, 1976, the House votes not to release the Pike Committee's final report in response to the assassination of CIA officer Richard Welch on December 23, 1975, in Athens, Greece.

February 28, 1975

CBS correspondent Daniel Schorr reports that President Ford had warned "associates" that should the recently-authorized congressional investigations of the CIA go far enough they would "uncover several assassinations of foreign officials involving the CIA."

May 1975

David Phillips retires as chief of the CIA's Western Hemisphere Division and along with retired CIA officials Ray Cline and Harry Rositzke forms the Association of Former Intelligence Officers. This new association launches an educational campaign to defend the CIA's record.

July 8, 1975

President Ford issues a finding authorizing the CIA to assist Angolan paramilitary movements headed by Jonas Savimbi and Holden Robert to destabilize the Marxist-led MLPA headed by Agostinho Neto. Senator Dick Clark subsequently uncovers this covert operation, code-named IA-FEATURE, during a fact-finding trip to Africa. In response, Clark proposes an amendment to the 1976 Defense Appropriation Act to terminate any funding for this Angolan covert operation. Clark's amendment is approved by the Senate by a vote of 54–22 on December 19, 1975, and by the House in a vote of 323–99 on January 27, 1976.

December 23, 1975

Masked gunmen assassinate Richard Welch, the CIA station chief in Athens, Greece, his identity as a CIA officer having been disclosed by the underground newspaper *Counterspy* with his name and address published in the English-language *Athens News*. Welch's murder leads to the enactment of legislation in 1982 to criminalize disclosing the identities of CIA officers.

January 26, 1976

Deputy Defense Secretary Robert Ellsworth, pursuant to a recommendation of the President's Foreign Intelligence Advisory Board, appoints a team of independent academic and policy experts (led by Harvard Professor Richard Pipes) to review CIA intelligence estimates of Soviet nuclear weapons capabilities and strategic objectives. This so-called Team B challenges the CIA's intelligence assessments as overly optimistic and endorses the need for increased military spending and a more aggressive foreign policy.

January 29, 1976

Senator Frank Church introduces S. Res. 400, authorizing the establishment of a permanent Senate intelligence committee. After deliberation and amendments, the Senate approves the amended bill on May 19, 1976, by a vote of 72–22.

February 11, 1976

CIA Director George H. W. Bush bans any CIA "paid or contractual relationship with any full-time or part-time news correspondent accredited by any U.S. news service, newspaper, periodical, radio or television network or station." Similar bans are imposed on CIA relations with American clergymen and missionaries.

February 16, 1976

The *Village Voice* publishes the full text of the Pike Committee's final report, in effect countermanding the House's action of January 29, 1976, prohibiting publication of the report until it had been "certified by the President as not containing information which would adversely affect the intelligence activities of the CIA."

February 18, 1976

President Ford issues Executive Order 11905, to "clarify the authority and responsibilities" of the U.S. intelligence agencies and to ensure that intelligence "activities are conducted in a Constitutional and lawful manner and never aimed at our citizens." Ford's order imposes stricter executive oversight over the intelligence agencies and requires all executive branch officials and government contractors to sign an agreement not to disclose information about "intelligence sources and methods."

July 14, 1977

The House approves H. Res. 658, creating a permanent House intelligence committee to oversee the U.S. intelligence agencies.

January 24, 1978

President Carter issues Executive Order 12036, authorizing a Policy Review Committee (chaired by the CIA director and including the vice president, secretaries of state and war, and chairman of the Joint Chiefs of Staff) to define the priorities for intelligence collection, analysis, and budgets. The order also establishes a special board to review proposed covert operations and subjects specific actions (assassinations, drug experiments) to the review of the attorney general to ensure their legality. Carter's order prohibits any intelligence operation against a U.S. citizen without a warrant "unless" authorized by the president.

February 9, 1978

Senator Walter Huddleston introduces S. 2525, the National Intelligence Reorganization and Reform Act, to spell out the authority of the U.S. intelligence agencies and to prohibit specified activities. Senate hearings were held that year (with the debate centering on whether the proposed charter legislation should specify the intelligence agencies' authority or should instead outline the general parameters with specific rules and regulations instituted by executive officials), but this bill was never enacted, having been sidetracked by the Iran hostage crisis of 1979–1980 and then the election of Republican presidential nominee Ronald Reagan in 1980.

October 25, 1978

Congress enacts the Foreign Intelligence Surveillance Act, creating a special court to review in secret Justice Department applications for "electronic surveillance [installations] for foreign intelligence or counterintelligence purposes in the United States in which communications of U.S. persons might be intercepted."

November 4, 1979

Iranian militants seize the U.S. embassy in Teheran and hold American diplomats and support staff hostage, precipitating a domestic debate whether to reverse the administrative restrictions on the intelligence agencies' operations and authority imposed during the years 1975 through 1978.

October 14, 1980

President Carter signs the Intelligence Accountability (or Oversight) Act of 1980, amending the 1974 Hughes-Ryan Act to reduce from eight to two (the House and Senate intelligence committees) the number of committees to which presidents must provide "timely" notification.

October 15, 1980

Congress enacts the Classified Information Procedure Act clarifying federal classification policy and imposing new penalties for the unauthorized disclosure of classified information.

November 23, 1981

President Reagan approves NSDD-17 declaring U.S. policy to "assist in defeating the insurgency in El Salvador" by Cuba, Nicaragua, or "others." CIA officials recruit and train Nicaraguan paramilitary forces (the so-called contras) to overthrow the Sandinista government in Nicaragua. Subsequent disclosures that CIA personnel had mined a Nicaraguan port and that a CIA contract employee had prepared a training manual including a section on assassinations triggered congressional restrictions on CIA assistance to the contras (the so-called Boland amendments).

December 4, 1981

President Reagan issues Executive Order 12333, granting the CIA exclusive authority to conduct covert operations "unless the President determines that another agency is more likely to achieve a particular objective" and to conduct "administrative and support activities" within the United States and abroad if properly authorized. Reagan's order rescinds the restrictions imposed under President Carter's Executive Order 12036.

June 23, 1982

Congress enacts the Intelligence Identities Protection Act, criminalizing the public disclosure of the names of U.S. intelligence agents.

December 8, 1982

Congress enacts the first so-called Boland amendment banning the expenditure of any funds to provide direct or indirect training or other assistance to the so-called Nicaraguan contras. The second Boland amendment (attached to Public Law 98-473, appropriating funds for the continuing operation of the federal government), approved on October 12, 1984, prohibits any CIA military or paramilitary assistance to the contras for the period October 1984 through December 1985, a prohibition extended to "any other agency or entity involved in intelligence activities."

March 16, 1984

Islamic fundamentalists kidnap William Buckley, the CIA station chief in Beirut, Lebanon. Buckley dies in captivity on June 3, 1985, having been brutally tortured by his captors. His kidnapping influenced President Reagan's decision to authorize the covert operation wherein CIA and NSC officials traded arms to Iran to ensure the release of American hostages.

October 1984

Congress enacts the CIA Information Act, exempting CIA "operational files" from the mandatory review and disclosure requirements of the Freedom of Information Act.

August 23, 1985

President Reagan approves the sale to Iran of weapons that the United States had supplied to Israel, to improve U.S. relations with Iran and ensure the release of American hostages in Lebanon. On September 14, 1985, an Israeli-chartered aircraft delivers 408 TOW missiles to Iran.

December 5, 1985

President Reagan signs a finding authorizing a CIA covert operation to secure the release of American hostages by shipping weapons to Iran. This finding retroactively approves the CIA's August action and stipulates that Congress not be notified (despite the requirement of the Intelligence Oversight Act of 1980). NSC Adviser John Poindexter secretly destroys this finding on November 11, 1986.

January 6, 1986

President Reagan signs a new draft finding authorizing the CIA to transfer arms to Iranians in order to improve relations with Iran and again stipulating that Congress not be notified. Reagan signs the revised version of this finding on January 17, 1986.

February 1, 1986

CIA Director William Casey establishes a Counterterrorist Center headed by Duane Clarridge for the purpose of promoting better coordination among U.S. intelligence agencies and within the various divisions of the CIA.

March 1986

President Reagan approves NSDD-166 to defeat Soviet intervention in Afghanistan through military assistance to the so-called *mujahedeen* (Islamist rebels).

October 5, 1986

The Nicaraguan military shoots down an American (but CIA-contract) cargo plane carrying supplies to the contras. The one surviving crew member, Eugene Hasenfus, claims to have been a CIA contract employee and to have worked with two CIA officers at Ilopango air base in Honduras.

November 3, 1986

Al Shiraa, a Lebanese newspaper affiliated with Muslim fundamentalists, alleges that the Reagan administration had engaged in arms-for-hostages negotiations with Iranian militants. In response to press and congressional inquiries, a Justice Department investigation is launched on November 25, 1986, Attorney General Edwin Meese III confirms that arms had been traded to the Iranian government to ensure the release of American hostages held in Lebanon with the proceeds from these arms sales diverted to fund the so-called contras' attempt to overthrow the Sandinista government in Nicaragua.

December 1, 1986

President Reagan issues Executive Order 12575, creating the President's Special Review Board (chaired by former Senator John Tower) to investigate the Iran-Contra affair. The board's report is released on February 26, 1987.

December 19, 1986

Lawrence Walsh is appointed Independent Counsel to investigate any criminal activities of senior White House, administration, CIA, and other federal officials during the Iran-Contra affair. The investigation's three-volume report is released on August 4, 1993.

January 7, 1987

The House and Senate authorize a special Joint House and Senate investigation of the Iran-Contra affair. Public hearings begin on May 5, 1987, lasting until August 3, 1987, with the joint committee's final report and multivolume hearings released on November 18, 1987.

June 20, 1988

Joseph Fernandez, the CIA station chief in San Jose, Costa Rica, is indicted on five counts of conspiracy to defraud the U.S. government, obstruction of the Tower Commission inquiry, and making false statements to U.S. agencies. Federal Judge Claude Hilton dismisses the indictment on November 24, 1989, when Attorney General Richard Thornburgh refuses to disclose relevant classified information to the defense.

November 9, 1989

The Berlin Wall falls, coinciding with the collapse of communist governments in Eastern Europe and the Balkans and marking the end of the Cold War. Then, on December 25, 1991, Mikhail Gorbachev resigns as president of the dissolved Soviet Union with the formation of the Commonwealth of Independent States, of which the newly renamed Russian Federation is a leading component.

July 9, 1991

Alan Fiers, Jr., the chief of the CIA's Central American Task Force, pleads guilty to two counts of withholding information from Congress about secret efforts to aid the Nicaraguan contras. Sentenced to one year probation and 100 hours of community service, Fiers is pardoned by President George H. W. Bush on December 24, 1992.

August 15, 1991

Congress enacts Public Law 102-88, Intelligence Authorization Act, Fiscal Year 1991, defining what constitutes covert action and requiring presidents to "fully and currently" inform Congress "in a timely fashion" of their findings that such covert operations are in the national interest—on the understanding that such findings should be reported "in a few days."

September 6, 1991

CIA Deputy Director for Operations Clair George is indicted on ten counts of perjury, false statements, and obstruction of Congressional and grand jury investigations in the Iran-Contra affair. Convicted on December 9, 1992, on two of the counts, George is sentenced to five years in prison and fined $250,000. President George H. W. Bush pardons him on December 24, 1992.

October 28, 1991

Congress enacts Public Law 102-138, the Foreign Relations Authorization Act Fiscal Years 1992 and 1993, challenging the continued classification of records relating to the Foreign Relations of the United States series. This legislation establishes systematic declassification procedures to ensure the publication of relevant CIA records and granting review authority to an Advisory Committee composed of representatives from the historical, political science, international law, and archival associations.

November 26, 1991

Duane Clarridge, the chief of the CIA's European Division, is indicted on seven counts of perjury and false statements in connection with investigations into the Iran-Contra affair. His trial was set to begin on March 15, 1993, but President George H. W. Bush pardons him on December 24, 1992

October 26, 1992

Congress enacts Public Law 102-156, the John F. Kennedy Records Collection Act of 1992, establishing standards to ensure the release of formerly classified records (including those of the CIA) pertaining to the assassination of President Kennedy and authorizing an Assassination Records Review Board to identify and order the release of all records pertaining to the assassination.

February 21, 1994

Aldrich Ames, a 30-year CIA officer, is arrested for having spied on behalf of the Soviet Union since 1985. Ames had given Soviet agents the names of ten Soviet sources whom the CIA and the FBI had recruited and in addition thousands of classified documents. On April 28, 1994, Ames pleads guilty to charges of conspiring to commit espionage and tax fraud, and is sentenced to life in prison without parole.

September 11, 2001

Nineteen alien residents, Muslims of Middle Eastern descent, commandeer four commercial jets, flying two into the World Trade Center in New York City, a third into the Pentagon, with the fourth being forced down in western Pennsylvania. This suicide bombing operation results in the deaths of 2,973 individuals and billions of dollars in property damages and economic losses.

June 4, 2002

The House and Senate intelligence committees initiate joint executive session hearings to examine the U.S. intelligence agencies' monitoring of international and domestic terrorist activities prior to the September 11, 2001, terrorist attack. In its final reports, released in December 2002 and July 2003, the joint committee criticizes the quality of the intelligence agencies' analyses of a prospective terrorist threat and interagency coordination and recommends changes to ensure a more coordinated and coherent intelligence community, notably creating a Cabinet-level director of national intelligence.

November 18, 2002

President George W. Bush signs legislation creating an independent ten-member commission (the National Commission on Terrorist Attacks upon the United States) to investigate the failure of the U.S. intelligence agencies to have anticipated the September 11, 2001, terrorist attack and to recommend changes to prevent future terrorist attacks. In December he appoints Thomas Kean to head this commission.

November 25, 2002

President George W. Bush signs legislation creating a new Department of Homeland Security. Under this reorganization, the CIA retains its independent status but would report any information it developed about domestic terrorism to the new Department's intelligence division (empowered to analyze but not collect intelligence).

September 29, 2003

The Justice Department launches a criminal investigation to identify the senior Bush administrations officials who leaked the identity of CIA officer Valerie Plame to syndicated columnist Robert Novak in July 2003. On January 21, 2004, former CIA officers petitioned congressional leaders to investigate the source of this leak, reflecting their concern over the Justice Department inquiry.

January 23, 25, and 28, 2004

In interviews with Reuters (January 23) and the *New York Times* (January 25) and in congressional testimony (January 28), former chief CIA weapons inspector David Kay (who resigned on January 23) criticizes the CIA's intelligence assessment of Iraq's biological and chemical weapons programs during the 1990s and preceding the 2003 war on Iraq. Kay endorses the appointment of an independent commission to investigate this intelligence failure.

February 6, 2004

By executive order, President George W. Bush creates a presidential commission, the Commission on the Intelligence Capabilities of the United States regarding Weapons of Mass Destruction, to evaluate the intelligence used to justify the 2003 Iraq war and about the weapons programs of North Korea, Libya, Afghanistan, and Iran. Cochaired by former Judge Laurence Silberman and former U.S. Senator Charles Robb, the commission was to report its findings in March 2005.

February 12, 2004

The Senate Intelligence Committee expands its inquiry into CIA intelligence on Iraq's weapons of mass destruction (initiated in 2003) to assess whether the Bush administration's public statements "were substantiated by intelligence information."

June 24, 2004

When approving the Intelligence Authorization bill, the House of Representatives accepts a report of the House Intelligence Committee criticizing the CIA for mismanaging human spying operations, and specifically the Agency's "misallocation and redirection of resources, poor prioritization of objectives, micromangement of field operations, and a continued political aversion to operational risk."

July 9, 2004

The Senate Select Committee on Intelligence releases a critical report on CIA failures in intelligence collection and analyses regarding Iraq's prewar chemical, biological, and nuclear weapons programs and capabilities.

July 22, 2004

The National Commission on Terrorist Attacks upon the United States, the so-called Kean or 9/11 Commission, releases its final report sharply criticizing the CIA's intelligence collection and analytical activities and failure to coordinate with other intelligence agencies prior to the 9/11 terrorist attack. The Commission recommends creating a director of national intelligence and a National Counterterrorism Center, to be housed in the Executive Office of the President, and shifting the authority for covert action to the military's Special Operations Command.

December 17, 2004

President George W. Bush signs the Intelligence Reform and Terrorism Prevention Act, creating a Director of National Intelligence (DNI). The DNI would report directly to the president and would have oversight and budgetary authority over the CIA and the fourteen other U.S. intelligence agencies.

March 31, 2005

The Commission on Intelligence Capabilities of the United States regarding Weapons of Mass Destruction (the so-called Silberman-Robb Commission) releases its final report criticizing the lack of coordination among the U.S. intelligence agencies and the CIA's deficiencies in its collection and analysis of intelligence relating to Iraq's, Iran's, and North Korea's weapons of mass destruction programs and capabilities. The commission recommended creation of a new National Counterprofileration Task Force to coordinate and conduct intelligence on proliferation and of a Human Intelligence Division within the CIA to improve the recruitment of human sources.

June 29, 2005

President George W. Bush issues new orders to restructure the U.S. intelligence community. In doing so, the president rejected recommendations to reduce the CIA's covert operations role, and instead authorizes the Agency to coordinate human spying and covert operations in effect reaffirming the CIA's preeminence in the planning and oversight of such operations.

October 28, 2005

A federal grand jury returns a five count indictment of I. Lewis Libby, Jr., Vice President Cheney's chief of staff. Libby was indicted on one count of obstruction of justice, two counts of false statements to the FBI, and two counts of perjury. Announcing Libby's indictment, U.S. Attorney Fitzpatrick disclosed that the investigation was ongoing, suggesting the possibility of future indictments.

Annotated Bibliography

Athan Theoharis

Adams, James. *Sellout: Aldrich Ames and the Corruption of the CIA.* New York: Viking, 1995.
>Criticizes CIA failure to have uncovered the espionage activities of CIA officer Aldrich Ames.

Agee, Philip. *Inside the Company: CIA Diary.* New York: Stonehill, 1975.
>Critical, detailed memoir of former CIA officer describing his covert operation activities in Latin America and CIA methods and training. Agee also identified by name individuals and organizations "controlled, supported or used by the CIA."

———. *On the Run.* Secaucus, NJ: Lyle Stuart, 1987.
>Describes CIA monitoring of his activities and publication plans and his own activities to "expose" and discredit the CIA.

Aldrich, Richard. *The Hidden Hand: Britain, America and Cold War Secret Intelligence.* London: John Murray, 2001.
>Surveys British liaison relationship with CIA during 1947–1963 (including CIA funding of cultural and European unification activities).

Allen, George. *None So Blind: A Personal Account of the Intelligence Failure in Vietnam.* Chicago: Ivan Dee, 2001.
>Former CIA analyst surveys the role of intelligence in the Vietnam war.

Allen, John K., John Carver, and Tom Elmore, eds. *Estimative Products on Vietnam 1948–1975.* Washington, DC: National Intelligence Council, 2005.
>Reprints 38 of the 174 estimates on Vietnam prepared by the CIA during the years 1948–1975, introduced by a brief historical survey of U.S. policy toward Vietnam written by historian Lloyd Gardner.

———. *Tracking the Dragon: National Intelligence Estimates on China During the Era of Mao, 1948–1976.* Washington, DC: National Intelligence Council, 2004.

Reprints seventy of the CIA's National Intelligence Estimates on China issued during the years 1948 through 1976.

Andrew, Christopher. *For the President's Eyes Only: Secret Intelligence and the American Presidency from Washington to Bush*. New York: HarperCollins, 1995.
Surveys presidential uses of CIA intelligence and covert operations from presidents Harry Truman through George H. W. Bush.

Bamford, James. *A Pretext for War: 9/11, Iraq, and the Abuse of America's Intelligence Agencies*. Garden City: Doubleday, 2004.
Critical survey of the Bush administration's and the intelligence community's (including the CIA) failure to anticipate the 9/11 terrorist attack and assessment of Iraq's weapon capabilities.

———. *The Puzzle Palace: A Report on America's Most Secret Agency*. Boston: Houghton Mifflin, 1982.
Detailed history of the National Security Agency that cursorily surveys the NSA's liaison relationship with the CIA and CIA intelligence and counterintelligence operations.

Bearden, Milt, and James Risen. *The Main Enemy: The Inside Story of the CIA's Final Showdown with the KGB*. New York: Random House, 2003.
Journalistic survey of recent CIA counterintelligence operations directed against the Soviet Union and the Russian Federation during the 1980s and 1990s, notably the Edward Howard, Aldrich Ames, and Robert Hanssen cases.

Benjamin, Daniel, and Steven Simon. *The Age of Sacred Terror*. New York: Random House, 2002.
Criticizes the failure of U.S. intelligence agencies (FBI, CIA) to have monitored al Qaeda operatives aggressively and to have anticipated the September 11, 2001, terrorist attack.

Benson, Robert, and Michael Warner, eds. *Venona: Soviet Espionage and the American Response 1939–1957*. Washington, DC: National Security Agency/Central Intelligence Agency, 1996.
History of the VENONA project (the interception and deciphering of Soviet consular messages sent from Washington and New York during World War II), reprinting representative sample of the more important deciphered messages.

Berghahn, Volker. *America and the Intellectual Cold War in Europe: Shepard Stone between Philanthropy, Academy and Diplomacy*. Princeton: Princeton University Press, 2001.
Biography of Shepard Stone and his role with the Ford Foundation and the International Association for Cultural Freedom and the funding of the Congress for Cultural Freedom. Offers limited insights into CIA funding of anticommunist cultural activities during Cold War years.

Berman, Jerry, and Morton Halperin, eds. *The Abuses of the Intelligence Agencies*. Washington, DC: Center for National Security Studies, 1975.
Surveys CIA abuses of power during Cold War years—both illegal domestic surveillance and covert operations abroad.

Bissell, Richard M., Jr. *Reflections of a Cold Warrior: From Yalta to the Bay of Pigs*. New Haven: Yale University Press, 1996.
> Senior CIA official's memoir of his career in the CIA from 1953 through 1962. Provides insights into 1954 Guatemala coup, the development of the U-2, plans to eliminate Lumumba, and the Bay of Pigs invasion.

Borosage, Robert, and John Marks, eds. *The CIA File*. New York: Grossman, 1976.
> Critical essays that survey CIA organization, covert operations, and methods.

Breckinridge, Scott. *CIA and the Cold War: A Memoir*. Westport, CT: Praeger, 1993.
> CIA officer's memoir of his service from 1953–1979 including at the Agency's Inspector General's office. Provides insights into training, operations, and procedures.

―――. *The CIA and the U.S. Intelligence System*. Boulder: Westview, 1986.
> Former CIA officer employed in Office of Inspector General surveys the Agency's history, organization, methods, and authority.

Center for the Study of Intelligence Bulletin.
> Newsletter of the CIA's Center for the Study of Intelligence containing feature articles and reports on declassified records, on recent publications, and on conferences and symposia.

Clarridge, Duane, with Digby Diehl. *A Spy for All Seasons: My Life in the CIA*. New York: Scribner, 1997.
> Memoir of senior CIA official (who served from 1955 to 1988) provides general information on training, methods, and activities. While Clarridge played a key role in the Iran-Contra affair and headed the Counterterrorist Center (when established in 1986), his memoir offers little new information about these operations.

Clifford, Clark. *Counsel to the President: A Memoir*. New York: Random House, 1991.
> Former White House counsel and secretary of defense recounts the role of the Truman White House, first in drafting, and then in helping enact and implement legislation creating the CIA in 1947; also recounts conflict between the CIA director and the president's Foreign Intelligence Advisory Board during the Kennedy administration.

Cline, Marjorie, Carla Christiansen, and Judith Fontaine, eds. *Scholar's Guide to Intelligence Literature*. Frederick, MD: University Publications, 1983.
> Dated but useful bibliography of books and articles (identified by subject matter) relating to intelligence, including publications about the CIA.

Cline, Ray. *The CIA under Reagan, Bush & Casey*. Washington, DC: Acropolis Books, 1981.
> Memoir of former CIA deputy director surveying the history of CIA intelligence and covert operations activities from the creation of the Office of Coordinator of Intelligence in 1941 and the creation of the CIA in 1947 through the Reagan administration.

Codevilla, Angelo. *Informing Statecraft: Intelligence for a New Century*. New York: The Free Press, 1992.

Surveys CIA intelligence, counterintelligence, and covert operations in formulation and execution of U.S. foreign policy.

Colby, William. *Honorable Men: My Life in the CIA*. New York: Simon and Schuster, 1978.
Memoir of former OSS and then CIA officer (dating from 1950) and CIA director (1973–1975) describing his role and selected history of the CIA since its creation in 1947.

Coll, Steve. *Ghost Wars: The Secret History of the CIA, Afghanistan, and Bin Laden, from the Soviet Invasion to September 10, 2001*. New York: Penguin, 2004.
Criticizes the CIA's Afghan programs dating from 1979 and relations with the Clinton and George W. Bush administrations.

Constantinides, George. *Intelligence and Espionage: An Analytical Bibliography*. Boulder: Westview, 1983.
Dated but useful annotated bibliography of studies of intelligence policy and espionage.

Cooper, Phillip. *By Order of the President: The Use and Abuse of Executive Direct Action*. Lawrence: University Press of Kansas, 2002.
Surveys presidential "direct action" activities that bypass Congress through use of executive orders, memoranda, proclamations, and secret directives, including authorization of CIA covert operations.

Corn, David. *Blond Ghost: Ted Shackley and the CIA's Crusades*. New York: Simon and Schuster, 1994.
Critical biography of senior CIA officer Theodore Shackley (1951–1979); provides insights into CIA covert operations (Germany, Cuba, Laos, Vietnam, Chile) and attempts to prevent publication of Philip Agee's and Frank Snepp's exposés of CIA operations.

Corson, William. *The Armies of Ignorance: The Rise of the American Intelligence Empire*. New York: Dial Press, 1977.
Solid if at times speculative and dated history of the CIA's creation and expansion.

Corson, William, Susan Trento, and Joseph Trento. *Widows*. New York: Crown, 1989.
Surveys CIA (and FBI) counterintelligence responses to suspected Soviet espionage cases during the Cold War years (Kronhal, Paisley, Shadrin, Sigler).

Counterspy.
Periodical that publishes critical articles on CIA history and operations.

Covert Action Information Bulletin.
Periodical that publishes critical articles on CIA operations, secrecy procedures, and court cases.

Cullather, Nick. *Secret History: The CIA's Classified Account of Its Operations in Guatemala, 1952–1954*. Stanford: Stanford University Press, 1999.

Reprints his own (partially redacted) classified history of the CIA's covert operation to overthrow the Arbenz government in Guatemala, including plans to assassinate high-level Communist leaders and sympathizers.

Darling, Arthur. *The Central Intelligence Agency: An Instrument of Government, to 1950*. University Park: Pennsylvania State University Press, 1990.

Formerly classified internal history of the creation and expansion of the CIA, written by a CIA historian and publicly released in 1989. Provides insights into the bureaucratic conflicts over the issue of "centralized intelligence" that led to the Agency's creation in 1947 and that continued to bedevil Truman administration and CIA officials in the ensuing years (to 1950).

Diamond, Sigmund. *Compromised Campus: The Collaboration of Universities with the Intelligence Community, 1945–1955*. New York: Oxford University Press, 1992.

Criticizes CIA funding of academic research and research institutes (notably Harvard University's Russian Research Center).

Doyle, David. *True Men and Traitors: From the OSS to the CIA, My Life in the Shadows*. New York: John Wiley, 2001.

Former CIA officer's memoir of his activities in the United States, Asia, Africa, and Europe as an employee (1949–1975) of the Agency's Directorate of Operations. Provides some detail but few insights; criticizes the actions of CIA defectors and foreign spies (Agee, Stockwell, Ames, Nicholson).

Dulles, Allen. *The Craft of Intelligence*. New York: Harper & Row, 1963.

Memoir of the former CIA director (1953–1961) that offers little new information about specific CIA operations and programs instituted during his directorship.

Earley, Pete. *Confessions of a Spy: The Real Story of Aldrich Ames*. New York: Putnam's, 1997.

Biography that focuses on CIA officer Aldrich Ames's recruitment as a Soviet spy, apprehension in 1994, and conviction (based on privileged interviews with Ames).

Epstein, Edward. *Deception: The Invisible War between the KGB and the CIA*. New York: Simon and Schuster, 1989.

Criticizes CIA-FBI counterintelligence conflict in the Yurchenko affair, the code-named WIN operation, the Fedora-Nosenko-Golitsyn defections, and suspected KGB infiltration of the CIA; offers a sympathetic portrait of CIA counterintelligence chief James Angleton.

Fain, Tyrus, with Katherine Plant and Ross Milloy, eds. *The Intelligence Community: History, Organization, and Issues*. New York: R. R. Bowker, 1977.

History of the creation, authority, methods, and operation of the CIA. Reprints selected documents: texts of executive directives; congressional hearings, reports, and debates; Rockefeller Commission report.

Final Report of the Independent Counsel for Iran/Contra Matters. 3 vols. Washington, DC: Office of Independent Counsel, 1993.

Report of the independent counsel chronicles the role of the CIA, NSC, and Reagan administration officials in the planning and execution of the Iran-Contra affair.

Ford, Harold. *CIA and the Vietnam Policymakers: Three Episodes 1962–1968*. Washington, DC: Central Intelligence Agency, 1998.
Briefly surveys CIA intelligence analyses concerning three crucial issues relating to U.S. commitments in Vietnam and their impact on Kennedy's and Johnson's policies during 1962–1968.

Frazier, Howard, ed. *Uncloaking the CIA*. New York: The Free Press, 1978.
Critical, although nonspecific and often speculative essays on CIA covert operations, secrecy, and methods.

Garthoff, Douglas. *Directors of Central Intelligence as Leaders of the U.S. Intelligence Community 1946–2005*. Washington, DC: Center for the Study of Intelligence, 2005.
Concise, helpful survey of the leadership of CIA directors from Hillenkoetter through Goss (including brief surveys of CIG Directors Souers and Vandenberg) and their contributions to U.S. intelligence policy.

Gates, Robert. *From the Shadow: The Ultimate Insider's Story of Five Presidents and How They Won the Cold War*. New York: Simon and Schuster, 1996.
Memoir of CIA officer (who, since 1966, briefly served on NSC staff and ultimately as CIA director from 1991–1993) that offers limited substantive information about CIA intelligence, counterintelligence, and covert operations.

Gleijeses, Piero. *Conflicting Missions: Havana, Washington, and Africa, 1959–1976*. Chapel Hill: University of North Carolina Press, 2002.
Criticizes CIA intelligence and covert operations in Cuba and the Congo (Zaire) in the 1960s and in Angola during the mid-1970s.

———. *Shattered Hope: The Guatemalan Revolution and the United States, 1944–1954*. Princeton: Princeton University Press, 1991.
Criticizes CIA covert operation to overthrow the Arbenz government in Guatemala.

Godson, Roy. *Dirty Tricks or Trump Cards: U.S. Covert Action and Counterintelligence*. Washington, DC: Brassey's, 1995.
History of CIA covert operations and counterintelligence methods during the Cold War years.

———, ed. *Intelligence Requirements for the 1980s: Clandestine Collection*. Washington, DC: National Strategy Information Center, 1982.
General discussion of intelligence collection methods, needs, and uses.

———, ed. *Intelligence Requirements for the 1980s: Counterintelligence*. Washington, DC: National Strategy Information Center, 1980.
General discussion of counterintelligence needs and capabilities in addressing the Soviet and broader terrorist threats in the 1980s.

———, ed. *Intelligence Requirements for the 1980s: Covert Action*. Washington, DC: National Strategy Information Center, 1981.
  General discussion of the role of covert operations in promoting security and policy interests.

———, ed. *Intelligence Requirements for the 1980s: Intelligence and Policy*. Lexington, MA: Lexington Books, 1986.
  General discussion of the role of intelligence in the formulation and execution of foreign and military policy.

Godson, Roy, Ernest May, and Gary Schmitt, eds. *U.S. Intelligence at the Crossroads: Agendas for Reform*. Washington, DC: Brassey's, 1995.
  Surveys CIA intelligence, counterintelligence, covert operations methods, priorities, and practices.

Goldberg, Robert A. *Enemies Within: The Culture of Conspiracy in Modern America*. New Haven: Yale University Press, 2001.
  History of conspiratorial thinking in modern America that briefly recounts, as one of many theories about President Kennedy's assassination, CIA involvement and cover-up.

Goodman, Allan, Gregory Treverton, and Philip Zelikow. *The Report of the Twentieth Century Fund Task Force on the Future of U.S. Intelligence*. New York: Twentieth Century Fund Press, 1996.
  Criticizes the role and importance of intelligence in the Cold War and post–Cold War eras.

Grose, Peter. *Gentleman Spy: The Life of Allen Dulles*. Boston: Houghton Mifflin, 1994.
  Biography of CIA Director Allen Dulles (1953–1961) that provides insights into Dulles's role and CIA activities from 1947–1961.

———. *Operation Rollback: America's Secret War behind the Iron Curtain*. Boston: Houghton Mifflin, 2000.
  Surveys CIA covert operations in Eastern and Western Europe, the Balkans, and the Soviet Union (psychological, economic, and political warfare; sabotage; propaganda) during early Cold War years—including the establishment of Radio Free Europe and Radio Liberty.

Haines, Gerald, and Robert Leggett, eds. *CIA's Analysis of the Soviet Union 1947–1991*. Washington, DC: Central Intelligence Agency, 2001.
  Briefly surveys submissions of CIA's Office of Reports and Estimates (renamed Office of National Estimates, Office of Research and Reports, Office of Current Intelligence, Office of Political Research, and Office of Soviet Analysis) to the White House concerning Soviet political, economic, and military plans and capabilities during years 1947–1991. Reprints a representative sample of forty-nine of these reports.

Halperin, Morton, Jerry Berman, Robert Borosage, and Christine Marwick. *The Lawless State*. New York: Penguin, 1976.
  Critical history of U.S. intelligence agencies, including CIA intelligence and covert operations.

Helgerson, John. *Getting to Know the President: CIA Briefings of Presidential Candidates 1952–1992*. Washington, DC: Central Intelligence Agency, n.d.
Surveys (based on interviews and presidential and CIA records) CIA briefings of presidential candidates during the period 1952–1992, provides insights about international developments and the quality of CIA intelligence analyses and capabilities.

Helms, Richard, with William Hood. *A Look over My Shoulder: A Life in the Central Intelligence Agency*. New York: Random House, 2003.
Autobiography of former CIA director (1966–1972) that also surveys the history of the Agency.

Hersh, Burton. *The Old Boys: The American Elite and the Origins of the CIA*. New York: Scribner's, 1992.
Critical history of CIA covert operations from 1947 through 1961 that focuses on leading CIA officials and their values.

Holt, Pat. *Secret Intelligence and Public Policy: A Dilemma of Democracy*. Washington, DC: Congressional Quarterly, 1995.
Textbook history (if fairly comprehensive) of CIA methods, operations, and relationships.

Howard, Edward. *Safe House: The Compelling Memoirs of the Only CIA Spy to Seek Asylum in Russia*. Bethesda, MD: National Press, 1995.
Critical memoir of disaffected CIA officer (who served only three years and was fired having failed a polygraph test) who defected to the Soviet Union in 1986.

Hulnick, Arthur. *Fixing the Spy Machine: Preparing American Intelligence for the Twenty-first Century*. Westport, CT: Praeger, 1999.
Former CIA officer's brief but comprehensive survey of CIA training, recruitment, intelligence, counterintelligence, and covert operations.

Hunt, E. Howard. *Memoirs of an American Secret Agent*. New York: Berkley, 1974.
Memoirs of famed "Watergate burglar" that sketchily surveys his career as CIA officer (1949–1970) in the conduct of covert operations (most notably the Bay of Pigs invasion).

Immerman, Richard. *The CIA in Guatemala: The Foreign Policy of Intervention*. Austin: University of Texas Press, 1982.
Detailed history of CIA covert operation to overthrow the Arbenz government of Guatemala.

Intelligence and National Security.
Periodical that publishes articles of academics and intelligence professionals about various aspects of intelligence policy and history.

International Journal of Intelligence and Counterintelligence.
Periodical that publishes articles of academics and intelligence professionals on CIA intelligence and counterintelligence programs.

Jeffreys-Jones, Rhodri. *The CIA and American Democracy*. New Haven: Yale University Press, 1989.

Comprehensive survey of the history of the CIA dating from its creation in 1947 through the 1980s.

————. *Cloak and Dollar: A History of American Secret Intelligence*. New Haven: Yale University Press, 2002.
Episodic, impressionistic history of secret intelligence activities (including those of the CIA) dating from the American Revolution with the subtheme that intelligence officials often operated as "confidence men" in a quest for increased funding authority.

Jeffreys-Jones, Rhodri, and Christopher Andrew, eds. *Eternal Vigilance? 50 Years of the CIA*. London: Frank Cass, 1997.
Disparate essays (unsystematic and uneven coverage) on selected aspects of the CIA's history, role, and activities.

Johnson, Loch. *America's Secret Power: The CIA in a Democratic Society*. New York: Oxford University Press, 1989.
History of the CIA's intelligence, counterintelligence, and covert operations activities and of Congress's oversight to promote national security and preclude abuses of power.

————. *A Season of Inquiry: The Senate Intelligence Investigation*. Lexington: University Press of Kentucky, 1985.
Detailed inside account (written by former Church Committee aide) of the Church Committee's 1975–1976 investigation of the U.S. intelligence agencies.

————. *Secret Agencies: U.S. Intelligence in a Hostile World*. New Haven: Yale University Press, 1996.
History of CIA intelligence and covert operations activities and of congressional oversight that focuses on the role and effectiveness of the U.S. intelligence agencies since World War II.

Johnson, Loch, ed., with James Wirtz. *Strategic Intelligence: Windows into a Secret World: An Anthology*. Los Angeles: Roxbury, 2004.
Collection of essays that survey history, uses, and methods of CIA operations and analyses.

Karalekas, Anne. *History of the Central Intelligence Agency*. Laguna Hills, CA: Aegean Park Press, 1977.
Brief history of the CIA originally prepared for the Church Committee in April 1976 and published as one of the Commitee's final reports.

Kessler, Ronald. *Inside the CIA: Revealing the Secrets of the World's Most Powerful Spy Agency*. New York: Pocket Books, 1992.
Journalistic, often anecdotal history of CIA since 1947 that focuses on the post–1975 period, based on interviews and secondary literature.

Kim, Jin-hyun, and Chung-in Moon, eds. *Post–Cold War, Democratization and National Intelligence*. Seoul: Yonsei University Press, 1996.
Contains a brief reflective essay by former CIA Director William Colby on the CIA's role in a democratic society. The essays on other (Soviet, South Korean, Japanese) intelligence agencies provide a comparative perspective.

Kinzer, Stephen. *All the Shah's Men: An American Coup and the Roots of Middle East Terror.* New York: John Wiley, 2003.
    History of CIA covert operation, Operation TPAJAX, to overthrow the Mossadegh government in Iran.

Kirkpatrick, Lyman B., Jr. *The U.S. Intelligence Community: Foreign Policy and Domestic Activities.* New York: Hill and Wang, 1973.
    Cursory, dated history of the U.S. intelligence community, and specifically of the CIA, during the Cold War years.

Knott, Stephen. *Secret and Sanctioned: Covert Operations and the American Presidency.* New York: Oxford University Press, 1996.
    Focuses on late eighteenth and nineteenth centuries, but critically surveys congressional oversight of the CIA from 1947 through the Iran-Contra affair.

Kohli, M. S., and Kenneth Conboy. *Spies in the Himalayas: Secret Missions and Perilous Climbs.* Lawrence: University Press of Kansas, 2003.
    Surveys CIA intelligence operations in northern India during the 1960s and 1970s intended to uncover Chinese nuclear capabilities.

Lamphere, Robert, and Tom Shactman. *The FBI/KGB War: A Special Agent's Story.* New York: Random House, 1986.
    Lamphere's autobiography focuses on his FBI career in counterintelligence and liaison with the code-named Venona project; offers limited insights into FBI-CIA liaison relationship.

Laquer, Walter. *The Uses and Limits of Intelligence.* New Brunswick: Transaction, 1993.
    History of CIA intelligence methods, analyses, and uses of intelligence product.

Leary, William. *Perilous Missions: Civil Air Transport and CIA Covert Operations in Asia.* Tuscaloosa: University of Alabama Press, 1984.
    History of CIA proprietary Civil Air Transport and use during Asian covert operations.

Lewis, Jonathan. *Spy Capitalism: Itek and the CIA.* New Haven: Yale University Press, 2002.
    Detailed history of the relationship between Itek (a private corporation manufacturing satellite reconnaissance cameras) and the CIA's Corona project during the 1957–1965 period.

Loftus, John. *The Belarus Secret.* New York: Knopf, 1987.
    Prosecutor in Justice Department's Nazi war crimes unit recounts CIA recruitment of German Nazis (notably Reinhard Gehlen and Gustav Hilger) and Ukrainian Nazi collaborators to obtain intelligence and conduct guerrilla warfare against communist governments in Eastern Europe, Albania, and the Soviet Union after 1948—some of whom were allowed to immigrate to the United States and were later employed in Radio Liberty and Radio Free Europe.

Lowenthal, Mark. *U.S. Intelligence: Evolution and Anatomy.* Westport, CT: Praeger, 1992.

History of the CIA's organization and role in promoting U.S. international objectives and the national interest.

Maas, Peter. *Killer Spy: The Inside Story of the FBI's Pursuit and Capture of Aldrich Ames, America's Deadliest Spy*. New York: Warner Books, 1995.
    Criticizes CIA officials' failure to uncover the pro-Soviet espionage activities of CIA officer Aldrich Ames.

Mangold, Thomas. *Cold Warrior: James Jesus Angleton: The CIA's Master Spy Hunter*. New York: Simon and Schuster, 1991.
    Critical biography of CIA counterintelligence chief James Angleton and of CIA counterintelligence operations conducted under Angleton's direction.

Marchetti, Victor, and John Marks. *The CIA and the Cult of Intelligence*. New York: Knopf, 1974.
    Critical but dated history of CIA organization, intelligence, and covert operations, coauthored by former CIA officer Marchetti. CIA prepublication review ordered 339 passages deleted. Filing a court suit, the authors were able to publish 171 of these passages, which were published in bold print (with withheld passages cited as deleted) in the printed text.

Martin, David. *Wilderness of Mirrors*. New York: Harper and Row, 1980.
    Surveys CIA operations against the Soviet Union during the 1950s and 1960s, focusing on the role of CIA officials William Harvey and James Angleton.

McAuliffe, Mary, ed. *CIA Documents on the Cuban Missile Crisis, 1962*. Washington, DC: Central Intelligence Agency, 1992.
    Reprints declassified CIA documents relating to the 1962 Cuban Missile Crisis—including maps of U-2 flights, CIA intelligence estimates, notes on key NSC meetings, memos relating to Operation MONGOOSE, and briefing papers given to the president, senior administration officials, members of Congress, and key allies.

McCoy, Alfred. *The Politics of Heroin: CIA Complicity in the Global Drug Trade*. New York: Lawrence Hill, 1991.
    Criticizes CIA complicity in Southeast Asian, Asian, and Central American drug trafficking (Laos, Burma, Afghanistan, Panama, Nicaragua, Corsica).

McGehee, Ralph. *Deadly Deceits: My 25 Years in the CIA*. New York: Sheridan Square, 1983.
    Former CIA officer's (1952–1977) critical account of CIA covert operations in Thailand and Vietnam and of CIA training.

Melanson, Philip. *The Murkin Conspiracy: An Investigation into the Assassination of Dr. Martin Luther King, Jr*. New York: Praeger, 1989.
    Highly speculative, conspiratorial analysis of the role of U.S. intelligence agencies in King's assassination and specifically CIA role as reflected in redacted reports pertaining to the Agency's monitoring of King and the civil rights movement and liaison relations with local police (notably in Memphis).

Mendez, Antonio, with Malcolm McConnell. *The Master of Disguise: My Secret Life in the CIA*. New York: William Morrow, 1999.

Memoir of CIA officer (employed in the Technical Service Division, 1965–1990) about CIA disguises, false documents, and other clandestine techniques and their various uses.

Mendez, Antonio, and Jonna Mendez with Bruce Henderson. *Spy Dust: Two Masters of Disguise Reveal the Tools and Operations That Helped Win the Cold War*. New York: Atria Books, 2002.
Memoir of husband-and-wife employees of CIA Office of Technology Services recounting various CIA training and clandestine techniques (disguises, document forgery).

Mills, Ami Chen. *CIA Off Campus: Building the Movement against Agency Recruitment and Research*. Boston: South End, 1991.
Detailed history of the student-led movement to prevent CIA recruitment and funding of research on college campuses.

Montague, Ludwell. *General Walter Bedell Smith as Director of Central Intelligence, October 1950–February 1953*. University Park: Pennsylvania State University Press, 1992.
Detailed history (written by CIA historian) of former CIA Director Walter Bedell Smith and of the evolution of the CIA during the Agency's formative years, 1947–1953.

Moynihan, Daniel Patrick. *Secrecy: The American Experience*. New Haven: Yale University Press, 1998.
Survey of overclassification and secrecy policy of the U.S. government during the twentieth century that unnecessarily immunized government agencies from public scrutiny.

National Commission on Terrorist Attacks upon the United States. *The 9/11 Commission Report: Final Report of the National Commission on Terrorist Attacks upon the United States*. New York: Norton, 2004.
Based on access to relevant CIA and other classified records. Criticizes the CIA's pre-9/11 intelligence collection, analyses, and covert operations and the failure to coordinate with other U.S. intelligence agencies (notably, the FBI).

Odom, William. *Fixing Intelligence: For a More Secure America*. New Haven: Yale University Press, 2003.
Semi-critical survey of the U.S. intelligence community by former NSA director that argues both for greater secrecy and for greater coordination and centralization.

Olmsted, Kathryn. *Challenging the Secret Government: The Post-Watergate Investigations of the CIA and FBI*. Chapel Hill: University of North Carolina Press, 1996.
In-depth survey of the Church and Pike Committees' investigations of the CIA.

Peake, Hayden, ed. *The Reader's Guide to Intelligence Periodicals*. Washington, DC: NIBC Press, 1992.
Useful guide to periodicals that publish articles on CIA history, operations, and methods.

Peake, Hayden, and Samuel Halpern, eds. *In the Name of Intelligence: Essays in Honor of Walter Pforzheimer*. Washington, DC: NIBC Press, 1994.
> Disparate essays on aspects on intelligence policy and the role of CIA as well as personal reflections on the long CIA career of Walter Pforzheimer.

Pedlow, Gregory, and Donald Welzenbach. *The CIA and the U-2 Program, 1954– 1974*. Washington, DC: Central Intelligence Agency, 1998.
> History of the U-2 aerial reconnaissance program from planning stage in 1954 through 1974.

Persico, Joseph. *Casey: From the OSS to the CIA*. New York: Viking, 1990.
> Biography of William Casey that focuses on his directorship of the CIA during the Reagan administration and the Iran-Contra affair.

Petersen, Neal. *American Intelligence, 1775–1990: A Bibliographical Guide*. Claremont, CA: Regina Books, 1992.
> Helpful bibliographical guide of books, articles, and congressional hearings on the subject of intelligence agencies, policy, and activities. The guide is not annotated but does list published works around themes (chronological, topical, presidential, and method).

Phillips, David Atlee. *The Night Watch*. New York: Atheneum, 1977.
> Former CIA officer's sympathetic, anecdotal history of CIA training, recruitment, and covert operations.

Pisani, Sallie. *The CIA and the Marshall Plan*. Lawrence: University Press of Kansas, 1991.
> Surveys CIA's role during early Cold War years to contain communist influence in Western Europe, and particularly in connection with the Marshall Plan.

Powers, Thomas. *The Man Who Kept the Secrets: Richard Helms and the CIA*. New York: Knopf, 1979.
> Political biography of CIA Director Richard Helms that concurrently surveys the history of the CIA from 1947 through 1976.

Prados, John. *Lost Crusader: The Secret Wars of CIA Director William Colby*. New York: Oxford University Press, 2003.
> Critical biography of William Colby, CIA officer (since 1950) and director (1973–1975), that also reviews important CIA covert operations in the Baltic states, Italy, Laos, Vietnam, Indonesia, and Angola.

———. *Presidents' Secret Wars: CIA and Pentagon Covert Operations since World War II*. New York: Morrow, 1986.
> History of CIA covert operations from 1947 through 1985 (before revelations of the Iran-contra affair of 1985–1986).

———. *The Soviet Estimate: U.S. Intelligence Analysis & Soviet Strategic Forces*. Princeton: Princeton University Press, 1986.
> Criticizes CIA (and other intelligence agencies') analyses and methods relating to Soviet strategic, military, and nuclear capabilities and plans.

Prouty, L. Fletcher. *The Secret Team: The CIA and Its Allies in Control of the United States and the World*. Englewood Cliffs, NJ: Prentice Hall, 1973.
   Memoir of Air Force colonel who served as liaison officer to the CIA during 1955–1963 that criticizes CIA covert operations and the secrecy shrouding CIA operations.

Ranelagh, John. *CIA: A History*. London: BBC Books, 1992.
   Brief, fairly comprehensive history of the CIA from the Agency's creation in 1947 through 1988 (originally a BBC television series).

Ranson, Harry Howe. *The Intelligence Establishment*. Cambridge: Harvard University Press, 1970.
   Dated but useful history of CIA role and activities, liaison relations, and congressional oversight.

Report to the President by the Commission on CIA Activities within the United States. Washington, DC: U.S. Government Printing Office, 1975.
   The report and recommendations of the so-called Rockefeller Commission (established by President Ford on January 4, 1975) of its investigation of CIA domestic surveillance activities.

Richelson, Jeffrey. *A Century of Spies: Intelligence in the Twentieth Century*. New York: Oxford University Press, 1995.
   Cursory history of espionage, intelligence activities, codebreaking, and communication interception conducted by the United States and other nations during the twentieth century, including an assessment of the role and capabilities of the CIA.

———. *The Wizards of Langley: Inside the CIA's Directorate of Science and Technology*. Boulder: Westview, 2001.
   Detailed history of the evolution of CIA science and technology initiatives and the contributions of scientific personnel to U.S. intelligence policy and operations.

Richelson, Jeffrey, and Desmond Bell. *The Ties That Bind*. Cambridge: Unwin Hyman, 1990.
   Briefly surveys CIA role and liaison with Australian, Canadian, and British intelligence; the FBI; and the U.S. Air Force.

Riebling, Mark. *Wedge: The Secret War between the FBI and CIA*. New York: Knopf, 1994.
   Impressionistic history of the FBI's and the CIA's conflicting liaison relationship, which the author attributes to FBI Director Hoover's bureaucratic politics.

Roosevelt, Kermit. *Countercoup: The Struggle for the Control of Iran*. New York: McGraw-Hill, 1979.
   CIA officer's inside account of the CIA coup to overthrow the Mossadegh government in Iran.

Rositzke, Harry. *The CIA's Secret Operations: Espionage, Counterespionage, and Covert Action*. New York: Reader's Digest Press, 1977.

Memoir of senior CIA officer (1947–1970) that selectively recounts CIA intelligence, counterintelligence, and covert operations.

Rudgers, David. *Creating the Secret State: The Origins of the Central Intelligence Agency, 1943–1947.* Lawrence: University Press of Kansas, 2000.
    Detailed survey of the CIA's creation in 1947 focusing on the bureaucratic rivalries of the World War II and early Cold War years over the issue of centralized intelligence.

Ruffner, Kevin. *Corona: America's First Satellite Program.* Washington, DC: Central Intelligence Agency, 1995.
    History of the CIA's Corona satellite reconnaissance program from its inception in August 1960. Reprints selected reports and some reconnaissance photographs and charts.

Salisbury, Harrison. *Without Fear or Favor: An Uncompromising Look at The New York Times.* New York: Ballantine, 1980.
    Inside account of the history of the *New York Times* provides insights into the CIA's covert relationship with *Times* publisher Arthur Sulzburger and the *Times's* coverage of CIA operations.

Saunders, Frances Stonor. *The Cultural Cold War and the World of Arts and Letters.* 1999. Reprint. New York: The New Press, 2000.
    Published in London in 1999 by Granta under the title *Who Paid the Piper? The CIA and the Cultural Cold War.* Surveys CIA secret cultural intelligence activities, including funding the journal *Encounter* and the Congress for Cultural Freedom; the filming of George Orwell's *1984* and *Animal Farm*; and subsidizing thousands of academic books (notably by Frederick A. Praeger, Inc.).

Scheuer, Michael (Anonymous). *Imperial Hubris: Why the West Is Losing the War on Terror.* Washington: Brassey's, 2004.
    Senior CIA analyst's critical assessment of CIA counterterrorism policies and decisions during the 1990s through September 11, 2001.

Schlesinger, Stephen, and Stephen Kinzer. *Bitter Fruit: The Untold Story of the American Coup in Guatemala.* Garden City: Doubleday, 1982.
    Critical history of CIA covert operation to overthrow the Arbenz government in Guatemala.

Scott-Smith, Giles. *The Politics of Apolitical Culture: The Congress for Cultural Freedom, the CIA, and post-War American Hegemony.* New York: Routledge, 2002.
    Detailed survey of the CIA's covert subsidization of the Congress for Cultural Freedom and the anticommunist cultural war of American intellectuals.

Shulsky, Abram. *Silent Warfare: Understanding the World of Intelligence.* Washington, DC: Brassey's, 1991.
    General commentary on intelligence methods, operation, and policy, but contains few direct references to the CIA.

Simpson, Christopher. *Blowback: America's Recruitment of Nazis and Its Effect on the Cold War.* New York: Weidenfeld & Nicolson, 1988.

Critical assessment of CIA recruitment of German Nazis and Nazi collaborators to conduct intelligence and covert operations during the early Cold War years, including bringing some to work with émigré groups inside the United States or to work with Radio Liberty and Radio Free Europe.

Smist, Frank. *Congress Oversees the United States Intelligence Community, 1947–1994.* 2nd ed. Knoxville: University of Tennessee Press, 1994.
History of congressional authorization and oversight of CIA during the years 1947–1994.

Snepp, Frank. *Decent Interval: An Insider's Account of Saigon's Indecent End Told by the CIA's Chief Strategy Analyst in Vietnam.* New York: Random House, 1977.
Memoir of former CIA analyst criticizing the politicization and manipulation of CIA analyses and of CIA officials' failure to protect sources with the collapse of the South Vietnamese government in the closing days of the Vietnam War.

Snider, L. Britt. *Sharing Secrets with Lawmakers: Congress as a User of Intelligence.* Washington, D.C.: Center for the Study of Intelligence, 1997.
Surveys CIA liaison relations with Congress from 1947 through the 1990s.

Stafford, David. *Spies Beneath Berlin.* London: John Murray Ltd., 2002.
Detailed account of CIA's Berlin tunnel project, Operation GOLD, to tap Soviet communications, compromised by British intelligence officer George Blake.

Steury, Donald, ed. *Sherman Kent and the Board of National Estimates.* Washington, DC: Central Intelligence Agency, 1994.
Administrative biography of Sherman Kent, head of the CIA's Board of Estimates from 1952–1967, who earlier served as an analyst in COI and OSS. Provides insights into Kent's leadership role in CIA intelligence analysis.

Stockwell, John. *In Search of Enemies: A CIA Story.* New York: Norton, 1978.
Former CIA officer's critical history of CIA covert operations in Angola in 1975–1976.

Studies in Intelligence.
Unclassified edition of articles on aspects of the CIA's history, including reminiscences of and interviews with key CIA officials, published by the CIA's Center for the Study of Intelligence.

Sullivan, John F. *Of Spies and Lies: A CIA Lie Detector Remembers Vietnam.* Lawrence: University Press of Kansas, 2002.
Surveys CIA lie detector testing of CIA case officers during the Vietnam War era.

Taubman, Philip. *Secret Empire: Eisenhower, the CIA and the Hidden History of America's Space Espionage.* New York: Simon & Schuster, 2003.
Detailed history of the CIA's covert space reconnaissance program directed at the Soviet Union, that led to the development of the U-2 spy plane.

Terrell, Jack, with Ron Martz. *Disposable Patriot: Revelations of a Soldier in America's Secret Wars.* Washington, DC: National Press Books, 1992.

An insider's critical account of CIA funding and other assistance to Nicaraguan contras during 1980s.

Theoharis, Athan. *Chasing Spies: How the FBI Failed in Counterintelligence But Promoted the Politics of McCarthyism in the Cold War Years.* Chicago: Ivan Dee, 2002.
Briefly recounts the role of CIA director Dulles in the Joseph Alsop matter.

———. *Spying on Americans: Political Surveillance from Hoover to the Huston Plan.* Philadelphia: Temple University Press, 1978.
Briefly surveys the history of the creation of the Church Committee and of CIA domestic surveillance activities.

———, ed. *A Culture of Secrecy: The Government versus the People's Right to Know.* Lawrence: University Press of Kansas, 1998.
Surveys CIA secrecy procedures, court cases involving such procedures, CIA compliance with the Freedom of Information Act, and CIA restrictions on access to foreign policy records.

Thomas, Evan. *The Very Best Men: Four Who Dared: The Early Years of the CIA.* New York: Simon and Schuster, 1995.
Assessment of the social and class background of CIA officials Frank Wisner, Desmond Fitzgerald, Tracy Barnes, and Richard Bissell, offering insights into the early history of CIA intelligence and covert operations.

Trento, Joseph. *The Secret History of the CIA.* Roseville, CA: Forum, 2001.
Critical, if melodramatic and gossipy, history of CIA intelligence and counterintelligence failures.

Treverton, Gregory. *Covert Action: the Limits of Intervention in the Postwar World.* New York: Basic Books, 1987.
Critical history of CIA covert operations during the Cold War era.

———. *Reshaping National Intelligence in an Age of Information.* Cambridge: Cambridge University Press, 2001.
Surveys the history of CIA intelligence collection, analyses, covert operations, and coordination with the purpose to define U.S. intelligence role in post–Cold War years.

Troy, Thomas. *Donovan and the CIA: A History of the Establishment of the Central Intelligence Agency.* Frederick, MD: University Publications of America, 1981.
Administrative biography of OSS Director William Donovan (1942–1945) that also surveys the drafting and enactment in 1947 of legislation creating the CIA.

———. *Wild Bill and Intrepid: Donovan, Stephenson and the Origins of CIA.* New Haven: Yale University Press, 1996.
History of the creation of the COI and OSS and of the roles of COI/OSS director Donovan and Canadian intelligence officer William Stephenson in the creation of the CIA.

Tully, Andrew. *CIA: The Inside Story.* New York: Morrow, 1962.
Dated, popular history of the CIA; provides few insights into CIA operations and activities.

Turner, Stansfield. *Secrecy and Democracy: The CIA in Transition*. Boston: Houghton Mifflin, 1985.

Memoir of former CIA director (1977–1981) relating his experiences, changes, and decisions—useful, although providing little substantive information.

Twentieth Century Fund. *The Need to Know: The Report of the Twentieth Century Fund Task Force on Covert Action and American Democracy*. New York: Twentieth Century Fund Press, 1992.

Assessment of CIA covert operations and problems these posed for a democratic society.

U.S. House, Select Committee on Intelligence. *U.S. Intelligence Agencies and Activities Committee Proceedings* (94th Cong., 1st sess.), 1975; *Committee Proceedings II* (94th Cong., 2nd sess.), 1976; *U.S. Intelligence Agencies and Activities: Intelligence Costs and Fiscal Procedures* (94th Cong., 1st sess.), 1975; *U.S. Intelligence Agencies and Activities: Risks and Control of Foreign Intelligence* (94th Cong., 1st sess.), 1975; *U.S. Intelligence Agencies and Activities: The Performance of the Intelligence Community* (94th Cong., 1st sess.), 1975.

Surveys authority, role, and effectiveness of the CIA.

U.S. Senate, Select Committee on Intelligence. *Report on U.S. Intelligence Community's Prewar Intelligence Assessments on Iraq* (108th Cong., 2nd sess.), 2004.

Critical assessment of CIA intelligence collection and analyses regarding Iraq's chemical, biological, and nuclear weapons programs and capabilities.

U.S. Senate, Select Committee on Intelligence and Committee on Health and Scientific Research. *Joint Hearings on Project MKULTRA, the CIA's Program of Research in Behavioral Modification* (95th Cong., 1st sess.), 1977.

Surveys CIA drug testing and behavioral modification program, code-named MKULTRA, and destruction of records pertaining to that program.

U.S. Senate, Select Committee on Intelligence and U.S. House, Permanent Select Committee on Intelligence. *Report on Joint Inquiry into Intelligence Community Activities before and after the Terrorist Attacks of September 11, 2001* (107th Cong., 2nd sess.), 2003.

Critical assessment of the failure of the CIA (and other U.S. intelligence agencies) to have anticipated the September 11 terrorist attack. Recommends the creation of a Cabinet-level director of intelligence.

U.S. Senate, Select Committee to Study Governmental Operations with respect to Intelligence Activities. *Interim Report: Alleged Assassination Plots involving Foreign Leaders* (94th Cong., 1st sess.), 1975; *Hearings on Unauthorized Storage of Toxic Agents*, Vol. 1 (94th Cong., 1st sess.), 1975; *Hearings on Huston Plan*, Vol. 2 (94th Cong., 1st sess.), 1975; *Hearings on Mail Opening*, Vol. 4 (94th Cong., 1st sess.), 1975; *Hearings on Covert Action*, Vol. 7 (94th Cong., 1st sess.), 1975; *Final Report on Foreign and Military Intelligence, Book I* (94th Cong., 2nd sess.), 1976; *Final Report on Intelligence Activities and the Rights of Americans, Book II* (94th Cong., 2nd sess.), 1976; *Final Report on Supplementary Detailed Staff Reports on Intelligence Activities and the Rights of Americans, Book III* (94th Cong., 2nd sess.), 1976;

Final Report on Supplementary Detailed Staff Reports on Foreign and Military Intelligence, Book IV (94th Cong., 2nd sess.), 1976; *Final Report on Investigation of the Assassination of President John F. Kennedy; Performance of the Intelligence Agencies, Book V* (94th Cong., 2nd sess.), 1976; *Final Report on Supplementary Reports on Intelligence Activities, Book VI* (94th Cong., 2nd sess.), 1976.

Surveys history of CIA authority, intelligence role, covert operations (including planned assassinations), domestic surveillance, and the Kennedy assassination.

Volkman, Ernest. *Espionage: The Greatest Spy Operations in the Twentieth Century.* New York: John Wiley, 1995.

Critical survey of selected CIA espionage, counterespionage, and covert operations.

Warner, Michael, ed. *The CIA under Harry Truman.* Washington, DC: Central Intelligence Agency, 1994.

Surveys history (and reprints relevant documents) of the creation and authorization of the CIA, the CIA's intelligence and covert operations activities, and the exemption of CIA expenditures from congressional budgetary and accounting requirements.

Watson, Bruce, Susan Watson, and Gerald Hupple, eds. *United States Intelligence: An Encyclopedia.* New York: Garland, 1990.

Useful compendium of information, including selected (although not annotated) bibliography, glossary of terms and acronyms, brief biographies, and reprints of selected legislation and executive orders.

Weber, Ralph, ed. *Spymasters: Ten CIA Officers in Their Own Words.* Wilmington, DE: Scholarly Resources, 1999.

Reminiscences of former CIG Director Sidney Souers and CIA officials Allen Dulles, Richard Bissell, Samuel Halpern, Lyman Kirkpatrick, Robert Amory, Ray Cline, John McCone, Richard Helms, and William Colby.

Weiner, Tim, David Johnston, and Neil Lewis. *Betrayal: The Story of Aldrich Ames, an American Spy.* New York: Random House, 1995.

Biography of CIA officer Aldrich Ames that surveys CIA failure to uncover Ames's espionage activities.

Westerfield, H. Bradford, ed. *Inside CIA's Private World: Declassified Articles from the Agency's Internal Journal, 1955–1992.* New Haven: Yale University Press, 1995.

Reprints selected formerly classified articles written by CIA personnel that range from reports on CIA collection methods to analyses and counterespionage.

Wilford, Hugh. *The CIA, the British Left and the Cold War: Calling the Tune?* London: Frank Cass, 2003.

Surveys CIA covert program of subsidizing the Congress for Cultural Freedom and *Encounter* magazine.

Wilson, Joseph. *The Politics of Truth.* New York: Carroll & Graf, 2004.

Discusses in detail his trip to Niger in 2002 (at the request of the CIA) to ascertain the validity of a report that Niger had sold uranium to Iraq, and the role of unnamed Bush Administration officials in leaking the name of his wife (Valerie Plame, a CIA officer) to syndicated columnist Robert Novak.

Winks, Robin. *Cloak & Gown 1939–1961: Scholars in the Secret War.* New York: Morrow, 1987.
    Recounts role of Yale University students, faculty, and staff as CIA recruits as well as recruiters for OSS and the CIA.

Wise, David. *The American Police State: The Government against the People.* New York: Random House, 1976.
    Critical but dated history of U.S. intelligence agencies that focuses on the FBI and the Nixon White House but cursorily surveys CIA intelligence and covert operations.

———. *Molehunt: The Secret Search for Traitors that Shattered the CIA.* New York: Random House, 1992.
    Detailed account of CIA counterintelligence operations that provoked internal CIA and CIA-FBI conflicts over the Golitsyn-Nosenko-Kulak-Polyakov defections and questions about a Soviet mole in the CIA.

———. *Nightmover: How Aldrich Ames Sold the CIA to the KGB for $4.6 Million.* New York: HarperCollins, 1995.
    Criticizes CIA counterintelligence failure to uncover CIA officer Aldrich Ames's Soviet espionage activities.

———. *The Spy Who Got Away: The Inside Story of Edward Lee Howard, the CIA Agent Who Betrayed His Country's Secrets and Escaped to Moscow.* New York: Random House, 1988.
    Detailed account of recruitment, training, and then defection to the Soviet Union of CIA officer Edward Howard and of the CIA's and FBI's bungled handling of Howard's flight to Moscow.

Wise, David, and Thomas Ross. *The Invisible Government.* New York: Random House, 1964.
    Dated, journalistic history of CIA intelligence and covert operations.

Woodward, Bob. *Veil: The Secret Wars of the CIA 1981–1987.* New York: Pocket Books, 1987.
    Journalistic account of CIA covert operations in Central America and the Middle East conducted under CIA director William Casey from 1981 culminating in the Iran-Contra affair of 1985–1986, based primarily on interviews and accessible primary Sources.

Wyden, Peter. *Bay of Pigs: The Untold Story.* New York: Simon and Schuster, 1979.
    Detailed account of the CIA's covert operation to overthrow the Cuban government of Fidel Castro.

Zegart, Amy. *Flawed by Design: The Evolution of the CIA, JCS, and NSC.* Stanford: Stanford University Press, 1999.
    Critical assessment of presidential, congressional, and bureaucratic roles in the creation and evolution of the CIA, and the Agency's organizational design and flaws.

Index

Hunt, Everett Howard, 199–202, 232, 273–274, 284, 323, 344
HUNTER program, 316–317
Hussein, Saddam, 64, 67–69, 71–77, 79, 81, 118–119, 130, 152, 225, 227, 289, 296–297, 302
Huston, Tom Charles, 195, 322
Huston Plan, 195–196, 322

IAFEATURE, 51, 177–178, 325
Ibarra, Jose Velasco, 167
ICBM. *See* Intercontinental Ballistic Missile
IDEALIST, 315
IMINT. *See* Imagery Intelligence
Imagery Intelligence, 54, 87, 111
India, 254, 267, 346
Indochina, 157
Indonesia, 157, 257; CIA covert operation, 166, 316
Inman, Bobby, 65, 265
Inouye, Daniel, 218
INR. *See* Bureau of Intelligence and Research
Inside the Company, 234, 337
Intelligence Authorization Act of 1991, 182
intelligence collection and analysis, 20, 34, 38–39, 42–43, 46–47, 53–54, 60–63, 68, 72–79, 81, 90, 99, 112, 122–123, 125–132, 134–145, 149–156, 206–209, 211–212, 225–228, 282, 287, 296–297, 299–300
Intelligence Community Staff, 299
Intelligence Identities Protection Act of 1982, 171, 208, 226, 229, 233, 235, 286, 303, 325, 328
Intelligence Oversight Act of 1980 (aka Intelligence Accountability Act), 108, 179, 181, 182, 208, 216, 219, 251, 301, 329
Intelligence Oversight Board (IOB), 89
Intelligence Reform and Terrorism Protection Act of 2004, xviii, 83, 85, 89, 96–97, 151, 153, 187, 225, 245, 270
Intercontinental Ballistic Missile, 32, 128–129, 133, 139
Intermediate Range Nuclear Forces Treaty, 63
International Atomic Energy Agency (IAEA), 75, 225–226

International Court of Justice, 59, 180
International Drug Control Program, 119
International Telephone and Telegraph Corporation (ITT), 47, 283, 322, 323
Iran, 15, 60–61, 127, 144, 265, 302; CIA covert operation, 25–26, 160–161, 181–182, 255, 290, 304, 344, 348; hostage crisis, 54–57, 176, 185, 215, 255, 299, 326–327; Iran-Contra, 216–221, 255
Iran-Contra, xix, 59–61, 82, 101, 104–105, 179–185, 189, 215–221, 245, 250–251, 254, 265, 268, 301–302, 330, 341–342, 356
Iraq, 79, 296–297; CIA covert operation, 64, 72, 297; First Gulf War, 64, 153, 302; Second Gulf War, 71–77, 114, 152–153, 225–229, 296–297
Iraq Survey Group, 77, 79
Iraqi National Accord (or Wafik), 64
Iraqi National Congress (INC), 64, 77, 79
Israel, 145, 240, 296, 316
Italy, 157; CIA covert operation, 16, 18, 21, 159, 239, 257, 311

Jackson, William H., 13–14, 19, 275–276
Jagan, Cheddi, 167
Japan, 127; CIA covert operation, 167, 261, 262
Jaruzelski, Wojciech, 59
Jawbreaker, 71
Jeremiah, David, 152
JFK (movie), 198, 320
John Paul II (pope), 59, 143, 266
Johnson, Clarence "Kelly," 30–31
Johnson, Lyndon B., 23, 40, 45–46, 133, 177, 193, 197, 210, 253, 263; CIA, 136, 175, 202, 248, 257, 271, 283, 288, 322
Joint Chiefs of Staff (JCS), 5–6, 81, 125, 136, 190, 195, 291, 308
Joint House-Senate Intelligence Committee, September 11, investigation, xix, 80, 105–106, 152, 186, 222–223, 244–245, 269, 330, 332, 354
Joint Intelligence Committee, 121
Joint Intelligence Group, 125
Joint U.S. Military Advisory Group (Philippines), 279
Jordan, 255
Josselson, Michael, 312

About the Editor
and Contributors

ATHAN THEOHARIS is a professor of history at Marquette University whose research has focused on government secrecy, Cold War politics, and the history of the FBI. He is the author, coauthor, and editor of eighteen books, including *The FBI and American Democracy* (2004), *Chasing Spies* (2002), *A Culture of Secrecy* (1998), *The FBI: A Comprehensive Reference Guide* (1998), *From the Secret Files of J. Edgar Hoover* (1991), *The Boss: J. Edgar Hoover and the Great American Inquisition* (1988), and *Spying on Americans* (1978). Theoharis has also published numerous articles in academic and popular journals, including *Journal of American History*, *Political Science Quarterly*, *Intelligence and National Security*, *The Judges' Journal*, *Wayne Law Review*, *Cornell Law Review*, *Criminal Justice Review*, *Crime and Justice*, *Journalism History*, *Authors Guild Bulletin*, *Government Publications Review*, *USA Today*, *The Nation*, *First Principles*, and *Los Angeles Times*. He has received numerous awards, including the American Library Association's selection of the FBI guide as an outstanding reference work, the American Bar Association's Gavel Award, the Binkley-Stevenson Award, Marquette University's Lawrence Haggerty Award for Research Excellence, and selection as a fellow by the Wisconsin Academy of Arts, Sciences, and Letters.

RICHARD IMMERMAN is currently a professor of history at Temple University where his work has focused on U.S. foreign policy and intelligence policy. He is the author or coauthor of seven books, including *John Foster Dulles* (1999), *Waging Peace* (1998), *How Presidents Test Reality* (1989), *The CIA in Guatemala* (1982), and *Ike's Spies: Eisenhower and the Espionage Establishment* (1981). Immerman has also published numerous articles, essays, and encyclopedia entries, including those in *Political Science Quarterly*, *Journal of American History*, *Diplomatic History*, *American National Biography*, *Oxford*

Companion to Military History, Encyclopedia of U.S. Foreign Relations, Encyclopedia of Latin American History and Culture, and *Dictionary of American Biography.* He has received numerous awards, including Temple University's Paul Eberman Faculty Research Award, the Stuart Bernath Lecture Prize, the Stuart Bernath Book Prize, and the Richard Neustadt Book Award.

LOCH JOHNSON is currently Regent Professor of political science at the University of Georgia and the editor of *Intelligence and National Security.* He had served as special assistant to the chair of the Senate Special Committee on Intelligence Activities (the so-called Church Committee), special assistant to the Senate Committee on Foreign Relations, and staff director of the House Permanent Select Committee on Intelligence. He is the editor and author of twenty books on U.S. foreign policy, intelligence policy, and national security, including *Fateful Decisions: Inside the National Security Council* (2003), *Strategic Intelligence* (2003), *Bombs, Bugs, Drugs, and Thugs* (2002), *Secret Agencies* (1996), *America as a World Power* (1991), *America's Secret Power: The CIA in a Democratic Society* (1989), *A Season of Inquiry: The Senate Intelligence Investigation* (1985), and *The Making of International Agreements* (1984). Johnson has also published numerous articles in academic and popular journals, including *White House Studies, Intelligence and National Security, Comparative Strategy, International Journal of Intelligence and Counterintelligence, Washington Monthly, Foreign Policy, Journal of Conflict, World Intelligence Review, American Intelligence Journal, Congress and the Presidency, American Journal of International Law, Journal of Politics, Harvard Journal of Law and Public Policy, International Studies, First Principles, Presidential Studies Quarterly, The Nation,* and *The New Republic.* Johnson has received numerous teaching awards at the University of Georgia and his publications have been awarded the V.O. Key Award and the Certificate of Distinction (from the National Intelligence Study Center).

KATHRYN OLMSTED is currently an associate professor of history at the University of California–Davis. She has done extensive research of Cold War domestic politics and the role of U.S. intelligence agencies, and is the author of *Challenging Secret Government: The Post Watergate Investigations of the CIA and the FBI* (1996) and *Red Spy Queen: A Biography of Elizabeth Bentley* (2002). Olmsted has also published articles in *Presidential Studies Quarterly, Journalism History,* and *Intelligence and National Security.* She is currently writing a book titled *Governing Conspiracies: Conspiracy Theories about the U.S. Government from World War I to September 11.*

JOHN PRADOS, a senior researcher at the National Security Archive, has published extensively on U.S. intelligence and counterintelligence policy, the presidency, and U.S. military, foreign, and national security policy. He is the author or editor of twenty books, including *Lost Crusader: The Secret World of CIA Director William Colby* (2003), *Hoodwinked: The Documents that Reveal*

How Bush Sold Us a War (2004), *Inside the Pentagon Papers* (2004), *America Confronts Terrorism* (2002), *Presidents' Secret Wars* (1996), *Combined Fleet Decoded: The Secret History of U.S. Intelligence and the Japanese Navy in World War II* (1995), *The Hidden History of the Vietnam War* (1995), *Keepers of the Keys: A History of the National Security Council from Truman to Bush* (1991), and *The Soviet Estimate* (1986). Prados has also published extensively in newspapers and academic and popular journals, including the *New York Times*, *Washington Post*, *Los Angeles Times*, *American Prospect*, *Journal of American History*, *Political Science Quarterly*, *Diplomatic History*, *Intelligence and National Security*, *Journal of American-East Asian Relations*, *MHQ: The Quarterly Journal of Military History*, *Strategy and Tactics*, *Strategic Survey*, and *Bulletin of Atomic Scientists*. His books have been awarded numerous prizes, including the annual book award of the New York Military Affairs Symposium, Notable Naval Book of the Year, and the annual book prize from the National Intelligence Study Center.